YA
646.7
T 21

D1568173

silly goose
productions, LLC

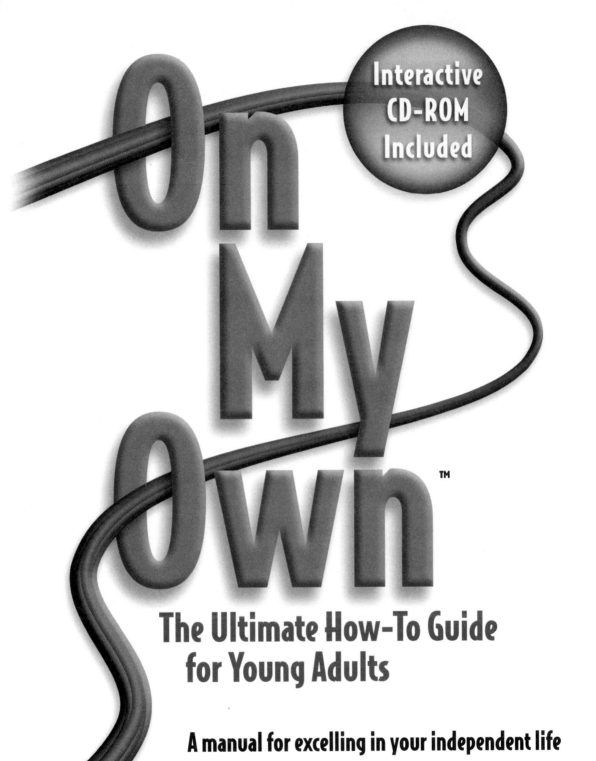

On My Own™

The Ultimate How-To Guide for Young Adults

A manual for excelling in your independent life

Sally Taylor

WEST BEND LIBRARY

Interactive CD-ROM Included

To my nephew, Erek
You continue to teach me about life and love every day.

To read Erek's story, go to Chapter 12, page 427.

Acknowledgments

*"The future belongs to those who believe in the
beauty of their dreams."*

~ Eleanor Roosevelt

Amazingly, this project has been completed in a year's time. The people who have helped with it have been phenomenal. Their faith in me is, at times, a bit overwhelming. And their talents are awesome!

Kerry, my husband, is my biggest inspiration. He is one of those rare individuals who truly defines "integrity." I joke that I'm not a lucky person (having only won a paper kite at my first-grade Halloween party), but I am truly blessed to be loved by Kerry. My cats, Snickers, Texan, and Giggles, have also been a huge support. I probably wouldn't have taken any breaks if it hadn't been for them!

My family spares nothing to let me know how proud they are of me. My parents, Jim and Dianne, are two of the most generous and compassionate people I know. (Mom is great at selling this book!) My siblings are also my friends: Cindy, Tammy, Jimmy, and Lorey. They've been a tremendous help with this book. I have gotten so much joy as an aunt to Erek, Alisa, Luke, and Paul. They're the best! Mark, Randy, Debbie, Devin, and Mario have been a wonderful addition to the family. And my parents-in-law, Max and Carolyn, have been amongst my biggest supporters.

The many talents of the production partners amaze me: Digital Lagoon; Pneuma Books; Central Plains Book Manufacturing; EMI Manufacturing; BookExpo America; Morgan Chilson; Pam Denman; Lloyd Rich; Beate Pettigrew; Coughlin Indexing Services, Inc.; Print Time; Bankrate, Inc.; Express Card & Label Co., Inc.; Silver Lake Bank; the photographers; and the young adults who gave of their time and talents.

I am grateful to my friends: Morgan, Alisa C., Carla, Laurie, Elaine, Peggy, Kathryn, Bridget, Danny, Toni, Barb, Nelson, Krissy, Chuck, Stan, Steve, Patti, Thom, Mary, Donnie, Jeremy, Courtney, Rem, and so many others who have believed in me.

Linda VandeGarde, MA, LSCSW; Nina Bryhn, M.D.; and Tim Hallbom are amongst the best in their fields.

And to all those who believed in this project — and in me — thank you. I couldn't have done it without you!

Also see "Thank Yous" on page 567 and "Credits & Copyright Approvals" on page 575.

Table of Contents

Table of Figures

Chapter 7 – Relationships

Chapter 8 – Sex

Chapter 9 – Health

Chapter 10 – Personal Safety

Chapter 11 – Alcohol & Drugs

Chapter 12 – Depression & Suicide Prevention

Chapter 13 – Pet Care

Chapter 14 – Charities & Giving Back

Chapter 15 – Car Ownership

Chapter 16 – Government

Foreword

As a judge hearing juvenile cases for the past 13 years, many times I've wished for an informative book to give to young adults as they make their first forays into the adult world. Today, we have a perception that young people know far more than they really do. Between the media blitz they undergo daily and the shocking realities on the news, we all know they grow up fast.

But growing up fast doesn't mean they know how to find a good job, balance a checkbook, or do laundry. There is basic knowledge that many young adults need to begin a responsible life as an adult — and far too often, they don't have that knowledge. The juveniles I deal with in the justice system often are relying on information they've received from sources who are just as uninformed as they are. Making choices with inadequate knowledge can bring devastating consequences to the lives of these young adults.

That is why I was so pleased to read *On My Own!*™ *The Ultimate How-To Guide for Young Adults*. This book offers a wonderful compilation of information that is relevant — and necessary — for young men and women who are transitioning into their adult lives.

While many agencies have brochures or pamphlets with information for young adults, most are soon lost or tossed by the wayside. *On My Own*™ is a handy reference that young adults can refer to again and again.

Sally Taylor has approached this book with determination because of her love, concern, and compassion for young people and the decisions they have to make. I hope her book will find its way into the hands of all young adults — and that each book has many tattered pages from being referred to time and again. And the CD-ROM is an excellent tool for individuals who have difficulty in reading and comprehending — and it's fun ... which makes learning much easier for everyone!

The time of transition into adulthood is rocky, at best. Change is hard for everyone, whether you're young or old. I know that *On My Own*™ is a tool that can help young adults face those changes with confidence. It should be put in the hands of all young adults to help them face the challenges put before them as they make their mark within our society.

~ Judge Tom B. Webb

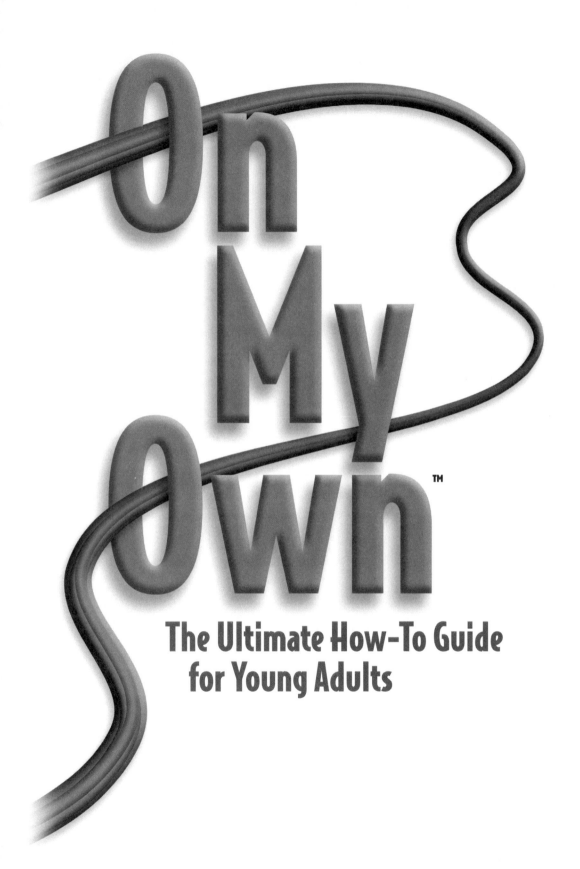

On My Own™

The Ultimate How-To Guide
for Young Adults

Introduction

 Introduction

Want to be in control of your life? Want to be independent? How do you know what needs to be done when you're living on your own? How do you find an apartment, change your address, hook up utilities, get cable installed? What about finances? How are you going to pay rent? And utilities? And your phone bill? And food? Will you have any money left over for fun? How do credit cards work? How do you balance a checkbook? (And, no, you don't have money in the bank just because you have checks left!)

Are you going to college or trade school? What if you want to go, but your parents can't afford to send you? How will you pay for it? Or are you going to work? How do you find a good job? What skills do you need? What if you don't have any work experience? How much money will you make? Which taxes will be taken out of your paycheck – and how do you pay income taxes each year?

On My Own,™ with its interactive CD-ROM, can help you find the answers to these questions — and many more!

How do I use this book?

On My Own™ contains 16 chapters of how-to information you need to know to be a responsible and independent adult. The book and CD-ROM are written in question-and-answer format. For help in finding the answers to your questions, refer to the "Table of Contents" at the front of the book or the "Index" at the end of the book. A list of the main topics covered are listed at the beginning of each chapter in question format and begin with this icon:

The CD-ROM has interactive elements on it. The following icons refer you to those segments:

- Each chapter begins with a quiz. Photocopy the quiz in the book so you can use it again and again or go to the CD-ROM for the interactive version.

- A movie of this segment is shown on the CD-ROM.

- This segment is automatically calculated on the CD-ROM.

- Download this form and print it from the CD-ROM.

- The CD-ROM is linked to many websites so you can gain further information.

- Download screensavers from the CD-ROM for use on your personal computer (Chapter 13 only).

How do I use this CD-ROM?

The CD-ROM is both MAC- and PC-compatible. Just insert the disk in your CD-ROM drive and the program will load itself. It's that easy. Click on a chapter — and then a question — and you're on your way. If you need help, go to the main menu of a chapter and click the HELP key in the lower left corner of your screen. The HELP screen explains how the CD-ROM works:

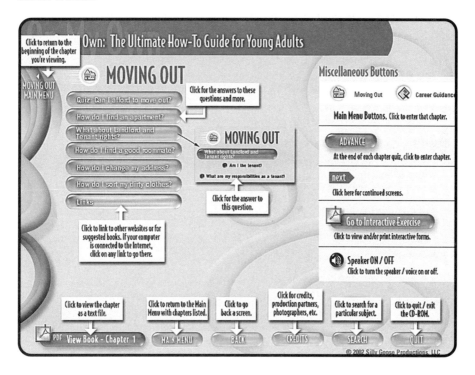

Can I afford to move out?

Interactive CD-ROM

Quiz

So, you want to live on your own. Can you afford to? Have you done the math? Complete the following quiz to help you decide if you're ready to move out — or if you need to stay where you are for a few more months to save some money.

Section A. Am I independently wealthy?   Yes _____ No _____
If **Yes**, you don't need to take the rest of this quiz. If **No**, continue with Section B.

Section B. Do I have a job?   Yes _____ No _____
If **Yes**, continue with Section C. If **No**, how are you going to pay rent and other expenses? Get a job, and then continue with Section C.

Section C. Subtract all the monthly expenses that apply to you:
How much money do I bring home each month? $ _____

1. Subtract my rent payment   – _____
2. Subtract my electric payment   – _____
3. Subtract my water payment   – _____
4. Subtract my sewer payment   – _____
5. Subtract my trash payment   – _____
6. Subtract my telephone/cell phone/pager payment   – _____
7. Subtract my cable TV payment   – _____
8. Subtract my Internet connection fee   – _____
9. Subtract my tuition payment   – _____
10. Subtract my transportation/car payment/gas   – _____
11. Subtract my auto insurance payment   – _____
12. Subtract my rental insurance payment   – _____
13. Subtract my health insurance payment   – _____
14. Subtract my food expenses   – _____
15. Subtract pet care costs (food, etc.)   – _____
16. Subtract my clothing expenses   – _____
17. Subtract my investment in myself (savings/investing)   – _____
18. Subtract my fun and entertainment expenses   – _____

Do I have any money left over? $ _____

continued...

Figure 1A

Moving Out

Have you been dreaming of your first apartment since you became a teenager? Oh, the freedom you'll have ... No one to tell you what to do, when to do it, or how to do it. In theory, it sounds fun. In reality, though, it's work! First, can you afford to move out? And stay out? Learn the basics of having your own place: from finding an apartment to using the *Yellow Pages* to doing your laundry.

 How do I find an apartment?

How do I find an apartment or house to rent?

Check the yellow pages of your phone book for "Apartments"; look in the classified ads in the newspaper; pick up free magazines listing rental properties in your area (usually found at the entrances of grocery stores); ask friends and co-workers; check with local real estate offices; check bulletin boards at the bank, the Laundromat, school, etc. Check with your local Housing & Credit Counseling office. Check the Internet at *www.AptsForRent.com*. You might even drive by an apartment complex that has a sign advertising "Apartment for Rent." Visit as many rental properties as you can, so

Can I afford to move out?

...continued

Monthly rent and utilities should cost no more than 30 percent of your total gross monthly income. How much can you afford to spend on rent and utilities each month?

1. My salary $____/hour × ____hours/week
   × 4.5 weeks/month = Gross Monthly Income. $ _____

2. Gross Monthly Income $____ × .30 = $ _____
   (Total I can afford to spend each month on rent/utilities).

3. Now, add other debt payments (lines 6 thru 18 above)
   to the total I can afford to spend on rent.
   Other debts $____ + $____ (rent/utilities: Lines 1 thru 5)
   = $ _____
   (Total Monthly Debt)

Is your Total Monthly Debt less than what you bring home each month? If not, you have a major problem! You have more bills than you can afford to pay.

- Is there something you can eliminate from your debts, such as a cell phone, cable TV, call-waiting, etc.?

- Can you find a roommate to help pay expenses?

- Can you live with your parent(s) until you save more money, find a better-paying job, or get more hours at work?

- Can you find a cheaper apartment with cheaper utilities?

Figure 1A (continued)

you'll have a good idea of the quality and size of apartment you can get for the amount of money you have to spend.

What about renting a house?

Houses are usually more expensive to rent. They require more maintenance, inside and out. They cost more money to heat and cool, and the ones you can afford when you're just starting out may not be in the best repair — or the best neighborhood. However, if you have several roommates to split the costs, houses are great. Some cities have a limit on the number of unrelated people who can live together in the same house, so check your area's zoning laws or ask the landlord.

What should I look for in a rental property?

Price and location are the two most important factors. View the actual apartment you are considering renting. Don't look at a "similar" one. See the apartment during the day in natural light. Find an apartment you can afford in a safe area with an easy commute to work and/or school. For other considerations, ask the landlord the questions on page 4.

 ## What about Landlord and Tenant rights?

Am I the tenant?

You, as the person renting the apartment, are the tenant. The landlord is the person who owns the house or apartment you rent.

What are my responsibilities as a tenant?

As a tenant, you may be legally responsible to do the following:

● Pay rent on time — every month. Rent is paid in advance. For instance, you pay rent on May 1st to live in the apartment from May 1st through May 31st. You pay again on June 1st to live there through the month of June. Also, if you move in during the middle of the month, you'll have to pay rent on a pro-rated basis. So, if you move in on May 23rd, you'll have to pay rent from May 23rd until May 31st, and then again on June 1st for the month of June.)

● Pay any agreed-upon utilities on time.

How do I find an apartment?

Interactive CD-ROM

Print It!

1. How much is rent? $ _____
    When is it due? _____
2. Who is responsible for paying utilities?
    - ◉ Electricity ○ I pay ○ Landlord pays   ◉ Water ○ I pay ○ Landlord pays
    - ◉ Trash   ○ I pay ○ Landlord pays   ◉ Gas   ○ I pay ○ Landlord pays
    - ◉ Cable TV   ○ I pay ○ Landlord pays   ◉ Other ○ I pay ○ Landlord pays
3. What deposits are required? _____
4. How long does the lease last?   ○ One month   ○ Six months   ○ One year
    Is there a penalty to break the lease?   ○ Yes ○ No
5. Does the apartment come with all appliances?   ○ Yes ○ No
    Do they work?   ○ Yes ○ No
6. Does the shower have adequate water pressure?   ○ Yes ○ No
    Is there plenty of hot water?   ○ Yes ○ No
    Do the faucets work? ○ Yes ○ No   Does the toilet flush? ○ Yes ○ No
7. Are there smoke alarms installed? ○ Yes ○ No   Do they work? ○ Yes ○ No
    Are there at least two ways to exit the residence?   ○ Yes ○ No
8. Are washers and dryers in the building?   ○ Yes ○ No
    What does it cost to use them? $_____
9. Are pets allowed? ○ Yes ○ No   Is there a deposit? $ _____
10. Is there a designated parking place?   ○ Yes ○ No
    Is it included with rent?   ○ Yes ○ No
    Where do guests park? _____
11. Where is the nearest mass transit?_____
12. What security does the apartment have? _____
    Is the main entrance always locked securely?   ○ Yes ○ No
    Are there locks on windows and doors?   ○ Yes ○ No
    Are entryways, parking areas, and area streets well lit? ○ Yes ○ No
    Are there many thefts or vandalisms in this neighborhood? ○ Yes ○ No
13. Is the building clean?   ○ Yes ○ No
    Is the area around the building clean?   ○ Yes ○ No
14. Are the carpets clean and the walls freshly painted?   ○ Yes ○ No
15. If you don't have furniture, is it furnished?   ○ Yes ○ No
    Is the furniture clean and in good shape?   ○ Yes ○ No
    If you do have furniture, will it fit in the apartment?   ○ Yes ○ No
16. How many electrical outlets and phone jacks are there? _____
    Where are they located?_____
    Are high-speed Internet connections available in this location? ○ Yes ○ No
17. How much closet space is available? _____
    If needed, is there extra storage available in the building? _____
18. Is there noise from trains, airports, dogs, construction, or neighbors? ○ Yes ○ No
19. Have there been any complaints about the neighbors?_____
20. If a pool is present, does it have a fence with a locked gate? ○ Yes ○ No

- Keep the rental unit clean.

- Dispose of trash properly.

- Use plumbing, electrical, heating, cooling. and appliances properly.

- Inform the landlord in writing of needed repairs as soon as they are discovered. Don't do any repair or re-decorating (painting, wallpapering, etc.) without the prior written consent of the landlord.

- Respect your neighbors. Don't do any actions that unreasonably disturb the peace and quiet of other tenants. Refrain from intentionally or carelessly damaging the property. You, as the tenant, are also responsible for the actions of your family, friends, guests, or pets in this regard.

- Let the landlord know if you'll be gone more than seven days so he won't think you've abandoned the property.

- When moving out, restore the property to the same condition as when you moved in, excluding normal wear and tear.

- Obey all rules and regulations of the lease and other laws governing landlord/tenant relationships.

What are the landlord's responsibilities?

Specific laws governing the landlord/tenant relationship vary by city and state, but some general rules apply across the country. Most landlords must abide by an "implied warranty of habitability," which means that the house or apartment must be fit for humans to live in. The landlord must:

- Keep floors, stairs, walls, and roofs safe and intact.

- Maintain all common areas (hallways, stairways, courtyards) in a safe and clean condition. (If you're renting a house, you may have to maintain the outside/yard yourself. Ask the landlord before signing a lease.)

- Keep electrical, plumbing, heating, ventilating, and air-conditioning systems and elevators operating safely and properly; and make needed repairs in a reasonable time and manner after being notified.

- Supply running water and reasonable amounts of hot water and heat (although you, the tenant, may be required to pay the utility bills).

- Provide trash receptacles and arrange for trash removal, unless the city or county government does.

- Install and maintain required safety devices, such as smoke detectors, fire alarms, or sprinkler systems.

- Keep other tenants, their families, friends, guests, or pets from unreasonable disturbances. That is, if a complaint is lodged against a tenant in the apartment, the landlord must take action to correct the situation.

- Abide by any other agreements contained in the lease and obey all local laws governing landlord/tenant relationships.

How do I rent the apartment?

Fill out a rental application, to include the following information: your name and current address, social security number, age, name(s) of all parties who will be living in the rental property; your residence history (for most, that would be your parent(s) address); employment and income references (they want to make sure you can pay the rent); bank, credit, and character references; description of pet(s) (if allowed); number of cars (for parking spaces), physical modifications; and an emergency-contact person. The landlord may check personal, financial, and credit records before accepting you as a tenant.

What's a lease — and do I have to sign it?

A lease is any written or oral agreement (preferably written) between a landlord and a tenant. It's a legal contract and must be respected by all parties. You'll probably have to sign a lease before moving into a rental property. Before signing, though, read the lease carefully.

If you have roommates, all of them should sign the lease to make sure they know the commitment and legal responsibilities. (Don't rush to be the most independent of your roommates by putting the apartment, phone, and utilities in your name. You could be the one footing the entire bill — and possibly harming your credit rating.)

What's included in a lease?

A lease contains information that you, the tenant, and the landlord must abide by while you reside in the rental property. It typically includes the following:

Rent

States the amount of rent you must pay each month and what date it is due. Pay your rent by check or money order only. Never pay by cash because it provides no proof that you paid.

Term

States how long the lease is in effect. A typical lease is for a month-to-month rental for a year. This means that you pay rent monthly for a year. At the end of the year, you can choose to sign another year's lease, or you can choose to move somewhere else. If you move before your lease has expired, you are responsible for paying the remainder of the rent due until the lease is complete. So, if you sign a one-year lease, make sure you're going to live there for one year.

Security Deposit

A security deposit is usually due when renting a home, and can be equal to first and last month's rent. This means that if the rent is $300 per month, you would have to pay the landlord $900 upon signing the lease: $300 for this month's rent plus $600 for the deposit. When you move out, the landlord will use your deposit to cover past-due rent (if any), damages to the property (above normal wear and tear), and/or expenses the landlord has incurred if you do not comply with the terms of the lease. The landlord will return the balance of the security deposit, with a list of deductions (if any), to you within 30 days after you have vacated the property. Give your landlord a forwarding address so your deposit can be returned.

> The security deposit cannot be used during the term of your lease for rent or other charges that you owe the landlord.

Rent Raise

Written notice to raise the price of your rent must be made to you at least 45 days before the end of your lease so you can decide whether to sign a new lease at the increased rental price or give a 30-day written notice to move. If you have a signed lease stating that you pay "x" dollars for "x" months, your landlord cannot raise the rent until that lease is up. Read the lease carefully to make sure this is included.

Sub-Leasing

If you decide to move before your lease is up, you cannot let someone else move in and take over your lease without the written consent of the landlord.

Utilities

Utilities will be paid by you or the landlord, and will be stated in the lease. Utilities include electricity, gas, water, sewer, trash, and cable TV. If utilities are not included in the price of your rent, you will have to pay for them. This will add to your monthly expenses. Many utility companies also require a deposit to hook up services.

Inspections

Within five days of moving into your apartment, you should do a walk-through inspection of your new home with the landlord so you can both agree on the condition of the apartment and its contents. Write a detailed record during the walk-through, have both the landlord and you sign this inventory, and each keep a copy. If the landlord fails to do a walk-through with you, do one alone and send a copy to the landlord. Keep a copy for your own records.

Lead-Based Paint Disclosure

Federal regulations require both the landlord and tenant to sign a disclosure recognizing any known presence of lead-based paint and/or lead-based paint hazards in the rental unit.

Repairs

If something needs to be repaired in your apartment, you should notify your landlord, preferably in writing, during business hours unless it's an emergency. Many cities set limits on the time allowed for repairs. For example, if you are without hot water, heat, or electricity, it might have to be repaired within 24 hours.

Landlord and Tenant Warrants

The landlord agrees to the Landlord's Responsibilities, and the tenant (you) agrees to the Tenant's Responsibilities. (See "What are the landlord's responsibilities?" and "What are my responsibilities as a tenant?")

Landlord Entry

The landlord can enter your apartment at reasonable times, with your consent, to inspect the premises, make necessary repairs, spray for bugs, perform routine maintenance, or show the apartment to potential renters. A landlord is free to enter anytime there is a genuine emergency that threatens life or property.

Pets
The lease will state whether you're allowed to have pets, and if so, what size, kind, etc. There may be an additional security deposit for a pet.

Termination of Lease by Tenant
Most leases state that you must give a 30-day written notice when you plan to move. (See "What if I want to move?")

Termination of Lease by Landlord
If you don't pay your rent on time, the landlord can give you a written notice stating that you must either pay all rent due or vacate the premises within five days (number of days varies by state). The landlord can sue you for back rent, expenses to collect back rent from you, and expenses to find a new tenant. Failure to pay your rent can also result in immediate action for eviction, which means that the landlord has legal means to remove you from your apartment.

Pay your
rent
on time!

Signatures
The tenant (you) and the landlord must sign and date the lease. If you have roommates, all should sign the lease so you are not the only party responsible.

Who pays for utilities?
Utilities include electricity, gas, water, sewer, trash, and cable TV. Some utilities are included in the price of your rent — others you may have to pay in addition to your rent. You may have to pay a deposit on these utilities, too. The deposit will be credited or refunded to you after you've paid your bill on time for a set number of months. You might also be billed for installation charges. Keep this in mind when budgeting for your rent.

Utilities are paid monthly. If you have to pay utilities, call the utility companies *before* you sign the lease to ask what the average monthly charge has been for the property. If it's too expensive, find another place to live.

If you can't pay your bill, let the utility company know. Some companies offer a payment plan. If you don't pay, your service may be disconnected, without notice, and any remaining deposit will be added to your final bill. It may be difficult for you to get utilities hooked up the next time and you may have to pay a higher security deposit.

If utilities are billed under your name, it's your responsibility to have your service turned off when you move. If you don't, the next tenant may use the utilities under your name — and you would be responsible for paying the bill.

Look under the following headings in the yellow pages of your phone book for the numbers to call to get utilities hooked up:

- **Electricity**: Electric Light & Power Companies (or check *www.wattage-monitor.com or www.energyguide.com*)

- **Gas**: Gas Companies

- **Water**: Water Companies — Utility

- **Trash**: Trash Hauling

- **Telephone**: Telephone Companies

- **Cable TV**: See Television — Cable CATV & Satellite

Do I have to pay a security deposit?

A security deposit is usually due when renting a home and can be equal to first and last month's rent. This means that if the rent is $300 per month, you would have to pay the landlord $900 upon signing the lease: $300 for this month's rent plus $600 for the deposit. When you move out, the landlord will use your deposit to cover past-due rent, damages to the property (above normal wear and tear), and expenses the landlord has incurred if you

> The security deposit cannot be used during the term of your lease for rent or other charges that you owe the landlord.

don't comply with the terms of the lease. The landlord will return the balance of the security deposit, with a list of deductions (if any), to you within 30 days after you have vacated the property. Give your landlord a forwarding address so your deposit can be returned.

What if I can't pay my rent on time?

If you don't have enough money to pay your rent, contact your landlord immediately to explain the situation. Many landlords are willing to work with you to come up with a payment plan. If you don't cooperate, or try to skip out, legal action may result — and your credit rating may be damaged.

If your rent is late, your landlord only needs to give you a written three-day notice (72 hours) before beginning eviction proceedings. During this 72 hours, you have the opportunity to pay the debt in full or to move. If you do neither of these, the landlord can hire an attorney and begin legal action to evict you. (Evictions can take place even if a tenant is pregnant or ill.)

What if something needs to be repaired?

The best time to ask for repairs and improvements is before you sign the lease. If the landlord agrees to repair something, get it written as part of the lease before you sign it. Don't rely on verbal assurances. Write a letter informing the landord of the items in need of repair. Indicate you would prefer to be present when the repairs are made. See the suggested letter on page 12.

What if I want to move?

If you want to move, most states require you to give a 30-day written notice to your landlord. For instance, if you want to move out on March 1st, your 30-day notice would be given February 1st — 30 days before you plan to move out. If you move out before your lease is up, you can be held financially responsible for the remainder of rent that's due until your lease officially ends. See the suggested letter on page 13.

What if I don't have any furniture?

Apartments can be rented with or without furniture. Rented furniture usually includes living room and bedroom furniture. Furnished apartments cost more to rent because you are renting the apartment and the furniture. Most apartments have major appliances included (stove, refrigerator, and dishwasher). If you're renting a house, you may have to pro-

(Today's Date)

Dear (*Landlord's Name*):

The following item(s) need to be repaired at my house/apartment/trailer at (*address*):

_____

_____

_____

I would like to be home when the maintenance work is done. I can arrange for myself or someone else to be there. Please call me at (*your phone number*) to let me know when the repair(s) will be done so I can make arrangements.

Thank you,

(*Your Printed Name and Signature*)

Figure 1C

(*Today's Date*)

Dear (*Landlord's Name*):

The purpose of this letter is to give you my legal 30-day notice. When I have finished moving out, I would like to do a move-out inspection with you to ensure the return of my security deposit. When it gets closer to the move-out date, I will call you to arrange a time that is at our mutual convenience. I plan to be entirely out and have the keys returned to you by (*date*).

Sincerely,

(*Your Printed Name and Signature*)

Figure 1D

vide appliances before you sign the lease. Check before you sign the lease because that's an additional expense.

 ## Why is the phone book my best reference tool?

Why is the phone book my best reference tool?

Because it holds the answers to any questions you may have. If you really want to be independent, get in the habit of looking in your phone book first — and making a few phone calls on your own to find answers. The phone book contains the following sections:

Residential Pages

This is usually the white pages that list home phone numbers and addresses. (Unlisted phone numbers and cell phone numbers are not included.)

Business Pages

This section lists business phone numbers and addresses.

Government Pages

These are usually in the middle of the phone book between the white pages and yellow pages. Government pages include phone numbers and addresses of city, county, state, and federal government offices. They also include area schools, area codes for your state, zip codes for your state, and addresses of elected government officials.

Yellow Pages

The yellow pages contain businesses sorted by type of business. An index is at the back of the phone book so you can easily search for anything you may need. If you can't find what you're looking for under a certain heading, think about other headings you could look under. For example, *Cable TV* is listed under *Television* — not *Cable TV*. If you're not sure you've found the company that can answer your question, call and ask. Most people are glad to help!

How do I choose a phone company?

It can be a bit overwhelming deciding which phone company to use. There are so many choices available: local phone companies, long-distance phone companies, cellular phones, roaming charges, nationwide service, companies providing phone and Internet access, pre-paid phone cards, nighttime rates, daytime rates, weekend rates, in-state rates, state-to-state rates, and more. So, how do you decide? First, you can ask friends, family, and co-workers for referrals of companies to use — and companies *not* to use. You can also do some research by calling several companies to compare their rates.

Do I need to read my phone bill each month?

Read your bill carefully and ask questions. Call your carrier every three months and ask, *"Am I on the cheapest calling plan?"* New plans come up regularly, but companies don't bother to tell you about them. Watch for monthly minimum fees you didn't expect. Also watch for "cramming" — when you're billed for special services you didn't order; and "slamming" — switching your telephone carrier without your knowledge or permission. (Slammers often distribute contest or sweepstakes forms that contain fine print switching your telephone service, so never fill out entry forms without reading the fine print carefully.)

If you don't use long distance a lot, consider dropping your long-distance carrier. Instead, use pre-paid phone cards, which are sold at many retail outlets. Just be sure you have a low-cost card. The package should disclose the rates and fees. Be sure to use your minutes before they expire.

What's the cheapest way to get Directory Assistance?

Major carriers charge $1.99 per call to look up a phone number for you — even if they can't find the number or find the wrong one. Your local phone company's 1-411 service costs about half that. Ask your phone company for rates or check free sites on the Internet: *www.anywho.com, www.whitepages.com,* and *www.yellowpages.com.*

What if I'm getting obscene and harassing calls?

State and federal laws make it a crime to place obscene or harassing phone calls. The penalty is a fine and/or imprisonment. If you receive an obscene phone call, remember the following:

- You control the phone — not the caller. Hang up at the first obscene word.

- Hang up if the caller remains silent after the second time you say *"hello."*

- Don't give your name or address unless you know who's calling.

● If unwanted calls persist, call your phone company to report it. They can provide Caller I.D., Call Blocker, or Call Trace. (These may cost you a small fee.)

How can I stop telemarketers from calling?

According to Congress, Americans lose an estimated $40 billion each year due to fraudulent sales of goods and services over the telephone. Telemarketers who rip off consumers are committing a crime. These callers may say you are eligible to win a prize, ask for a contribution to a bogus charity (See Chapter 14, "How do I know if a charity is bogus?"), or promise to get money back that you lost in an earlier telemarketing scam.

To stop telemarketers, get Caller I.D. Many "unknown" or "out of area" callers are telemarketers. Tell each telemarketer that you want to be on the "**DO NOT CALL**" list. Your reply might be, *"No, thank you. I'm not interested. Please remove my name from your list."*

You can also send a request to have your name removed from telemarketers' lists to the Direct Marketing Association (DMA). (Not all telemarketers belong to the DMA, so you may still get some calls.)

> **Telephone Preference Service**
> Direct Marketing Association
> Dept. P
> PO Box 9014
> Farmingdale, NY 11735-9014

Don't pay to get a prize. It's illegal for any company to make you pay to enter a contest. (Your chances of winning are not improved by making a purchase.) Don't allow any caller to intimidate or bully you into buying something. Don't give any caller your bank account number unless you are authorizing a payment to be deducted. Don't give your credit card number to anyone unless you made the call and are making a purchase. Don't wire money or send money by an overnight delivery service unless you initiated the transaction.

If you are a victim of telemarketing fraud, call your state's attorney general to report it. Also report it to the National Fraud Information Center (NFIC) at 1-800-876-7060 or *www.fraud.org.*

How do I find a good roommate?

How do I find a good roommate?

Ask your friends first. It's always safest to live with someone you know. If no one is in need of a new place to live, search the following sources:

- Friends — and friends of friends.

- Co-workers or classmates.

- Classified ads in newspapers. (You can place your own ad, too.)

- Bulletin boards in community places (banks, Laundromats, work, etc.).

- College bulletin boards and newspapers.

- Landlords and apartment-finder companies.

- Internet sites.

Where do we meet?

If you must find a roommate but don't know anyone, keep personal safety in mind. Meet the potential roommate in a coffee shop or restaurant. Do *not* meet the person in your home.

What do I ask?

Respecting each other is the most important thing you need for a roommate-relationship to work. Be honest with the potential roommate (and yourself) about what you really want. Look for compatibility with your lifestyle. Ask pointed questions to screen out those who aren't compatible with you. Do you smoke? What kind of music do you like? What are your hours? Do you have a job (or a way to pay your share of the rent)? Do you have a significant other that will be at the apartment a lot? (This may be an issue if you end up paying rent for the boyfriend or girlfriend that seems to have moved in.) Are you clean? Will you buy your own groceries? Do you stay up late or sleep late? Ask for references and call them.

Do I need renters insurance?

Do I need renters insurance?

Renters insurance is not required by law (like auto insurance is), but if you rent a house or apartment, rental insurance is recommended to cover theft or damage to your personal property. It also provides liability protection, which can insure you for damages caused by you, your family or guests, or pets. Insurance companies can tailor a policy to fit your rental needs.

Renters may assume that since the landlord has insurance, they don't need it. While landlords do have insurance, it's only for the building itself — not for the people who live in the building (or their possessions). Landlords are not responsible for protecting renters' property. As a renter, you have no coverage if your possessions are lost in a fire or burglary or if someone sues you for getting hurt on your property or for property damage you, your guests, or your pets may cause.

What is personal property insurance?

Coverage that protects your household belongings, such as your TV, sound system, computer, clothes, furniture, jewelry, appliances, and most other personal items if they're stolen or damaged. Personal possessions in your car or trunk that are stolen are usually covered under renters (or homeowners) policies — not auto policies. Check with an insurance agent.

Most renters' policies are "named perils" policies. This means that the insurance company will only pay for property stolen or damaged by one of the specific perils or reasons listed in the policy (usually theft, vandalism, fire, smoke, lightning, windstorms, and hail). Exclusions typically include animals, birds, or fish; motor vehicles, including equipment and accessories; flood water damage; water damage from sewer backup; neglect; earthquakes; or power failure. Separate policies may need to be purchased if you live in a flood zone or earthquake zone. Check with an insurance agent.

Do I get "actual cash value" or "replacement cost?"

Most companies insure the contents of your rental home on an **actual cash value** basis. You can insure your belongings at **replacement cost**, but the premium will be 15 to 40 percent higher.

To get an idea of how each works, let's pretend ...

You purchased a couch in 2000 for $700. The couch was destroyed in 2002. The value is now $300. You have an insurance deductible of $200. A new couch, similar in style, now costs $900.

If you have an **actual cash value** policy, coverage entitles you to the following:

Current value of the couch	$300
Minus your deductible	- 200
Your reimbursement	$100

($100 to purchase the new $900 couch)

If you have a **replacement cost** policy, coverage entitles you to the following:

Current value of the couch	$300
Minus your deductible	- 200
Your initial reimbursement	$100

($100 to purchase the new $900 couch)

Your replacement cost*	+ 600
Total reimbursement	$700

(Replacement Cost minus your deductible.)

* Reimbursed when you show proof of purchase to your insurance company.

Your policy should be based on the quality and expense of your possessions. And, no matter what the value, the amount you actually receive will always be reduced by the amount of your deductible. (Your deductible is paid "per incident" not "per item.") Proof of purchase is a must to get your full reimbursement for replacement cost. Also, if you buy a more expensive replacement item, the insurance company will not reimburse you for that cost. They will only reimburse you for the replacement of a product "equal" to the one you had insured. Any additional cost is out of your pocket.

What is personal liability insurance?

Liability insurance covers you for damages caused by you, your family, or your pets, whether you're at home or somewhere else, subject to some special limits and exclusions. Liability insurance also includes damage to property of others, usually covering about $500 in damages. Liability is another term for responsibility. What if you accidentally started a fire? You could be sued for property loss or injuries to others. Or what if a friend falls down while coming into your house and breaks a leg? Your renters policy would cover the medical payments up to your policy's limits and your legal fees if sued.

How much coverage do I need?

The easiest way to determine how much coverage you need is to make an inventory of all your belongings. List the item, the date purchased, and the actual cost. Take photos or videos of your stuff. Keep receipts for big-ticket items.

The amount of property and liability coverage you choose determines the cost of the policy. Standard coverage ranges from $25,000 to $100,000. The medical expenses part of the policy usually pays up to $2,000 for medical expenses if someone is injured in your home by you, your family, your guests, or your pets.

Don't over-insure. The insurance company won't pay more than the actual cost of repairs or replacements. And ask for discounts. Discounts are offered for multiple policies with the same insurance company (such as auto and renters), and for home safety devices such as burglar alarms, smoke detectors, and sprinkler systems. Another way to save is to increase the amount of the deductible. The higher your deductible, the lower your premium (the cost you pay for the policy).

How do I get renters insurance?

Ask family, friends, or co-workers for the name of the insurance company/agent they use, or look in the yellow pages of the phone book. Call several companies to compare costs. First, you'll get what's called a "quote" — the price of the policy. To get an accurate quote, you'll usually need to provide the following:

- Coverage and limits you want.

- Description of your home and possessions.

- History of other losses.

- Square footage of your rental property.

- Fire and security devices.

- Distance you live from the nearest fire department and fire hydrant.

Ask an insurance agent the following questions when calling for a quote:

- How much would I save if I increase my deductible?

- What is not covered?

- Is my coverage actual cash value or replacement cost?

- Does coverage include water damage or sewer back-up?

- Does the policy cover my jewelry, antiques, or special collections?

- What proof do I need in case of loss?

- Do you have monthly payment plans available?

How do I change my address?

How do I change my address?

Your local post office has a Mover's Guide that includes the information needed to change your address. Send a *Change of Address* form (PS Form 3575) to your local post office at least one month prior to moving (or as soon as you know your new address if it's less than one month).

If your move is temporary, for a season or a semester, notify the post office of your address change with the official *Change of Address* form. The post office will forward your mail until the Stop Date listed on your form.

How do I notify companies that I've moved?

It's your responsibility to notify all companies of your new address. It is *not* the post office's responsibility. Mail an *Address Notification Card* (PS Form 3576) to businesses and people that send you mail (credit card companies, insurance companies, the IRS, family, friends, magazines, catalogs, newspapers, etc.). These cards are free at the post office.

Most states require that you get a new driver's license within 30 days from the date you move. (Replacement costs are only a few dollars.) If you own a car, you'll also need to contact the Department of Motor Vehicles to change your vehicle registration.

And, you'll need to register to vote in your new district. Call the County Election office.

Will the post office forward my mail?

The following mail will be forwarded at no charge for the period indicated:

- 12 months for first-class, priority, and express mail.

- 60 days for newspapers and magazines.

- 12 months for packages weighing 16 ounces or more if your new address is in the same *local* area. You pay forwarding charges if you move outside the local area. (If you don't want this class of mail forwarded, contact your local post office.)

- Circulars, books, catalogs, and advertising mail under 16 ounces will not be forwarded unless requested by the mailer. You must contact the companies to change your address.

If you receive mail with a yellow label attached, that means you must notify the sender. The sender doesn't have your new address — and the post office won't continue forwarding. If mail is received after the above dates expire, the post office will return your mail to the sender.

What does the yellow label on my mail mean?

If you receive mail with a yellow label attached, notify the sender. The sender doesn't have your new address — and the post office won't continue forwarding.

Should I notify the IRS?

Many refund checks are returned to the IRS each year because the post office, by law, cannot forward them. To notify the IRS of your move, call 1-800-829-3676 and request Form 8822 or download one at *www.irs.gov.*

What about pet tags?

Pets can't ask for directions — so, if you have a pet, order a tag with your new address on it.

How can I stop getting so much junk mail?

Americans spend an average of eight years opening junk mail. One of the not-so-positive things about living on your own is that the junk mail will soon begin. You'll get credit card offers, magazine offers, telephone offers, and more. When junk mail comes with a prepaid envelope, write *"Please remove from your mailing list."* by your address and return the envelope. Don't return the product registration or warranty card when you purchase a new product. (Your warranty is still good.) Don't fill out entry forms to win a free car, a cruise, a trip, etc. (You won't win anyway!) To remove your name from four major credit-reporting agency lists, block unauthorized access to your credit record, and stop unwanted credit card and loan offers, call toll free 1-888-567-8688. You can also write a letter stating that you don't want to receive junk mail from the Direct Marketing Association:

> Direct Marketing Association
> Mail Preference Services
> Direct Marketing Association
> PO Box 9008
> Farmingdale, NY 11735-9008

Check out *www.junkbusters.com* to learn more techniques to reduce junk mail.

 ## What household safety should I be aware of?

What if my home is on fire?

Always crawl close to the floor in smoke. Feel each door for heat before opening it. If your clothing catches on fire, stop, drop to the floor, and roll over and over again to put out the flames. (Remember what you learned in grade school?) Call the fire department from a neighbor's phone.

For home fire prevention tips, go to *www.nfpa.org* or *www.sparky.org*.

Do I need a smoke detector?

Yes. Nearly half of all home fires and three out of every five fire-related deaths in the U.S. occur in residences *without* smoke detectors. Install smoke detectors on each floor of your home. Test the detector each month by pressing the test button. Change the batteries every six months when you change your clocks for daylight savings time.

If your rental property doesn't have a smoke detector, ask your landlord to install one. Many fire departments also offer free or low-cost smoke detectors.

What about smoking in bed?

Despite all the warnings about smoking in bed, it remains the most common reason for fatal house fires.

Any tips for electrical safety?

Electrical Cords

Don't create a fire hazard by overloading extension cords. Use a power strip, like you would for a computer. Make sure that cords don't have cracks, frays, or breaks, and that plugs and prongs are not loose when plugged into outlets. Never yank a cord from an outlet. Place cords where they won't be tripped over or receive excessive wear. Placing cords under rugs, furniture, or through doorways wears out the insulation, which can lead to a fire.

AC Adapters

Be careful not to overload wall outlets with AC adapters (those little black boxes used to power answering machines, cordless phones, handheld vacuums, and other appliances). Avoid putting AC adapters behind a bed, couch, or heavy curtain, which can cause them to overheat and spark a fire.

Ground Fault Circuit Interrupters

In the bathroom and kitchen, have ground fault circuit interrupters (GFCIs) installed for outlets near all water supplies. Know where the fuse box or circuit breaker is and how to operate it. (Ask your landlord.) Unless you are qualified, get expert help with wiring improvements in your home.

TV, VCR, Stereo Equipment

These appliances are responsible for 2,000 blazes per year. Allow plenty of ventilation for the machines. Do not stack newspapers, magazines, or anything else on your TV. The piles can block air vents, causing the interior to overheat. Also, don't set plants on the TV because dripping water can cause the wires to short out. Avoid talking on the telephone during a lightning storm. You could get shocked.

Small Appliances

Many appliance fires can be traced to problems with power cords. Avoid tugging on the power cords of small appliances, such as blow dryers or electric blankets. It can short out the wires. Turn off any appliance that sputters, stalls, sparks, or gives the slightest shock. Always unplug an appliance to clean it. Make sure your hands and feet are dry when using electric appliances.

Portable Heaters

Keep blankets, clothing, curtains, furniture, and anything that could get hot and catch fire away from portable heaters. Plug heaters directly into the wall socket (not an extension cord) and unplug them when they're not in use.

Can irons cause fires?

A cotton shirt left beneath a hot iron can burn within two minutes, and can go up in flames in 20 minutes. Always stand your iron upright when you're done ironing. Never leave it face-down on the ironing board. Unplug the iron when not in use.

What about the lint trap in the dryer?

Dryers account for 14,500 fires, so remove the lint from the dryer after each load. When lint builds up and clogs airflow in the dryer or ductwork, the appliance's components overheat.

Any tips for safe cooking?

An unattended pot on a stove is one of the most common causes of house fires. If you must answer the phone or leave the kitchen, turn off the stove and carry a spoon with you to remind yourself that you're cooking. Keep pot holders, towels, pizza boxes, etc. away from the stove and other appliances. Keep appliances clean.

In the event of an oven or microwave fire, keep the door closed. Oxygen will feed the fire. The fire is usually contained in the oven — and the microwave should be turned off and unplugged. Built-up grease catches fire easily. In a grease fire, smother the flames with a lid or larger pan. Don't put water or flour on a grease fire. It will splatter and spread the fire. Never try to carry a pan with a flaming grease fire outdoors. You may burn your arms and spread the fire.

Small, heated appliances set off 3,900 blazes per year, a significant number of them started by toasters. The major cause: a jamming cartridge mechanism caused by holding down the pop-up mechanism to make your English muffin a littler crisper. This causes the toaster to overheat, damaging its electrical parts, and increasing the chances for a future fire. Also, don't store anything on top of a toaster oven.

Keep a Class ABC fire extinguisher in the kitchen. If you don't know how to use one, stop by the fire department. They'll show you.

Do I need deadbolt locks on my doors?

Install a deadbolt lock on all of your exterior doors. If your rental property doesn't have deadbolt locks, ask the landlord to install them. If he refuses, ask if he'll split the cost with you or offer to pay to have them installed. Your safety is worth a few dollars.

What basic tools do I need?

Your first toolkit should include the bare minimum of a flashlight, hammer, flat-head screwdriver, Phillips-head screwdriver, adjustable crescent wrench, nails for hanging pictures, safety goggles, a bucket, and a First Aid kit.

 ## What are the basics of keeping my home clean?

Can I decorate to fit my own style?

Emphasize your own personal flair. Group things together — a collection of cars, books, fast food toys, whatever. Displaying a collection of your favorite items adds interest to any room. And, it's your home — you get to decorate any way you want! One of the cheapest and best things you can do to make your home look better is to simply make it neater. Clutter makes a room look smaller. Painting is also another cheap way to make a room look better (but check with your landlord before painting to see if it's allowed).

Any tips for keeping my kitchen clean?

Why bother with cleaning? Because bacteria can double every 20 minutes if given the right conditions. That means a single bacterium on a wet countertop can reproduce to nearly 17 million in just eight hours. Buy a package of dishrags at a discount store. (They usually come in packs of 12 for about $4.) Use a clean dishrag and hot, soapy water to wipe off your counters. Wipe behind any appliances or other items on your counter. Crumbs collect behind them — inviting roaches. Wipe off the front of your refrigerator and the handles, and the inside of it. Wipe water spots off your sink edge and faucet handles. Sweep weekly, or more often, if needed. Mop as often as needed. Wipe up spills as they happen. Buy a $4 plastic plate cover for your microwave. They work wonders for stopping the splattering of food in your microwave. Organize your cupboards, drawers, and refrigerator.

Should I buy two sets of sheets?

Buy two sets of sheets so you can change sheets weekly — and still be able to go to bed if you haven't done the laundry. Vacuum your bedroom weekly. Organize your closets and drawers.

What about my living room?

Vacuum weekly. Dust as often as needed. (The *Swiffer Sweeper* pads are wonderful for dusting and for sweeping hardwood floors and tile!) If you snack in the living room, take your dirty dishes to the kitchen when you're done. Pick up clutter each night before heading to bed. Allow smoking outdoors only. Use coasters for drinks.

How often should I clean the bathroom?

Change your shower curtain liner when the mold and mildew start growing. Yuck! Invest in a bathroom, tub and tile cleaner; a toilet bowl brush; and toilet bowl cleaner. Clean the bath/shower, toilet, and sink weekly. Wipe off faucets and mirrors. Sweep weekly. To clean bathroom grout, wet the grout and apply baking soda with a small scrub brush and rinse well. Spot-treat stubborn mildew stains with diluted chlorine bleach.

What cleaning needs to be done when I move in?

When you move in, do a thorough cleaning of everything with an antiseptic cleanser. You never know how clean or not-so-clean the tenant before you was. Here's a tip for filling in small picture holes in walls: If the walls are flat-white, fill the holes with white toothpaste (not the gel kind). If the walls are brightly painted, add a dab of watercolor paint to the toothpaste.

What basic food safety do I need to know?

Why sing *Happy Birthday* when I wash my hands?

Hands spread germs, so when preparing food, wash your hands before and after handling, as well as after touching pets and using the bathroom. Wash your hands with warm, soapy water for at least 20 seconds. (That's how long it takes to sing the *Happy Birthday* song — twice.)

What basic food safety should I know?

Bacteria can double every 20 minutes if given the right conditions — which means that a single bacterium can reproduce to nearly 17 million in just eight hours. Use basic food safety to reduce your risk of food poisoning:

Meats, Fish, and Poultry

The safest way to eat meats is to cook them until they are no longer red in the middle and juices run clear. Never allow raw meat, poultry, and fish to come in contact with other foods.

Raw Eggs

Foods containing raw eggs, such as homemade ice cream, cake batter, eggnog, and mayonnaise carry a Salmonella risk, so keep them refrigerated.

Leftovers

When reheating leftovers, be sure the food reaches a temperature of 165 degrees to kill microorganisms. Hot foods should be refrigerated within two hours after cooking. Don't keep food if it's been standing out for more than two hours. Don't taste it, either. Even a small amount of contaminated food can cause illness. Leftovers should be eaten within three to five days. If in doubt, throw it out.

Thawing Foods

Thaw foods on plates on your refrigerator's bottom shelf; the microwave oven; or put the package in a water-tight plastic bag submerged in cold water, changing the water every 30 minutes. Foods defrosted in the microwave oven should be cooked immediately after thawing. Do not thaw meat, poultry, and fish products on the counter or in the sink without cold water; bacteria can multiply rapidly at room temperature.

Food Storage

Avoid storing food in cabinets that are under the sink; or that have water, drain, or heating pipes passing through them because it can attract insects and rodents through openings that are difficult to seal adequately. Seal packages tightly to prevent food from becoming stale.

The Fridge

The temperature in your fridge should be between 35 and 40 degrees. Higher temperatures allow bacteria to grow at an unacceptable rate and create a health risk for you. (Any temperature below 32 degrees will freeze your milk.)

Are cutting boards safe?

More than one-third of food-borne illnesses in the home are caused by cross-contamination where "clean" food picks up bacteria from tainted cutting boards, knives, and other utensils. After exposure to raw meat juices, wash cutting boards and utensils in hot, soapy water; rinse; then allow to air dry. Washing with a damp cloth will not remove bacteria.

What about the sink and countertops?

On average, 229,000 germs per square inch are found on frequently-touched kitchen faucet handles. The kitchen sink and drain are breeding grounds for germs, and are often overlooked. Clean the sink, faucets, and refrigerator doors and handles with hot, soapy water, or wipe them with a sanitizing cleanser.

Countertops also have germs, however, 99.9 percent of the time, cleaning the surfaces with hot, soapy water takes care of the debris that could harbor organisms. Disposable paper towels are best for countertop cleanup.

Do sponges contain the most germs?

Some 700 million microorganisms lurk in a typical damp household sponge, more than are found in any other spot in the kitchen or the bathroom. If you must use sponges, soak them three times a week in a solution of 3/4 cup bleach to one gallon of water. Let the sponges air-dry. Use paper towels instead to clean up spills, especially juices from raw meats.

Any safety tips for washing dishes?

To prevent contamination of freshly-washed dishes, pots, and pans, allow them to air-dry rather than using a dish towel to dry them. That goes for any dishes or pans in the dishwasher that may have a few drops of water on them when the cycle is finished. Make sure bowls, cups, pans, and other dishes are completely dry before you store them.

For the dishwasher, scrape off large food pieces and bones. Soaking and pre-washing is generally only recommended in cases of burned-on or dried-on food. Be sure the dishwasher is full, but not overloaded. Let your dishes air-dry. If you don't have an automatic air-dry switch, turn off the control knob after the final rinse and prop the door open a little so the dishes will dry faster.

 ## How do I sort my dirty clothes?

Interactive CD-ROM

Movie

How do I sort my dirty clothes?
Sort your dirty clothes by color, soil content, and fabric type. Each type listed below should be a separate load of laundry:

- 1 load = whites (socks and underwear)

- 1 load = light colors

- 1 load = similar medium or dark colors

- 1 load = heavily-soiled clothes (work clothes)

- 1 load = delicates (lingerie, lace, machine-washable silks)

- 1 load = towels

- 1 load = sheets and blankets

How do I remove stains?
Pre-treat or pre-soak stains before washing. Treat stains as soon as possible for best results. To pre-treat small stains, apply undiluted liquid detergent or a paste of granular detergent and water directly to the stain. Dish soap also works well to treat food and grease stains. Allow the product to soak in, then rub gently. Don't mix or combine stain removal products, especially ammonia and chlorine bleach.

For deep-set soils, old stains, or extensive staining, soak items in the hottest water safe for the fabric (read the label) for up to 30 minutes using a detergent with bleach.

Air-dry stained clothes until the stain is removed. If you put the clothing in the dryer, the heat can permanently set the stain.

How do I wash my dirty clothes?

When you take your clothes off and throw them in the dirty clothes pile, turn everything right-side out ... your socks, shirts, jeans ... and empty all your pockets. Make this a lifetime habit. It will make laundry a much easier task.

Interactive CD-ROM

Movie

To wash your clothes, follow the directions on the washer and the detergent packaging to determine how much detergent to use and when to add it. Some washers suggest putting the detergent in the washer first — then adding your clothes. Other washers have a container that holds detergent.

Drop items in the washer loosely and evenly. Don't wrap laundry around the agitator (that thing in the middle of the washer). Avoid overloading the washer and don't shove laundry in the washer too tightly. Over-packing can cause poor cleaning, create excessive lint, and wear items out faster.

Add non-chlorine, color-safe bleaches for your really tough laundry problems. You can use a liquid fabric softener (added in the wash) or dryer sheets to soften and freshen your laundry. Dryer sheets also help control static cling.

Remove your wet laundry from the washer so it won't mildew.

How do I dry my laundry?

When you take your clothes out of the washer, shake them lose as you put them in the dryer. (The dryer doesn't have to work so hard to dry your clothes and they won't get as wrinkled.) Fold your clothes or hang them up when they're dry.

Remove the lint from the dryer after each load of laundry, otherwise you create a fire hazard.

What can I recycle?

What can I recycle?

Recycling saves natural resources. The average American uses 142 steel cans per year, with two million tons of steel cans put in landfills each year. It takes 95 percent less energy to produce an aluminum can from an existing can than one from ore. The most common recyclables include glass, newspapers, aluminum, magazines, cardboard, pop cans, tin cans (such as canned vegetables), plastic, and paper. Paper makes up 40 percent of the trash in our landfills.

What is household hazardous waste?

Several common products around your home could be hazardous to your health and to your clean water supply, if handled improperly. These include household cleaners (drain, toilet, and oven cleaners), pesticides, paints and stains, used motor oil, spot and stain removers, waxes, car batteries, and polishes. Read and follow disposal instructions on hazardous waste because they eventually contaminate rivers and lakes when they are thrown in the trash, down a drain, or on the ground. Check the yellow pages in your phone book for recycling centers near you or visit Earth's 911 at *www.1800cleanup.org* to find out how to dispose of hazardous products.

 ## Additional Information for this Chapter

Books

- *I'm Outta Here! Facing the Tough Choices After High School* by Len Woods

- *Your Own Two Feet (and How to Stand on Them): Surviving and Thriving after Graduation* by Ingrid Meyer

- *Reality 101: Practical Advice on Entering and Succeeding in the Real World* by Fran Katzanek

- *How to Do Just About Everything: 1,001 Easy-to-Follow, Step-by-Step Instructions from the Web's Most Comprehensive Source of Practical Information* by Courtney Rosen and the eHow Editors

Web Links

- *www.AptsForRent.com*

- *www.apartmentguide.com*

- *www.imove.com*

- *www.artofmoving.com*

- *www.move-n-storage.com*

- *www.roomiematch.com*

- *www.rentlaw.com*

- *www.wattagemonitor.com*

- *www.energyguide.com*

- *www.anywho.com*

- *www.feist.com*

- *www.whitepages.com*

- *www.yellowpages.com*

Interactive CD-ROM

Click to the web from the CD-ROM!

Web Resource

- *www.junkbusters.com*

- *www.fraud.com*

- *www.usps.com*

- *www.irs.gov*

- *www.eHow.com*

- *www.homestore.com*

- *www.1800cleanup.org*

- *www.cleaning101.com*

- *www.sparky.org*

- *www.nfpa.org*
(National Fire Prevention Association)

Do I control my money?

Do you control your money or does it control you? If you think you're in control, this chapter will give you a few pointers that might help you even more. If you don't think you're in control, following the guidance in this chapter can make the rest of your life easier. How do you know if you're in control? Ask yourself the following questions:

**Interactive
CD-ROM**

Calculator

- Do you pay your bills on time? Do you save 10 percent of your paycheck each month? Do you have enough cash to get through the month? If you answered YES to these questions, you're in control of your money.

- Do you use your credit card to pay for groceries, personal items, or other daily needs because you don't have any other way to pay for them? Do you have very little cash, if any, left over at the end of the month? Do you have any to save or invest? Do you make only the minimum monthly payment on your credit card? Do you worry about money? Are you working overtime or taking an extra job just to keep up with your spending? Are you always late with bill payments? Are you getting calls or letters from creditors about overdue bills? If you answered YES to these questions, you're NOT in control of your money. It's controlling you.

Experts suggest that your debt should be no more than 10 percent of your total take-home pay. Use the following calculator to compute your Debt-to-Income Ratio.

Debt-to-Income Ratio

Calculate your Debt-to-Income Ratio to determine whether you're in financial trouble. Continue to calculate it every three months until you're either completely out of debt or satisfied with your debt ratio. Then, check your ratio every six to 12 months to make sure you stay in control of your finances.

Debts	*Minimum Monthly Payment*
Credit Card(s)	$ _____
Car Loan/Lease	$ _____
Student Loan	$ _____
Department Store Credit	$ _____
Gas Card	$ _____
Other Loan(s)	$ _____
Other Loan(s)	$ _____
Other Loan(s)	$ _____

continued...

Finances

Chapter 2

It's not the amount of money you make that's important. It's how you manage the money you make that counts. Do you have enough money to pay all your expenses each month? Do you know how to balance a checkbook? Should you carry a balance on your credit card? When do you start planning for retirement? And what happens if you get in over your head? Take control of your money — and you'll take control of your life.

The information in this chapter is intended for informational purposes only. It is

not all-inclusive and cannot substitute for professional financial or legal guidance.

 ## How much money do I need?

Do I need a budget?

Does the idea of planning for your financial future seem too complex or confusing? Do you live paycheck to paycheck, with no spending plan, no savings plan, and no idea when you're going to be out of debt? Do you think you shouldn't even bother since you don't earn enough money to make ends meet now? You're wrong! You just need a plan.

People who know how they spend their money are in control of their finances. Whether you earn $5,000 or $500,000 a year, a budget is the first

Do I control my money?

...continued

1. Total Monthly Payments * $ _____
   *Does not include housing expenses of
   rent and utilities.

2. Monthly Take-Home Pay $ _____
   Your income after taxes are withheld —
   the amount of your paycheck.

3. Debt-to-Income Ratio   _____
   (Percentage of after-tax money that pays   Divide Line 1 by Line 2.
   your monthly non-housing debts.)

4. Debt-to-Income Percentage   _____%
                                         Multiply Line 3 by 100.

SCORES

Ratio	Percentage	Rating
0.0 to 0.05	0% to 5%	Excellent! You're a money marvel!
0.06 to 0.10	6% to 10%	Good. Now concentrate on paying off a creditor.
0.11 to 0.15	11% to 15%	Not good, but you can still recover. Read this chapter.
0.16 to 0.19	16% to 19%	You're in trouble. Call your creditors and a credit counselor.
0.20+	20% or more	You're out of control! Seek credit counseling now!

and most important step you can take to put your money to work for you. A budget is simply a tool to make you aware of how and where you spend your money — and a guideline to help you spend your money on the things that are most important to you. A budget gives you freedom to achieve your goals.

How much money do I need?

Gather your pay stubs, bank statements, and credit card statements for the past year to see where you're spending your money — and then get busy implementing your money plan! The **Monthly Expense Plan** and the **Monthly Money Plan** will walk you through the process of establishing a budget. Use the forms on pages 39 – 41 or print them from the interactive CD-ROM. Then follow these steps:

1. Complete the **Monthly Expense Plan**. List all of your expenses. If you don't know how much you spend on an item, keep a daily spending log for a few weeks by writing down everything you buy. List the monthly expenses and then multiply that amount by 12 to get the annual total. (Personalize the list. If you need to add or delete something from it, do so.)

2. Transfer your expense totals to the **Monthly Money Plan**. (This is your budget.)

3. List all sources of monthly income. All earnings should be the net amount — after taxes. This is what you take home in your paycheck. (If you listed your gross pay, you would have to deduct taxes because that's not money you have available to spend. It's already spent.)

4. Subtract your TOTAL MONTHLY EXPENSES from your TOTAL MONTHLY INCOME. Do the same for the annual totals.

5. How many times do you get paid each month? Once, twice, four times? Divide your TOTAL MONTHLY EXPENSES by the number of paychecks you get each month. (For example, if you get paid twice a month, you would divide your total by two.) This gives you the amount of money you need from each paycheck to pay your bills.

If your TOTAL MONTHLY EXPENSES is greater than your TOTAL

MONTHLY INCOME, you need to decide how you can reduce your monthly expenses or find a way to earn more income.

6. Stick with your **Monthly Money Plan**. Review your plan each month. At the end of each month, compare actual expenses against what you budgeted. Did you come close? If not, adjust the amount(s) for the next month's budget. Continue making a plan each month. That's how you maintain control of your money! (See "Can I afford to move out?" for more information on budgeting.)

Do I need to buy budgeting software?

No. While good software will make budgeting easier, it's not necessary. A piece of notebook paper and pen work just as well. Or print the **Monthly Expense Plan** and the **Monthly Money Plan** forms to use. What's important is that you create a budget, set goals — and then follow through.

Can I be a millionaire?

It won't happen overnight — but you can be. If you create a plan and stick with it, being a millionaire is very possible. And it doesn't depend on how little or how much money your parent(s) make. It depends on you — and your commitment to the goal! For example, if you invest $14 a day in an account that pays eight percent interest, in 35 years, you'll have accumulated $1,000,000! If you put the $14 under your bed every day for 35 years, you would only earn $178,850. Compounded interest is a wonderful thing ... especially if you start saving young! (See "What is compounded interest?" for more information.)

Monthly Expense Plan

Instructions: Grab your pay stubs, bank statements, credit card statements — and then fill in your BEST GUESS on what you'll spend each month for the following items. If you don't use an item on the list, leave it blank. If something is missing, list it in the "Other" column.

Interactive CD-ROM

Print It!

	Monthly	Annual		Monthly	Annual
Shelter (30% of take-home pay):			**Transportation (15%):**		
Rent	_____	_____	Car Insurance*	_____	_____
Electricity/Gas	_____	_____	License/Registration*	_____	_____
Water/Sewer	_____	_____	Car Maintenance	_____	_____
Trash	_____	_____	Gas/Oil	_____	_____
Telephone	_____	_____	Parking/Tolls	_____	_____
Cable TV	_____	_____	Bus/Train/Taxi	_____	_____
Internet Service	_____	_____	Other	_____	_____
Renters Insurance*	_____	_____	**Total Transportation**	_____	_____
Household Supplies	_____	_____			
Other	_____	_____	**Education:**		
Total Shelter	_____	_____	Tuition/Fees*	_____	_____
			Textbooks/Supplies	_____	_____
Food (10%):			Computer	_____	_____
Groceries	_____	_____	Activities/Sports	_____	_____
Lunches/Snacks	_____	_____	Other	_____	_____
Other	_____	_____	**Total Education**	_____	_____
Total Food	_____	_____			
			Personal (5%):		
Credit Payments (10%):			Haircuts	_____	_____
Credit Card(s)	_____	_____	Personal Care	_____	_____
Car Loan/Lease	_____	_____	Cigarettes	_____	_____
Student Loan	_____	_____	Hobbies	_____	_____
Department Store Credit	_____	_____	Other	_____	_____
Gas Card	_____	_____	**Total Personal**	_____	_____
Other	_____	_____			
Total Credit Payments	_____	_____			

continued...

Figure 2B

...continued

	Monthly	Annual		Monthly	Annual
Savings (10%):			**Clothes (5%):**		
Emergency Fund	_____	_____	New Clothes/Shoes	_____	_____
Savings Account	_____	_____	Cleaning/Laundry	_____	_____
Work Retirement Plan	_____	_____	Other	_____	_____
IRA	_____	_____	**Total Clothes**	_____	_____
Investments	_____	_____			
Financial Counseling	_____	_____	**Entertainment (5%):**		
Other	_____	_____	Dining Out	_____	_____
Total Savings	_____	_____	Movies/Videos	_____	_____
			Books/Subscriptions	_____	_____
Family Needs:			Vacations*	_____	_____
Pet Care	_____	_____	Other	_____	_____
Child Care	_____	_____	**Total Entertainment**	_____	_____
Child Support	_____	_____			
Alimony	_____	_____	**Miscellaneous:**		
Life Insurance*	_____	_____	Donations	_____	_____
Gifts/Cards	_____	_____	Membership Dues*	_____	_____
Other	_____	_____	Taxes (if not withheld)*	_____	_____
Total Family Needs	_____	_____	Other	_____	_____
			Total Miscellaneous	_____	_____

Total Monthly Expenses: _____
Total Annual Expenses: _____

Transer the category totals to your Monthly Money Plan.

*These expenses may not occur on a regular basis. Set money aside each month to pay them when they're due. For example, car insurance of $240 may be due every six months. Divide that into monthly payments of $40 — and save that amount. (Don't spend it on something else.)

Figure 2B (continued)

Monthly Money Plan

Income	Monthly	Annual	Expenses	Monthly	Annual
Paychecks	_____	_____	Shelter	_____	_____
Tips	_____	_____	Food	_____	_____
Commissions	_____	_____	Credit Payments	_____	_____
Bonuses	_____	_____	Savings	_____	_____
Interest	_____	_____	Family Needs	_____	_____
Dividends	_____	_____	Health Care	_____	_____
Gifts	_____	_____	Transportation	_____	_____
Child Support	_____	_____	Education	_____	_____
Alimony	_____	_____	Personal	_____	_____
Tax Refund(s)	_____	_____	Clothes	_____	_____
Student Loan(s)	_____	_____	Entertainment	_____	_____
Other	_____	_____	Miscellaneous	_____	_____
Total Income:	_____	_____	**Total Expenses:**	_____	_____

Total Income – Total Expenses = _____ *

Interactive CD-ROM

Print It!

* Total Income – Total Expenses = Money you have left over each month.

If the amount is negative, you need to figure out where to cut expenses or how to get more income.

Figure 2C

Any tips to help me stick with my plan?

- Turn off the lights when you leave a room.

- Stop using Directory Assistance. Use a free web-based directory. *www.Theultimates.com* lets you search six directories at once.

- Cut back on cable or satellite TV. Do you really need that many channels?

- Set your thermostat at 68 degrees and put on a sweater.

- Instead of buying books, check them out from the library.

- Find a cheaper long-distance phone company and cancel luxury items like Call Waiting.

- Clip coupons. See *www.couponmaker.com*.

- Eat one less pizza per week and save over $150 in a year.

- Stop impulse buying.

- Drop some "guilty pleasures." Skip the morning coffee on the way to work.

- Brown bag your lunch.

- Spend less than you earn.

- Control your day-to-day spending so you can afford to do the things you enjoy.

- Buy food items at grocery stores and non-food items at discount stores.

- Buy cosmetics at a discount store.

- Bargain shop.

- Look for sales.

- Leave your credit cards at home.

- Spend cash only.

- Drink water instead of soda. Your restaurant tab will be 20 percent cheaper — and you'll probably lose a few pounds.

- Quit smoking.

- Quit drinking.

- Quit spending.

- Start saving.

- Keep a detailed list for a month of what you spend your money on.

- Personalize your budget to reflect the way you actually spend money.

- Maintain a calendar and address book.

- Set up a filing system to keep all your paperwork in one place.

- Pay for your *needs* before your *wants*.

- Educate yourself. Check your local library for books and magazines on personal finance.

- Study finances on the Internet.

- Review your credit report once a year.

- Use the many calculators available on the Internet to help you figure out how much money you save, need for retirement, pay in interest.

- Don't base decisions on gut feelings. Do some research before handing over your hard-earned money.

- Budget your money — and stick to your budget.

- Be in control of your money.

- Learn the Rule of 72.

- Know that your *credit past* is your *credit future*. Bad credit decisions stay on your credit report for seven years!

- Save for repairs, accidents, or illnesses.

- Compute your credit card interest on a monthly and yearly basis. Look at your statements each month and start a log of the amount charged. That'll give you good reason to pay those cards off!

- Credit is not income or cash. It's a loan that must be repaid.

- If a deal sounds too good to be true, it probably is. Walk away.

- Don't let greed or desperation overcome common sense. Both can get you in serious trouble.

- If in debt, get help. Doing nothing can lead to problems much larger that the ones you have now.

- Find a bank that doesn't charge ATM fees.

- Enjoy inexpensive pleasures. You don't have to spend money to have fun.

- Ask yourself these three questions: Do I really need it? Do I really need it today? What would happen if I don't buy it now?

- Fund your 401(k) to the max.

- Contribute to an IRA.

- Stay with the same employer for at least five to seven years. Changing jobs costs you retirement money.

- Be responsible for your debts. Pay them on time, every time

- Know what your take-home pay is. If your gross salary is $15,000 per year, you only take home about 75 percent or $11,250. (The rest pays taxes). That means you have $11,250 to pay all debt, not $15,000.

- Start saving now!

- Learn how compounded interest works — and then let it work for you!

- Borrow only what you can repay.

- Don't expect something for nothing. It just doesn't happen.

- Tap into your savings to pay off debt. Your debt's interest is higher than the interest you'll make on your savings. Once your debt is paid off, though, put the money you've been spending on your debt into an investment account.

What if I get discouraged?

You probably will. Especially since you're just starting your financial life ... You didn't learn to walk, talk, eat, ride a bike, or play football in one day — or even one month. For the first few months, be open to adjusting your plan to fit your needs. Don't quit! Stick with it. Each month will get easier and you'll get much better at anticipating and planning your monthly expenses. If you do quit, the odds are that you'll be living your life paycheck to paycheck — so commit yourself to controlling your money and your **Monthly Money Plan**!

If you need help with budgeting, contact the Consumer Credit Counseling Service® (CCCS), a non-profit organization that offers free or low-cost financial counseling to help people solve their financial problems. CCCS can help you analyze your situation and work with you to develop solutions. There are more than 700 CCCS offices nationwide. Call 1-800-388-2227 for the office nearest you.

What if I don't have enough money?

Is there an easy way to pay bills?

Yes! It's a matter of getting organized — and of being committed every payday to take a few minutes to pay your bills.

Interactive CD-ROM

Movie

1. Set up your system. This is the part that takes the longest — but you only do it once. Start by gathering all your bills. Use a spiral note-book to write down all of your **Bills to be Paid**. Include the due date, who you owe, and how much you owe (and a total balance if you're only paying part of the bill, such as with a loan or credit card.) Once you've done that, re-write your bills on a clean sheet of paper in due-date order.

   (If a bill is due on the 1st of the month, list it first. If you haven't re-ceived a bill for the month yet, include the bill but leave the amount due column blank for now.)

   Leave the last three columns blank until you pay the bill.

2. How many paychecks do you get each month? Do you get paid once a month, twice a month, every week? Use your last paystub or figure your "best-guess" for what an average paycheck would be? (Include only your take-home pay. Don't include money that's deducted for taxes.)

3. Determine which bills you can pay from each paycheck. If you get paid once a month, it's easy. You pay all your bills with one pay-check! If you get paid twice a month, which bills will you pay on the 1st and which on the 15th? If you get paid weekly, which bills will you pay each week? (If you get paid weekly, it may help to put a 1, 2, 3, or 4 beside each bill to remind you which paycheck/week you need to pay that bill. Also, if a bill is due on the 1st and you don't get paid until the 8th of the month, the bill will have to be paid out of the previous month's paycheck. Otherwise, your payment will be late.)

   Do you have enough money to pay your bills? What happens if you're short? Complete the **Debt-to-Income Ratio** to see where you stand and then complete the **Monthly Expense Plan** and the **Month-ly Money Plan**. These will help you gain control over your bills.

Bills to be Paid

for the month of _____ May _____ , 200 2

Date Due	Name of Billing Company	Amount Due	✓	Amount Paid	Date Paid
5/1	Rent	$175.00	✓	175.00	4/30
5/1	Electricity	$38.18	✓	38.18	4/30
5/4	Water	$17.54	✓	17.54	4/30
5/15	Savings	$20.00			
5/16	Student Loan	$69.00			
5/24	Cable TV	$28.00			
5/25	Mom (loan)	$20.00			
5/26	Newspaper	$8.00			

Figure 2D

4. When your bills arrive, put them in a folder marked "Bills to be Paid."

5. On payday, sit down with your "Bills to be Paid" list, folder, and your checkbook — before you go shopping or partying! Review your bills to make sure they're correct. Was last month's payment credited? If there's an error on a bill, contact the creditor immediately to resolve it. If your bills are correct, do the following steps:

   ● Add any missing information to your "Bills to be Paid" list, such as amount due.

   ● Write a check to pay for each bill that's due (and/or that you can afford to pay).

   ● Put a checkmark after the "Amount Due" column on the "Bills to be Paid" list. Write in the amount and date paid on your list.

   ● List all the checks you wrote in your checkbook register and do the math to find your new balance. If you have any electronic payments, deduct those from your checkbook register, too. You don't want to bounce any checks.

   Ideally, you should now be able to put your bills away and not worry about them until the next payday.

   Mail your checks at least five to seven days before the due date. Don't put your bills in your mailbox with the flag raised. It alerts thieves. Instead, drop your payments in a postal drop box. When you insert your bill into the envelope, be sure the address side of the bill is facing the window. Many people have had payments returned to them simply because the bill was put in the envelope backwards. (This could incur late charges and future credit problems for you.) Also, if you don't have enough time to mail the bill before the due date, many companies accept payments over the phone and deduct them electronically from your checking account.

6. Set up a filing system. Buy a box of manila folders and make a folder for each bill you pay. When the bill is paid, insert the statement into the appropriate file. Do *not* file your bills until they're paid!

7. On the next payday, repeat Step 5. Make a new "Bills to be Paid" list for the next month. Write in new due dates and balances due. By doing this every month, you're in control — not your money, not the creditors, not the bank. Do this for each payday of the month — every month for the rest of your life!

To simplify this even more, order your *Ultimate Bill-Paying Tablet* at *www.onmyown.com*.

Do I need to keep records?

Recordkeeping is part of "being a responsible adult." It's *your responsibility* to pay your bills. It's also *your responsibility* to keep track of your payments. Recordkeeping is really very simple. File any paperwork you think is important. Here's a list of basic records:

Keep for two to three years:

- Bills that have been paid*

- Bank statements

- *   Make a folder for each billing.

Keep as long as in force/owned:

- Insurance information

- Auto information

- Warranties

Keep indefinitely:

- Income Tax Returns *

- Personal records **

- School transcripts

- Health information

    * Save your tax returns for at least seven years.

    ** Personal records include birth certificates, marriage licenses, divorce decrees, wills, etc.

What if I don't have enough money?

If you're having trouble paying bills, the first step is to admit that you have a problem. A credit problem doesn't go away by itself … it only gets worse. You're responsible for your debts, so if you don't have enough money, take the following steps:

> My dog
> is worried about
> the economy because
> Alpo is up to 99 cents a
> can. That's almost $7 in
> dog money.
>
> *~Joe Weinstein*

Talk with your creditors immediately. (Your creditors are the companies you owe money.) Contact your creditors before you miss a payment. Don't wait until your account is turned over to a debt collector. Explain your situation and try to work out a payment plan. Most creditors are willing to work with you if they believe you're acting in good faith and the situation is temporary. Some creditors may reduce or suspend payments for a short time. If you have a credit card or loan payment, you may be able to change your due date to a time during the month that works better for you.

Contact Consumer Credit Counseling Service® (CCCS) for free or low-cost financial counseling.

Consider borrowing money from family or friends — and make sure you pay them back before you buy or do anything else. Many friendships have been ruined over money.

Check with your financial institution to see if you can get a consolidation loan. A consolidation loan typically pays your credit accounts off, leaving you with just the one monthly loan payment.

If absolutely necessary, file bankruptcy. If you apply this chapter, however, bankruptcy should never be an option.

Can CCCS help me pay my debts?

Consumer Credit Counseling Service® (CCCS) provides help to people who have money problems. Interviews are confidential and can be held in person, by phone, by mail, and on the Internet. There is a one-time $20 counseling fee. No one, however, is turned away because they can't afford to pay the fee. This service is available to anyone, 24 hours a day, seven days a week, regardless of race, sex, creed, social, or financial position. CCCS can help you solve debt problems, avoid bankruptcy, and learn to manage your money.

CCCS offers creditor relations (to help you work with creditors); budget counseling; debt management planning (to help you pay all your debts); and education to teach you good money-management skills. CCCS can negotiate and manage debt repayment plans for clients. Some payments may be adjusted and paid over a longer period of time — but they will be paid in full. CCCS also offers individual and group training on using credit wisely, budgeting, and good money management. Some offices also offer mortgage default and rental relations, home ownership, and consumer and community options. CCCS is located nationwide. To find an office near you, look in the yellow pages of your phone book under *Credit Counseling* or call 1-800-388-2227.

Ask yourself these questions to see if you're in financial trouble. If you're doing one or two of the following, you're in financial trouble — and should call CCCS immediately.

- Do you pay only the minimum amount on credit card balances?

- Do you find that each month's credit card bill seems higher?

- Are you missing payments or paying bills late?

- Do you frequently use your overdraft privileges?

- Do you use credit or savings to pay routine bills?

- Do you receive telephone calls or letters from your creditors?

- Do you argue at home over money problems?

- Do you depend on overtime pay and bonuses to cover regular living expenses?

- Do you have little or no money in a savings account?

● Do you take out new loans to pay old ones?

What if a debt collector calls me at work?

You are responsible for your debts. If you don't pay your bills on time or an error is made on your account, your account may be turned over to a debt collector. A debt collector is any person, other than the creditor, who regularly collects debts owed to others. This includes lawyers who collect debts on a regular basis.

If you've gotten behind on your payments, and have not worked out a payment plan with your creditor (or have not complied with it), your account can be turned over to a collection agency. Under the Fair Debt Collection Act, a debt collector may not call you before 8 a.m., after 9 p.m., or at work if the collector knows that your employer doesn't approve of the calls. Collectors may not harass you, make false statements, or use unfair practices when they try to collect a debt. Debt collectors must honor a written request from you to cease further contact.

Don't let your bills get to this point. It goes on your credit report — and stays there for seven years. Instead, review your options in "What if I don't have enough money?"

Can a credit repair company erase my debts?

No. Avoid credit repair companies that offer the promise of cleaning up credit reports for a fee. They don't — and can't — deliver. They can't do anything for you that you can't do for yourself. The Federal Trade Commission cautions consumers about using repair clinics that use ads like the following:

> *Consolidate your bills into one monthly payment without borrowing.*

> *Stop credit harassment, foreclosures, repossessions, tax levies, and garnishments. Keep your property!*

> *Wipe out your debts! Consolidate your bills!*

> *Use the protection and assistance provided by federal law. For once, let the law work for you!*

Such phrases often involve bankruptcy proceedings that you're not even aware of until it's too late. This can hurt your credit tremendously and cost you attorney's fees. Before you do business with any company, find out what services the business provides and what it costs; get all promises in writing; and check out any company with your local consumer protection agency or the Better Business Bureau in the company's location. They can tell you whether other consumers have registered complaints about the business. (See "Should I hire a credit repair company?" for more information.)

For a copy of *Credit Repair: Self-Help May Be Best*, call 1-877-382-4357 or visit the Federal Trade Commission's website at *www.ftc.gov*.

Should I file bankruptcy?

Not unless you absolutely have to. Personal bankruptcy is considered the last option for debt management because it stays on your credit report for 10 years. These long-lasting effects make it difficult for you to acquire credit, buy a car, get insurance, or even get a job — for 10 years!

There are two primary types of personal bankruptcy: Chapter 13 and Chapter 7. Both are filed in federal bankruptcy court. Both may get rid of unsecured debts and stop foreclosures, repossessions, garnishments, utility shut-offs, and debt collections. Both also provide exemptions that allow people to keep certain assets, although exemption amounts vary. Personal bankruptcy usually does not erase child support, alimony, fines, taxes, and some student loan obligations. And unless you have an acceptable plan to catch up on your debt under Chapter 13, bankruptcy usually does not allow you to keep property if your creditor has an unpaid mortgage or lien on it.

Chapter 13

Chapter 13 allows people with steady incomes to keep property, like a mortgaged house or a car, that otherwise might be returned to the creditor. In Chapter 13, the court approves a repayment plan that allows you to use your future income to pay off a default during a three- to five-year period, rather than surrender any property. After you have made all payments under the plan, you receive a discharge of your debts.

Chapter 7

Chapter 7, known as straight bankruptcy, involves liquidation of all assets that are not exempt. Exempt property may include cars, work-related tools, and basic household furnishings. Some of your property may be sold by a court-appointed official or turned over to your creditors. You can receive a discharge of your debts through Chapter 7 only once every six years.

Where'd all my money go?

Where'd all my money go?

You have to pay taxes — just as sure as you have to breathe. Let's say you work full-time (40 hours per week) and earn $7 an hour. How much money will be in your paycheck at the end of the week?

Weekly Gross Pay ($7×40 hours per week)	$280.00
FICA/Social Security Tax (6.2%)	- 17.36
Medicare Tax (1.45%)	- 4.06
Federal Tax*	- 26.00
State Tax (3.5% — taxes vary by state)	- 9.80
Local Tax (2% — taxes vary by community)	- 2.80
401(k) Retirement Fund (10%**)	- 42.00
Take-Home Pay	**$179.98**

* Federal Tax figured for one allowance for being single with one job When you're hired, you'll fill out a **W-4 form** (Employee's Withholding Allowance Certificate). You claim allowances on the W-4 to determine how much of your paycheck is withheld for federal income taxes. For example, if you're single and have only one job, you can claim one allowance. However, if your parent(s) claim you as a dependent on their income taxes, you cannot claim an allowance for yourself.

By January 31st of each year, your employer must give you a **W-2**, a statement showing how much you earned in wages, tips, and other compensation during the previous year — and how much was withheld for taxes. If you had more than one employer during the past year, each employer must send you a W-2. Use the W-2 to file your income tax. Keep a copy with your income tax for at least three years.

** 401(k) plan at 10% with company matching 5%.

How often will I get paid?

How often you're paid has a big impact on how you pay your bills. Companies pay employees weekly, every other week, twice a month, or monthly. The following terms will help you understand your paycheck:

Minimum Wage

The Fair Labor Standards Act sets minimum wage standards and overtime regulations for employees of companies covered under this law. Minimum wage is $5.15 as of September 1997. Employees who receive tips are paid less than this, assuming tips will make up the difference. According to federal law, all tips must be counted as "earned income" on your income taxes.

Gross Pay

Hours worked × rate per hour = gross pay.

> **Example:** $5.15 per hour × 40 hours per week = $206 gross pay.

Take-home Pay

Your gross pay minus all deductions. Deductions average about 25 percent of your paycheck. (See "Where'd all my money go?" for details.)

Payroll Deductions or Withholdings

Your employer deducts a certain amount from your paycheck to pay for taxes. This tax money funds many specific programs, including Social Security (FICA), Medicare, worker's disability, and more. Federal, state, and local taxes are also deducted from your paycheck.

Tips

If you receive more than $20 a month in tips, you must report the amount to your employer. To keep track of tips, keep a daily "Tips Earned" log to write down the exact amount of tips you earn each day. Share the monthly total with your employer who will deduct and pay federal, state, and local taxes for you.

Overtime Pay

Rate paid for any hours worked over 40 hours per week. Rate is usually $1\frac{1}{2}$ times your regular pay.

> **Example:** You're paid $6 per hour and worked 47 hours this week. 40 hours × $6 + 7 hours × $9 ($1\frac{1}{2}$ × $6) = $240 + $63 = $303 gross pay.

Direct Deposit

Payroll and government checks are electronically deposited in your bank account. The deposit is credited at the start of the business day making your money available to use and/or earn interest. Direct deposit eliminates problems caused by stolen, lost, or mutilated checks.

What if I'm paid on commission?

Commission sales can be tricky. Because there is no set amount of money you earn each payday, it can be hard to maintain a budget and stay out of financial trouble. Before taking a job that pays commissions, be sure the base pay (if offered) is enough for you to pay your bills.

Salary

Fixed wages regardless of hours worked.

> Example: Retail Store Manager is paid $16,500 per year, or $317 per week, regardless of number of hours worked.

Salary Plus Commission

Fixed wages + commissions earned.

> Example: $317 (fixed wage) + $128 ($.32 per unit × 400 units made) = $445 for week.

Straight Piece Rate

Number of units produced × rate per unit.

> Example: 400 units × $.32 per unit = $128.

Differential Pay Rate

Rate is related to number of pieces produced.

> Example: 1-300 units = $.45 per unit; 301-500 units = $.65 per unit.
>
> If 437 units are produced:
> (300 units × $.45) + (137 units × $.65) = $135 + $89 = $224.

Straight Commission

Total sales × commission rate.

> Example: $12,000 sales × 5% commission =
> $600 commission.

Variable Commission

Commission is related to number of pieces sold.

> Example: 1-200 pieces sold = 5% commission;
> 201 to 500 pieces = 6% commission.
>
> If 386 pieces are sold:
> (200 pieces × 5%) + (186 pieces × 6%).

What if I just need $100 until payday?

The ads are everywhere — get cash fast! These small, short-term, high-interest-rate loans work by having you (the borrower) write a personal check payable to the lender for the amount you wish to borrow — plus a fee. Your check is usually post-dated to your next payday. The company then gives you a check for the amount borrowed.

Fees charged for payday loans are usually a percentage amount borrowed or a fee charged per amount borrowed — and can be as high as 800 percent or more to borrow money for just two weeks. One company advertised on the Internet charges 608 percent to borrow $100 for 15 days — and a whopping 3,042 percent to borrow $100 for just three days.

If you do decide to use a payday loan, only borrow as much as you can afford to repay with your next paycheck — and still have enough left over to make it to the next payday.

What are the alternatives to payday loans?

Before getting a payday loan, consider the following options:

- Ask your creditors for more time to pay your bills.

- Find out if you have, or can get, overdraft protection on your checking account. What are the repayment terms? Some overdrafts have to be paid back within a month.

- Consider a small loan from your credit union, an advance from your employer, or a loan from family or friends.

- A cash advance on a credit card may also be an option, but it may have a high interest rate. Find out the terms before you decide.

- When you need credit, shop carefully. Compare offers. Look for the credit offer with the lowest APR (Annual Percentage Rate). And don't borrow more than you can pay back.

If you find you routinely have trouble making it from paycheck to paycheck, go to "Do I need a budget?" and learn how to take control of your money. Avoid unnecessary purchases, even small daily items like a soda from the vending machine. They add up fast. Also, build some savings, even small deposits can help, to avoid borrowing for emergencies. If you need help developing a budget, contact your local Consumer Credit Counseling Service®, a non-profit group in each state that offers credit guidance to consumers. These services are available at little or no cost.

 ## Do I have to pay taxes?

Why do I have to pay taxes?

Paying taxes is *not* voluntary. Everyone must pay taxes so the government can provide needed and wanted services. Your tax dollars pay for police, fire and rescue squads; court systems; armed forces; food, beverage, and drug inspections; health departments; public schools and libraries; building and maintenance of roads and highways; conservation of wildlife, forests, and natural resources; and emergency relief and aid for droughts, floods, and other natural disasters. (A large portion of your tax dollars pays for welfare, disability, Social Security, and education.)

> If you make any money, the government shoves you in the creek once a year with it in your pockets, and all that don't get wet you can keep.
>
> ~*Mark Twain*

What taxes do I have to pay?

Individual income taxes are paid on the money you earn. These taxes include federal, state, and local income taxes. Federal taxes include income,

Social Security, and Medicare taxes — and everyone has to pay them. State and local taxes are determined by voters — and are different in every state. Many cities and states also require you to pay sales and property taxes and motor vehicle registrations. Some states require sales tax on everything but food items. Some states have no sales tax at all. Estate, inheritance, and gift taxes are also collected by the government.

How do I file an income tax return?

The IRS requires you to file a tax return by April 15th of each year. You may be able to use the 1040-EZ. Kiplinger's *TaxCut* and Quicken's *TurboTax* let you file a 1040-EZ online free of charge. The 1040 form can also be used if your taxable income is less than $50,000 and you don't itemize deductions.

You'll need your W-2 from each employer you had in the previous year to complete your income tax. (A W-2 lists total wages earned and taxes paid in the previous year.) Your employer must give you a W-2 by January 31st. If you don't receive one, contact your employer.

If you don't receive tax forms in the mail, you can pick them up at the local library, grocery store, financial institution, college, and many other locations. You can also download forms.

Contact the IRS at the following:

- 1-800-829-3676 for blank forms and publications.

- 1-800-829-4477 for recorded messages on over 140 tax topics.

- 1-800-829-1040 for a person to answer your federal tax questions.

You can also log onto *www.irs.gov* or visit *www.kiplinger.com/software/tax-cut.htm* or *www.quicken.com/freedom*.

Do I have to file state income taxes?

State income taxes are not collected in Alaska, Florida, Nevada, South Dakota, Texas, Washington, and Wyoming. These states rely on other taxes (such as property and sales taxes) to pay for government. (Delaware and New Hampshire require income taxes on interest and dividends only.) All other states require a state income tax return. Complete your state return at the same time you do your federal return. The IRS now has an e-file program that allows you to file federal and state income taxes at the same time from your home computer. As of October 2001, it is available in 37 states and the District of Columbia.

What if I can't afford to pay taxes that are due?

Call the IRS at 1-800-TAX-1040 to set up an installment plan. Call before April 15th.

What happens if I don't pay income taxes?

If caught (which you most likely will be with computer technology), you can be liable for tax evasion, fraud, and other criminal charges. You can also be charged penalties and interest on any unpaid taxes. (And the penalties are severe!) If you owe taxes and can't afford to pay, contact the IRS by April 15th to work out a payment plan.

What if I don't receive my refund?

If you've moved and your old address is on your tax form, your check was probably returned to the IRS. The U.S. Post Office, by regulation, cannot forward government checks. Contact the IRS at 1-800-TAX-1040.

Can I file my taxes electronically?

Taxpayers can file their taxes with personal computers and tax preparation software. The information goes directly to the IRS and the IRS can directly deposit refunds into the taxpayer's bank account. According to the IRS, there is no better way to reduce the number of errors on your return, ensure that the IRS receives your return, and get your refund in just a few weeks. In 2000, more than 25 million taxpayers sent their returns to the IRS electronically rather than by paper. Anyone who submits a 1040, 1040A, or 1040-EZ can file electronically. You must fill out Form 8453 authorizing the electronic transmission of your tax information. And if you owe money, you can file anytime before April 15th and mail your payment with form 1040-V on April 15th.

How do I balance my checkbook?

Are there different types of checking accounts?

There are many types of checking accounts available. Their names may vary by financial institution, but they basically offer the same services. Decide on your needs, then compare costs and benefits to find the right account for you. Although a few may seem out of your reach right now (like the Money Market account with a $10,000 minimum deposit required), keep them in mind once you set your goals and start achieving financial independence.

Basic Checking Account

Use a basic checking account if you don't maintain a high balance and do little more than bill-paying and daily expenses. Some basic accounts require direct deposit or a low minimum balance to avoid monthly fees.

Student Checking Account

Student accounts vary at different financial institutions, but may include free checks, free ATM use, and better rates on loans and credit cards.

Interest-Bearing Checking Account

This account usually requires a minimum balance to open and a high balance (such as $10,000) to maintain the account. Interest is paid monthly.

Joint Checking Account

A joint account is owned by two or more people, with each co-owner having equal access to the account. It is recommended that you don't have a joint account with anyone unless you're married.

Money Market Checking Account

This account combines checking with savings or investments and usually requires a high minimum deposit to open ($1,000 to $10,000). It also usually allows a limited number of checks to be written from the account each month.

Should I order duplicate checks?

When you open a new checking account, the financial institution will give you a supply of temporary checks. It's your responsibility to order permanent checks that list your name, address, and phone number.

If you order checks from your financial institution, the cost is automatically withdrawn from your account. Some financial institutions charge up to $24 for an order of checks. Be sure to deduct it on your checkbook register when you order the checks so you won't bounce a check.

You can also order checks from an outside check printer for less than $10 per box. Many of these companies, such as Artistic Checks, the Check

Gallery, or Checks Unlimited, have fliers in the Sunday newspaper and ads in various magazines. You must have an active checking account and a temporary check to order from a printer.

Order checks that have carbon — or duplicate — copies. With carbon checks, you don't have to stand at the checkout stand filling in your checkbook register. You can do it once you get home. Don't rely on your memory to keep track of checks you've written. If you forget to deduct any checks from your register, you could pay a lot of money in finance charges and harm your credit rating.

Checks are like money — so keep all checks in a secure place. This includes your checkbook, as well as the box of checks you're not using. Keep your deposit slips in a secure place, too, since they have your account number on them. If your financial institution offers a code word to access your account, use it. And don't hand over a blank check to anyone.

How do I fill out a checkbook register?

All transactions on your account *must* be written in your checkbook register. So, if you write a check, withdraw cash, deposit money, use an ATM or debit card, or get charged a fee, you must enter it in your register. The checkbook register is the only way you'll know how much money you have available to spend at all times.

The register is easy to keep track of. When you order duplicate checks, you have a copy of each check you write. Put the check information in your checkbook register. Then subtract the amount from your balance. When you make a deposit, write it in the register and add it to your balance.

Refer to the example on page 63 for an easy way to write different entries in your register.

- List all transactions that deduct money from your account in the "Amount of Payment" column.

- List all transactions that add money to your account in the "Amount of Deposit" column.

- Calculate the "Balance Forward" column by either adding or subtracting each transaction.

Sample Check Register

Check No.	Check Issued To or Description of Deposit	Amount of Payment (-)	✓	Amount of Deposit or Interest (+)	Balance Forward
					$300.00
1009	On My Own — book	34.95			265.05
1010	Creekside Apt. — rent	175.00			90.05
SC	Service Charge — May	4.50			85.55
ADJ	Adjust Check #1001			.05	85.60
I	Interest — May			.18	85.78
T	Transfer from savings			50.00	135.78
TF	Transfer fee	3.00			132.78
1011	USC — tuition	100.00			32.78
C	Cash	10.00			22.78
D	Deposit -- XYZ Co.			225.00	247.78
DW	Electric	43.18			204.60
CR	Credit Check #1003			25.00	229.60
ATM	Cash for movie	15.00			214.60
DEB	Groceries	23.78			190.82

List all transactions that deduct money from your account in the "Amount of Payment" column.
List all transactions that add money to your account in the "Amount of Deposit" column.
Calculate the "Balance Forward" column by either adding or subtracting each transaction.

Figure 2E

● Develop a simple key that works for you — one that you'll remember from month to month.

Suggested Key

SC = Service Charge. This will appear on your monthly bank statement.

ADJ = Adjustment made when balancing checkbook. For example, you wrote $13.95 in your checkbook, but the bank deducted $13.90. Write the $.05 adjustment as a deposit because it should be added back to your account.

I = Interest earned on your account. (Not all checking accounts earn interest.)

T = Transfer. If you transfer money from one account to another, such as from your savings to your checking account.

TF = Transfer fee. Most banks charge a fee for transfers under a set amount.

C = Withdrawal of cash.

D = Deposit.

DW = Draft Withdrawal. This is for electronic payments. The amount is electronically withdrawn from your account on a set day each month.

CR = Credit. For example, your check register is balanced through check #1007, but you decided not to mail check #1001. Instead of crossing out all the transactions between checks #1001 and #1007, you can write a credit for #1001. (Put a ✓ by check #1001 and by the credit. They cancel each other out.)*

ATM = ATM card transaction.

DEB = Debit card transaction.

* The ✓ means that the transaction has "cleared" the bank. It has been added or subtracted from your account at the bank and has appeared on your monthly bank statement. (See "How do I balance my checkbook?" for more information.)

Can't I just call the bank for my balance?

No! What if some of your checks haven't cleared the bank yet? If you rely on the bank, here's what could happen:

You call the bank and ask for your balance. The bank shows a balance of $125, so you write check #2008 for $100.

That same afternoon, a check you wrote last week (check #2005 for $75) clears the bank. Now the bank shows you have a balance of $50.

When check #2008 is cashed, it bounces. The check will be returned because you have insufficient funds to cover it. Now you'll have to pay the bank a $30 charge — and you'll have to pay the creditor a $30 charge.

Wouldn't it just be easier — and cheaper — to keep track of your own checking account balance? You can buy a calculator for $5 ... and make it a habit to balance your checkbook each day you write a check.

How do I balance my checkbook?

One of the most important things you *must* do each month is balance your checkbook. If you use an ATM or debit card, keep your receipts and deduct them from your checkbook register each time you use them. Forgetting to deduct ATM transactions is an easy way to become overdrawn. If you don't write down the transaction immediately, put your receipts in one place (your checkbook or rubber-banded around your card). Update your checkbook register each day you make a transaction.

Balancing your checkbook is as easy as 1-2-3! Get your checkbook, your monthly bank statement, a ruler, and a calculator — and follow these steps:

1. Use a ruler on your bank statement to track each transaction. Slide the ruler down the list of transactions so you don't miss any. For each item listed on your bank statement, you **must** also have that same transaction listed in your checkbook register. Put a ✓ on the bank statement and a ✓ in your checkbook register for each item that matches. If something on your bank statement doesn't match your register or you don't have it listed, circle it and come back to it when you're finished with this step.

2. For any transactions circled, figure out why it doesn't match your register. Did you forget to list it? If so, write it in your register and then put a ✓ by it.

   Is the amount wrong (even by a penny)? If so, make an adjustment in your checkbook register. Write ADJ in the "Check #" column, write *Adjust Check* # _____ in the "Check Issued To" column, enter the amount of the adjustment, and then put a ✓ by it. Put a ✓ by the original check #, too. By checking the original check and the ADJ line, you're "matching" the transaction that's listed on your bank statement. (See ADJ example in "How do I fill out a checkbook register?")

   Is there a fee you didn't have written in your register? Enter it and put a ✓ by it. Adjust your "Balance Forward" column in your checkbook register to reflect any new transactions.

   Flip back through the pages in your checkbook. If you have a page that has a ✓ by every transaction, but an ✗ on the bottom right-hand corner of that page. This will help when you look for outstanding transactions. The ✗ will show that there are no outstanding transactions on that page. (Outstanding transactions are ones that haven't appeared on a bank statement yet.)

3. On the back of most bank statements, there's a Reconciliation form. Use this form to reconcile — or balance — your checkbook. Start by

listing any outstanding transactions that are in your checkbook, including checks, and ATM and debit card transactions. Go through your checkbook register and write all the outstanding checks in the appropriate column. (Some forms have columns for both the check numbers and the amounts. Just write the amounts.) Add up the outstanding transactions.

Follow the steps on the Reconciliation form to complete the balancing process:

1. Write the "Ending Balance" shown on your bank statement.

2. Add any "Deposits" in your checkbook that haven't appeared on a bank statement yet.

3. Sub-Total the "Ending Balance" and "Deposits."

4. Subtract your outstanding transactions (checks, ATM, debit) from the sub-total.

5. This gives you your "Adjusted Ending Balance." This number should match the last entry on the "Balance Forward" column in your checkbook register.

   If the balance doesn't match, find the problem. Repeat the steps above first. Did you miss anything? Re-calculate your "Balance Forward" column in your register. It's easy to make a math mistake. If you can't find where the difference is, call your bank and ask if they'll help. Some may charge a small fee for this — but it's cheaper than having checks bounce! Keep in mind, too, that banks do make mistakes. If there's a mistake, contact your bank immediately with proof of the mistake.

Will the bank return my cancelled checks?

Cancelled checks are checks that have "cleared" your account at your financial institution. That means the money has been deducted from your account. Do you get these checks back? Depends. Some financial institutions return your cancelled checks with your statement each month. Others keep a microfiche or imaged copy and provide you with a photocopy upon request.

Should I get overdraft protection?

Some financial institutions offer overdraft protection on checking accounts. If you don't have enough money to cover a transaction, overdraft protection allows you to "borrow" the needed funds for a limited amount and limited time. (Be aware, though, that these are very short-term loans, usually only a month or so.) Find out what the charge is for this service. It may be high. Here's an even better idea: Keep track of your checkbook balance and don't bounce checks!

What if I bounce a check?

You waste a lot of money! Don't write checks if you don't have enough money in your account to cover them. Let's say you wanted to buy a snack at the local convenience store. You know you don't have any money left in your checking account, but you think … *"I'm only writing it for $2.97. The bank will cover that."* **Wrong!** The bank will most likely return the check to the store. You could end up paying $62.97 for that snack!

NSF(non-sufficient funds)fee to your bank	$30.00
NSF fee to the convenience store	+30.00
Amount of the check	+2.97
Total cost of snack	**$62.97**

Now consider this: If your check is submitted to your bank a second time, and you still don't have enough money to cover it, the bank will return the check again. And will charge you the NSF fees again. So, on top of the $62.97 you pay for the first return, add another $60 for the second return. That makes that snack worth $122.97! It would be less stressful (and damaging to your credit) to just light a match to your money …

If you do bounce checks, you'll waste a lot of money — and you may loose your check-writing privileges, too. If that happens, you'll have to purchase money orders or cashier's checks to pay your bills. (Never use cash to pay bills unless you get a receipt.) Money orders and cashier's checks can cost as much as $3 each — and if you have several creditors to pay, that can add up fast.

Should I use direct deposit?

Direct deposit is a wonderful option for receiving your paycheck. Have your employer deposit your paycheck automatically into your checking account. It saves you a trip to the financial institution to make the deposit.

To set up direct deposit, you and your employer must complete a simple form and attach one of your blank, voided checks. Once your direct deposit begins, usually two weeks, you'll receive a voucher from your employer instead of a paycheck. The voucher will include information about taxes, benefits, and other deductions.

What if my bank "floats" my check?

In banking terms, "float" is the time between when you deposit a check and when the money becomes available. Some financial institutions have instant access to deposited money — while others have a two- to five-day wait. Financial institutions use this "float" time to verify that the check is legal and that funds are available to deposit in your account. Legislation requires financial institutions to make money from local checks available within two business days of deposit. Money from checks written from out-of-state financial institutions must be available within five business days. (You might consider using Western Union if you're having money sent from out-of-state and need it immediately.)

Can a bank "blacklist" me?

As many as 90 percent of banks and many credit unions consult ChexSystems, a company that blacklists banking customers for five years. ChexSystems handles a database of over seven million names that have been blacklisted. If you get put on the list, you probably won't be able to open a new checking account for five years. Banks report you if they close your account because you bounce checks or use overdraft protection and don't repay quickly. You're also reported if you close an account and mistakenly still owe the bank money — even if it's only $5. If you have electronic bill payments set up, those must be cancelled, too. If a payment comes through after you close the account, you could be blacklisted.

If you do have a problem, you can get a copy of your ChexSystems report at *www.chexhelp.com* or call 1-800-428-9623.

 ## Should I use a debit or ATM card?

Should I use a debit card?

When you use a debit card, the money is deducted from your checking account — and you can't spend more than you have in your account. Write every transaction in your checkbook register immediately so your account doesn't become overdrawn.

If your debit card is lost or stolen, report it to your financial institution immediately because someone could take all the money you have. Under federal law, you must notify your financial institution about a lost or stolen debit card within *two business days* to limit your loss to $50. After *three days*, your responsibility increases to $500. After *60 days*, you could lose your entire bank balance, plus the amount of any overdraft protection.

If your debit card is lost or stolen, close that account and open a new account with a new PIN (Personal Identification Number). Keep your receipts so you can verify them when you get your statements. And don't throw away any receipts without shredding them first.

Should I use an ATM card?

The automated teller machine (ATM) gives you access to your money 24 hours a day, seven days a week. While convenient, ATM cards are an easy way to become overdrawn on your account if you forget to deduct money you've withdrawn in your checkbook register.

If your ATM card is lost or stolen, report it to your financial institution immediately. If you report your ATM card missing within *two business days* of losing it, you won't be responsible for more than $50 for unauthorized use. However, if you don't report your card missing for *two weeks*, you could lose up to $500 for unauthorized use. If you fail to report unauthorized use within *60 days* of receiving your bank statement, you risk unlimited loss. You could lose all the money in your account and, if established, any unused line of credit for overdrafts.

Is it safe to use an ATM at night?

Use common sense when using an ATM, especially at night. Be aware of your surroundings and if you feel uncomfortable, don't use the machine. Have your ATM card in your hand as you approach the ATM, instead of fumbling for it when you get there. Use your body to block the keypad so no one can see you enter your PIN. Put your money inside your pocket, purse, or wallet and count it later in a safe place. Don't count or display your money as you leave the ATM. Take your ATM receipt after completing a transaction. If you use a drive-up ATM, lock all car doors and roll up your windows. If you have a problem with the ATM, contact the financial institution, not the stranger waiting in line behind you. Report all crimes to the police and the financial institution. At night, try to find a drive-up ATM. If not, park in a well-lit area and take another person with you. If the lights at the ATM aren't working, look for another one or wait until morning.

What's a smart card?

Smart cards contain computer chips that act like credit or debit cards. They also allow customers to transfer cash value to a card. Smart cards haven't gained much popularity in the U.S. Stored-value cards, however, are very popular. They include prepaid cards for telephone services, transit fares, highway tolls, library fees, school lunches, and more.

Can I write my PIN on my ATM card?

Statistics show that in one-third of ATM fraud cases, the PIN (Personal Identification Number) was written on the card or a slip of paper kept with the card. How lucky for the thief! When choosing a PIN, use a number that will be difficult for a thief to figure out. Avoid using your address, telephone number, Social Security number, or birthday. Memorize your PIN. Don't write it on a piece of paper in your purse or wallet — or on your card. And never give your PIN to anyone.

Do I use a bank or credit union?

Your lifestyle, your income, and your preferences will determine which financial institution is best for you. Banks are owned by stockholders. Credit unions are member-owned. When choosing a financial institution, choose a bank that is insured by the Federal Deposit Insurance Corporation (FDIC) or a credit union insured by the National Credit Union Administration (NCUA). Both protect your deposits up to $100,000. (Look for stickers on doors and windows.)

With today's banking, you're more likely to pick and choose services in order to find a financial institution that works for you. Decide what products and services you need and then compare costs of at least three banks and credit unions in your area:

- Is it located near my home or work?

- Is it open on nights or weekends?

- Are there student or new customer discounts?

- What are checking account service charges?

- Is there a minimum balance I have to maintain each month?

- Is there a limit to the number of checks I can write each month?

- Is there a limit to the number of withdrawals I can make each month?

- Are there per-check fees? If so, what are they?

- Is there overdraft protection? How much does it cost? How do I get it?

- What are NSF (non-sufficient fund) fees if I bounce a check?

- Are cancelled checks returned? If not, what are the fees for providing copies?

- What are the fees for stopping payment on a check?

- What are savings account service charges?

- Are ATM cards available? What is the monthly fee?

- Is there a limit on the number of ATM transactions I can use each month?

- Are there per-transaction fees for using the ATM?

- How many ATMs are in your network?

- What are the fees if I use another financial institution's ATM?

- Are debit cards available? What is the monthly fee?

- Are there fees to see a live teller?

- Does it cost to do a balance inquiry?

- Are there fees to close my account?

Also consider future uses such as credit card rates, loan rates, and certificates of deposit rates. See "Are there different types of checking accounts?" for more information.

Should I bank online?

Today, the Internet can be used for gathering information, shopping, investing — even banking and paying bills. You can conduct many banking transactions electronically via your personal computer. For instance, you can view your account balance, request transfers between accounts, and pay bills. Before signing up for online banking, ask the following questions:

- Is the online bank insured through the FDIC (Federal Deposit Insurance Corporation)?

- How secure are my online transactions?

- How quickly will my bills be paid?

- How much does it cost?

- What are the minimum balance requirements to avoid monthly fees?

- What are the current checking and savings account interest rates?

- If those rates are promotional, when do they change and to what rate?

- What happens if I make a mistake?

- How easy is it to set up? Do I need to install special software?

- Can I download transactions directly into Intuit's *Quicken®* or *Microsoft Money®*?

- Does the account have free ATM access?

- Can I close an account easily?

Is it safe to make electronic payments?

When conducting business on-line, practice the following safety tips:

- Use a secure browser (a software program that encrypts or scrambles the information you send over the Internet) to guard the security of your on-line transactions. Most computers have a secure browser already installed. You can also download free browsers from the Internet. Make sure your connection to the Internet, or browser, features 128-bit encryption, the highest security level available.

- Understand services offered before using them. Most online financial institutions offer training or online help. Read the fine print before signing. Print and file your contract or order, the confirmation, and any electronic messages you get. You might need them for verification at some point. Check your e-mail regularly for notices or changes in prices or terms.

- Know who you're doing business with. Give payment information only to businesses you know and trust, and only in appropriate places like order forms. If a website doesn't have a privacy policy, consider shopping elsewhere. There are many scams out there.

- Keep records of your on-line transactions. Be prompt about reviewing your monthly bank and credit card statements for any billing errors or unauthorized purchases. Notify your financial institution or credit card company immediately if your credit card or checkbook is stolen.

- Never give your password or PIN to anyone, not even your Internet Service Provider (ISP). Choose a password that is difficult to guess. Use a combination of capital and lowercase letters and numbers.

- Keep your personal information to yourself. Don't disclose your address, telephone number, Social Security number, or e-mail address unless you know who's collecting the information, why they're collecting it, and how they'll use it.

- Don't download files sent to you by strangers or click on hyperlinks from people you don't know. Opening a file could expose your computer to a virus.

Can I pay my bills online?

While banking online may seem convenient, it only works if you keep excellent records of your bills and your checkbook register. Many financial institutions now offer customers the ability to pay bills online with the click of a button. You decide which bills to pay and when to pay them. The financial institution then safely and quickly issues a check or transfers the correct amount of money from your account to the payee.

Automated bill payments, also known as direct payments, are a quick, safe, and convenient method to pay for everything from insurance premiums to school loans to utility bills. You should receive a printed bill in the mail at least 10 days before a scheduled payment date if the company is a regulated utility (gas, water, electric) or if the bill exceeds the range you authorized. For fixed payments (the same date and amount due each month), a company should state in the authorization agreement if it will stop mailing a printed bill.

If you use automatic bill-paying, *you must deduct the transaction in your checkbook register* ... or you might end up with bounced checks (and you will be charged non-sufficient fund (NSF) fees averaging $60 per transaction). Your liabilities are the same as if you wrote a check. The date and payment amount of each transaction, along with the payee name, will appear on your monthly checking account statement. Like a cancelled check, that statement serves as proof of the transaction. Review your checking account statement carefully each month. Again, paying bills online only works if you keep excellent records of your bills and your checkbook register.

If you get your bank statement and find there was an error in the payment, contact the billing company first so they can correct it. If not, you have 60 days to notify your financial institution. You may be required to sign a written confirmation that the payment is unauthorized. With proper notification, your financial institution should credit you for unauthorized or incorrect payments.

If you want to stop direct payments, review your original agreement. It outlines the procedures for revoking direct payment authorization. You generally must make the request in writing at least one billing cycle before termination.

If your e-mail address or account changes, you *must* notify all the companies you do automatic bill-paying with. E-mail isn't forwarded — and you can be charged with NSF fees as if you had bounced a check. You might also have to pay late charges with the company and even get your interest rate increased. Don't assume that just because you close your account, the billing company will know to stop your automatic payments. You'll end up with several NSF charges and could ruin your credit rating — and even be denied when you attempt to open a checking account at another institution.

Personal financial software like Intuit's *Quicken*® and *Microsoft Money*® may be linked directly to your financial institution account if your financial institution offers online banking services. This allows you to download account transactions directly into your software or pay bills online.

Many companies aren't equipped to accept electronic payments, so your financial institution would just end up mailing them a check. This can take an extra week or so for payment to arrive, which could lead to late payments for you. If the company doesn't have electronic payment, write a check yourself.

Can I get a loan?

When you apply for a loan, creditors look for an ability to repay debt and a willingness to do so — and sometimes a little extra security to protect their loans. They consider the Three Cs: capacity, character, and collateral.

Capacity

Can you repay the debt? Do you have a steady job? How long have you been at your present job? How much are you paid? Do you have any other loan payments? What are your current living expenses? What are your current debts? Do you have any dependents?

Character

Will you repay the debt? Have you used credit before? Do you pay your bills on time? Do you have a good credit report? Do you have character references? How long have you lived at your current address? Do you rent or own your home? How often do you borrow? From your credit history, do you seem to be honest and reliable in paying your debts?

Collateral

Is the creditor fully protected if you fail to repay? What property do you own? Do you have a savings account? Do you have any investments? Can you list anything that the bank can take if you don't make payments?

The Equal Credit Opportunity Act does not guarantee you will get credit. You must still pass the creditor's tests of credit-worthiness. But the creditor must apply these tests fairly and impartially. The Act bars discrimination based on age, gender, marital status, race, color, religion, and national origin. The Act also bars discrimination because you receive public income such as veteran's benefits, Social Security benefits, or welfare. (Go to "Why do I need a good credit record?" for more information.)

What if I don't get the loan?

You must be notified within 30 days after your application has been completed whether your loan has been approved or not. If credit is denied, this notice must be in writing and it must explain the specific reasons that you were denied credit or tell you of your right to ask for an explanation. If you are denied credit, be sure to find out why. You can also request a copy of your credit report free within 60 days of being denied credit. If you really need the loan to make ends meet, go to "What if I can't pay my bills?"

Should I co-sign a loan?

What would you do if a friend or relative asked you to co-sign a loan? Before you answer, make sure you know what co-signing involves. When asked to co-sign, you're being asked to take a risk that a financial institution won't. In most states, if you co-sign and your friend or relative misses a payment, the lender can immediately collect from you without first pursuing the borrower. In addition, the amount you owe may be increased by late charges and attorney's fees if the lender decides to sue to collect. If the lender wins the case, your wages and property may be taken. Ask the lender to agree, in writing, to notify you if the borrower misses a payment.

If you do co-sign, be sure you can afford to pay the loan. If you're asked to pay and can't, you could be sued or your credit rating could be damaged. Even if you're not asked to repay the debt, your liability for the loan may keep you from getting other credit because creditors will consider the co-signed loan as one of your debts.

If you need a co-signer to get a loan, make sure you can pay the loan. *Do not allow the loan to default so that your co-signer has to pay for it*. The financial institution can sue you — and the co-signer can sue you. And it's probably not something you want to spend the rest of your life feeling guilty over. If you really need the loan, see "What if I can't pay my bills?"

How long will it take to pay off my credit card?

How do I "shop" for a credit card?

Many first-time credit card holders take the first credit card that is offered them. That may not be the best route to take. You should shop for a credit card based on what you'll be using it for. For example, if you expect to pay your balance in full each month, the grace period, annual fee, and other charges may be more important that the periodic rate and the Annual Percentage Rate (APR). If you expect to use your credit card to get cash advances, the APR, balance computation method, and grace period may be most important to consider. (This is an expensive way to borrow money since credit cards can charge 19.99 percent or more for cash advances.) If you plan to pay for purchases over time, the APR and balance computation method are definitely major considerations.

Federal law prohibits issuers from sending you a card you didn't ask for. However, an issuer can send you a renewal or substitute card without your request. Issuers may also send you an application or solicitation or ask you by phone if you want a card. If you receive a notice stating that you're "pre-approved" for a credit card, that doesn't guarantee you'll get the card. Your credit record and employment information will be checked once the application is submitted.

How do I qualify for a credit card?

A credit card is a loan — not an invitation to go on a shopping binge. It can give you a lot of freedom ... but it can also cause you serious problems if you fail to manage it responsibly. If you don't use it carefully, you could end up owing more than you can repay, damage your credit rating, and create credit problems for yourself that can be difficult to fix. If you're at least 18 years old and have a regular source of income, you're well on your way to qualifying for a credit card. But despite the invitations from card issuers, you still have to demonstrate that you're a good risk before they grant you credit. The proof is in your credit record. If you've financed a car loan or other purchase, you probably have a record at a credit reporting bureau. This credit history shows how responsible you've been in paying your bills and helps the credit card issuer decide how much, if any, credit to extend. Before you submit an application for a credit card, get a copy of your credit report to make sure it's accurate. (See "Why do I need a good credit rating?")

How much credit can I afford?

Experts advise never borrowing more than 15 percent of your yearly take-home pay. For example, if your paycheck averages $120 per week, you should never have more than $936 in total outstanding debt. This does not include the cost of your housing. ($120 × 52 weeks = $6,240 × 15% = $936).

Your monthly payments should be less than 10 percent of your take-home pay also. For instance, your paycheck is $120 per week, or $520 per month. Ten percent of $520 per month means your total monthly payments should be no higher than $52 per month. This does not include the cost of your housing.

What does APR mean?

The APR, or Annual Percentage Rate, is the cost of credit expressed as a yearly rate. It is key when comparing costs of credit, regardless of the amount of credit or how long you have to repay it. It also must be disclosed before you become obligated on the account and it must be included on your account statements. Many credit card companies are now using your credit history to determine the amount of interest you'll be charged on your credit card, which is very important if you carry a balance from month to month. If your credit rating isn't so good, you'll probably be offered a high APR. See the example of the "Comparison of Annual Percentage Rates" on page 80.

Many credit card companies often offer their credit card for low or zero percent introductory rates. Make sure you read the fine print before accepting. What is the APR after the introductory period? What fees are involved? If you do receive pre-approved credit card offers in the mail, tear them into small pieces or shred them before throwing them away. Amazingly enough, thieves will steal these offers and get credit cards issued to them under your name.

What other credit card terms do I need to know?

A credit card is a form of borrowing that often involves charges. Credit terms and conditions affect your overall cost. It's wise to compare terms and fees before you agree to open a credit or charge card account. The following are some important terms to consider that generally must be disclosed in credit card applications or in solicitations that require no application. Compare these terms when shopping for a credit card:

Comparison of Annual Percentage Rates (APRs)

Suppose you want to buy a $7,500 car. You put $1,500 down and need to borrow $6,000. What's the total cost of the car?

Loan Terms	Creditor X	Creditor Y	Creditor Z
Amount Borrowed	$6,000	$6,000	$6,000
APR	14%	14%	15%
Length of Loan	3 years	4 years	4 years
Monthly Payment	$205.07	$163.95	$166.98
Total Finance Charge	$1,382.52	$1,870.08	$2,015.04
Total Payments	$7,382.52	$7,870.08	$8,015.04
Down-Payment	$1,500.00	$1,500.00	$1,500.00
Total Cost	$8,882.52	$9,370.08	$9,515.04

Figure 2F

Periodic Rate

The periodic rate is applied to your outstanding balance to figure the finance charge for each billing period. For example, if your APR is 18 percent, your monthly periodic rate would be 1½ percent (18 percent per year ÷ 12 months per year). The periodic rate must be disclosed by the card issuer.

Variable Rate

Some credit cards change the APR when interest rates or other economic indicators change. Rate changes raise or lower the finance charge on your account. If you're considering a variable rate card, the card issuer must disclose the following information to you:

1. that the rate may change;

2. how the rate is determined — which index is used and what additional amount, or "margin," is added to determine your new rate;

3. how often (usually quarterly) your rate may change; and

4. how much your rate may change.

Credit Limit

The credit limit is the amount of money a credit card company authorized for you to "borrow" on your credit card. If you charge more than your credit limit, you may be charged a fee of $25 or more and you risk having your APR increased and/or your account closed.

Finance Charge

The finance charge is the total dollar amount you pay to use credit. It includes interest costs, service charges, and some credit-related insurance premiums. Under the Truth-in-Lending law, creditors must tell you in writing and before you sign any agreement what the finance charge and annual percentage rate are.

Grace Period

Also called a "free period," the grace period lets you avoid finance charges by paying your balance in full before the due date. If you plan to pay your card off each month (which you should do!), this is very important. Without a grace period, the card issuer can impose a finance charge from the date you use your card or from the date the transaction is posted to your account. If your card includes a grace period, the issuer must mail your bill at least 14 days before the due date to give you enough time to pay.

Annual Fee

Many credit card companies charge an annual membership, ranging from $25 to $100. Some companies don't charge a fee.

Transaction Fees or Other Charges

Some card issuers charge a fee if you use the card to get a cash advance, make a late payment, or exceed your credit limit. Some charge a monthly fee whether you use the card or not. If your payments are late or you exceed your credit limit a certain number of times, your interest rate will probably be raised. These rates sometimes exceed 20 percent. Just be sure to pay your bill on time and stay under your credit limit.

How is my finance charge calculated?

If you don't have a grace period, or if you expect to pay your balance over time, it's important to know what method the issuer uses to calculate your finance charge. This can make a big difference in how much you pay for finance charges — even if the APR and your buying patterns remain relatively constant. If you don't understand how your balance is calculated, ask your card issuer. An explanation must appear on your billing statements. For examples of balance computation methods, please refer to the "Balance Computation Methods" table on page 83.

What does "average daily balance" mean?

This is the most common calculation method. It credits your account from the day payment is received by the issuer. To figure the balance due, the issuer totals the beginning balance for each day in the billing period (usually monthly) and subtracts any credits made to your account that day. The total is then divided by the number of days in the billing period to get the "average daily balance."

Adjusted Balance

This is usually the most advantageous method for card holders. Your balance is determined by subtracting payments or credits received during the current billing period from the balance at the end of the previous billing period. Purchases made during the billing period are not included. This

Balance Computation Methods

	Average Daily Balance w/New Purchases	Average Daily Balance w/No New Purchases	Adjusted Balance ***	Previous Balance ****
Monthly interest rate	$1^1/_2$%	$1^1/_2$%	$1^1/_2$%	$1^1/_2$%
APR	18%	18%	18%	18%
Previous balance	$400	$400	$400	$400
New purchases made	$50 on 18th	$50 on 18th	na	na
Payments made	$300 on 15th	$300 on 15th	$300	$300
Average daily balance	$270 *	$250 **	na	na
Finance charge	$4.05 ($1^1/_2$% × $270)	$3.75 ($1^1/_2$% × $250)	$1.50 ($1^1/_2$% × $100)	$6.00 ($1^1/_2$% × $400)

* Average Daily Balance w/New Purchases:
($400 × 15 days) + ($100 × 3 days) + ($150 × 12 days) ÷ 30 days = $270

** Average Daily Balance w/No New Purchases:
($400 × 15 days) + ($100 × 15 days) ÷ 30 days = $250

*** Adjusted Balance:
$400 - $300 = $100

**** Previous Balance:
$400

Figure 2G

method gives you until the end of the billing cycle to pay a portion of your balance to avoid the interest charges on that amount.

Previous Balance

This is the amount you owed at the end of the previous billing period. Payments, credits, and new purchases during the current billing period are not included. Some creditors also exclude unpaid finance charges.

Two-Cycle Balances

Card issuers sometimes use various methods to calculate your balance that make use of your last two months' account activity. Read your agreement carefully to find out if your issuer uses this approach, and, if so, what specific two-cycle method is used.

Should I pay the minimum monthly payment?

No. You should always try to pay more than the minimum required. If you have an outstanding balance of $2,000 with 18.5 percent interest and a low minimum monthly payment, it would take over 11 years to pay off the debt and would cost you an additional $1,934 just for interest! Use the interactive calculator on the CD-ROM to figure out how to pay off your credit cards. Visit *www.Bankrate.com* for more interactive calculators.

What if my credit card is lost or stolen?

If your card is lost or stolen, report it immediately. If a thief uses your card before you report it missing, the most you will owe for unauthorized charges is $50 per card. After the loss, review your credit card statements carefully. If there are any unauthorized charges, send a letter to the credit card company describing the charges. Mail the letter to the address given on your statement for "Billing Errors" within 60 days. Don't send it with your payment unless you're directed to do so.

What if I find an error on my statement?

If you find a mistake on your bill, you can dispute the charge and withhold payment on that amount while the charge is being investigated. The error might be a charge for the wrong amount, for something you didn't order or accept, or for an item that wasn't delivered as agreed. Of course, you still have to pay any part of your bill that's not in dispute, including finance charges.

To dispute a charge, write to the credit card company at the address indicated on your statement for "Billing Inquiries." Include your name, address, account number, a description of the error, and a copy of your statement. Send your letter immediately. It must reach the creditor within 60 days after the bill containing the error was mailed to you. (If you fail to report the error within 60 days, you may have little or no recourse. Under federal law, the credit card company has no obligation to conduct an investigation if you have missed the 60-day deadline.) Your creditor must acknowledge your complaint in writing within 30 days of receipt, unless the problem has been resolved. At the latest, the dispute must be resolved within two billing cycles, but not more than 90 days.

What if I lose my statement or mailing envelope?

Look on your credit card for an 800 number to call. There is usually an automated answering service that will tell you your balance due and where to mail your payment. You can also look on previous statements for the address. Don't wait until the next statement to arrive before you make a payment. That will only hurt your credit, cost you a late fee, and raise your interest rate — and if done more than once, it could result in your credit card being cancelled.

Any safety tips for using a credit card?

- Credit cards are like a loan — you have to pay what you owe. Keep track of how much you spend. Incidental and impulse purchases add up fast.

- Never give out your credit card number or expiration date over the phone unless you know you're dealing with a reputable company. Keep your account information to yourself.

- Carry only those cards you think you'll need.

- Don't lend your card to anyone — not even a friend. Your credit privilege and history are too important to risk.

- Don't sign a blank charge slip. Draw a line through blank spaces on charge slips above the total so the amount cannot be changed. Destroy carbon copies of receipts or any paperwork that has your credit card number listed.

- Report mistakes or discrepancies within 60 days to the "Billing Errors" address on your statement.

- Never put your account number on the outside of an envelope or on a postcard.

- Cut up expired cards.

- Tear up credit card offers you get in the mail before throwing away.

- Read the fine print on the papers that come with your credit card and file in a safe place.

Do I need to buy additional credit card protection?

No. The Federal Trade Commission has issued a "scam alert" to young adults, particularly college students, about credit card protection rackets that have cost consumers at least $25 million. Telemarketers call and frighten you into paying several hundred dollars to protect yourself against credit card loss or theft. Sometimes they pose as *Visa* or *MasterCard* representatives. They post unauthorized charges to your account after persuading you to give them your credit card number. Don't fall for the scam. Under federal law, you are only responsible for up to the first $50 in unauthorized purchases if your card is lost or stolen.

Why do I need a good credit record?

What is a credit report?

A good credit rating is very important. Businesses can inspect your credit history when they evaluate your applications for credit, insurance, employment, leases, and more. Your credit record maintains information about your income, debts, and credit payment history. It also indicates whether you have been sued, arrested, or have filed for bankruptcy. Credit reports are maintained and sold by credit bureaus.

It's a good idea to get a copy of your credit report once a year. Credit bureaus are listed in the Yellow Pages under *Credit Reporting Agencies*. The three large national credit bureaus supply most credit reports and can charge up to $8.50 for a copy. You're entitled to a free copy if:

1. you're unemployed and plan to look for a job within 60 days;

2. you're on welfare;

3. your report is inaccurate because of fraud; or

4. you've been denied credit, insurance, or employment within the past 60 days because of your credit report.

You can contact the credit bureaus at the following addresses:

> **Experian**
> PO Box 2002
> Allen, TX 75013
> 1-888-397-3742
> *www.experian.com*

> **Choicepoint** (formerly Equifax)
> PO Box 740241
> Atlanta, GA 30374-0241
> 1-800-685-1111
> *www.equifax.com*

> **TransUnion**
> PO Box 1000
> Chester, PA 19022
> 1-800-916-8800
> *www.tuc.com*

If you live in Colorado, Georgia, Maryland, Massachusetts, New Jersey, or Vermont, you are eligible by law to receive a free copy of your credit report once a year.

What information is in a credit report?

A credit report includes four types of information:

Identifying Information

Your name, nicknames, current and previous addresses, Social Security number, date of birth, and current and previous employers. This information comes from any credit application you have completed and its accuracy depends on your filling out forms clearly, completely, and consistently each time you apply for credit.

Credit Information

Specific information about each of your accounts, including the date opened, credit limit or loan amount, balance, monthly payment, high/low balances, and your payment pattern during the past several years. The report also states whether anyone else besides you (a co-signer, spouse, etc.) is responsible for paying the account. This information comes from companies that do business with you.

Public Record Information

This information comes from public records, such as Federal district bankruptcy records, state and county court records, tax liens, and monetary judgments, and in some states, overdue child support payments.

Inquiries

Inquiries include the names of those who have obtained a copy of your credit report for any reason. This information comes from the credit reporting agency, and it remains available for as long as two years according to federal law. If you apply for a lot of credit cards, each company will be listed here. (And that doesn't look good for you!)

Why do I need a good credit rating?

Financial institutions use a credit report to determine if you'll get a loan. Credit card companies use it to determine if you'll be issued a credit card and how high your interest rate will be. Insurance companies use it to determine how much your premiums will be. Employers sometimes use a credit report to hire and evaluate employees for promotion, reassignment, or retention.

How do I establish a credit history?

If you haven't financed a car, a computer, or some other major purchase, consider applying for a credit card issued by a local store and use it responsibly. Ask if they report to a credit bureau. If they do — and you pay your bills on time — you'll establish a good credit history. Open a checking and/or savings account. (These do not begin your credit file, but may be checked as evidence that you have money and know how to manage it.)

You might also consider applying for a "secured" credit card. A secured credit card requires that you open and maintain a bank account or other asset account at a financial institution as security for your line of credit. Your credit line will be a percentage of your deposit, typically from 50 to 100 percent. For example, you may have to deposit $250 in the account in order to get a credit limit of $500. Unsecured cards usually carry a higher interest rate and you may have to pay application and processing fees.

As a last resort, consider asking a relative to co-sign a credit card account if you don't qualify on your own. The co-signer promises to pay your debts if you don't. Repay your debts promptly so you can build a credit history and apply for credit on your own in the future.

Who is allowed to see my credit report?

Only the following requesters are allowed to view your credit report:

- Creditors who are considering granting or have granted you credit.

- Employers considering you for employment, promotion, reassignment, or retention.

- Insurers considering you for an insurance policy or reviewing an existing policy.

- Government agencies reviewing your financial status in connection with issuing certain licenses or government benefits.

- Anyone else with a legitimate business reason for needing the information (such as a potential landlord).

Credit reports can also be reviewed by court orders or federal jury subpoenas. And they can be issued to a third party if you give them written instructions to do so.

What if my credit application is denied?

According to the Fair Credit Reporting Act, you are entitled to a free copy of your credit report if you've been denied credit, insurance, or employment within the last 60 days. If your application for credit, insurance, or employment is denied because of information supplied by a credit bureau, the company you applied to must provide you with that credit bureau's name, address, and telephone number. If you're turned down for credit, find out why. It may be that you don't have a strong credit history, haven't been at your job or address long enough, or that you don't have enough income to meet the criteria.

What if there's negative information on my report?

If the negative information isn't true, you are entitled to have the information investigated by the credit reporting agency. You can dispute mistakes or outdated items for free. Ask the credit reporting agency for a dispute form or submit your dispute in writing, along with any supporting documentation. Don't send original documents. If you disagree with the findings, you can file a short statement (100 words or less) in your record giving your side of the story. Future reports must include this statement or a summary of it.

If the negative information is true, you're stuck with it on your credit report for at least seven years! If your file contains accurate negative information, only time and good money habits will restore your credit-worthiness. Pay any balances that you owe so creditors can update your file. Wait for the required length of time to elapse for negative information to be removed from your file (10 years for bankruptcies, seven years for everything else). You can write a statement (100 words or less) to be included in your credit report.

Should I hire a credit repair company?

Everything a repair company can do for you legally, you can do for yourself at little or no cost. Companies nationwide appeal to consumers with poor credit histories. They promise, for a fee, to clean up your credit report so you can get a car loan, buy a house, get insurance, or even get a job. They can't deliver. After you pay them hundreds or thousands of dollars in up-front fees, these companies do nothing to improve your credit report. Many may simply vanish with your money.

You've seen their ads on TV, on the Internet, and in newspapers. You hear them on the radio. You get fliers in the mail. You may even get calls from telemarketers offering credit repair services. None of them can repair your credit. No one can legally remove accurate and timely negative information from your credit report.

> *Credit problems? No problem!*

> *We can erase your bad credit — 100% guaranteed!*

> *Create a new credit identity — legally.*

We can remove bankruptcies, judgments, liens, and bad loans from your credit file forever!

- Beware of companies that want you to pay for credit repair services *before* any services are provided. Under the Fair Credit Repair Organizations Act, credit repair companies cannot require you to pay until they have completed the promised services.

- Beware of companies that don't tell you your legal rights and what you can do yourself for free.

- Beware of companies that recommend that you *not* contact a credit bureau directly.

- Beware of companies that suggest you try to invent a *new* credit report by applying for an Employer Identification Number (EIN) from the IRS to use instead of your Social Security number.

- Beware of companies that advise you to dispute all information in your credit report or take any action that seems illegal, such as creating a new identity.

- It's a federal crime to make false statements on a loan or credit application, to misrepresent your Social Security number, and to obtain an EIN from the IRS under false pretenses. If you follow illegal advice and commit fraud, you may be subject to prosecution. You can also be charged and prosecuted for mail or wire fraud if you use the mail or telephone to apply for credit and provide false information. (For more information, see "Can a credit repair company erase my debts?")

What is credit scoring?

Credit scoring is a system creditors use to help determine whether to give you credit. Information about you and your credit experiences (such as your bill-paying history, the number and type of accounts you have, late payments, collection actions, outstanding debt, and age of your accounts) is collected from your credit application and your credit report. Using a statistical program, creditors compare this information to the credit performance of consumers with similar profiles. A credit scoring system awards points for each factor that helps predict who is most likely to repay a debt.

A total number of points — a credit score — helps predict how credit-worthy you are; that is, how likely it is that you will repay a loan and make the payments when due. Credit scoring is based on real data and statistics and treats all applicants objectively. Scoring models evaluate the following types of information in your credit report:

Have I paid my bills on time?

Payment history is a significant factor. Your score will be affected negatively if you have paid bills late, had an account referred to a collection agency, had several checks bounce, or declared bankruptcy. Many landlords also report to credit bureaus, so pay your rent on time.

What is my outstanding debt?

Many scoring models evaluate the amount of debt you have compared to your credit limits. If the amount you owe is close to your credit limit, it's likely to have a negative affect on your score.

How long (or short) is my credit history?

The length of your credit track record can affect your credit score. An insufficient credit history may have an affect on your score, but can be offset by other factors, such as timely payments and low balances.

Have I applied for new credit recently?

Many scoring models consider whether you have applied for credit recently by looking at "inquiries" on your credit report when you apply for credit. Each time you submit an application for any type of credit, it shows up as an inquiry on your credit report. If you've applied for too many new accounts, it may negatively affect your score. Inquiries by creditors who are monitoring your account or looking at credit reports to make "pre-screened" credit offers are not counted.

How many and what types of credit accounts do I have?

Although it is generally good to have established credit accounts, too many credit card accounts or too many types of credit accounts may have a negative affect on your score.

Scoring models also consider information from your credit application, your job or occupation, length of employment, or whether you own a home. To improve your credit score, concentrate on paying your bills on time, paying down outstanding balances, and not taking on new debt.

What is the FICO credit scoring system?

Many loans are based entirely on your FICO score, a credit scoring system created by Fair, Isaac and Co. of San Rafael, California. Scores range from 300 to 850. Most lenders are looking for a score of 700 or higher.

- Excellent scores are above 730.

- Good scores are 700 to 729.

- Consumers who need a closer look score 670 to 699.

- Higher risk consumers score 585 to 669.

- And those who score below 585 receive no credit or limited credit.

- Here's how your FICO score is calculated:

Payment Record

Whether you've paid your bills on time or not accounts for 35 percent of your FICO score.

Amounts Owed

Your total amount of debt, including balances on credit cards, car loans, and student loans, accounts for 30 percent of your score.

Credit History

How long you've had credit makes up 15 percent of your score. FICO scores consider both the age of your oldest account and the average age of all your accounts. If you have old credit cards you're no longer using, don't close them out. You might shorten your credit history, lowering your FICO score.

New Debt

Ten percent of your score is based upon your application history — the number of times you apply for credit. Shopping around for lower-interest cards is not a good thing. Lenders want someone who will establish credit with them and keep it.

Credit Mix

The remaining 10 percent is based on how much credit you have and the types of debt you have incurred. Having too many accounts could harm your score.

To learn your score, go to *www.myfico.com* or the three national credit bureau websites, *www.equifax.com*, *www.experian.com*, and *www.tuc.com*. There is a small fee.

How can I stop getting credit card offers?

If you'd like your name removed from mailing lists for pre-approved credit cards, contact the following:

> **Choicepoint Options**
> PO Box 740123
> Atlanta, GA 30374-0123
> 1-800-759-5979
> (formerly Equifax)

> **Experian**
> Consumer Opt Out Service
> PO Box 7245
> Fullerton, CA 92834
> 1-800-241-2858

> **TransUnion**
> Consumer Relations Department
> PO Box 919
> Allen, TX 75013
> 1-800-392-1122
> 1800-353-0809

Include your complete full name, full address, Social Security number, and signature.

 ## Am I too young to worry about retirement?

Am I too young to worry about retirement?

No. Start planning now so your money will earn even more money for your retirement. To calculate how much you'll need to retire, use the online retirement calculators at *www.quicken.com*, *www.asec.org/ballpark/*, and *www.financenter.com*. Since you're just starting your career, you might try putting in your desired salary to determine how much you'll need to save.

Continue to re-calculate your retirement needs each time you get an increase in your salary.

What is the Rule of 72?

The Rule of 72 enables you to determine how long it will take your money to double. How does it work? With simple math! You just divide 72 by your interest rate.

For example, if you have $1,000 in a savings account that pays 4 percent interest, it will take 18 years for your money to double ($72 \div 4 = 18$). In 18 years, your $1,000 will double to $2,000.

If you take that same $1,000 and put it in a mutual fund that pays 8 percent interest, it will only take nine years to double your money ($72 \div 8 = 9$).

The Rule of 72 works in reverse, also. Do you want your money to double in six years? Here's the formula: $72 \div 6$ (years) = 12 (percent). If you want your money to double in six years, you'd have to find an investment that pays a return of 12 percent.

How does compounded interest benefit me?

When you deposit money in an investment account, you earn interest on your money. If the interest is compounded, you'll earn interest on the interest. Sound confusing? It's really not. It'll help to define simple interest first — and then compounded interest.

Simple Interest

Let's assume you put $3,000 in a three-year investment account that earns five percent interest. For simple interest, your money would earn $450 in interest:

Year 1 ($3,000 × 5%)	$150
Year 2 ($3,000 × 5%)	+150
Year 3 ($3,000 × 5%)	+<u>150</u>
Total	$450

Compounded Interest

Now if you take that same $3,000 at five percent interest compounded annually, you'll earn $473:

Year 1
($3,000 × 5%) $150
Year 2
($3,000 + $150 interest earned = $3,150 × 5%)   +158
Year 3
($3,150 + $158 interest earned = $3,308 × 5%)   +165
                                                  Total $473

To give you an idea of why it's so important to start saving now, let's look at that $3,000 in 20 years: Simple interest earned is $3,000. Compounded interest earned is $5,319. What a difference! That's just on the original $3,000 investment. Just think what could happen if you continued to invest money in the compounded-interest account during that 20 years.

What's the best investment I can make?

Paying off the balance on your credit card(s) is the best "investment" you can make. Suppose you pay 18 percent interest on your card. If you pay off that card, it's like earning 18 percent — tax-free, risk-free! Think about it. Where can you earn a guaranteed 18 percent return on your money? The stock market isn't even that good — and you have to pay taxes on profits and dividends. And, if you keep a balance on your credit card, your lifestyle is 18 percent more expensive than it needs to be. Pay off your credit cards and then use that same amount of money to invest in your future.

Why did I steal $5 from Dad?

Are you still feeling guilty about money from your childhood? What's your first memory of money? Suze Orman's book, *The 9 Steps to Financial Freedom: Practical and Spiritual Steps So You Can Stop Worrying*, illustrates how your past holds the key to your financial future. In Step 1, Ms. Orman writes,

> *Messages about money are passed down from generation to generation, worn and chipped like the family dishes. Your own memories about money will tell you a lot, if you take that step back and see what those memories taught you about who you were — and whether those memories are still telling you who you are today.*

The 9 Steps to Financial Freedom: Practical & Spiritual Steps So You Can Stop Worrying by Suze Orman.

© 1997 by Suze Orman. (Crown Publishers, ISBN 0-517-70791-8)

The book uses personal stories and simple exercises to help you gain financial freedom. *Read the book!* (Or listen to the audio tapes.) It will change the way you think about money — and about yourself!

What can I invest in?

There are many options for investing — and this book is only a tool to help you understand those options. Do your own research and talk to financial experts before you start investing. Don't invest in the first thing, or the easiest thing, that comes along. Your basic options include 401(k); employee pension or profit-sharing plan; IRA; stocks; mutual funds; checking, savings, and money market accounts; certificates of deposit (CDs); bonds; and insurance policies.

401(k)

Many companies allow you to invest a set percent of your pre-tax salary in a 401(k) or similar retirement program. If your employer offers this, invest the maximum amount. You pay no income taxes on the amount you invest or on its earnings until you begin taking the money out for retirement. Many employers will match a set percent of what you invest. If you change jobs, roll your retirement fund over to your new employer's fund, or roll it into an IRA. If you spend it, you'll have to pay federal and state income taxes and a 10 percent early-withdrawal penalty.

Employee Pension or Profit-Sharing Plan

A traditional pension is a function of salary and tenure with an employer. It builds up as your pay and years with the company increase.

IRA

You can invest up to $2,500 a year in a Roth or regular Individual Retirement Account (IRA) For most people, the Roth IRA is a better option because the earnings on your contributions continue to grow tax-free forever. You can withdraw up to $10,000 tax-free to purchase your first home or for qualifying educational expenses if the funds have been invested for five years. With a regular IRA, you get a tax-deduction of $2,500 a year (if you itemize your taxes), but your money grows tax-deferred, not tax-free. (Tax-deferred means you don't pay taxes on the money until you withdraw it.)

Stocks

Companies sell shares of ownership in their company, called stock, to raise money to finance operations. Stocks are traded in stock markets like the

New York Stock Exchange or the NASDAQ. Stock prices go up and down on a daily basis. Stocks have produced the highest long-term returns over the past several decades.

Mutual Funds

A mutual fund is an investment that combines the money of many investors who have common financial goals into a professionally-managed portfolio. The portfolio holds many different stocks, bonds, and other securities. You can buy mutual funds for as little as a few hundred dollars.

Checking, Savings, and Money Market Accounts

A savings account or money market fund might be ideal to save for a rainy day — and your money is easily accessible. Money market accounts usually require a minimum balance of $1,000 to $2,500 and pay a higher rate of return than a savings account.

Certificates of Deposit

You can invest in a Certificate of Deposit (CD) at your financial institution. CDs pay a fixed amount of interest during a fixed amount of time.

Bonds

Bonds are basically IOUs issued by corporations and the government in exchange for your loan to them. More than 55 million Americans own U.S. Savings Bonds worth nearly $185 billion. Savings bonds are the most secure investment. You don't have to pay state or local income tax on interest earned. Savings bonds can earn interest for 30 years, but can be cashed after six months. (There may be a fee to cash a bond within the first five years.) For more information, go to *www.savingsbonds.com*.

Insurance Policies

Some view permanent life insurance (also known as "cash-value") as an investment or tax shelter because a portion of your premium is put in a reserve fund where it earns interest or dividends.

How are interest rates determined?

Interest rates are affected by a number of factors. The Federal Reserve, which is charged with maintaining the stability of the nation's financial system, raises or lowers short-term interest rates it charges banks in an effort to maintain that stability. The banks, in turn, raise or lower short-term interest rates to consumers. The Federal Reserve regularly takes these actions in response to economic expansions and contractions that the country goes through on a fairly routine basis.

When the economy is slowing down, short-term interest rates are lowered to make it less expensive to borrow money. Businesses and consumers can then buy more products and services and speed the economy up a bit. This keeps the economy from sinking into a recession. A recession happens in a cycle of consumers holding onto their money; companies not producing as many products; and employees losing their jobs.

How does inflation affect me?

Inflation is caused when there's too much money to spend on too few products. Inflation decreases the value of your dollar — which makes it more expensive to buy or manufacture products. For example, between 1939 and 1995, inflation grew at a rate of 4.4 percent each year. While that may seem like a small amount, it adds up fast. Inflation makes a 1939 dollar worth 998 percent more than a 1995 dollar. (Do you remember hearing stories about when new cars cost just $400? That same car would cost almost $40,000 today!)

 ## Will I get Social Security when I retire?

What is Social Security?

Social Security is based on a simple concept: When you work, you pay taxes into the system — and when you retire you collect benefits. (Benefits can also be paid to you if you become disabled or to your spouse and/or dependents if you die.) Almost all American workers pay Social Security and Medicare taxes. Social Security is deducted from your paycheck under the heading FICA (Federal Insurance Contributions Act). As of July 2000, the tax rate of 7.65 percent covers both Social Security and Medicare. The Social Security tax is 6.2 percent of gross wages, up to $76,200. Your employer matches your Social Security tax payment.

The Social Security Administration also manages the Medicare system. Medicare taxes are deducted from each paycheck at a rate of 1.45 percent of all earnings. (Medicare is our country's basic health insurance program for people 65 or older and for many with disabilities.)

For more information, visit *www.ssa.gov* or call 1-800-772-1213 (TTY 1-800-325-0778).

Why do I need a Social Security number?

You need a Social Security number to get a job and pay taxes. Your Social Security number is used to keep a record of your earnings throughout your lifetime. Make sure your name and number are correct on your pay stub and W-2 (year-end Wage and Tax Statement).

Will I get Social Security when I retire?

Yes. Social Security law has changed over the past 60 years to meet the needs of the American people — and will continue to change to meet your needs when you reach retirement age. Keep in mind, though, that Social Security should not be your only source of retirement income. Most financial advisors say that you'll need 70 percent of pre-retirement earnings to live comfortably when you retire. Social Security only pays an average of 40 percent. Start investing for your retirement today. Go to "What can I invest in?" for information on investment options.

How do I get a Social Security number?

If your parent(s) didn't get a Social Security card for you when you were younger, contact your local Social Security office or call 1-800-772-1213. To get an original card, you'll need to complete an application and provide documents that show your age, identity, and citizenship/birth certificate (or lawful alien status), and marriage or divorce certificates. All documents must be originals or certified copies. Social Security cards are free.

When do I replace my card?

Replace your card if you get married, divorced, or change your name. If your card is lost or stolen, contact your local Social Security office to get a replacement card. Your same number will be given to you. If you change your name, you need to show one or more documents that identify you by your old name and your new name. Replacement cards are free.

If you move, become a parent or adopt a child; are imprisoned; or leave the United States (to live or work), you should contact your local Social Security office.

Should I give my number to others?

Be careful with your Social Security number. It is the key to identity theft.

Giving your number is voluntary, even when asked for the number directly. If requested, ask the following questions:

- Why is my number needed?

- How will it be used?

- What law requires me to give my number to you?

- What are the consequences if I refuse to give you my number?

(See "What if someone steals my identity?" for more information.)

What are Social Security benefits?

Benefits are paid monthly, not in one lump sum, and are based on your earnings. Payments are also based on the annual cost-of-living index.

Retirement Benefits

Retirement benefits are paid to more than 30 million retired workers and their family members. More than 90 percent of retirees receive Social Security. Full retirement benefits are paid at age 65 for those people born before 1938, with reduced benefits available as early as age 62. The age for full benefits is gradually rising, until it reaches age 67 in 2027 for people born in 1960 or later. (Reduced benefits will still be available at age 62.) Social Security replaces about 40 percent of an average-wage earner's salary.

Disability Benefits

Disability benefits are paid to workers who become severely disabled. Under Social Security, workers are considered disabled if they cannot do work they did before and Social Security officials decide that a worker cannot adjust to other work because of his/her medical condition(s). The disability must be expected to last for at least 12 months or to result in death.

Survivor Benefits

Survivor benefits are paid to a deceased worker's family. Benefits may be paid to children under 18; under 19 but still in high school; and 18 or older who become disabled before age 22. Benefits are paid to widows or widowers who are caring for children under age 16; disabled; age 60 or older; and age 50 or older who are disabled.

 **Do I need insurance?**

Do I need auto insurance?

Auto insurance is used to protect yourself against expenses you could not otherwise afford due to an accident. If you own a car, you *must* also buy auto insurance. Requirements vary by state. (See Chapter 15, "What car insurance do I need?" for more information.)

Do I need health insurance?

Going without personal medical insurance is risky. You may feel perfectly fine today, but you could be sick or injured tomorrow. Not having health insurance could mean financial ruin. Unfortunately, there are no cheap choices. If you do buy health insurance, it's expensive. If you don't, and you get sick or hurt, healthcare will be very expensive. (See Chapter 9, "Do I need health insurance?" for more information.)

Do I need life insurance?

If you're single with no dependents (spouse and/or children), you probably don't need life insurance. The main purpose of life insurance is to provide cash to your family after you die. Most young adults buy life insurance when they get married. There are basically two types of life insurance: term and permanent.

Term Life Insurance

Term life insurance is a more cost-effective choice for young families and healthy people. Term insurance pays your beneficiary (the person you designate to receive the money) if you, as the policy holder, die within a specified amount of time (such as a term of 5, 10, or 20 years). With a **level-term** policy, you pay the same amount in premiums throughout the life of the policy. The premiums only increase if you choose to renew the policy when it expires. **Annual-renewable** premiums increase each year as you age.

Permanent Life Insurance

Permanent life insurance (also known as "cash-value") provides lifelong protection. As long as you pay the premiums, the death benefit will be paid. Some view cash-value life insurance as an investment or tax shelter because your premiums (payments) are divided to pay for the amount due your survivors if you die (death benefit), with the remainder put in a reserve fund where it earns interest or dividends. If you decide to end the policy, you get some of the savings back (cash-surrender value). The premiums for permanent policies are higher than for term policies, but the premiums are typically the same for the duration of the policy.

Policy holders have a choice of three types of permanent insurance premiums. **Whole life** remains in effect for your lifetime or until you stop paying the premiums. **Universal life** allows the policy holder flexibility in choosing and changing the terms of the policy. **Variable life** gives the policy holder the choice of investing in stocks, bonds, and money market funds.

What is a beneficiary?

A beneficiary is the person you choose to receive the income of your life insurance when you die. You may choose more than one beneficiary. Most young adults choose a parent or other family member until they marry.

Do I need renters insurance?

Renters insurance is not required by law (like auto insurance is), but if you rent a house or an apartment, rental insurance is recommended to cover theft or damage to your personal property. It also provides liability protection. (See Chapter 1, "Do I need renters insurance?" for more information.)

What are industry ratings?

Ratings are an objective way to determine an insurance company's stability and financial strength. Several organizations rate insurance companies. Use companies that have had high ratings for five years or more. Check the following sources on the Internet or at your local library for free ratings before buying insurance:

- A.M. Best

- Moody's Investors Services

- Standard and Poors

What are insurance scores?

The insurance industry uses your credit information to compile a score that will predict insurance claim losses. Statistics that show a direct correlation between an individual's credit history and his/her chances for filing an insurance claim are used. Insurance companies generalize that drivers with poor credit histories submit at least 50 percent more claims and that homeowners and renters with poor credit histories file twice as many claims and collect three times more in claim payments as individuals with excellent credit histories. (See "Why do I need a good credit report?" for more information.)

How do I file a complaint about my insurance company?

Talk to your company or agent first. Many problems are resolved at this level. When you contact your insurance company, have your policy number and information ready to fully explain your concern. Keep copies of documents and phone notes in case you file a complaint. If you've tried unsuccessfully to resolve the problem with the company and/or agent, you can call or write your State Insurance Department. Look in the government pages of the phone book for the number.

What is insurance fraud?

Insurance fraud is a crime. People who commit insurance fraud steal an estimated $20 billion a year. Who pays? Everyone does — by paying higher insurance premiums. Fraud is committed when false information is given about accidents, injuries, or losses. Examples include staged auto accidents, faked auto thefts, phony or inflated medical bills or auto repair bills, burglary, and arson for profit. (If you file a claim to get your car repaired and buy a stereo instead, you're committing fraud.) Be honest with your insurance company. It is not a financial institution and does not owe you just because you pay a premium. In the long run, you'll end up paying even more when you really need it.

If you suspect fraud, call your insurance agent or the National Insurance Crime Bureau's toll-free fraud hotline at 1-800-TEL-NICB.

 ### How does someone steal my identity?

Identity theft occurs when a criminal uses your personal information to take on your identity. Identity thieves get your personal information through a variety of means. They steal your purse or wallet (even at work). They steal your mail. They rummage through your trash looking for personal data. They illegally obtain your credit report posing as a landlord, employer, or someone who may have a legitimate need (and legal right) to the information. They get your business and personal records at work. They find personal information in your home. They get information from the Internet. They also "buy" personal information from "inside sources," such as store employees.

 ## Should I buy the service contract?

You probably don't need one — no matter what the salesman says. Service contracts are often called "extended warranties" — but they aren't warranties. Warranties are included in the price of the product. Service contracts provide repair and/or maintenance for a specific time. They cost extra and are sold separately. Do you need to buy the service contract? Does the warranty already cover the repairs and the time period of coverage of the service contract? Is the product likely to need repairs? If so, what are potential repair costs? How long does the service contract last? What is the reputation of the company offering the service contract?

 ## Do I have to leave a tip?

Do I have to leave a tip?

Tipping is an important part of American life. It lets people know their service is valued. There are no all-purpose guidelines for tipping. Some people tip a standard 15 percent. Others tip based on quality of service. Some tip everyone who provides a service to them, while others tip only at restaurants. Although people in the service field are paid low wages, with employers expecting tips to compensate, you're still not obligated to tip. Tipping is voluntary to reward good service. You should also treat service people with respect. Your attitude is just as important as the tip you leave. The following are some common tipping practices:

- Waiter / Waitress

    - 15 percent of the pre-tax bill.

    - 20 percent if it's a nice restaurant or if the service is exceptional.

    - 10 percent at buffets (or no tip if the server didn't assist you).

    - For large parties, the tip may be added to the bill automatically.

- Bartender — 5 to 15 percent of bar bill.

- Hairstylist or Barber — 15 percent.

- Taxi Driver — 15 percent.

- Food Delivery Person — $1 to $5, depending on the size of the delivery.

- Flower Delivery Person — $3 to $5.

- DJs — $1 or more if you ask for a song to be played.

- Restroom Attendant — $1.

- Valet/Car Park Attendant — $2 to $5.

- Coffee Bar Attendant — $1 or your change in the jar on the counter.

- Coatroom Attendant — $1.

What can I do to earn better tips?

Making good tips as a waiter or waitress is easy— just care about the customer. This means that when you're on the clock, you want everyone at your table(s) to have a good experience. What can you do to make your customers happy? With customers, it truly is "the little things" that make the difference. Take their orders promptly — and then check back on them several times after you've served the meal. Even if they don't need anything, it shows you care enough to ask. If something doesn't go well (such as a hair in the soup or taking too long for an order to be served), apologize for the mishap and then do what you can to fix it. If your customers complain, they just need to be heard. Acknowledge their complaint (and their feelings). Do what you can to turn the experience back into a pleasant one — and show that you care. Let your customers know you care and your tips will increase — and so will your job satisfaction.

What does RSVP mean?

RSVP stands for *"Répondez s'il vous plaît,"* or *"Reply if you please."* It's listed in the finances chapter because it can cost a host a lot of money if invited guests don't RSVP.

Why do some people not reply?
Some people think that if they don't reply, the host should assume they're not attending. Some people forget to RSVP but show up for the event anyway. If you don't RSVP, you leave the host guessing ... Did you get your invitation? Are you coming? Should I begin the event without you? Should I wait five more minutes? Do I order food just in case you do show up? Do I reserve a room for 20 or 40?

Respond promptly when you receive an invitation with an RSVP. Your friend was nice enough to include you — so be respectful enough to RSVP even if you can't attend.

Additional Information for this Chapter

Books

- *Get in the Game: The Girl's Guide to Investing* by Vanessa Summers

- *Getting Rich in America: 8 Simple Rules for Building a Fortune and a Satisfying Life* by Dwight R. Lee and Richard B.McKenzie

- *Kiplinger's Practical Guide to Investing* by Ted Miller

- *The Millionaire Next Door* by Thomas J. Stanley, Ph.D. and William D. Danko, Ph.D.

- *The Motley Fool's Rule Makers: The Foolish Guide to Picking Stocks* by David and Tom Gardner

- *The Motley Fool's You Have More than You Think: The Foolish Guide to Investing What You Have* by David and Tom Gardner

- *The 9 Steps to Financial Freedom: Practical & Spiritual Steps so You Can Stop Worrying* by Suze Orman

- *Rich Dad, Poor Dad* by Robert T. Kiyosaki with Sharon L. Lechter, C.P.A.

- *The Road to Wealth: A Comprehensive Guide to Your Money* by Suze Orman

- *Think and Grow Rich* by Napoleon Hill

- *Yes You Can: Achieve Financial Independence* by James E. Stowers

Web Links

- *www.pueblo.gsa.gov*

- *www.bbb.org*
  (Better Business Bureau)

- *www.consumer.gov*

- *www.ssa.gov*
  (Social Security
  Administration)

- *www.irs.gov*

- *www.ftc.gov*
  (Federal Trade Commission)

- *www.savingsbonds.gov*

- *www.savingsbonds.com*

- *www.experian.com*

- *www.equifax.com*

- *www.tuc.com* (TransUnion)

- *www.bankrate.com*

- *www.ambest.com*

- *www.moodys.com*

- *www.standardandpoors.com*

- *www.jumpstartcoalition.org*

- *www.creditpage.com*

- *www.myfico.com*

- *www.familymoney.com*

- *www.suzeorman.com*

- *www.fool.com*

- *www.money.com*

- *www.smartmoney.com*

- *www.debtfree.org*

- www.asec.org

- www.richdad.com

- www.missingmoney.com

- www.quicken.com

- www.chexhelp.com

- www.financenter.com

- www.turbotax.com

- www.kiplinger.com

- www.insurance.com

- www.insure.com

- www.startsampling.com

- www.couponmaker.com

- www.TheUltimates.com

- www.ChecksUnlimited.com

- www.ArtisticChecks.com

- www.CheckGallery.com

Will I get the job?

When you interview for a job, you'll be asked a lot of questions. Answer the following interview questions and practice saying your answers out loud until you're comfortable with them.

Interactive CD-ROM

Quiz

1. What can you tell me about yourself? _____

   _____

   Talk about business life, not personal life. Make a short, organized statement of your education and achievements. Briefly describe your qualifications and the contributions you can make to the company. Don't ramble in the interview.

2. Why should I hire you? _____

3. What are your strengths? _____

4. What are your weaknesses? _____

   Turn this question back to your strengths. Does your weakness make you do something better?

5. What do you want to be doing five years from now? _____

6. Why do you want to work for this company? _____

7. What are your salary expectations? _____

8. What skills can you offer this company? _____

9. What is your education? _____

10. Do you have a job now?   ○ Yes ○ No

11. If selected, when can you begin? _____

    (Do you need to give a notice at your current job?)

12. What work experience do you have? _____

13. What were your duties and responsibilities? _____

14. How long did you work for that company? _____

15. Why did you leave your last job? _____

    Avoid using negative statements about your last job and/or boss.

16. What do you know about this company? _____

17. Would you be willing to take a drug test?   ○ Yes   ○ No

18. What's the most difficult situation you faced and how did you handle it? _____

    _____

19. Do you prefer working alone or with others?   ○ Alone   ○ With others

20. What do you do in your spare time? _____

21. Do you have any gaps in your education or employment dates?   ○ Yes   ○ No

22. What did you do during those gaps? _____

23. Do you feel you can do this job?   ○ Yes   ○ No

24. Do you have any questions?   ○ YES! (Come prepared with your own questions.)

25. Are you married? Do you plan to have children? How old are you?
    (These are questions interviewers are not allowed to ask.)

Check the end of this chapter for more interview questions to practice.

Career Guidance

Write the résumé that will get you an interview for the job you want! With a thorough knowledge of the business world, you can avoid sweaty palms and a racing heart as you prepare for that all-important job interview. Know how to dress and what questions you can expect to answer. Remember: Knowledge is power and the more prepared you are, the better you'll do!

Chapter 3

How do I find a job?

What do I want to do?

Before you find a job, you have to know what kind of job you want to find. Make a list of things you enjoy doing. The following questions will help you begin:

- What do I like to do?

- What skills and abilities do I have?

> Opportunity
> is missed by most
> people because it is
> dressed in overalls and
> looks like work.
> ~ Thomas A. Edison

- What are my interests?

- What volunteer work have I done?

- What motivates me?

- What kind of school activities do I like?

- What experience do I have?

- What kind of social activities do I like?

- What are my accomplishments?

- What kind of sports activities do I like?

If you're currently employed, or have been employed, write things about your job that you like and things you don't like. Use the form on page 113. If this will be your first job, imagine things you would like and dislike.

Study your list. Focus your search on jobs that fall within the "likes" column. What did you like about these things? What skills did you acquire by doing them? What challenges did they offer? What skills can you improve on? Do you need more training or any specialized training? (If so, go to Chapter 3, "College & Skill Guidance.")

You might also consider taking a skills test. There are several available, including the Strong Interest Inventory, the Campbell Interest and Skills Survey, and the Myers-Briggs Type Indicator. An excellent book that can help is *What Color is My Parachute?* by Richard Nelson Bolles.

How do I find a job opening?

You alone are responsible for your success! With that in mind, make a plan to have a successful job search. Choose the type of position you want. Choose the type of company you want to work for. Choose the type of people you want to work with. Choose to remain in control of your search to find the job that fits you, not a job that you can fit into. And keep

> Well,
> yes, you do have
> great big teeth;
> but, never mind that.
> You were great to at least
> grant me this interview.
>
> ~ *Little Red Riding Hood*

Do I like my job?

Things I Like to Do

1. _____
2. _____
3. _____
4. _____
5. _____
6. _____
7. _____
8. _____
9. _____
10. _____
11. _____
12. _____
13. _____
14. _____
15. _____
16. _____

Things I Don't Like to Do

1. _____
2. _____
3. _____
4. _____
5. _____
6. _____
7. _____
8. _____
9. _____
10. _____
11. _____
12. _____
13. _____
14. _____
15. _____
16. _____

Figure 3B

in mind that your first job will probably not be your last. The average American has three to five careers and 10 to 12 jobs during a lifetime.

The best jobs with the least competition aren't advertised in the newspaper. They're found through networking and informational interviews. On average, only five percent of people who respond to newspaper ads receive an interview. One of the best ways to get an interview and a job offer is to *never ask for a job!* Do an *informational search* with companies you're interested in. Call to ask for information, advice, referrals — and to be remembered for any openings in the future. Make a friend in the company!

Networking is one of the most important tools in finding a job. In his book, *Dig Your Well Before You're Thirsty: The Only Networking Book You'll Ever Need*, Harvey Mackay says,

> *"One reason that people are so afraid to network is that they don't want to hear the word 'no.' But 'no' is the second-best answer there is. At least you know where you stand."*

Even though companies spend millions of dollars to advertise job openings, 40 to 50 percent of employees are hired based on recommendations from current employees, family members, or friends. Make a list of contacts. Include everyone you can think of (former co-workers, bosses, professors, your trainer at the gym, your hairdresser). Network with people who already work in the job you hope to have. Community volunteering is also a great way to network.

The following are sources you can use to help in your search:

- Informational searches

- Newspapers

- Friends and relatives

- Internet

- Networking

- Professional associations

- Volunteering

- Alumni associations

- High school guidance counselors

- Job fairs

- College placement offices

- Trade and business magazines

- Temporary-help agencies

- Bulletin boards

- Career assistance networks with local non-profit agencies (some provide training, too)

- Headhunters and executive recruiters (usually for upper-management positions)

Dig Your Well Before You're Thirsty: The Only Networking Book You'll Ever Need by Harvey Mackay.

© 1997 by Harvey Mackay. (Doubleday, ISBN 0-385-48546-8)

How do I keep track of my job search?

Get a notebook to use for your job search. Keep it organized by including the following information:

- All companies you contacted. Include date and method of contact (mailed résumé, called, e-mailed, etc.). If you don't hear from a company within a week, call to see if they've received your résumé.

- All informational searches you've done. Who have you called? Who have you met? With what companies? In what positions? When did you contact? How did you contact? What were the results?

- A copy of all letters you've sent.

● Notes on your interview preparation — and answers to interview questions.

 How do I write a résumé?

Why do I need a résumé?

There are four uses for a résumé:

1. for you to record and remember your experience and accomplishments;

2. to inform potential employers of your skills so they can call you for an interview;

3. to use as an agenda during an interview; and

4. to help the interviewer remember you after the interview.

> **20** seconds is all you get! That's the average time a manager takes to scan a résumé and determine if the applicant should be granted an interview!

How do I write a good résumé?

The following tips can help you write a résumé; however, a good résumé will not get you a job. It might get you an interview, though. Employers look for the candidate with the best experience, skills, education, and attitude. Think of your résumé as a tool to get you in the door for an interview.

Use your own words so that if you're asked about something during an interview, you'll know the answer. If you hire someone to write a résumé for you, work closely with that person so the words used reflect you. Don't copy words from another résumé. You can copy style, though. Check your library for books that show samples of résumés, cover letters, and thank you notes.

Be specific with experience, awards, accomplishments, volunteer activities, summer jobs, etc. Highlight your accomplishments by adding numbers or percentages, if possible. Think hard about the things you've done. In each task, you probably learned some sort of skill. Never start sentences with *"I."* Use short, clear sentences with action words. Make paragraphs no longer than six sentences long. Here's a sample of action verbs:

achieved	designed	implemented	performed	supervised
added	eliminated	increased	planned	trained
assisted	established	initiated	produced	transformed
broadened	evaluated	maintained	purchased	utilized
consolidated	expanded	managed	reduced	verified
created	generated	negotiated	saved	worked
developed	identified	organized	simplified	wrote

For example, if you worked behind the counter at McDonalds, state how many people you served on an average day with no complaints. This shows that you have good people skills and communications skills and that you can perform under pressure. If you were in charge of a cash drawer, state how much money you were in charge of — with no shortages.

Did you know that 1 in 8 workers has at some point been employed at McDonalds?

~from Fast Food Nation

by Eric Schlosser

Tell the truth. If you lie about your education, job experience, or any other information, you'll probably live to regret it. If you've had periods of unemployment, don't adjust dates on other jobs to cover that fact. If a prospective employer does a background check and discovers that you lied, you won't get the job. Also, don't include reasons for leaving a job on your résumé; or personal information, such as marital status, age, race, etc.

Use the chronological format if you have a consistent work history. (It's preferred by most employers.) Start with your most recent job. If you don't have much work experience, use a functional résumé to highlight your accomplishments instead of your lack of work experience.

Make it easy for someone to contact you. Include your address and phone number (and e-mail address, if you have one). Get an answering machine or voice mail and *return calls immediately*. Also, make it easy for someone to contact past employers and references by including their addresses and phone numbers.

Check for typos and grammatical errors. Use your computer's spellchecker. Have someone proof your résumé. Don't use the word "résumé" on the résumé. Put your "Objective Statement" in your cover letter, not on your résumé.

Use one page — but don't reduce the type/font size to make it fit. (Standard font size is 12-point.) Use two pages only if the information on the second page answers the question, *"Why should we hire you?"* Print your résumé on expensive-looking paper. You can buy a few sheets at a time from a printer, office supply store, or stationery store. If you don't have access to a computer, some print shops rent computers by the hour.

Save your résumé on a disk so you can update it and/or make changes depending on the job you're trying to get.

Do I need references?

Yes. References are used by potential employers to get an idea of an applicant's skills, work habits, communication abilities, and motivation. Choose three people who can verify your work history and your personal character — in a positive manner. *Ask* these people for permission to list them as a reference. Do you know any teachers, adult friends of the family, co-workers, co-volunteers who would be a good reference? Typically, former supervisors or bosses are not listed as references because they'll be notified for work history. Family members are also not used for references.

List your references on your résumé. Include names, job titles, work addresses, and work phone numbers. You might also ask if they would write a letter of recommendation that you can photocopy for future use. If you put *"References available upon request"* on your résumé, you'll just be adding to someone's workload. Save them a step and include your references.

How do I send my résumé to the company?

Always include a cover letter with your résumé. In the first paragraph, include the job opening you're applying for and how you heard about it. In the second paragraph, briefly answer this question: *Why should we hire you?* List your skills, qualifications, and education. In the last paragraph, ask for a meeting and list how you can be contacted. Keep a copy of the letter in your job search notebook.

Contact the company, preferably the person hiring, to get his/her preference for how to send your résumé. Should it be mailed, faxed, or e-mailed?

Can I apply on-line?

More than two million jobs are now posted online and many companies accept résumés that are sent via e-mail. Search as many sites as possible, especially those that are specific to the industry you want to work in. Find out where you'd like to work, who to contact, and then send a targeted résumé. You can find this information on a company's website.

Adjust your paper résumé for the Internet. Emphasize key words using *nouns*, not verbs. (Use *manager* instead of *managed*.) To maximize the "hits" between a search and your résumé, use words everyone knows. Use lots of white space and *text only*. Plain text files don't recognize bullets, bold facing, underlining, or italics, so use asterisks (*), plus symbols (+), and capital letters to help outline your résumé. And read the privacy policy. Some websites let you block where your résumé will be posted (such as on your present employer's job board), while others allow anonymity. Some allow absolutely no privacy at all.

Format your résumé in ASCII as an e-mail text file. ASCII text files (.txt file extension) are plain files that are universally accessible. (Don't attach it as a Word document unless you know the person you're sending it to can open it.) To format your résumé into an ASCII document, write your résumé in a word processing program (as you normally would). Set your margins at 0 and 65 characters to make your résumé easier to read and safe to print. When you save the document, use the "Save As" command. Save your résumé as an ASCII or MS-DOS text document and change the file extension to .txt.

Send your résumé to yourself and a friend before you send it to a company to make sure the margins and layout translate well.

Write or paste a cover letter in the same file, noting where you found the ad. In the subject line, include the job title and reference number, if available. Follow up with an e-mail or phone call in a week.

Do I need to fill out an application?

That depends on the job and the company. If you do have to complete an application, do so *honestly*. If your application isn't accurate, you can be fired immediately, regardless of your performance. The best policy is to be honest with your potential employer. Fill in all the required blanks. If they don't apply to you, write "NA" (for "Not Applicable"). If you'll be filling out an application at the company, take along a cheat sheet that includes employment history with names, dates, phone numbers, and addresses. Have the names, addresses, and phone numbers of your references available, too.

What happens in an interview?

How do I practice for an interview?

> Don't go around saying the world owes you a living. The world owes you nothing. It was here first.
>
> *~ Mark Twain*

Hiring and training new employees is very expensive, so employers want to make sure they hire the right employee. While your GPA, work experience, references, résumé, and community experience are important, they are not as important as the actual face-to-face interview. The interview determines whether or not you'll get the job. Think of it as an exchange of information between you and the company. The company wants to get information to see if you are qualified for the job and will fit in with the company. You want to get information to help you determine if this is the company and the job you want.

The single most important stage of a job search is the interview. Make a good impression at the interview by doing a bit of research before you go. The interviewer will be impressed by your motivation and interest — and you'll be able to explain what you can do for the company. Don't be under the impression that you'll only have to do one interview. You may have to do 10, 20, 30 interviews before you find the right job for you. This is good, though. Remember, practice makes perfect. You'll want to get a few interviews under your belt before you interview for the job you really want.

You seldom get a second chance, so it's very important that you practice interviewing with family or friends. If you have a video camera (or can borrow one), tape your practice interview. (If you don't have access to a video camera, use a cassette recorder.) Watch the video at least twice so you can study the content of your answers and how you're projecting yourself. Are you using *"um"* or *"like"* too much? How are you sitting? What does your body language say?

Some companies will do a "screening" interview. This is typically a phone call that is used to select those who will actually come in for a face-to-face interview. A telephone interview allows an employer to find out how well you handle yourself on the phone — and on the spot. If you don't pass this test, you won't get an interview.

How do I prepare before the interview?

Interactive CD-ROM

Movie

- Arrive in the company's office at least ten minutes early to show commitment, dependability, and professionalism.

- Take a test drive a day or so before the interview to find out how long it takes to get there and where to park.

- Take a bathroom break before the interview so you don't have to excuse yourself.

- Get a good night's sleep so you'll be fresh and alert.

- Prepare a list of questions to ask.

- Bring several copies of your résumé, work samples, letters of recommendation, and a notepad and pen to the interview.

How do I greet the interviewer?

Interactive CD-ROM

Movie

When the interviewer approaches you, stand up fully and extend your hand (yes, ladies, too!). Say something like, *"Hi. I'm _____(your first and last name). It's nice to meet you."* Then let the interviewer take the lead. Don't sit down in a room until the interviewer does or tells you to do so. When you sit, lean forward just slightly. If you lean back in the chair, it may seem that you want to move away from the interviewer. Make eye contact frequently. Mirror the interviewer's body language by leaning forward if the interviewer leans forward, using similar hand gestures, etc.

Do I shake the interviewer's hand?

A good handshake could make the difference in getting the job. Practice shaking hands with a friend until you feel confident that you have a firm handshake. For men, shaking hands is not a test of strength or a competition. For ladies, if you have a weak handshake, that may be the message that you're sending to others about yourself. Your handshake affects how people perceive you, so when you meet someone, initiate a firm handshake and say, *"Hello. It's good to see/meet you."*

If you have clammy hands, carry a small container of powder with you and apply it to your hands before you go into the interview. (If you drive, you can apply the powder in the car. If you take another method of transportation, use a bathroom before you check in for your interview to apply the powder.)

What should I do during the interview?

Employers are looking for education and experience — but also for friendliness, competency, honesty, credibility, likeability, spontaneity, and enthusiasm. Employers hire people they like — so smile often.

- Take slow, deep breaths.

- Be polite and courteous.

- Be professional.

- Show respect for the interviewer and everyone you meet.

- Show interest and enthusiasm for the position and the company, but don't exaggerate.

- Think of the interview as a conversation, rather than an interrogation.

- Listen to the interviewer by focusing your attention on what the person is saying.

- Let your voice show excitement for the opportunity to have this job.

- Use good English and talk loud enough to be heard.

- Know the question behind the question: *"Why should we hire you?"*

- Convey all the relevant information about yourself in 15 minutes.

- Stress your positive qualities and strengths.

- Talk about yourself only if what you say offers some benefit to that company and its problems.

● Answer all the questions accurately, honestly, and promptly.

● Experts estimate that the words you say and your tone of voice account for only 45 percent of what people actually communicate. Your body language — your facial expressions and body movements — speaks louder than your words, so relax.

● Be yourself.

● Act spontaneous, but be prepared.

● Sit tall.

● Nod your head in agreement (at appropriate times).

● Make and keep eye contact. (Don't stare, though.)

● Walk and sit with an air of confidence (even if you're not feeling very confident at the moment).

● Lean toward an interviewer to show interest and enthusiasm.

● Focus on the present moment.

What shouldn't I do during the interview?

● Don't talk too fast or too slow. (If you talk fast when you're nervous, take a few deep breaths.)

● Don't talk too much.

● Don't mumble.

● Avoid talking negatively.

● Avoid arguments and don't criticize anyone.

● Don't use first names (unless asked). You're not his/her buddy. Use Mr., Mrs., or Ms.

- Don't mention any personal, domestic (home), or financial troubles.

- Don't discuss equal rights, sex, race, national origin, religion, or age.

- Don't leave the interview without getting your own questions answered.

- Don't smoke (even if invited to do so).

- Don't chew gum.

- Don't look at your watch.

- Don't bring your cell phone or pager into the interview.

- Don't be late. There are few good excuses.

- Don't take anyone to the interview with you.

- Don't close yourself off physically by folding your arms across your chest.

- Don't sit down until motioned to do so.

- Don't show anxiety or boredom.

- Don't show samples of your work (unless asked).

- Don't assume a passive role.

- Don't bad-mouth anyone! State your most previous experiences in the most positive terms. When you speak negatively of a person, you run the risk of appearing to be a troubled person who may have difficulty working with others. If you make negative comments, it usually turns out to be a strike against you — not the person you're bad-mouthing. Many interviewers assume that if you're openly criticizing your past boss, you'll show the same disrespect when discussing current employers.

- Don't be discouraged if you're nervous and don't do your best. Learn from it! Don't be discouraged if you don't get the job. You'll do better on the next interview!

What do I do at the end of the interview?

Interactive CD-ROM

Movie

End the interview with a handshake and a thank you. State your interest in the job again (if you're still interested). Ask if you can call in a few days to check on the status of the job. Go home and write a thank you note and mail it.

What questions will I have to answer?

Every question you're asked will be to answer just one simple question: *"Why should the company hire you?"* Study the questions in "Will I get the job?" and "Any other interview questions I can practice?"

Should I ask questions at the interview?

At most interviews, you'll be given a chance to ask questions. Do your own research on the company before the interview and ask questions concerning the job, the boss, the department, the company, and/or the industry. Here are some basic questions you can ask:

- What are the duties and responsibilities of this job?

- Is this a new position?

- Why is this position open?

- What kind of person are you looking for?

- Who does this position report to?

- What are the promotional opportunities in this company?

- What are your expectations from the person hired?

- Have there been any problems associated with this job?

- What's the corporate culture like?

● What is the normal pay range of this job? (Ask only *after* the interviewer asks about your salary requirements.)

If you don't understand anything that has been addressed in the interview, ask for clarification. Don't ask questions that raise warning flags, such as *"Do I have to work weekends?"* Don't ask questions about compensation, such as salary or vacations. You might seem more interested in paydays and time-off than in the actual job. Save these questions until you're offered the job.

Can the interviewer ask me anything?

The Civil Rights Act of 1964 makes it illegal for employers *not* to hire you based on discrimination of race, sex, religion, or national origin. You cannot be asked questions about your marital status, weight, height, age, religion, debts, sexual orientation, or arrest record. Ladies, you cannot be asked about your views on children, marriage, what your husband or boyfriend thinks, or whether or not you want children. If you're asked any of these questions, you can answer the question, ask if it's a qualification for the position, or decline to answer. Unfortunately, if you do either of the last two suggestions, you might not get the job ... but then, would you really want to work for someone like that?

Should I send a thank you note?

Send a thank you note within 24 hours of your interview! Emphasize your interest in the job and the company and why you feel you're ideal for this job. Find some areas discussed during the interview and expand upon them in your note. The company may still be deciding who to hire — and your thank you card will be a plus for you. Even if you aren't selected for the position, send a note thanking the interviewer for meeting with you and ask to be considered for future openings.

How do I dress for the interview?

Research shows that first impressions are made during the first two minutes of an interview — and are seldom changed during the remainder of the interview. You've heard the phrase, *"You never get a second chance to make a good first impression."* This is absolutely true when interviewing. What you wear is absolutely critical to the first in-person impression an interviewer has of you.

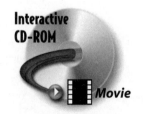

Interactive
CD-ROM

Movie

Dress in clothing that is appropriate to the job. For instance, if you're interviewing for a construction job, don't wear a three-piece suit. Instead, wear a clean pair of blue jeans and a nice shirt. If you're interviewing for a position in a corporate office, forget the blue jeans. Invest in a nice outfit or suit to wear for interviewing. Dress for the position you want, not the one you have.

The safest look is traditional and conservative. It's better to over-dress rather than under-dress. The interview is *not* the place to exhibit your independence and freedom of style. Have clean hair and fingernails. Hide the tattoos. Take out the earrings. Avoid bright colors. You might even want to invest in an inexpensive briefcase to carry a notepad, pen, and your keys.

For men, wear a suit to interview for all office jobs. (Avoid black suits and trendy suits.) Wear something classic with a white or light blue long-sleeved shirt. If the job is not in an office, wear dressed-up casual (like khakis and a button-down shirt or polo shirt). Your belt and shoes should match in color. "Permanent press" means it might still need to be ironed a bit. Don't wear wrinkled clothes. Have a clean-shaven face or a neatly-trimmed mustache and/or beard. Use just a bit of cologne or aftershave.

Ladies, you have more options — but you should still dress appropriately for the job you want. Wear a suit, a dress appropriate for business (not for dates), or a nice pantsuit. Don't wear "suggestive" or "sexy" clothes to an interview. If you wear a suit or dress, wear pantyhose to the interview. Wear makeup or perfume sparingly. Wear simple jewelry. Don't take a purse with you to the interview.

How do I negotiate my salary?

Never be the first to mention money. Let the employer name the first price. Base your price on facts, not on what you "feel" you should earn. Have a good understanding of the job and its responsibilities before you talk money. Many people have unrealistic expectations about the amount of money an employer should pay. Discuss salary at the end of an interview — after you have convinced the interviewer of your value to the company. If the interviewer asks what salary you want, don't give a dollar amount. You may be asking too much or too little. Instead, ask what salary range this job falls into.

When asked what salary you desire, have your answer ready. Also, know what the least amount you need to earn is. How much do you need to earn to pay your bills, buy food, see a movie? (See Chapter 1, "Can I afford to move out?" for more information.) Set a minimum amount, as well as the amount you'd like to make. When negotiating for your salary, the results must be a win-win situation for both sides. Don't accept an offer on the spot and don't issue an ultimatum.

Check your library, the Internet, or newspaper ads to see what comparative jobs are paying in your area. Before you can determine how much you should earn, you need to know your value to employers. Learn what employers pay for the job you want. Information on pay is readily available at your local library and on the Internet. Check the *American Salaries and Wages Annual Survey, American Almanac of Jobs and Salaries, Jobs-Related Almanac,* and the *Occupational Outlook Handbook* published by the U.S. Bureau of Labor Statistics. It's also available at *www.bls.gov.*

And don't just think in terms of how much money you can make. Will this be a job that you'll enjoy? Will you be able to grow personally and professionally in this job? What benefits are offered? Is the culture one you would enjoy and feel comfortable in?

Will the company do a background check on me?

Many companies are now conducting extensive background checks. There is good reason for companies to be concerned about the backgrounds of people they hire. A recent study reported by the Associated Press estimates that high-tech theft costs American businesses $4 billion a year. And theft isn't the only problem employers face. If an employee proves to be dangerous to co-workers or customers, an employer can be sued for negligent hiring or retention. Background checks are essential now because of increasing court cases involving companies and employees. Background checks include calling previous employers, verifying educational information, running criminal conviction and civil case searches, and checking credit histories.

 ## What happens if I'm offered the job?

What happens if I'm offered the job?

You accept or decline, or start negotiating salary and benefits. (Most jobs paid by the hour have a limited range for salary negotiations.) If you al-

> The only place success comes before work is in the dictionary.
>
> *~ Author Unknown*

ready have a job, give your two-weeks notice to your supervisor. And re-member this: You were not hired to do a job. You were hired to solve a problem.

What benefits are available?

In a study by the National Association of Colleges and Employers, 5,500 new college graduates were asked what was most important in a job. *Bene-fits* ranked number five on the list. The top three were (1) enjoying what you do; (2) having opportunities to use your skills and abilities; and (3) having opportunities for personal development. Are you surprised that *making lots of money* ranked number nine?

Companies offer a wide variety of benefits. You may or may not be entitled to them — or offered them. Negotiate benefits when you negotiate salary. Some examples of benefits include 401K and other retirement programs; insurance (health, dental, life, accidental death); paid sick leave, paid va-cation days, personal days off, profit-sharing; stock options, tuition reim-bursement, flex-time (or a flexible work schedule), and disability compen-sation plans.

Will I have to take a drug test?

Since the 1980s, drug testing of employees and job applicants has become a standard practice because it is believed that people who use illegal drugs will be poor workers and may endanger the lives of their co-workers. Drug testing is the analysis of body fluids to determine whether a person is using illegal drugs. Modern drug testing employs accurate and reliable biochem-istry techniques. Generally, the procedure involves sending a urine sample to a laboratory for an initial screening test. If there are no illegal drugs in your body, the test result will be negative. (This is the result you want!) If the result of that test is positive, a second test is done to confirm the results. The laboratory won't report a positive test unless both tests show the pres-ence of an illegal drug. In addition, positive test results are typically re-viewed by a physician to determine whether the individual has a legal rea-son to use the drug.

What if I don't get the job?

Don't be discouraged. The most qualified person isn't necessarily the one who gets the job. The one who gets the job is the one who *convinces* the in-terviewer that he or she is the most qualified for the job. You should still be actively involved in your job search. Don't stop interviewing just because you interviewed somewhere and are waiting for a call. Keep looking. If you don't get the job, call and ask why. You can learn from the experience and improve your interviewing skills for the next interviews.

What are my responsibilities at work?

Watch your thoughts; they become words.
Watch your words; they become actions.

Watch your actions; they become habits.
Watch your habits; they become character.

Watch your character; it becomes your destiny.

~ Frank Outlaw

What are my basic responsibilities at work?

Show up every day on time. Go to lunch on time. Come back from lunch on time. Take only the breaks you're allowed. (If you smoke, you're not allowed a break every time you feel the need to light a cigarette.) Do your job. Do any other related duties that will help your department, your company — and you. Continue to learn. Treat everyone with respect. Be responsible for yourself and your actions. Drop the excuses.

What are work ethics?

Ethics deals with what is good and bad. It's a set of moral principles or values of conduct governing an individual or a group. Unethical workplace conduct includes stealing a pencil, sharing company secrets with competitors, doing something illegal at work, lying to your supervisor, using drugs or alcohol on the job, falsifying records or reports, or even cheating the time clock out of 10 minutes. You should also know that every piece of equipment your employer allows you to use during your employment still belongs to the employer.

If you make decisions hoping no one will find out, they're probably not ethical decisions. If you have a decision to make, and you're wondering if it's ethical, ask yourself these questions:

- Does it pass the test of sportsmanship?

- If everyone followed the same course of action, would the results be beneficial for all?

- What affect will my action(s) have on others?

- What affect will it have on me?

- Will I think well of myself when I look back on what I've done?

- How would the person I most admire handle this situation?

- Will it bother me if everyone knows about my decision, especially my family and friends?

What about my attitude?

Your attitude is your most valuable possession. It's the way you communicate your mood to yourself and to others. Is the glass half full or half empty? Do you roll with the punches — or do you punch back? Are you too negative? Do you feel as though the world is out to get you? If you find it hard to keep a positive attitude, consider the following:

> *There is nothing you cannot be,*
> *nothing you cannot do,*
> *nothing you cannot have,*
> *if you have a positive attitude.*

When you're optimistic, you present a positive image and people tend to respond favorably. A positive attitude shows your enthusiasm. It enhances your creativity. It causes good things to happen.

When you're pessimistic, you tend to expect the worst and your attitude is often negative. A negative attitude speaks so loudly that no words are necessary. You show it in the way you carry yourself, your facial expressions, your gestures. People tend to avoid pessimists. Are you in need of an attitude adjustment? Do you find yourself being critical and cynical, complaining, and comparing everything? Do you find fault in everything and everyone? Are you unappreciative? Do you think no one can be trusted? If so, you are definitely in need of an attitude adjustment. Charles Swindoll wrote:

The longer I live, the more I realize the impact of attitude on life. Attitude, to me, is more important than facts. It is more important than the past, than education, than money, than circumstances, than failures, than successes, than what other people think or say or do. It is more important than appearance, giftedness, or skill. It will make or break a company ... a church ... a home.

The remarkable thing is we have a choice every day regarding the attitude we will embrace for that day. We cannot change the past. We cannot change the fact that people will act in a certain way. We cannot change the inevitable. The only thing we can do is play on the one thing we have — and that is our attitude.

I am convinced that life is 10 percent what happens to me and 90 percent how I react to it.

What about good manners?

"Good manners are free, but they are also priceless," said Harvey Mackay. Be polite and courteous to everyone. You don't have the right to be rude to anyone. Hold the door open for the person behind you. Say *"please"* and *"thank you."* Say *"excuse me"* and *"you're welcome."* Answer the phone with a pleasant voice and identify yourself. Fill the copier with paper if you used the last of it. Make a new pot of coffee if you drink the last cup. Be considerate.

Good manners show your maturity and ability to respond to business situations. There's an old saying that goes, *"It's nice to be important, but it's more important to be nice."*

We make character judgments within the first 30 seconds of meeting someone. Grooming and manners are noticed. Here are some examples of bad manners: people who dominate the conversation, men who sit down before ladies are seated, people who begin eating before everyone is seated, people who don't hold the door open, people who leave their cell phones on in public places, people who don't say *"please"* or *"excuse me."* Can you add any other behaviors to the list? Are you guilty of any of them?

Try this exercise for a few days. Smile and be polite when you meet someone — a clerk in the grocery store, the person at the drive-up window, a
co-worker. Do you get a polite response back? Most times you will. Keep
trying it. In three weeks it will become a habit — a good habit.

Am I responsible for customer service?

Yes! And it's so easy to give people what they want — to be appreciated!

- Say *"Thank you"* more often.

- Say *"You're welcome"* when someone thanks you.

- *Smile.* It makes you seem likable.

- *Be friendly* before you know who it is.

- *Listen* to what the customer is saying.

- Be polite — even when you're busy. Being busy doesn't give you
  permission to be rude. You're never too busy to be nice.

- Say *"I don't know but I'll find out."* if you really don't know. Don't
  guess ... because a wrong guess can be very costly for the customer,
  the business, and you.

How do I dress for work?

Dress appropriately for your job. Sloppy dress affects morale and work
habits. It also projects a bad image of you and the company — and offends
customers and co-workers. What message are you sending to others with
the clothes you wear? Leave your weekend clothes for the weekend. Don't
wear sexy or provocative clothes to work (unless your job warrants). Keep
your underwear under your clothes. Always wear a belt and socks. Dress
for the position you want. If you want to be a manager, dress like a manager. If you're allowed to dress casually at work, wear conservative casual —
not something you'd wear to wash the car. Khakis and corduroys are a safe
bet for men and women. Wear clothes that are clean and pressed; stain-
free and odor-free; and don't have any rips, tears, or frays.

What is proper e-mail etiquette?

Be cautious of the words you use in your e-mails. You never know how your words are being taken — and they can be easily misunderstood. You can dig your own grave before you even realize your message didn't come across as you had intended. Keep in mind, too, that messages are easily forwarded — both by mistake and intentionally. Don't hide behind e-mail. Pick up the phone and call every now and then.

What is proper phone etiquette?

Answer the phone with a smile. Say the company's name and then your first name, *"XYZ Company. This is Alisa."* Don't interrupt someone who is on the telephone by gesturing or using some form of sign language. Don't eat while on the phone. Try to answer by the third ring.

Do I have privacy at work?

According to the U.S. Department of Commerce, employers lose more than $40 billion annually to theft. The majority of this theft is committed by employees. Because of this, many U.S. companies monitor employees by recording and/or reviewing phone conversations, e-mail, Internet connections, and/or computer files. Spy cameras may be installed, so don't even steal a pencil. (Spy cameras are legal to install in public work areas, but not private areas like restrooms or lounges.) According to the American Management Association:

- 78 percent of U.S. companies actively monitor their employees.

- 63 percent monitor employees' Internet connections.

- 47 percent store and review employee e-mail.

- 27 percent have fired employees for misuse of Internet or e-mail.

- 15 percent videotape employees at work.

- 10 percent do not inform employees of surveillance.

Your best defense is to assume you're being monitored — and don't write or say anything at work that you will later regret.

How do I ask for a raise?

How do I get promoted?

It is your responsibility to manage your career. Promote yourself. Let your boss know that you're interested in "upward mobility," that is, moving to positions of greater responsibility, challenge, and pay. In many companies, jobs are posted for current employees first. This means you have a chance to be interviewed and hired first. It's a great way to get promoted — and is often how people "climb the corporate ladder."

> If you want them to show you the money, you better show them the reason.
>
> ~ *Harvey Mackay's Moral*

If you want to get promoted, people have to know who you are and what you're doing. Don't wait for someone to notice how hard you're working. Today, people are promoted because of what they offer a company. Do you have the ability to cut costs, increase productivity, do things faster and cheaper?

Here are some simple guidelines that will help you get promoted: Arrive early and be ready to start on time. Maintain a positive attitude. Read everything possible about the job, the company, and the industry. Do more than your share. Minimize breaks. Don't leave early. Participate in training. Encourage teamwork. Ask about cross-training opportunities. Ask for feedback on projects. Make friends in every department, not just the one you work in. Let those who can promote you know that you're interested in being promoted. (Don't expect anyone to read your mind. Remember, you are responsible for your career — not your boss or anyone else.)

What's a sure way NOT to get promoted?

If you're an employee who says, *"It's not my job," "That's not what they hired me to do,"* or *"They don't pay me to do that,"* you're probably not going to get any gold stars. Do you enjoy your job? Do you lack challenges? Do you like the people you work with? Do you think you're too good to do certain jobs? Are you afraid to take new risks? Whatever your reasoning, get over it. It's your job to do what you can to help the company. If you don't want to do that, it might be time to look for another job.

What if I want to quit my job?

Do I have to give notice?

Yes. Don't burn your bridges because your boss today will be a reference in the future. You never know who your boss knows — and it may be the person who is interviewing you next. You never know when a former employer will be contacted for a reference. Leave on good terms. If you're needed to train the person who's been hired to replace you, do so gladly. Even if you don't feel loyal to the company after giving your notice, be loyal to yourself in leaving the job doing the best you can until the very end.

When you leave a job, leave gracefully and on good terms with the company. Give at least a one- to two-week notice at your current job and offer to train your replacement. Be vague about giving a reason for leaving the company. Say something like *"I want to pursue other interests"* or *"I found a job that furthers my career plan."* Be positive and thank your boss and co-workers for the training and experience.

Can I just walk out if my boss is a jerk?

Walking out will only hurt you in the long run. Even if your boss is a jerk, a huge lesson for you to learn is that there are no perfect work situations — so, figure out a way to get along or give your two-week notice and find a new job. If you get mad and walk out, perhaps you're struggling with some of your own issues. Some companies offer counseling services. It's best for you to keep your emotions in check. If you want to yell, don't. Instead of blowing up, try putting your hands in your pockets, take a deep breath, and count to 20.

If you do quit in the heat of a moment, you're out of a job. How are you going to pay rent? Make your car payment? Buy food to eat? Wouldn't it be wiser to learn to control your responses to "jerks" rather than continue a life pattern of walking out of jobs? In addition to the immediate loss of income, you also have to deal with the fact that your permanent employment record will reflect your "voluntarily quit" status. So, as emotionally satisfying as it may be to quit your job in protest, the satisfaction only lasts a short while until the reality of having to find another job sets in. If you find this situation happening quite often, ask yourself this question: *"What am I doing to contribute to these situations?"* Instead of changing jobs every six months, think about changing your behaviors.

What if I'm fired?

Count to 10 and stay in control. Don't lose your temper. Pay attention to what is being said so you get a clear picture of why you're being let go. Don't say anything negative about the company, your boss, or yourself. Maintain your dignity. Gather your things and leave. Remember, the boss who just fired you will be a reference for your next job. If you are fired, take a deep breath and calmly call your boss in a few days to discuss how to present your termination to a future employer so you can both agree on a statement.

Losing a job is considered one of the five most stressful life changes you can experience. It's normal to feel panic about paying your bills, anxiety about looking for a new job, and loneliness for your co-workers. Expect to feel the stages of grief following a dismissal: shock, denial, bargaining, anger, guilt, and acceptance. Talk to a counselor if you need to. This is a great opportunity for you to grow personally. Use the situation to learn more about your own behaviors. How did your behavior contribute to your being fired? And, proceed to "How do I find a job?" at the beginning of this chapter.

Depending upon your job and the company, you may be entitled to severance pay if you're fired. If your boss doesn't offer severance pay, check your employee manual. If there's no written policy, you're probably out of luck. If there is a policy, you may be entitled to a certain number of weeks of pay, such as one or two weeks. You may also be able to request payment for any unused vacation days. Severance pay is a benefit, not an entitlement or a right. The company does not owe you severance pay.

 ## What is the Americans with Disabilities Act?

A disability is defined as a physical or mental impairment that substantially limits one or more of a person's major life activities, a record of such impairment, or being regarded as having such an impairment.

The Americans with Disabilities Act (ADA) gives people with disabilities civil rights protection that is similar to that provided to individuals on the basis of race, sex, national origin, or religion. It guarantees equal opportunity for individuals with disabilities in employment, public accommodations, transportation, state and local government services, and telecommunications.

The Americans with Disabilities Act was signed into law in 1990, with the purpose of providing a clear and comprehensive national mandate to end discrimination against individuals with disabilities; providing enforceable standards addressing discrimination against individuals with disabilities; and ensuring that the federal government plays a central role in enforcing these standards on behalf of individuals with disabilities.

 ## How can I resolve conflicts at work?

Will this matter tomorrow?

Before getting into any conflicts, whether at work or elsewhere, ask yourself this question: *"Will this matter tomorrow?"*

Before you criticize someone or something, ask yourself this question. Before you lose your cool, ask yourself this question. Before you run to the boss, or alienate a co-worker, or hurt your friend's feelings, ask yourself this question. If the issue is too emotional for you, try this question: *"Will this matter next year?"*

Get in the habit of asking yourself these questions. You'll be amazed at how many things that upset you really don't matter tomorrow — or next year.

Is it okay to criticize co-workers?

Use extreme caution before criticizing someone because the person most likely to be wounded is you. Even if your complaint is entirely justified, you could be viewed as a backstabber or tattle tale. So, pick your battles carefully. If you feel you must say something, try to discuss *your* problem calmly with the person(s) involved. The only time you should say something to the boss is when someone's work (or lack thereof) is jeopardizing your ability to get your job done, but don't complain unless you can offer a suggestion or a solution. What do you hope to gain by criticizing? How would you feel if someone made the same criticism of you? If someone simply rubs you the wrong way, that's your problem - not your boss's or the company's problem. If you feel the need to complain, do it with a friend or counselor outside of work.

What if I can't get along with a co-worker?

Personality conflicts at work can create tremendous stress and make it hard to get your job done, but not all disagreements are destructive. When conflicts happen, people quickly blame the other person. If this happens, let the other person vent first. This way, you can find out what the other person's perspective is. It also allows you to see if there are any assumptions made that are incorrect. To resolve conflicts, you must have a willingness to change your own behavior. What are you contributing to the conflict? Once you figure this out, you can work to change your own behaviors. (This is a really great opportunity for you because conflicts don't just happen at work. Even a small change in behavior can make huge differences in your relationships with others.)

If the conflict seems to be a big issue, write down what your concerns are on a piece of paper. By writing them down, you'll be able to clarify what your issues really are. It also helps you think about what the other person will say about these concerns. Avoid using the word *you* because it tends to put responsibility on the person you're talking to. Try to define the problem, without blame, so that you can both work together to resolve it. If the problem can't be resolved, you can both agree to disagree on the subject. And then just leave it at that.

 ## What is sexual harassment?

What is sexual harassment?

Sexual harassment is a form of sex discrimination that violates Title VII of the Civil Rights Act of 1964. Sexual harassment is illegal. Basically, harassment is unwelcome behavior of a sexual nature that makes someone feel uncomfortable or unwelcome in the workplace by focusing attention on his/her gender instead of his/her professional qualifications. It applies to both men and women. The victim as well as the harasser may be a woman or a man. The harasser can be the victim's supervisor, a co-worker, a supervisor in another area of the company, or a customer or vendor. The victim does not have to be the person harassed but could be anyone affected by the offensive conduct.

Unwelcome sexual advances, requests for sexual favors, and other verbal or physical conduct of a sexual nature constitutes sexual harassment when submission to or rejection of this conduct affects a person's employment, unreasonably interferes with a person's work performance, or creates an intimidating, hostile, or offensive work environment.

Sexual harassment is about individual perception. If one person perceives something as harassment, then it is harassment, regardless of what other people's perceptions of the situation may be. It may be as direct as an actual or attempted rape or sexual assault — or as subtle as hanging around a person.

Sexual harassment is not the same as flirting. Sexual harassment feels bad. Flirting feels good. Sexual harassment is unwelcome. Flirting is wanted. Sexual harassment is degrading. Flirting is flattering. Sexual harassment is one-sided. Flirting is reciprocal. Sexual harassment lowers self-esteem. Flirting raises self-esteem.

What is spoken sexual harassment?

Spoken sexual harassment may include, but is not limited to, any of the following:

- Telling a dirty joke in front of others, even if some find the joke funny.

- Unwanted pressure for sexual favors.

- Whistling at someone.

- Cat calls.

- Unwanted pressure for dates.

- Sexual comments.

- Unwanted sexual teasing, jokes, remarks, or questions.

- Referring to a female as a girl, doll, babe, honey, bitch, etc.

- Referring to a male as a hunk, stud, doll, babe, honey, etc.

- Asking about sexual fantasies, preferences, or history.

- Personal questions about social or sexual life.

- Sexual comments about a person's clothing, anatomy, or looks.

- Telling lies or spreading rumors about a person's sex life.

What is written sexual harassment?

Written sexual harassment may include, but is not limited to, any of the following:

- Unwanted letters or materials of a sexual nature.

- Giving personal gifts.

- Sexually-suggestive pictures or graphics.

- Graffiti in bathrooms.

What is physical sexual harassment?

Physical sexual harassment may include, but is not limited to, any of the following:

- Putting your arm around someone.

- Unwanted deliberate touching, leaning over, cornering, groping, or pinching.

- Neck massage.

- Touching or rubbing oneself sexually around another person.

- Hugging, kissing, patting, or stroking.

- Touching an employee's clothing, hair, or body.

- Standing close or brushing up against a person.

What is gesturing sexual harassment?

Gesturing sexual harassment may include, but is not limited to, any of the following:

- Kissing sounds, howling, and smacking lips.

- Staring at someone.

- Unwanted sexual looks or gestures.

- Looking a person up and down.

- Facial expressions, winking, throwing kisses, or licking lips.

- Making sexual gestures with hands or through body movements.

Is physical assault considered sexual harassment?

Physical assault, including rape and attempted rape, is considered sexual harassment. Along with legal implications for the actual assault, additional charges of harassment can be added.

What if I'm being harassed?

If you're experiencing sexual harassment, there are several things you can do:

- Ignore the harassment. (This usually doesn't work and the harasser may actually interpret your lack of response as encouragement!)

- Speak up at the time of the harassment. Tell the harasser firmly that the behavior is offensive to you and that you want it to stop.

- You can choose to make a formal or informal complaint. If the harassment is continual, keep a record of it, including dates, times, locations, and a description of the incidents. Also list the names of any witnesses.

- Companies with more than 15 employees are mandated by law to have a sexual harassment policy, so find out who in the company handles it. If the company does not deal with your complaint, you can file a complaint with the EEOC (Equal Employment Opportunities Commission), a federal agency that enforces federal anti-discrimination laws.

- If all else fails, consult an attorney and bring charges. Unfortunately, this is a very lengthy and expensive option and should not be taken lightly.

What if I'm accused of harassing someone?

Depending upon the nature and duration of the offense, the disciplinary action may only be a quiet closed-door chat — or it may be as extreme as termination of employment. Charges of sexual harassment are serious. If you are accused, get all the information you can about the situation. Learn about your company's policies and procedures, as well as state laws.

Informal Charges

If someone accuses you of sexual harassment, listen carefully to understand the person's point of view. Making a joke of your behavior or the incident is inappropriate and will likely make the situation worse. Respect the other person's point of view and stop doing the behavior that is offending the other person. You cannot retaliate or get even with this person, either. Retaliation is illegal. And further harassment may result in formal charges being filed against you. You might also seek counseling.

Formal Charges

If you are formally charged with sexual harassment by an authority in the company, immediately contact the human resources department or the person who handles harassment policies in the company. Affirmative action offices are charged with investigating and resolving issues of sexual harassment fairly and confidentially. Most affirmative action offices are interested in resolving the situation, so your cooperation will help you tremendously. Don't do anything that would seem to be retaliation or getting even. It's illegal.

Can I join the military service?

Can I join the military service?

The branches of the U.S. Armed Forces offer tremendous opportunities for today's young adults. All branches of the Armed Forces offer benefits like college funds, technical training, job security, free medical and dental care, and travel. The military also offers pride of belonging, courage, and self-discipline.

For more information, contact the following:

U.S. Marine Corps
1-800-MARINES
www.marines.com

U.S. Air Force
1-800-423-USAF
www.airforce.com

U.S. Coast Guard
1-800-GET-USCG
www.uscg.mil

U.S. Army
www.goarmy.com

U.S. Navy
www.sealchallenge.navy.mil

The National Guard and Reserve components of the military are also great part-time jobs. You work one weekend a month and two weeks per year for annual training—and receive excellent benefits in return. Build your career while serving your community and your country. For more information about the National Guard or Reserve, log onto the websites listed above or look in the government pages of your phone book under *Recruiting*.

Have I registered with Selective Service?

Selective Service Registration is the process by which the U.S. government collects names and addresses of men 18 through 25 to use in case a national emergency requires rapid expansion of the Armed Forces. With few exceptions, all male U.S. citizens and male immigrant aliens residing in the U.S. and its territories must register within 30 days of their 18th birthday. (This has been a requirement since 1948.)

How do I register?

To register, stop at any post office and fill out the form or register online at *www.sss.gov*. Within 90 days after registering, you should receive in the mail a Registration Acknowledgement from Selective Service. Keep this document since it will serve as official proof of your registration. It is your responsibility to verify that your registration has been received, so if you don't receive this acknowledgement, call 1-847-688-6888 or write to:

Selective Service System
Registration Information Office
PO Box 94638
Palatine, IL 60094-4638

What if my address changes?

If you move before your 26th birthday, you must let Selective Service know. The law requires you to keep Selective Service informed of your address changes so you can be reached without delay. You can change your address by writing to the above address or you can go to any post office for a Change of Information form (SSS Form 2), fill it out, and mail it to Selective Service. You can also change your address online.

Will I be drafted?

You don't join the military when you register. The fact that a man is required to register does not mean that he will be drafted. No one has been drafted since 1973. No one can be drafted into the military unless ordered by Congress and the President. A draft would most likely occur only in the event of war or national emergency.

What happens if I don't register?

Young men convicted of failure to register may be fined up to $250,000, imprisoned for up to five years, or both. In addition to being subject to prosecution, failure to register may cause you to *permanently* forfeit eligibility for certain benefits, such as federal student loans. *Not registering is a felony.*

What is the formula for success?

Long ago, the people of a very successful civilization thought they had all the answers to success. The king called the wisest people in the kingdom together and said, *"I want you to write down all the reasons why we are successful so future generations will be able to read it and duplicate our success."*

> There are many formulas for success, but none of them works unless you do.
>
> ~ *Harvey Mackay's Moral*

They worked for almost two years and came back

with the answer. It consisted of nine volumes. The king looked at it and said, *"This is impressive, but it's too large."* He then challenged them to simplify their findings.

They worked for another year and narrowed it down to one book. *"This is better,"* said the king, *"but it is still too lengthy. Refine it."*

After another year of work, they reported back to the king. Their results now contained one page. The king said, *"You have done a great job, but it is still too long. Please reduce our formula for success to the lowest common denominator."*

For another year, they worked on it. The team reduced the formula to one paragraph. And the king said, *"That's an improvement, but it is still far too complicated. Keep working until everyone understands why we are so successful."*

Six months later, they came back to the king with their formula for success — one sentence. The king said it was perfect. *"If all future generations understood this, they would be in a position to conquer anything."*

The sentence read, ***"There ain't no such thing as a free lunch!"***

~ Author Unknown

 Any other interview questions I can practice?
Use the sample questions on pages 147 – 148 to prepare for your interview.

Sample Interview Questions

1. What is the lowest salary you will accept? _____

2. Do you have a résumé? ○ Yes ○ No

3. Do you have references? ○ Yes ○ No
   (Ask your references for permission to list them as references.)

4. May we contact them? ○ Yes ○ No

5. What would they say about you? _____

6. If you attended college, what did you major in? _____

7. Why?_____
   _____

8. What was your GPA? _____
   Do you have a copy of your transcript? ○ Yes ○ No

9. What subjects did you enjoy most? _____
   Least? _____

10. Have you ever been fired? ○ Yes ○ No
    If yes, why? _____

11. If hired, how long do you plan on staying with this company? _____

12. How do you feel about working for a large company? _____
    A small company? _____

13. Can you work nights and/or weekends? ○ Yes ○ No

14. See this pencil I'm holding? Can you sell it to me? _____
    _____

15. What kind of person do you find it difficult to work with? _____
    _____

16. Are you a team player? ○ Yes ○ No
    Give an example. _____

17. What was the last book you read? _____

18. If you've held several jobs in a short time, why? _____
    _____

19. Are you willing to take classes to learn new skills? ○ Yes ○ No

20. What are your short-term goals? _____
    _____

21. What are your long-term goals? _____
    _____

22. How do you work under pressure? _____
    _____

23. What are your three most important accomplishments so far in your career? _____
    _____
    _____

Figure 3C

continued...

...continued

24. Give an example of your creativity. _____
_____

25. Give an example of your analytical skills. _____
_____

26. Give an example of your administrative skills. _____
_____

27. Give an example of your leadership skills. _____
_____

28. How did you get along with your last boss? _____
_____

29. Why are you leaving your current job? _____
_____

30. How do you think you'll fit in with our company? _____
_____

31. How would you describe the "ideal" boss? _____
_____

32. How do you define "cooperation?" _____
_____

33. What suggestions have you offered former employers that were implemented? _____
_____

34. What is the most difficult assignment you have completed? _____
_____

35. What is the most rewarding assignment you have completed?
_____

The following are questions an interviewer should **not** ask you. If asked any personal questions like these, you can choose to answer the question, ask if it's a qualification for the position, or decline to answer.

1. How old are you?
2. What's your ethnicity?
3. Are you married?
4. Do you have children or do you plan to have children soon?
5. How tall are you?
6. How much do you weigh?
7. Do you have a boyfriend/girlfriend?
8. Do you have illnesses or mental or physical disabilities?

Figure 3C (continued)

Additional Information for this Chapter

Books

- *Beyond Business Casual: What to Wear to Work If You Want to Get Ahead* by Ann Marie Sabath

- *Blue Collar & Beyond: Résumés for Skilled Trades & Services* by Yana Parker

- *Complete Idiot's Guide to the Perfect Résumé* by Susan Ireland

- *Damn Good Résumé Guide* by Yana Parker

- *Pushing the Envelope All the Way to the Top* by Harvey Mackay

- *What Color is Your Parachute?* by Richard Nelson Bolles

- *Who Moved My Cheese?* by Spencer Johnson

- *Zapp! The Lightning of Empowerment* by William C. Byham, Ph.D. with Jeff Cox

Web Links

- *www.monster.com*

- *www.military.com*

- *www.jobweb.com*

- *www.armedforcescareers.com*

- *http://careers.yahoo.com*

- *www.marines.com*

- *www.jobsonline.com*

- *www.airforce.com*

- *www.damngood.com*

- *www.uscg.mil*

- *www.job-interview.net/*

- *www.goarmy.com*

- *www.mackay.com*

- *www.sealchallenge.navy.mil*

- *www.mapping-your-future.org*

- *www.sweaty-palms.com*

- *www.dol.gov* (U.S. Dept. of Labor)

- *www.bls.gov* (U.S. Bureau of Labor Statistics)

Do I want to go to college?

Why do you want to go to college? How important are the following reasons to you? Check YES if any of these reasons are important for YOU to go to college. Check MAYBE if they might be important reasons. Check NO if they are not important reasons.

Interactive CD-ROM

Quiz

Yes	Maybe	No	Reasons to go to college
O	O	O	1. I need a college degree to get a good job.
O	O	O	2. I need college to prepare for my career.
O	O	O	3. I want to be independent.
O	O	O	4. I want to develop my intellect.
O	O	O	5. I want to develop my talent(s).
O	O	O	6. I want to meet interesting people.
O	O	O	7. I need a college degree so I can go to graduate school.
O	O	O	8. I want to expand my cultural horizons.
O	O	O	9. I want to learn new subjects.
O	O	O	10. It will help me plan my life's goals.
O	O	O	11. I want to make important connections. It's who you know.
O	O	O	12. My parents want me to go.
O	O	O	12. My parents can afford for me to go.
O	O	O	14. Everyone else in my family has gone to college.
O	O	O	15. No one else in my family has gone. I'll be the first.
O	O	O	16. Everyone goes nowadays. It's "the thing" to do.
O	O	O	17. My boyfriend/girlfriend is going.
O	O	O	18. I think the social life will be fun.
O	O	O	19. The sports activities are excellent.
O	O	O	20. I don't know what else to do.

SCORE

If you answered a majority of the first 10 reasons with YES, you have a positive attitude about attending college. If not, you may have some major reservations about going to college right now. There is no correct score on this quiz because going to college is a personal choice. You can, however, review your answers to help you determine if you want to go to college — or if you want to pursue other opportunities.

College & Skill Guidance

Imagine getting up everyday and going to a job you love! That's what can happen when you take time to figure out what you like to do and what skills you have that will make you successful in the business world. Do you need a college degree or vocational education? Learn what it takes to flourish in the educational world — and make your dreams come true.

 ## How do I choose a college?

Are there different types of colleges?

There is no "one size fits all" college or university. Many students learn more readily in smaller classes with a focus on interaction and participation. Others prefer a larger, less intimate setting. Colleges are basically divided into two categories: vocational / technical schools and colleges / universities.

> If you are planning for a year, sow rice. If you are planning for a decade, plant trees. If you are planning for a lifetime, educate people.
>
> ~ *Chinese Proverb*

Chapter 4

Vocational Training Schools

Vocational training schools are specialized schools that offer specific career-focused educations. Training is available in a wide variety of careers, such as cosmetology, mechanical repair, court reporting, parale-

Interactive CD-ROM

Movie

gal services, travel services, secretarial, medical assistance, graphic arts, refrigeration, and many types of computer careers. Courses usually last from five to 12 months, but some may last from two to three years.

Technical Colleges

Technical colleges offer several different types of programs, including two-year Associate degrees, technical diplomas and certificates, and apprenticeships. Some examples of technical programs include accounting assistant, computer programmer, computer analyst, automotive maintenance, pharmacy technician, and dental hygienist. For those interested in working in an industrial or service trade, on-the-job apprenticeships are available. Such jobs can include carpenter, machinist, millwright, electrician, and landscape specialist.

Community Colleges and Junior Colleges

Community colleges and junior colleges offer two-year degree programs. They frequently offer technical programs that prepare you for immediate job entry. Some have programs set up with universities so you can receive an Associate's degree that is transferable to a four-year Bachelor's degree program.

Liberal Arts Colleges

Liberal arts colleges offer a broad range of courses for four-year degrees in humanities, social sciences, and sciences. Most liberal arts colleges are private and focus on undergraduate studies. On the smaller campuses (500 to 2,500 students), you will get to know many other students personally and quickly. Classes are small, so you can get to know your teachers, too. Colleges may also offer graduate programs.

Universities

Universities are big schools that offer many majors and research facilities. School population is often very large (3,000 to 30,000 students). You can select from a wide variety of courses, majors, activities, and events. You can be anonymous in a crowd or you can choose friends from among many types of people. You may face stiffer competition for grades, positions, and opportunities. Universities may also offer graduate programs. Public universities are subsidized by the states they are located in, so tuition for in-state students is typically much cheaper than for out-of-state students.

What type of degree do I want?

Your college and/or skill preparation should include thinking about what kind of degree you want to earn. Here are the most common degree programs:

Certificates or Diplomas

Certificates or diplomas are usually earned for employment in occupational fields, such as computer science, mechanics, interior design, nursing, and such.

Associate Degrees

Associate degrees are earned after completing two years of study. After earning an Associate's degree, you can transfer your credits to a four-year college to complete requirements for a Bachelor's degree.

> AA = Associate of Arts degree
>
> AS = Associate of Science degree
>
> AAS = Associate of Applied Science (technical or vocational programs)

Bachelor's Degrees

Bachelor's degrees are earned at four-year colleges. This is where you pick a major — a major course of study — and complete the requirements for earning the degree. A bachelor's degree averages around 120 credit hours of study. (Credit hours are based on the number of hours per week you meet for a class. For instance, if you earn three credit hours for a math class, it's because the math class meets for three hours a week during the semester. Most students average 12 hours per semester.)

> BA = Bachelor of Arts degree
>
> BS = Bachelor of Science degree

Graduate Degrees

Graduate degrees are earned after completing a Bachelor's degree. For instance, an MBA is a Master's degree in Business Administration and entails another 60 credit hours (or more) of study. Graduate degrees include Master's degrees, doctorates, or professional degrees (such as medical doctor or doctor of veterinary medicine).

What should I look for in a college?

As you search for the right college, consider the school's academic programs, size, location, and cost. If possible, visit the schools you're interested in. Ask these questions to help make your decision:

1. Do I meet the application requirements?

2. Does the college offer the major programs and opportunities I need and want?

3. Does this college, after a close look and visit, feel like a place I'd like to spend the next two to four challenging years?

4. How easy is it to register for classes?

5. Is it difficult to get into some classes?

6. What does it cost?

7. What education and experience does the faculty have?

8. Are faculty members interested in students and available outside of class?

9. What is the average class size? Is that what I want?

10. Am I comfortable with the size of the college?

11. Are courses flexible? Are there afternoon, evening, and weekend classes?

12. Are courses offered through TV or the Internet?

13. Is the library a good place to study and do research?

14. Does the school have the most up-to-date equipment? Do I get hands-on experience?

15. Will I have access to computers and other special equipment?

16. Are campus jobs readily available?

17. What is the job placement rate for recent graduates?

18. Are the residence halls pleasant and quiet enough to study in?

19. Are there fraternities or sororities?

20. What's the cafeteria like?

21. Does the campus offer extracurricular activities?

22. Are there campus or community activities that interest me?

23. What sports are available to play? To watch?

24. Do the students seem to be the kind of people I'd like to get to know?

25. Do I like the social atmosphere?

26. Do I like the surrounding town or city?

27. Is it too far from home? Too close to home?

28. If out-of-state, how much is tuition?

Can I use the College Comparison Worksheet?

Use the College Comparison Worksheet worksheet on page 156 to help you determine which college meets your criteria.

College Comparison Worksheet

In the first column, rate each detail on the following scale of importance to you. Then, in the "College" columns, fill in the details for each college you're interested in. Which college meets the criteria you feel is very important?

3 = very important   2 = somewhat important
1 = not important at all

Interactive CD-ROM

Print It!

College Name	Importance	College	College	College
Location				
Setting (rural, urban, suburban)				
Distance from home				
Academics				
Level of difficulty				
Desired major				
Accessible faculty				
Computer labs				
Campus				
Size of campus				
Social life				
Sports activities				
Cultural activities				
Safety				
Your comfort level				
Selectivity				
School reputation				
Difficulty getting in				
Costs				
Tuition				
Books				
Access to grants/aid				
Career Preparation				
Career services				
Internships				
Graduate school				
Other factors				
Your specific needs				
TOTAL				

Figure 4B

How do I apply for college?

If I'm in high school, how do I apply?

If you're in high school, the following suggestions can make applying for college easier for you:

> Tell
> me and I forget.
> Show me
> and I remember.
> Let me do
> and I understand.
> ~ *Confucius*

- Visit potential colleges during your junior year or in the first semester of your senior year of high school. If you can't visit in person, many schools offer virtual visits via the Internet or on video.

- Take the ACT or SAT by June before your senior year of high school.

- Do online searches for national scholarships. Apply early. Don't use online searches that charge you.

- Apply for admission to the college(s) you choose. Most colleges have an application fee, so be selective on the one(s) you apply to. Some also have application deadlines. Many colleges must follow state-mandated admissions requirements. These requirements vary by state, so check with each college for specific details.

- If you want to live on campus, apply early. Most campus housing is assigned on a first-come basis. Apply in the fall of your senior year.

- Pick up a Free Application for Federal Student Aid (FAFSA) in your high school counselor's office, the college's financial aid office, banks that offer student loans, or you can file online at *www.fafsa.ed.gov*. Applications are available beginning January 2nd and must be filed by March 1st for classes beginning in August. (You must have *applied to* and been *accepted at* a college in order for your financial aid application to be processed, so apply to college early.)

- Register for orientation and attend on your scheduled date. You'll enroll in your classes during orientation.

What if I've already graduated?

If you've already graduated from high school and have been working, finding yourself, or whatever, you can still go to college. You don't have to apply a year in advance. Contact the college you're interested in to find out what the requirements are. Also check with the college's financial aid department to complete the Free Application for Federal Student Aid (FAFSA).

 ## Do I have to take the ACT or SAT test?

What are the ACT and SAT tests?

There are two major tests that most students take to get into college: the ACT test and the SAT test. Many colleges will accept either test, however, some only accept one or the other. Check with the college you're interested in so you take the right test. Both tests are designed to assess high school students' general educational development and their ability to complete college-level work. The tests cover four skill areas: English, mathematics, reading, and science reasoning; and are a "standard" way to measure a student's ability to do college-level work. Because classes and grading scales vary widely from high school to high school, scores on the ACT and SAT are standardized to help colleges compare your academic achievements with those of students from different schools. Tests cost around $25. To find more information or to register online, go to *www.act.org* or *www.collegeboard.org* (for the SAT).

How do colleges use the ACT and SAT?

ACT and SAT test scores help admissions officials identify applicants who can benefit most from the programs the college offers. College academic advisors also refer to your test scores to help you determine which classes to take and at what level. For instance, if your math scores were low on the ACT, you may be enrolled in a remedial algebra class for your first semester. Some scholarships and loans also use test scores to identify qualified candidates. Your test scores are not the only items considered for any of these decisions, though. College officials may also consider your high school grades, accomplishments, extra-curricular activities, volunteer activities, recommendations, essays, employment, and your plans for your future.

How do I pay for college?

What if I can't afford to go to college?

Yes, you can! Many colleges offer needs-based aid or work-study programs. If you need money to pay for school, federal loans are a good first choice. There are all kinds. It has been estimated that nearly half of all students in public colleges and as many as 80 percent of those in private colleges receive some form of financial aid.

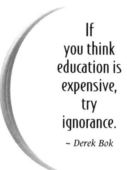

If
you think
education is
expensive,
try
ignorance.

~ Derek Bok

What is a Pell Grant?

A Pell Grant is a monetary gift given to qualified undergraduate students. (An undergraduate is a student who is working to complete a Bachelor's degree.) Eligibility is based on financial need and is limited to an annual amount of $2,700. It does *not* have to be repaid. You automatically apply for a Pell Grant when you complete the Free Application for Federal Student Aid (FAFSA).

What is the FSEOG?

The Federal Supplemental Educational Opportunity Grant (FSEOG) is a monetary gift awarded to undergraduate students. Eligibility is based on financial need. Priority is given to applicants who qualify for Federal Pell Grants. The annual amount given is limited to $4,000. (It may exceed $4,000 for study-abroad programs.) Due to limited funding, however, most awards are less than the maximum allowed. This grant does *not* have to be repaid.

What is the Federal Work Study Program?

Work study programs allow students to work part-time to earn money for college expenses. The school coordinates the job. Eligibility is based on financial need. Salaries are at least minimum wage, but may be more. Earnings are limited to the financial aid awarded. The financial aid office posts job openings, helps arrange interviews, recommends a work schedule (typically 10 to 15 hours per week), and monitors earnings.

What is a Federal Perkins Loan?

The Federal Perkins Loan offers a five percent* fixed interest rate where the school acts as the lender. Principal and interest charges are deferred while you're enrolled at least half-time. Eligibility is based on financial need. Up to $3,000 can be borrowed by undergraduate students (those working to complete a Bachelor's degree) and $5,000 for graduate students (those working toward a Master's or higher degree). Repayment begins nine months after the student graduates, falls below half-time enrollment (usually six hours), or leaves school. You may have up to 10 years to pay the loan off.

* Loan rates may vary. Check with your school or lending institution.

What are Federal Stafford Loans?

There are two types of Federal Stafford Loans: subsidized and unsubsidized. With a subsidized loan, the government pays your interest payments while you're in school. With the unsubsidized loan, you, the borrower, pay the interest accrued while in school, but it's usually deferred until you're out of school for six months. Both loans have an interest rate that is adjusted annually with an 8.25 percent maximum rate. You may have up to 10 years to pay the loan off.

> Repayment of the loan begins six months after graduating, leaving school, or whenever enrollment drops below half-time.

Subsidized Federal Stafford Loan

The subsidized loan is based on financial need and features deferment of principal and interest charges while enrolled at least half-time. The government pays interest for the subsidized loan until repayment begins.

Unsubsidized Federal Stafford Loan

The unsubsidized loan is for independent students and dependent students who do not qualify for the maximum subsidized version. Eligibility for the unsubsidized loan is *not* based on financial need. The borrower pays all interest charges for the unsubsidized loan, which may be deferred (at a cost to the borrower).

What are the borrowing limits?

As a student, you may borrow from both the subsidized and unsubsidized loan programs as long as the combined loan amount does not exceed the maximum allowed per year in school or the cost of attendance. The maximum loan amounts as of August, 2001, follow:

- $2,624 for your 1st year.

- $3,500 for your 2nd year.

- $5,500 for your 3rd and 4th years.

- $8,500 for graduate/professional studies.

Independent students* and dependent students whose parents aren't eligible for the PLUS loan can borrow additional funds in the unsubsidized Stafford loan program:

- $4,000 for your 1st and 2nd years.

- $5,000 for your 3rd and 4th years.

- $10,000 for graduate/professional studies.

*An independent student is one who meets one of the following criteria:

1. is 24 years or older;

2. is married;

3. has legal dependents;

4. is enrolled in a graduate or professional program;

5. is a veteran of the U.S. Armed Forces; or

6. is an orphan or ward of the court.

What is a Federal PLUS Loan?

The Federal Plus Loan is a loan for parents of undergraduate students. It is adjusted annually with a variable rate of interest. (Nine percent is the maximum rate.) Eligibility is determined by the school, but is *not* based on need. Parents may borrow up to the difference between school costs minus estimated financial assistance. Repayment begins within 60 days after the loan is fully disbursed or paid to the borrower.

How do I complete the financial aid form?

To qualify for any federal financial aid, you must complete the Free Application for Federal Student Aid (FAFSA). This is the all-important disclosure of your personal finances that everyone (schools, lenders, the government) will want to see. All families should complete the application, no matter how high or low the annual income. It may trigger other types of aid that are available.

The form is available each year on January 2nd. Complete and submit the application as soon as possible because funds are usually awarded on a first-come, first-served basis. (This means you and your parent(s) will have to do taxes early.) To estimate how much federal financial aid you're eligible for, log onto *www.act.org* and plug in your financial numbers.

Get an application at *www.fafsa.com*, from your high school or college, or call the Federal Student Aid Information Center at 1-800-433-3243.

How do I find scholarships?

If you're looking for scholarship money, check out the following *free* websites:

- *www.fastweb.com*

- *www.scholaraid.com*

- *www.collegeboard.org*

- *www.collegenet.com*

- *www.collegequest.com*

- *www.srnexpress.com*

- *www.college-scholarships.com*

These *free* sites require you to fill out a questionnaire. Your profile is then crunched against a catalog of tens of thousands of scholarships, instantly returning listings on all those for which you might qualify. Some scholarships can be applied for online. Don't pay for a scholarship application or search services.

Other places to look for scholarships include your high school guidance counselor or the college financial aid office. Also check locally with civic groups, churches, and merchants. They often give awards based on community involvement. Your parent's employer may offer tuition assistance. If you have a job, your own employer may offer some kind of assistance.

If you receive a scholarship, read the fine print. Many scholarships have strict requirements, such as maintaining a set GPA or taking a set number of classes.

Are there other sources for financial aid?

There are many sources of funding available, including the following:

State Aid

The 50 states collectively spend some $1.6 billion annually to help residents pay for education. All states offer need-based assistance, primarily to those who attend in-state public schools. Most states also have merit programs that provide assistance regardless of need. Eligibility guidelines and the amount of money available vary by state. Check with the school's financial aid office.

College Aid

Most colleges have established grant programs through alumni organizations, endowment funds, and gifts. Many colleges also offer their own installment plans, enabling you to pay tuition in installments spread throughout the semester — with low or no interest.

Special Needs

These grant programs address special needs and/or entitlements for specific groups, such as military veterans; physically-challenged students; minorities; and children of deceased or disabled veterans, policemen, or firemen. Applications are made to the specific administering agencies. Native Americans, for example, are eligible for aid through the Bureau of Indian Affairs.

Co-op Programs

More than 50,000 employers across the nation participate in co-op programs each year. In addition to paying students' salaries, these programs offer valuable work experience in the students' field of interest. Another advantage is that many co-op students have a job waiting for them when they graduate.

Private Funding Sources

Funding is also available from lenders and schools. Private loans may allow you to borrow larger amounts, but interest rates are usually higher than guaranteed student loans. Your own resources (insurance policies, home equity loans, etc.) can also be used to pay for college. Check with your bank or credit union for more information.

What about military benefits?

Under the Montgomery G.I. Bill, the Army, Navy, Air Force, Marine Corps, and Coast Guard (and the Reserve and National Guard) provide a cash incentive to encourage you to join and serve a tour of duty. The G.I. Bill benefit amounts change each year, but currently provide more than $9,000 for serving part-time in the Reserve or National Guard and more than $19,000 for a tour of active duty in the military services. Contact your local recruiter for more information.

The Army, Navy, and Marine Corps College Funds

These funds each provide tuition assistance in addition to the G.I. Bill. The Army and Navy funds increase the amount of support to as much as $50,000. The Marine Corps fund increases the amount of support to as much as $30,000.

ROTC Scholarships

ROTC scholarships provide you with money for college in exchange for a service commitment. You must take military science courses along with your other college courses, and upon graduation, enter the service as a commissioned officer. Full ROTC scholarships pay for almost all tuition, fees, and books for four years of college. ROTC scholarships also come in one-, two-, and three-year lengths. For more information, call the following:

- Air Force ROTC — 1-800-522-0033 (extension 2091)

- Army ROTC — 1-800-USA-ROTC

- Marine ROTC — 1-800-MARINES

- Navy ROTC — 1-800-USA-NAVY

U.S. Service Academies

Service academies are operated by each branch of the service as a four-year institution of higher education. All students receive a full scholarship with a small monthly stipend. Upon graduation, you're commissioned as a second lieutenant in the Air Force, Army, or Marine Corps; or as an ensign in the Navy or Coast Guard. Appointment to a service academy is extremely competitive. For more information, call the following:

- U.S. Military Academy at West Point — 1-800-822-8762

- U.S. Naval Academy — 1-800-638-9156

- U.S. Air Force Academy — 1-800-443-9266

- U.S. Coast Guard Academy — 1-800-883-8724

The Community College of the Air Force (CCAF)

The CCAF is a two-year college open only to enlisted men and women. It offers a variety of programs leading to an Associate's degree in more than 70 scientific and technical fields. The Air Force pays for up to 75 percent of the cost of college courses through its Tuition Assistance Program.

 # Can I live on campus?

Can I live on the campus?

Campus housing can include traditional residence halls or dorms with one- and two-person rooms; residence halls with apartment-style suites that can house up to four students; scholarship halls; and university-owned apartment complexes that house married students or students who are single parents. Contact the Student Housing office to find out what options are available at the school(s) you're interested in. Apply early, too. Most on-campus housing is filled on a first-come, first-served basis.

Residence hall fees can include basic cable TV, local telephone hook-ups (you pay the phone bill, though), and in-room connections for the Internet. Many residence halls also include a meal plan. Some residence halls are co-ed. (Both men and women live there.) Many are also smoke-free.

Can I live off-campus?

Off-campus housing includes fraternities and sororities; apartments;

rental houses; and living at home with your parent(s). Off-campus housing varies greatly in price, size, neighborhood, and condition. Be aware, too, that in some college towns, rental housing is very expensive — and you'll probably need a roommate or two to help pay the bills.

 ## What is a GED?

What is a GED?

Each year, about one-half million people earn their GED (General Educational Development) diplomas. If you left high school without graduating, earning a GED can make a big difference in your life. The tests are available in English, Spanish, and French. Special large-print, audio cassette, and Braille editions are also available, as well as adaptations to testing conditions for adults with disabilities. Visit *www.acenet.edu/ calec/ged/home.html* for more information.

> An education isn't how much you have committed to memory, or even how much you know. It's being able to differentiate between what you do know and what you don't.
>
> *~ Author Unknown*

What are the benefits of a GED?

The GED program provides an opportunity for adults to continue their education. Ninety-three percent of colleges accept GED graduates who meet their other qualifications for admission. A GED also documents that you have high-school level skills. Approximately 96 percent of employers accept the GED as equivalent to a traditional high school diploma. Many GED graduates also say they have increased self-esteem and self-confidence.

Am I eligible to take the GED tests?

If you left high school without graduating and your high school class has graduated, you are probably eligible to take the GED tests. If your class hasn't graduated, some states offer "alternative" high schools. Check with your area's GED testing center or the Department of Education for specific requirements and testing centers. There are more than 3,000 testing centers in the U.S. — and probably one not far from your home.

How do I prepare to take the GED tests?

Attend classes. To get information regarding a program in your area, contact your local high school, adult education program, or community college. Look in the Yellow Pages under *Schools, Education, Continuing Education*, or *GED*. If you can't find an adult education program in your area, study on your own. Many study materials are available through libraries, adult education centers, schools, colleges, and book stores.

What are the GED tests?

The GED tests measure important knowledge and skills expected of high school graduates. The five GED tests include Literature and the Arts, Mathematics, Science, Social Sciences, and Writing Skills.

The tests contain multiple-choice questions that test your ability to understand and use information or ideas. In many cases, you are asked to use the information provided to solve a problem, find causes and effects, or make a judgment. Very few questions ask about narrow definitions or specific facts. Instead, the focus of the questions is on the major or lasting skills and knowledge expected of high school graduates. The Writing Skills test also includes an essay, with very general topics so everyone can think of something to write.

Interpreting Literature and the Arts

- 45 questions

- 65 minutes to complete the test

Mathematics

- 56 questions

- 90 minutes to complete the test

Science

- 66 questions

- 95 minutes to complete the test

Social Sciences

- 64 questions

- 85 minutes to complete the test

Writing Skills

- 55 questions

- 75 minutes to complete the test

- 45 minutes to complete one essay

How are GED scores reported?

Separate scores are reported for each of the five GED tests. Test results are reported on a standard score scale ranging from 20 (lowest possible score) to 80 (highest possible score). Your score on the GED tests is not the number of correct answers or the percent correct.

What score do I need to pass?

Passing scores are set by the state in which you live. Although the requirements can vary slightly from one state to another, most requirements are stated in terms of a minimum standard score for each test and/or a minimum average standard score for all five tests. The highest score you can earn on each test is 80, the lowest is 20. The minimum passing standard set by the GED testing service is a minimum score of 40 on each test and an average of 45.

When did the founder of Wendy's get his GED?

When he was 60 years old! Dave Thomas, founder of the Wendy's chain of fast-food restaurants, grew up very poor — but he always wanted to finish his education. When he was 60 years old, he went back to high school and got his GED. He and his wife even attended the Senior Prom — and were voted Prom King and Queen. His fellow students voted him *"Most likely to succeed."*

What is e-learning?

E-learning is training that takes place through a network, usually over the Internet or a company Intranet. It allows people to take classes online from colleges in a variety of subjects. Online education is fast becoming an industry itself and is expected to generate $46 billion by 2005, according to the National Institute of Standards and Technology. More than 90 percent of traditional educational institutions offer, or plan to offer, some type of program via distance learning. There are two types of e-learning:

Synchronous e-learning

Synchronous e-learning is like a real classroom. Classes take place in real-time and connect instructors and students via audio, video, or a chat room.

A-synchronous e-learning

A-synchronous e-learning lets students access pre-packaged training on their own time, working at their own pace, and communicating with the instructor or other students through e-mail.

While e-learning might offer more flexibility for some students, it tends to isolate students physically. This can have negative effects on team building and sociability, which are important skills needed for most jobs. Those who are shy about speaking up in class, however, might be more likely to ask questions over the Internet. Both faculty and students report that online classes take more time and work than traditional classes. Faculty, for example, have a live audience in the classroom and get immediate feedback to questions. On the Internet, all communications have to be written — from every student and to every student.

And, even though colleges, universities, and other educational institutions are investing significant funds and courses into e-learning, no one knows for sure how e-degrees will be perceived by prospective employers. Companies are often skeptical of education programs that are totally online, so the degree alone may not be enough to get you hired. Having experience on your résumé with an online degree is very important.

What if I don't want to go to college?

Is college for everyone?

College is not for everyone. For some, college follows high school. Others want to get a few years of work experience. Some don't want a degree, they just want to take a class occasionally. And for others, college is definitely not an option — and never will be. And all of these options are okay!

A Bachelor's degree is still an asset if you're trying to make it in America. Going to college for four years can be an enriching experience. It's also a must for many careers, but not everyone needs to go to college right after high school — or ever — to succeed. It's still true that people with more education, on average, earn more money. But 28 percent of workers without a four-year degree earn more than the average worker with a Bachelor's degree, says Harlow G. Unger, author of *But What if I Don't Want to go to College?* Unger's guide lists educational alternatives to college. This doesn't mean you can walk into a great job right out of high school with no skills, no training, no effort.

To get a good job without a four-year college degree, you still need at least a high school education — and a skill that businesses want to pay you to do. You also need to know how to be a team player, how to communicate effectively, and how to learn.

Can I get some other kind of training?

Many jobs do require some sort of training. Which vocational training you need depends upon the job you choose. Community colleges and technical colleges offer some of the best vocational training, often specializing in areas such as graphic arts, hotel and restaurant management, and building trades. You can also attend a trade school that specializes in one field, such as hairstyling or auto mechanics.

Look for reputable, high-quality programs that are accredited, offer in-depth academic and vocational instruction, teach real skills for real jobs, provide hands-on work experience, help students in job-hunting, and are linked to potential employers.

If you don't want to go to college right out of high school, visit your library to review *The Occupational Outlook Handbook* or visit *www. stats.bls.gov*. It's published every two years by the U.S. Department of Labor and offers job descriptions and required training. What are you interested in? Do you like sports, gardening, animals, rocks? Believe it or not, there are many jobs that relate to almost any kind of interest you might have. (Go to Chapter 3, "Career Guidance" for more information.)

What if I can't afford to go to college?

If you want to go to college, but can't afford to, think again. The federal government has many grant and loan programs available for students. Complete a Free Application for Federal Student Aid (FAFSA). Go to "How do I pay for college?" for more information.

Can I go to college in a few years?

Yes. You can go to college when you're 80 years old, if you want to. Be open to the possibility that you might want to go someday. Go on your own timeline.

 ## What if I'm not smart enough to go to college?

Yes, you are! Thomas J. Stanley, author of *The Millionaire Mind*, says that many of today's millionaires were only so-so students. Though 90 percent of the more than 1,300 millionaires he surveyed are college graduates, they averaged only a 2.92 GPA and 73 percent had SAT scores under 1000. So, even if you struggled in high school, with a bit of effort, you can make it through college. Many have before you.

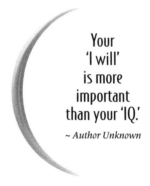

Your 'I will' is more important than your 'IQ.'

~ Author Unknown

 ## How do I study for tests?

How do I create a productive study space?

Try to create a study space that includes as many of the following elements as possible. You'll find that it's much easier to study.

- Arrange furniture so the phone, computer, and books are within easy reach.

- Choose a space with a window. Natural light aids in learning.

- Stick a *"Do Not Disturb"* sign and a notepad outside your door to reduce distractions.

- Have good lighting.

- Use a comfortable desk and chair.

- Avoid studying on your bed.

- Play soft instrumental music to help you concentrate. It drowns out distractions.

- Avoid loud rock music or music with lyrics. They're distracting.

- Study for 50 minutes, then take a 10 minute break.

- Don't take phone calls during study time. Use an answering machine or voice mail.

- Keep the temperature in the room a bit cool.

- Try to study at the same time and in the same location.

Any helpful study tips?

The following tips can make your time at college much easier:

- Go to class! Sit in the front of the classroom! (Professors do notice.) And talk in class — but listen, too. Try to schedule your classes all in the morning or all in the afternoon.

- Use a calendar or planner. Write all of your assignments for the semester on it. Set daily and weekly goals so you can meet these obligations. Write down all assignments. If not, you'll always forget one.

- Read ahead. The lectures will make more sense and it'll be easier to memorize. Work ahead in as many classes as possible, but don't get behind in other classes while concentrating on one.

- Get in the habit of reading your lecture notes at the end of each day, or at least at the end of each week, to eliminate a lot of cramming for tests. Spend at least two nights studying for any major exam. Allow even more time for writing papers, especially if research is required. Don't forget the time it will take to type and print the paper, especially if you need to schedule computer time.

- Write an outline. Even if you're rushed for time, take a few minutes to write an outline. It'll be easier to structure your paper when you start writing. Proofread all your papers, then have someone else proofread them. Always have a good dictionary and thesaurus handy. You might also invest in *20,000 Words Spelled and Divided for Quick Reference*.

- Drink plenty of water. Avoid caffeinated beverages like soft drinks and coffee.

- If a professor has office hours, visit him or her. It can raise a borderline grade.

- Be prepared to change your major several times, especially if you find you're not really interested in the subject matter.

What can I do about test anxiety?

Test anxiety can undermine a student's best efforts to do well on tests. Some students study the material thoroughly and then "freeze up" when it's time to take the exam. Others are so anxiety-ridden by the prospect of taking a test that they are unable to study effectively and go to school unprepared to take the test. Don't worry too much. A little test anxiety is normal and may be a good thing because it makes you more alert and motivates you to do your best. But, if the thought of taking a test makes you break out in a sweat, try the following strategies:

- Participate in class discussions.

- Do your homework.

- Spread out your studying time over a period of days or weeks.

- Read all directions carefully. If you don't understand, ask the teacher to clarify.

- Don't rush the test. Careless errors are made when you try to be the first one done.

- Answer every question, even if you have to guess.

- Use scratch paper.

- Drink water before the test and during the test. Bring bottled water to class.

- Be physically and mentally alert. Cramming the night before will probably not help.

- Look over the entire exam before you begin to see what types of questions are included. Then do the easy parts first, leaving plenty of time for more difficult problems.

- Don't spend too much time on one question. Make an "educated guess," put a mark next to it, and go back later to review it.

- Prepare for the test as fully as you can. When you've done all you can, relax. If you've prepared well, you'll do well.

Keep your fear of failure in check or it will become a self-fulfilling prophecy. If you believe that you're going to fail, then you will. Redirect your attention away from your fear of failure — and toward productive ways to do well on the test. Remember that one test usually doesn't count for your whole grade. Homework and class participation help your grade, too.

Any specific test-taking tips?

Essay Tests
State your answer to the essay question and then explain why you answered that way. Use the journalism model by answering the following questions: who, what, why, where, when, and how. Use details to make your essay more convincing. Think of your essay as an attempt to convince the reader of the correctness of your answer. Be sure your explanation supports your answer.

Math Tests

Look over the answer choices before beginning to figure out the answer. See how exact you need to be. For example, instead of an answer carried to three decimal places, the answer may not have a decimal at all. This will save you time in arriving at a solution.

Multiple Choice Questions

Cross off any answers that are clearly not correct. This narrows your options.

What if studying doesn't help?

If you find, early in the semester, that you're struggling with a class, are taking too many classes, don't like the instructor, or for some reason just don't want to be in a class, you might be able to drop the class or withdraw from the class so you won't hurt your GPA. If you just stop going to class, you'll end up with an F on your transcript. So, instead of failing the class, see if you can drop the class or withdraw from it. There are deadlines for each of these, so check your college handbook or Registrar's Office for details.

Drop/Add

If you've already enrolled, but need to change your schedule, you can do a drop/add. That means you drop one course, and add another. You can also just drop a course or just add a course. This is usually done during the first few weeks of school.

Withdraw

Don't just quit going to class ... unless you want an F on your transcript. You must withdraw officially from that class. There is a limited amount of time that you can do a withdrawal. You can't go in a week before semester ends, after not going to class all semester, and withdraw so you won't fail the class.

 ## Am I a cheater?

Am I a cheater?

In recent years, colleges have reported an increase in plagiarism and cheating on tests. (Plagiarism is the act of taking the writings of another person and passing them off as one's own.) In research conducted at 31 schools over the past decade, nearly 70 percent of students admit to cheating at some point during college. More than 15 percent of those said they were serious, repetitive cheaters.

When asked about cheating, students agree that cheating is "no big deal." Grades count, not learning. Students look over shoulders, use coughing codes to communicate to friends, and even flash answers on hands while pretending to stretch. Some have tried using pagers to send answers. Students have even been caught cheating in Ethics classes. Some students rationalize that it's okay to cheat if the class isn't required for their major, but is required for graduating (like math or English). Others assume cheating is a victimless offense. Many students say they cheat because their peers cheat and are getting away with it.

Keep in mind that research has found that cheaters are more likely to lie on résumés, expense reports, and insurance claims. Would you want to rely on a doctor who cheated throughout medical school?

Is it cheating if I find it on the Internet?

It's never been easier to cheat. With the Internet, students have access to a wide array of information they can use without giving proper credit to the author. It's seen as a great tool for term papers by cheating college students. Computer science graduates from the University of California, Berkeley, however, have created a program to catch would-be plagiarizers. Their website, *www.plagiarism.org*, allows teachers to upload term papers, which the site then compares with a database of manuscripts collected from other schools and from the Internet. An annotated copy of the paper is returned to the instructor, showing any similarities to other works. Last year, a neurobiology professor testing the program caught 45 of 320 students lifting passages or even entire term papers from Internet sources.

What happens if I get caught cheating?

If a professor catches you cheating, you will more than likely be confronted in private. Sometimes a judicial board (made up of faculty and students) reviews the case. If the accused admits cheating, the matter may be resolved with a punishment. The cases for students who deny cheating are often heard in formal proceedings, complete with evidence presented by witnesses. At many schools, punishment for first-time violators is an F on the assignment or in the course, or some form of disciplinary probation. More serious offenses, as well as second and third offenses, can result in suspension or expulsion from the college. Some colleges also put a mark on your transcript as a permanent part of your college record.

 ## What are four great lessons a college degree won't teach me?

Lesson #1

Everyone is important.

> During the second month of nursing school, the professor gave the class a pop quiz. I was a conscientious student and had breezed through the questions until I read the last one: *"What is the first name of the woman who cleans the school?"*
>
> Surely this was some kind of joke. I had seen the cleaning woman several times. She was tall, dark-haired, and in her 50s — but how would I know her name? I handed in my paper, leaving the last question blank. Before class ended, one student asked if the last question would count toward our quiz grade.
>
> *"Absolutely!"* said the professor. *"In your careers, you will meet many people. All are significant. They deserve your attention and care, even if all you do is smile and say, 'Hello.'"*
>
> I learned the cleaning woman's name was Dorothy.
>
> ~ Author Unknown

Lesson #2

Remember those you serve and who serve you.

> In the days when an ice cream sundae cost much less, a 10-year-old boy entered a hotel coffee shop and sat at a table. A waitress put a glass of water in front of

him. *"How much is an ice cream sundae?"* asked the boy. *"Fifty cents,"* replied the waitress.

The little boy pulled his hand out of his pocket and studied a number of coins in it. *"How much is a dish of plain ice cream?"* he inquired. Some people were now waiting for a table and the waitress was a bit impatient. *"Thirty-five cents,"* she said sharply.

The little boy again counted the coins. *"I'll have the plain ice cream,"* he said. The waitress brought the ice cream, put the bill on the table, and walked away.

The boy finished the ice cream, paid the cashier, and left the coffee shop. When the waitress came back, she began wiping down the table and then swallowed hard at what she saw. There, placed neatly beside the empty dish, were two nickels and five pennies — her tip.

~ Author Unknown

Lesson #3

The obstacle in your path is an opportunity.

In ancient times, a king had a boulder placed on a roadway. He then hid himself and watched to see if anyone would remove the huge rock. Some of the king's wealthiest merchants came by and simply walked around the rock. Many loudly blamed the king for not keeping the roads clear. None did anything about getting the big stone out of the way.

Then a peasant came along carrying a load of vegetables. On approaching the boulder, the peasant laid down his burden and tried to move the stone to the side of the road. After much pushing and straining, he finally succeeded. As the peasant picked up his load of vegetables, he noticed a purse lying in the road where the boulder had been. The purse contained many gold coins and a note from the king indicating that the gold was for the person who removed the boulder from the roadway.

The peasant learned what many others never understand: Every obstacle presents an opportunity to improve one's condition.

~ Author Unknown

Lesson #4

Attitude is everything.

Many years ago, when I worked as a volunteer at Stanford Hospital, I got to know a little girl named Liz who was suffering from a rare and serious disease. Her only chance of recovery appeared to be a blood transfusion from her five-year-old brother. Liz's little brother had miraculously survived the same disease and had developed antibodies needed to combat the illness.

The doctor explained the situation to the little brother, and asked the boy if he would be willing to give his blood to his sister. I saw him hesitate for only a moment before taking a deep breath and saying, *"Yes. I'll do it if it will save Liz."*

As the transfusion progressed, he lay in bed next to his sister and smiled, as we all did, seeing the color return to Liz's cheeks. Then his face grew pale and his smile faded. He looked up at the doctor and asked with a trembling voice, *"Will I start to die right away?"*

Being so young, the boy had misunderstood the doctor. He thought he was going to have to give his sister all of his blood.

~ Author Unknown

Additional Information for this Chapter

Books

- *ADD and the College Student* by Patricia O. Quinn, M.D.

- *America's Top Jobs for People Without a Four-Year Degree* by J. Michael Farr

- *Brain Gym* by Paul E. Dennison, Ph.D. and Gail E. Dennison

- *But What if I Don't Want to go to College?* by Harlow G. Unger

- *College Survival Guide for ADD and LD Students* by Kathleen G. Nadeau, Ph.D.

- *School Strategies for ADD Teens* by Kathleen G. Nadeau; Ph.D., Ellen B. Dixon, Ph.D.; and Susan H. Biggs, Ed.D.

- *20,000 Words Spelled and Divided for Quick Reference*

Web Links

- *www.Salliemae.com*

- *www.finaid.org*

- *www.ecollegetips.com*

- *www.studentcenter.org*

- *www.collegeview.com*

- *www.campustours.com*

- *www.fastweb.com*

- *www.fafsa.com*

- *www.fafsa.ed.gov*

- *www.act.org*

- *www.scholaraid.com*

- *www.srnexpress.com*

- *www.college-scholarships.com*

- *www.collegeboard.org*

- *www.votech.about.com*

- *www.ed.gov* (U.S. Dept. of Education)

- *www.plagiarism.org*

- *www.bls.gov* (U.S. Bureau of Labor Statistics)

- *www.collegenet.com*

- *www.collegequest.com*

- *www.acenet.edu/calec/ged/home.html*

How committed am I to my goal?

Set a goal. Complete the following sentence and then answer the questions that follow. Choose any goal you like. It can be something you want to do, be, have, see, or anything else.

Interactive CD-ROM

Quiz

Someday I'm going to _____

Yes	No	
○	○	Is this a goal I want to reach?
○	○	Is my goal achievable?
○	○	Is my goal challenging for me?
○	○	Am I motivated to accomplish this goal?
○	○	Do I take responsibility for accomplishing my goal?
○	○	If I fail, will I learn from it?
○	○	Will I maintain a positive attitude about my goal?
○	○	Am I passionate about my goal?
○	○	Am I committed to myself and my goal?
○	○	Am I willing to take risks?
○	○	Am I willing to ask for help if I need it?
○	○	Is my goal written down?
○	○	Is my goal flexible?

What are the specifics of my goal? _____

How will I know when I've reached my goal? _____

Do I need to break it down into smaller steps? _____

If so, what steps? _____

What is the deadline? _____

What can I work on today to accomplish my goal? _____

What can I work on this week to accomplish my goal? _____

What can I work on this month to accomplish my goal? _____

How will I celebrate when I accomplish this goal? _____

Can I visualize it? What does it look like? _____

Figure 5A

Dreams and Goals

Dream big and never lose sight of your goals — because nothing happens unless first you dream! And then set goals based on those dreams. Goals serve as a road map, laying out a path to success. By setting goals, you choose where you want to go in life. Grab control of your destiny!

 ## What do I want to be when I grow up?

> Happiness, wealth, and success are all by-products of goal-setting; they cannot be the goals themselves.
>
> ~ Marshall E. Dimock

What do I want to be when I grow up?

Someday I'm going to …. What do you want to be when you grow up? Don't know. That's okay. Most people have several jobs or careers as adults before they discover what they truly enjoy. And many adults end up doing something they never expected. Don't feel pressured. Discover what you believe in, what you like doing, what you're best at. Strive to become a better person. Dream big and never lose sight of your goals — because nothing happens unless first you dream!

Make a wish list. Write down who you want to be, what you want to do, what you want to see, where you want to go, and what you want to have. What's stopping you? What can you do today to turn your dreams into reality?

How can I visualize my dream?

Visualization is the most powerful way to achieve your goals. Success is no surprise to visionary people. They know what they want, determine a plan to achieve it, and expect positive results. They "see" themselves doing and being their dream. They visualize their dream as a reality. You can, too.

> Shoot for the moon. Even if you miss it, you will land among the stars.
>
> ~ *Les Brown*

Visualizing means painting a picture of your dreams. It allows you to see your ideal tomorrow. Learn to visualize. Use your imagination and create every detail of your goal. Project yourself into a successful situation. Dream every sight, every sound, every smell. Dream in color — bright, vivid color. Imagine different conditions. See yourself being and doing your dream. Success isn't so much *what* you think as *HOW* you think. If you can visualize it, you can make it happen.

How do I set goals?

Goals serve as a road map, laying out a path to success. If you don't set goals to determine where you're going, how will you know when you get there? By setting goals, you choose where you want to go in life.

> The most important thing about having goals is having one.
>
> ~ *Author Unknown*

Research shows that people who set goals suffer less from stress and anxiety, are happier, concentrate better and perform better, and show more self-confidence. Goals give you more than a reason to get up in the morning. They're an incentive to keep going all day. Reaching goals can have a huge impact on your confidence and self-esteem.

To set realistic goals, each of your goals must have the following:

> If you don't know where you're going, you will probably end up somewhere else.
>
> ~ *Dr. Laurence J. Peter*

Your goal must be your own.

If the goals you are setting are about you and your life, they need to be *your goals* — not the goals of your parents, your best friend, your teacher, or anyone else. Your goals must be something you want to achieve, not something someone else wants you to achieve. Consider what you want to achieve in your lifetime.

You can't set goals for other people.

You can't set a goal to change your co-workers, your boyfriend or girlfriend, or anyone else. You can only set goals for yourself. When you change yourself, however, chances are that others around you will also change.

Your goal must be achievable.

If your goals are unrealistic, you'll never achieve them. They will only discourage you and decrease your motivation. Set goals that you have control over, not ones that depend on someone else. Set priorities to avoid feeling overwhelmed by having too many goals. Focus on the most important ones. Break goals into smaller steps. If a goal is too large, it might seem that you are making no progress at all.

Your goal must be specific.

If your goals are vague and unspecific, how will you know when you've achieved them? Be specific about what you want, how you will achieve it, and when you will achieve it. Be precise. Put in dates, times, amounts. Know the exact goal to be achieved.

Your goal must have a deadline.

Deadlines provide a sense of urgency and a way to track your progress. Without deadlines, you won't take your goals seriously — and you're not likely to accomplish them. As Harvey Mackay once said, *"A goal is a dream with a deadline."* Set monthly goals and break them into weekly and daily goals.

Your goal must challenge you.

Demanding goals will motivate you to do your best. Dream big. Challenge yourself. Don't make your goals too easy, or you'll cheat yourself. Be action-oriented, but don't make your goals so hard that you give up on them.

Your goal must be written down.

Someone once said that an unwritten goal is merely a wish. Write your goals down and keep them visible. If you keep them in your head, they'll keep changing — and you'll never accomplish them. Writing your goals down makes them real — and motivates you to work on them. Write your goals using positive statements.

Your goal must be flexible.

Allow yourself the opportunity to change your mind — and the opportunity to change your goals. Don't cling to goals that are no longer achievable. Don't give up too quickly, either. You may just need to rethink how you're going to achieve your goals. Goals change as you mature. Adjust them as you grow to reflect the personal changes you make in your life.

Your goal must be celebrated when it's accomplished.

When you achieve a goal, take time to celebrate!

 ## Do I have to be responsible?

Do I have to take responsibility?

Yes! And be glad that you do! Take 100 percent responsibility for your life. Start using *"I"* statements. Take ownership of your life. Say *"I am doing this."* instead of *"This is happening to me."* Stop blaming your failures on others. Look to yourself. Be accountable. Be trustworthy. Be reliable. Answer for your own conduct.

> Success can be measured not so much by the position one has reached in life, as by the obstacles one has overcome trying to succeed.
>
> ~ *Booker T. Washington*

Eleanor Roosevelt once said, *"No one else can make you feel inferior without your consent."* The same is true of all other aspects of your life. You are responsible for your own situation and you're the one who has the power to take the steps necessary to change it. Regardless of your past, your future is up to you — and the best way to predict your future is to create it.

People spend too much time finding other peo-
ple to blame,too much energy finding excuses
for not being what they are capable of being,
and not enough energy putting themselves on
the line, growing out of the past, and getting
on with their lives.

~ J. Michael Straczynski

Do I need an attitude adjustment?

An attitude is defined as a feeling or emotion toward a fact. It is also defined as a negative or hostile state of mind. Is the glass half empty or half
full? Do you roll with the punches — or do you punch back? Are you too
negative? Do you feel as though the world is out to get you? If you find it
hard to keep a positive attitude, consider the following:

There is nothing you cannot be,
nothing you cannot do,
nothing you cannot have,
if you have a positive attitude.

Your attitude is your most valuable possession. It's the way you communicate your mood to yourself and to others. When you're optimistic, you
present a positive image and people tend to respond favorably. A positive
attitude shows your enthusiasm. It enhances your creativity. It can cause
good things to happen.

When you're pessimistic, you tend to expect the worst and your attitude is
often negative. A negative attitude speaks so loudly that no words are necessary. You show it in the way you carry yourself, your facial expressions,
your gestures. People tend to avoid pessimists. Are you in need of an attitude adjustment? Do you find yourself being critical and cynical, complaining, and comparing everything? Do you find fault in everything and
everyone? Are you unappreciative? Do you think that no one can be trusted? If so, you are definitely in need of an attitude adjustment.

The longer I live, the more I realize the impact
of attitude on life. Attitude, to me, is more im-
portant than facts. It is more important than
the past, than education, than money, than

circumstances, than failures, than success, than what other people think or say or do. It is more important than appearance, giftedness, or skill. It will make or break a company ... a church ... a home.

The remarkable thing is we have a choice every day regarding the attitude we will embrace for that day. We cannot change the past. We cannot change the fact that people will act in a certain way. We cannot change the inevitable. The only thing we can do is play on the one thing we have — and that is our attitude.

I am convinced that life is 10 percent what happens to me and 90 percent how I react to it.

~ Charles Swindoll

How do I adjust my attitude?

Try to look at the situation from another point of view. Did you learn something? Is there some humor that can be found in the situation? Did some good come out of it? Can you think of anyone less fortunate than you? Concentrate on the things you do well in life. Give the not-so-positive things less attention. Simplify your life. Lessen your involvement in activities. Refuse to accept responsibility for other people's problems. Don't worry about things you cannot control. Get a makeover. Create a balance between work/school and your personal life. Let go of relationships that bring you down. Be yourself.

View change as opportunity. Do something nice for someone else. Concentrate on what you can accomplish today. Exercise. Laugh. Spend time with positive people. Accept that life isn't fair. Take responsibility. As Abraham Lincoln said, *"Most people are about as happy as they make up their minds to be."* So, make up your mind to be happy. Take control of your life. That's a great attitude adjuster.

Isn't passion about sex?

Passion is the key to success. It's not about sex. It's about love. It's about loving what you're doing. Passion is defined as *"a strong liking or desire for or devotion to some activity, object, or concept."* Passionate people get things done. If you're passionate about your dreams and goals, your passion will sway others. You'll find that people want to be around you because they sense your commitment.

What is commitment?

Commitment is the difference between wishing and doing. The following words from Ella Wheeler Wilcox's poem, *"Will"* explain what commitment is: *"There is no chance, no destiny, no fate that can circumvent or hinder or control the firm resolve of a determined soul."* Commitment means that you obligate or pledge yourself to your goal. You stay focused on your goal, even if it means giving up some of the things you'd rather do (like hanging out with friends instead of studying). It means improving your talents because even if you already know how to do something, you can learn to do it better. (Everyone has room for improvement.) Commitment must come from within you. It is not something someone else can give you.

> Always bear in mind that your own resolution to succeed is more important than any other one thing."
>
> ~ *Abraham Lincoln*

Is managing personal change necessary?

Change is a part of your life. It is a part of everyone's life. Accept it. Deal with it. Welcome it. Even though change is sure to happen, many people respond negatively to it. Do you? Do you get headaches, rashes, stomach aches, or minor pains when there's a change that needs to be made? Do you feel exhausted? Do you feel confused? Do you find it hard to concentrate? Do you lose sleep? Do you forget details? Does your mind go blank? Do you get anxious, angry, or frustrated? Do you get depressed and withdraw? Do you feel afraid?

Someone once said, *"If you continue to do what you've always done, you'll continue to get what you've always got."* Maybe it's time to make some personal changes in your life. If you find yourself responding negatively to change, you can control your reactions by practicing the four Cs: challenge, control, commitment, and connection.

- Challenge. See change as a challenge and as an opportunity.

- Control. Focus your attention on things you can control.

- Commitment. Be committed to the change.

- Connection. Ask for help and support to stay connected with people.

Is it good to spend time alone?

Spending time alone is an essential part of being successful. Learn to keep yourself busy and interested. Learn the value of reading, writing, and creating —away from your peers. Don't fill every moment of your time. Be quiet. Stop to relax. Get to know yourself. Strive to find a sense of peace and calmness within yourself.

 ## Do I have a fear of failure?

Am I afraid to fail?

Failure is only feedback. Failure should be viewed as a positive learning experience. Just the fact that you tried something is important — and may even open doors that you never considered. People waste a lot of time being afraid and embarrassed over the smallest things. You can't die of embarrassment. It just feels that way sometimes. The important thing is to overcome your fear. Most people try to beat down their flaws or deny them altogether. Don't use your flaws as an excuse to quit or to not start at all. Don't be afraid to try new things — and if you are afraid, try them anyway.

> Fear doesn't exist anywhere except in the mind.
> ~ *Dale Carnegie*

> *Results! Why, man, I have gotten a lot of results. I know several thousand things that don't work. I found five thousand ways how not to make a light bulb.*
>
> ~ Thomas A. Edison

Fear is probably the main reason so many people don't set goals. Are you one who believes that "failure is bad?" If you write down a goal and don't reach it, does that make you a failure? Isn't it smarter not to have any goals at all since the easiest way to avoid failing is by not putting yourself in situations where you could fail? If you remove the possibility of failing, do you also remove the possibility of succeeding?

> *I've missed more than 9,000 shots in my career. I've lost almost 300 games. 26 times, I've been trusted to take the game-winning shot — and missed. I've failed — over and over and over again in my life.*
>
> *And that is why I succeed.*
>
> ~ Michael Jordan

Why do goals fail?

When a goal doesn't work out as planned, what lesson(s) can you learn? Did you have the skills or knowledge to accomplish the goal? Did you set an unrealistic time frame? Did you try as hard as you could? Did you break it into small enough steps? Did something or someone out of your control interfere? Did you give up too soon? Can you try a different method?

> When one door closes, another opens; but we often look so long and so regretfully upon the closed door that we do not see the one which has opened for us.
>
> ~ *Alexander Graham Bell*

Goals fail for many reasons. Here are some of the more common obstacles that might keep you from reaching your goals:

Goals are poorly planned.

Some goals fail because they are poorly planned. They might not be broken into small enough steps. The time frame may have been too short or too long to accomplish the goal. The goal may have relied on something or someone that was beyond your control. It may not have been written down. It may not have been specific enough. The reasons are limitless as to why goals fail. The key is to learn from the failures — and view them as opportunities to grow.

Past failures instill fear.

Elbert Green Hubbard said, *"The greatest mistake you can make is to be continually fearing you will make one."* Do you think that everything has to be perfect, including yourself? Do you feel boxed in by past mistakes, present circumstances or obligations, or by perceived limitations? The longer you stay in one place, the higher those walls seem to be — and the harder they are to knock down.

You have a fear of change.

Fear of failure is a very intense motivator for avoiding goals. You might prefer not to try rather than trying and failing. Fear of change, even positive change, can be just as paralyzing. How many people know they should give up smoking, but are afraid to try? How many people want to change jobs, but don't?

> The only man who never makes a mistake is the man who never does anything.
>
> *~Theodore Roosevelt*

You don't want to leave your comfort zone.

Working toward a goal means doing something new, leaving your familiar comfort zone. This can be a great adventure, but it can also be very scary. According to Julia Sorel, *"If you are never scared or embarrassed or hurt, it means you never take any chances."*

Goals are based on values that aren't yours.

Some of your values don't belong to you. They've been adopted from people you admire: family, friends, co-workers, boyfriends or girlfriends. You have your own set of core values, and those are the ones your goals must be based on. It takes great courage to stand up for your own values and live your life according to your own values, not those of others.

How do I overcome my fears?

"Remember the two benefits of failure. First, if you do fail, you learn what doesn't work; and second, the failure gives you the opportunity to try a new approach," said Roger von Oech. If you see failure as a way to learn, you'll be more willing to take risks. You'll be better prepared to live with the consequences. A good sense of humor is a must. In a difficult situation, humor can help you bond with others and see yourself as a survivor, rather than a victim. Be resilient. Resilient people are aware of what's right about their lives and remind themselves that others have lived through war, famine, and floods — and emerged intact.

When you lose, don't feel like a loser. Don't give up. It's amazing how many people give up at the least inconvenience or obstacle. Don't drown yourself in self-pity. Don't slack off or give less than you're capable of. A setback may be just the push you need to show what you have to offer.

Do I have any limiting beliefs?

Limiting beliefs are thoughts that make you feel helpless and hopeless. They encourage you to give up before you even start. Limiting beliefs ensure that you won't get what you want. A few examples of limiting beliefs include:

> The greatest mistake you can make is to be continually fearing you will make one.
>
> *~ Elbert Green Hubbard*

- I can't do this.

- I can't change.

- They don't care.

- I don't know how.

- I just can't learn this.

- It doesn't matter anyway.

- Life should be fair.

- I can't afford it.

- The future is going to get worse.

When people think negatively, they tend to act in ways that will ensure they don't get what they want. Have you heard of the "self-fulfilling prophecy?" A self-fulfilling prophecy means that *what you think* is *what you get*. If you continually believe that things won't work out — the odds are that they, in fact, won't work out. Limiting beliefs usually work to keep a person safe. You may not get what you want, but you also won't risk failure as long as you avoid trying anything new.

How can I change my limiting beliefs?

Four steps can keep you on track to more positive, empowering beliefs:

Cultivate positive influences.

Hang out with people who are positive. Avoid the negative ones because they drain your energy and drag you down to their level. Positive, action-oriented people, however, bring you up to their level of success. Their passion and enthusiasm will rub off on you.

Read inspirations.
Read something inspiring everyday — a book, a quote, an affirmation. Write in a journal.

Take a step.
Every journey begins with just a single step. If you're depressed, disillusioned, or unmotivated, the best thing you can do is take action. Write that letter. Make that phone call. The longer you wait, the harder it gets. If a task seems overwhelming, don't look at the task as a whole. Break it down into smaller steps. Once you get started, momentum takes over and you'll find it easier to focus on your goals.

Set goals and go after them.
Get past the obstacles and accomplish your goals. If your goal is fuzzy and you're not sure where you want to go, you'll bump into every stone and stump in your path. If, however, you have that goal in front of you, firmly planted in your mind, it will act as a magnet and draw you to it.

 ## How do I solve problems?

If you have a problem that needs to be solved, the first step is to define the problem. What is the real problem? Once you've defined the problem, you can work to resolve it. Break the problem into smaller pieces and solve each piece. Be creative in solving problems. Brainstorm. Explore as many options as you can think of. Don't become so rigid in your thinking that you believe there is

> You
> don't have
> a problem.
> You just have
> a decision to
> make.
>
> ~ Robert Schuller

only one way to solve a problem. Problems by themselves don't defeat people — it's the lack of a solution that defeats them. Ask yourself open-ended questions that require you to think and consider more options. Don't just ask yes/no questions. Make a list of pros and cons about the problem. That is sometimes the best way to make a decision. And trust yourself to solve the problem.

Keep in mind, too, that *not making* a decision *IS* a decision. You decide not to decide. Learn to problem-solve, and then making decisions won't seem so difficult.

 ## Is asking for help a sign of weakness?

Isn't asking for help a sign of weakness?

For some, asking for help is a sign of weakness. For others, it is frightening. Still others want to be independent at all cost. Asking for help, however, really is a very smart thing to do. What stops you from asking for help? Are you afraid someone will refuse? Do you worry that you'll feel obligated to take the advice?

> He who
> asks is a fool
> for five minutes,
> but he who does not ask
> remains a fool forever.
>
> ~ *Chinese Proverb*

Learn to ask for help. Make a list of people you could ask. It's human nature that people like helping people. So, keep this in mind: by not asking, you are robbing someone of the pleasure of helping you. And, if you do ask, what's the worst thing that can happen? They'll say *"no."* So, what? You're still alive. You're no worse off than you were before you asked. But, what if they say *"yes?"* Just think of the possibilities.

What is a mentor?

A mentor is someone who offers guidance, wisdom, experience, and encouragement. A mentor is a good role model, offering vision and insight, advice, support, encouragement, and constructive feedback. A mentor can be a leader who helps develop you into a leader. Mentors are those bigger-than-life people who keep you motivated — and can be anyone: a parent, a sibling, a friend, a teacher, a co-worker, a neighbor. Mentors enjoy helping others achieve their goals.

> People
> seldom improve
> when they have
> no other model but
> themselves to copy after.
>
> ~ *Oliver Goldsmith*

Mentors have been around for centuries. In Homer's *Odyssey*, Odysseus left home to undertake his mythic journey. He asked his trusted friend, Mentor, to act as guardian, teacher, and father-figure to his son, Telemachus, while he was gone.

The success of any mentoring relationship is determined by the level of commitment from both parties. Communication, trust, and honesty are keys to a strong mentoring relationship. You must have a desire to learn and grow. You must have a strong commitment to the mentoring relationship, goals, and personal responsibility. And you must have the ability to listen and follow through with directions.

How do I find a mentor?

Make a list of people you admire and respect. Choose the person you can learn the most from. Call this person and ask if he/she would be your mentor. Give this person the opportunity to help you grow. If the person refuses, don't take it personally. People are busy. Just go to the next name on your list.

Can I be a mentor?

You might already be a mentor. Do young kids look up to you? If so, then you're a mentor. There are many mentoring programs across the country. Big Brothers/Big Sisters of America recently teamed up with First USA to launch a program called *First Mentors* that puts kids with college students. For more information, go to *www.bbbsa.org*.

▶ What is Michael's story?

Michael is the kind of guy you love to hate. He is always in a good mood and always has something positive to say. When someone would ask him how he was doing, he would reply, *"If I were any better, I'd be twins!"* He was a natural motivator. If an employee was having a bad day, Michael was there telling the employee how to look on the positive side of the situation.

Seeing this style really made me curious, so one day I went up to Michael and asked him, *"I don't get it. You can't be a positive person all the time. How do you do it?"* Michael replied, *"Each morning I wake up and say to myself, 'I have two choices today. I can choose to be in a good mood or I can choose to be in a bad mood.' I choose to be in a good mood. Each time something bad happens, I can choose to be a victim or I can choose to learn from it. I choose to learn from it. Every time someone comes to me complaining, I can choose to accept their complaining or I can point out the positive side of life. I choose the positive side of life."*

"Yeah, right. It's not that easy," I protested.

"Yes, it is," Micheal said. *"Life is all about choices. When you cut away all the junk, every situation is a choice. You choose how to react to situations. You choose how people affect your mood. You choose to be in a good mood or a bad mood. The bottom line is that it's your choice how you live your life."*

I reflected on what Michael said. Soon thereafter, I left my job to start my own business. Michael and I lost touch, but I often thought about him when I made a choice about life instead of reacting to it. Several years later, I heard that Michael was involved in a serious accident, falling some 60 feet from a communications tower. After 18 hours of surgery and weeks of intensive care, Michael was released from the hospital with rods placed in his back.

I saw Michael about six months after the accident. When I asked him how he was, he replied, *"If I were any better, I'd be twins! Wanna see my scars?"* I declined to see his scars, but I did ask him what had gone through his mind as the accident took place.

"The first thing that went through my mind was the well-being of my soon-to-be-born daughter," Michael replied. *"Then, as I lay on the ground, I remembered that I had two choices: I could choose to live or I could choose to die. I chose to live."*

"Weren't you scared? Did you lose consciousness?" I asked.

Michael continued, *"The paramedics were great. They kept telling me I was going to be fine. But when they wheeled me into the ER and I saw the expressions on the faces of the doctors and nurses, I got really scared. In their eyes, I read, 'He's a dead man.' I knew I needed to take action."*

"What did you do," I asked.

"Well, there was a big burly nurse shouting questions at me," said Michael. *"She asked if I was allergic to anything. 'Yes, I replied.' The doctors and nurses stopped working as they waited for my reply. I took a deep breath and yelled, 'Gravity.' Over the laughter, I told them, 'I am choosing to live. Operate on me as if I am alive, not dead.'"*

Michael lived, thanks to the skills of his doctors, but also because of his amazing attitude. I learned from him that every day we have the choice to live fully. Attitude, after all, is everything.

~ Author Unknown

 ## Additional Information for this Chapter

Books

- *The Alchemist* by Paulo Coelho

- *Core Transformation: Reaching the Wellspring Within* by Connirae Andreas with Tamara Andreas

- *The Four Agreements: A Toltec Wisdom Book* by Don Miguel Ruiz

- *The Little Engine That Could* by Walter Piper

- *Oh, The Places You'll Go* by Dr. Seuss

- *The Tao of Pooh* by Benjamin Hoff

- *The Te of Piglet* by Benjamin Hoff

- *You Can Make It Happen: A Nine Step Plan for Success* by Stedman Graham

Web Links

- *www.helpmakingdecisions.com*

- *www.mentoring.org*

- *www.topachievement.com*

- *www.peoplesuccess.com*

- *www.nightingale.com*

- *www.incredible-life.com*

- *www.youcanmakeithappen.com*

- *www.bondlife.com*

- *www.attitudeiseverything.com*

- *www.asamanthinketh.com*

- *www.5passions.com*

- *www.dare2believe.com*

- *www.bbbsa.org*
  (Big Brothers/Big Sisters)

- *www.nlpca.com*

- *www.nlpco.com*

- *www.motivatorpro.com*

Do I manage my time well?

Time management means that you manage you — and how you use your time. It means you take time to make time. And, although the term implies it, it does not mean that you manage time — because time cannot be managed. Time is a gift most of us take for granted. We get so caught up getting through each day that we seldom stop to see how we're actually spending this gift.

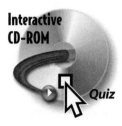

Interactive CD-ROM

Quiz

Have you ever said, "*I don't have enough time?*" The truth is, you do have enough time. There are 24 hours in each day. That's 1,440 minutes each day; 168 hours each week; 52 weeks each year. Are you in need of learning to manage yourself or your time better? Find out by checking YES or NO to the following statements:

Yes	No	
○	○	1. I spend a lot of time catching up on things.
○	○	2. I have free time to enjoy things I like.
○	○	3. I make up excuses often.
○	○	4. I choose how to spend my time.
○	○	5. I value my time.
○	○	6. I talk on the phone a lot.
○	○	7. I write my goals on paper.
○	○	8. I plan my days well.
○	○	9. I ignore interruptions when working.
○	○	10. I socialize with friends when my work is done.
○	○	11. I set deadlines.
○	○	12. I break projects into small, manageable steps.
○	○	13. I ask for help when I need it.
○	○	14. I worry a lot.
○	○	15. I learn from my mistakes.
○	○	16. I celebrate my accomplishments.

continued...

Figure 6A

Time Management

Chapter 6

Time is a gift most of us take for granted. We get so caught up getting through each day that we seldom stop to see how we're actually spending this gift. Time management means that you manage you — and how you use your time. You'll be amazed at how much you'll accomplish once you learn to manage your time.

 ## Where does all my time go?

Why do I need to manage my time and myself?

The biggest benefit of managing your time is that you can be more in control of your life. You'll feel less stress, less pressure, less chaos. You'll feel like you've accomplished something. You'll spend less time trying to catch up on things, less time doing tasks that aren't important. You'll have more energy. You'll succeed more easily because you'll set goals and priorities. And you'll

> There is only one time that is important — NOW! It is the most important time because it is the only time we have any power.
>
> ~ Leo Tolstoy, Russian novelist

...continued

○　○　17. I use a calendar or "To Do" list.

○　○　18. I say *"no"* to others.

○　○　19. I change habits that don't work well for me.

○　○　20. My projects can be imperfect.

○　○　21. I wait until the last minute to do things.

○　○　22. I only say *"yes"* when I mean it.

○　○　23. My home is organized.

○　○　24. I pay my bills on time.

SCORE　Add one point for each YES checked and zero points for each NO.

1 to 6 points　You're out of control and may be feeling a lot of stress right now. You need to learn to take time to make time. Read this chapter — and then read it again.

7 to 12 points　You're slipping — and may be too stressed to enjoy yourself. Read this chapter for ways to begin a plan today to regain control of your life.

13 to 18 points　You manage yourself and your time well — sometimes. With a bit more planning and time-saving techniques, you can accomplish your goals.

19 to 24 points　Good for you! You choose to manage yourself and your time well. You're in control of most situations and are probably meeting your long-term goals.

Figure 6A (continued)

have more free time to do the things you enjoy doing — even if you enjoy doing nothing at all.

How do I spend my time now?

Before you can manage your time, you have to know how you spend it. One of the hardest things to accept about managing your time is accepting the fact that *you* are usually the one who wastes most of it — not someone else.

Interactive CD-ROM

Print It!

First, wear a watch! How will you know how much time you're spending if you don't know what time it is? Second, keep a time log for a week or two to help you determine the activities that waste a lot of your time. Each day, write down the things you do and the time it takes. (Write them down as you do them, not at the end of the day.) Once you're aware of how you spend your time, you can begin to change those things that don't work well. See the sample Time Log on page 204.

Did you do all the things you needed to do? Or wanted to do? Were you rushed or panicked to do something? What was your most productive time of the day? Least productive? What did you spend most of your time doing? Did you waste a lot of time — and, if so, doing what? Were there a lot of interruptions, such as phone calls or friends stopping by? Did you procrastinate a lot? Did you spend a lot of time doing things that didn't really matter?

What is the "money model" of time?

You've heard of what you can do with your money: spend it, save/invest it, or waste it. Well, you can do the same thing with your time: spend it, save it, or waste it. You can also enjoy it. Time differs from money, however, in one very important way: no one has more time than anyone else. You have the exact same amount of time as the Pope, the President, a rock star, and a rocket scientist. And, unlike money, time cannot be accumulated. You cannot earn interest on time — once it's gone, it's gone.

How can I invest my time?

Invest your time in you. Use your time to become accomplished at something (sports, business, dancing, whatever) or in developing specific skills in order to have or do something else. Set goals — and then invest your time to accomplish those goals.

Daily Goals and Time Log

Goals For Today

Write down the activities and goals you have planned. Assign a
Priority rating to each. Note the time each needs to be completed by.

Priority Ratings

1 = Urgent (Does it have to be done today?)

2 = Important (Would you like to have it done today?)

3 = Routine (Does it have to be done today?)

4 = Wasted (Does it have to be done at all?)

Priority	Goal	Completion Time

Time Log for Daily Activity

Log all your daily activity to analyze how you spend your time. Use
the Priority Rating above.

Time	Activity	Minutes / Hours Used	Priority	Comments

Figure 6B

Isn't goal-setting for nerds?

Why should I set goals?

Setting goals is one of the best ways to ensure success — big or small. You have the power to choose whether you'll succeed in your life — or just drift along. Set goals that are important to you. Write your goals on paper. Put the list where you can see it daily. Keep in mind that your goals are not set in stone — you have the right to change them at any time. Write both personal and professional goals, as well as short-term and long-term goals. What do you want to accomplish today, tomorrow, and next week? Where do you want to be a year from now? Do you want to be in school, have a new job, move to a better apartment? What about five years from now? (See Chapter 5, "Dreams and Goals" to learn more about setting your goals.)

How do I know what my priorities are?

Priorities are the tasks that have to be done (work, school, paying bills) — and those that help you reach your goals. Setting priorities means determining what you can do today, tomorrow, or next week to help you accomplish your goals.

For instance, living on your own might be a goal you want to achieve. Paying rent would then be a priority. (Paying rent is something that must be done to accomplish the goal of living on your own.) So, having a steady job would be a priority. What if your friends want to see a movie, but you're supposed to work? Do you go to the movie with your friends or do you go to work? Which one is a priority for you — paying your rent or seeing a movie with friends? (Hopefully, you picked paying your rent. If you go to the movie, the odds are you won't be able to pay rent because you won't have your job for long.)

If you have drop-in visitors, don't hesitate to tell them that you're busy. You can say, *"Sorry, this really isn't a good time for me right now. Can we meet at …?"* Or set a time limit on their visit by saying, *"Thanks for stopping by, but I only have 10 minutes right now."* Do schedule in fun times with your friends, though.

How can I plan my day?

> Dance
> as if no one were
> watching. Sing as if no
> one were listening. And
> live every day as if it
> were your last.
>
> ~ *Irish Proverb*

How can I plan my day?

Planning is the key to a successful life for you. Planning and organizing help you stay in control of your life. Planning saves you time and effort. It helps you make better decisions, accomplish goals, reduce stress, solve problems quickly, avoid frustration, limit crisis situations, and it keeps you from wasting your valuable time on things that don't really matter. Practice the methods below to help you plan and stay in control of your life:

- Keep your end results in mind by staying focused on your goals. Stay motivated and make a commitment to yourself and your goals.

- Ignore interruptions and distractions. Make the task you're doing a priority. Find a place to work or study where you won't be distracted. Turn off the TV, the phone, the friends — whatever might distract you. Plan times to hang out with friends. If they drop by often and unexpectedly, set certain times for them to stop by.

- Set specific and realistic deadlines. Give yourself twice as long as you think you'll need to complete a project. This way you have a goal to reach and the project doesn't continue on aimlessly. Take a break occasionally because it's easy to make mistakes and get burned out when you're tired. And don't wait until the last minute — it only causes stress.

- Break projects or goals into small, manageable pieces. Complete your project one step at a time. If you only look at the whole project without breaking it into steps, it can seem overwhelming — and then it won't get done. Henry Ford once said, *"Nothing is particularly hard if you divide it into small jobs."*

- Ask for help. People enjoy helping other people — so let others help you if you need it. (Keep in mind that the worst thing that can happen if you ask is that they'll say *"no."*)

- Do the toughest tasks when you're mentally alert, not when you're too tired to focus.

● Stop worrying. It wastes a lot of energy — and usually doesn't accomplish much. Trust your intuition — your gut reaction. It's good to think ahead on some things, but sometimes it's good to "wing it." A quick response is sometimes the best solution.

A
stumble
may
prevent a fall.
~ English Proverb

● Learn from your mistakes. Everyone fails. You will fail many times throughout your lifetime. And you will get over it. No one is perfect — so don't be so hard on yourself if something doesn't go quite as planned. Just ask yourself, *"What can I learn from this?"* And forgive yourself. You are, after all, only human.

● Celebrate your accomplishments. Do something fun when you accomplish a goal.

Do I need to use a calendar?

To help you plan your days, weeks, and months, get in the habit of doing the following:

Use a calendar.

Get a yearly calendar with date boxes or lines big enough to write dates and times of work and school schedules, meetings, holidays, appointments, dates with friends, etc. Refer to your calendar daily and weekly to keep track of things that need to be done. (A vast array of calendars and planners are available, ranging in price from inexpensive $2 notebooks to $100 leather planners. Choose the kind that is most convenient and affordable for you.)

Make a daily "To Do" list.

Don't waste valuable brain space trying to remember all the things you need to do. Don't list more than you can accomplish. Highlight those items that are most important for you to accomplish. These are your priorities — and should be done first. Keep your list with you during the day and cross things off as you accomplish them. For items that aren't crossed off your list at the end of the day, reconsider the level of priority. If it's a high priority, can you move it to tomorrow's list? If it's not a priority, can you move it to next week's list — or forget about it? Are you doing too many things for others? If you're not getting things on your list accomplished, why not? Use a daily time log to find out what you're spending your time doing.

Make a weekly "To Do" list.

Get in the habit of planning your upcoming week. On Sunday, refer to your calendar and write down what you need and want to accomplish in the coming week. Keep your weekly list in a place you'll refer to each day. Use this list to help you plan your daily activities, too.

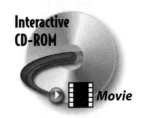

Interactive CD-ROM

Movie

 ### Do I have the power to choose?

You do have the power to choose. In fact, you have the power to communicate to your brain and body a clear picture of what you choose to do, when you choose to do it, and where you choose to start it. Learn to speak to yourself in positive language that focuses on positive results rather than on blame. Do you say the following to yourself:

> Those who make the worst use of their time are usually the ones who complain the most of its shortness.
>
> ~ *La Bruyere*

"I have to …" or *"I should have …?"* These two phrases create negative comparisons for you — from where you are to where you think you should be.

In *The Now Habit: A Strategic Program for Overcoming Procrastination*, Neil Fiore lists the following positive statements that you can choose to say instead of the negative statements:

- *"I choose to …"* instead of *"I have to…"*

- *"When can I start?"* instead of *"I must finish…"*

- *"I can take one small step."* instead of *"This project is so big."*

- *"I am human."* instead of *"I must be perfect."*

- *"I choose to take time."* instead of *"I don't have time."*

The Now Habit: A Strategic Program For Overcoming Procrastination by Neil Fiore. © 1989 by Neil Fiore. (J.P.Tarcher)

▶ Why can't I say "No?"

Do I have the "disease to please?"

Is it hard for you to say *"no?"* Do you end up doing things you really don't want to do? Do you feel guilty declining to do something? The inability to say *"no"* — the "disease to please" — is the main obstacle that keeps people from living the lives they want. Do you avoid saying *"no"* for any of these reasons?

- I don't want to disappoint others.

- I don't want to or know how to deal with the reactions others may have.

- I might regret saying *"no"* later.

- I'm afraid people won't like me.

- I'm afraid people will stop asking me.

- I'm afraid of serious consequences (losing my job or my boy or girl-friend).

- I don't want to make anyone angry.

- I don't want my relationship to end.

- I hate conflict.

- It's easier just to say *"yes."*

Can you guess what the common denominator is in these statements? *Fear.* Fear of hurting others. Fear of disappointing others. Fear of making mistakes. Fear of missing opportunities. If you have trouble saying *"no,"* find out why. Is it for any of the reasons listed above? Once you know what's motivating you to say *"no,"* you can work to overcome your under-lying fears — and have more time for you and your own goals. Think of it this way: saying *"no"* to others means saying *"yes"* to you! The key is to find a balance between honoring your own goals and doing things for those you care about.

Can I learn to say *"no?"*

Yes! You can learn to say *"no."* Keep your own goals and priorities in mind when someone asks you to do something. It's easy to just say *"no"* when your priorities are compelling and keep you motivated. Then *you decide* what you will do and won't do. If you say *"yes"* only to those things that you really want to do, you can avoid feeling frustrated or angry later on when you feel forced to do something you'd rather not do.

If you really want to take control of your life, you *must* learn to say *"no!"* In *Time Management from the Inside Out*, Julie Morgenstern offers the following tips to help you:

- You have a right to say *"no."*

- Be polite and considerate when you say *"no."*

- Be brief. You don't need to go on at length with excuses.

- Get good at saying *"no."* Practice with close friends and family.

  - Practice saying *"no"* out loud until it feels natural.

  - Practice saying *"I'm sorry. I can't."* out loud until it feels natural.

  - To decline an invitation, say something like, *"Thank you for thinking of me. I'd love to attend, but unfortunately, I can't make it."* (That's all you need to say. There's no need to give a reason why.)

  - To decline from doing a task, you might say, *"It sounds like a great project. I'm too busy to give it my full attention right now, but thank you for thinking of me."*

  - To a telephone solicitor, a good response is, *"Thank you for calling, but I'm not interested. Please remove my name from your list."* (Don't be rude, though. The person on the other end of the phone is just trying to earn a living.)

  - If someone keeps insisting, smile and repeat, *"I'm sorry. I can't."* (Don't keep giving excuses. You have a right to say *"no"* — so, just say *"no."*)

- Refrain from letting *"yes"* slip out of your mouth when you really mean *"no."* Tell the person you'll have to think it over first.

Time Management From The Inside Out by Julie Morgenstern.

© 2000 by Julie Morgenstern. Reprinted by permission of Henry Holt and Company, LLC.

 ## Why am I always late?

Are you always late? Have your friends started to make comments about it? Does your boyfriend/girlfriend hate that quality about you? Being late for appointments can become a habit — and it's not one that most people admire. Being late occurs for several reasons: you try to fit a few more tasks in before an appointment; you don't allow enough time to get wherever you're supposed to be; or you're arrogant and think that everyone should wait on you. Whatever the reason, try the habit-changing exercise below before your reputation is harmed. If you believe that showing up early is a waste of time, take something with you that you can do during those few minutes of waiting.

> You delay, but time does not.
> ~ *Benjamin Franklin*

 ## How can I break my bad habits?

How can I break habits that aren't helping me?

Do you have any habits that don't seem to be working for you anymore? Everyone does. You can choose to change those habits you don't like. Experts say it only takes three weeks to break a habit, so choose one habit you have that isn't working — and decide right now to change it.

Complete the following steps from the book, *Time Management Made Easy* by Peter Turla and Kathleen L. Hawkins, to help you break your self-defeating habits:

> We are what we repeatedly do. Excellence, then, is not an act, but a habit.
> ~ *Aristotle*

- Write the habit you want to change.

- Write your goal. Visualize the end result of your goal, not the process of you changing your habit.

- Write measurable results. How will you know when you've reached your goal? How will you measure your results?

- Write all the problems your habit creates for you.

- Write all the benefits you'll experience when you change your habit.

- Write positive statements and affirmations that will help motivate you to change your old habit. Don't let past failures interfere.

- Visually rehearse your new behavior. See yourself the way you want to be.

- Start working on your measurable results — one step at a time. Allow no setbacks. If you see yourself slipping back into the old habit, stop immediately. Take a deep breath and start again with the new habit.

- If necessary, ask others to help you stay on track.

- When you're no longer doing the undesired habit, reward yourself. What an accomplishment for you!

Time Management Made Easy by Peter Turla and Kathleen L. Hawkins.

©1994 by Peter Turla and Kathleen L. Hawkins. (Plume, ISBN 0-452-27202-5) www.timeman.com.

Is there a cheat-sheet I can use?

Print or copy the chart on page 213 to use in breaking habits that you choose to change.

Here's an example for using the habit-changing formula:

1. Habit I want to break: *Having a messy room.*

2. Goal I want to achieve: *My room is clean and organized.*

3. Measurable results: *(1) My dresser and closet are organized. (2) My clothes*

Plan for Breaking Habits

1. Habit I want to break: _____
   _____
   _____

2. Goal I want to achieve: _____
   _____
   _____

3. Measurable results: _____
   _____
   _____

4. Problems my habit creates: _____
   _____
   _____

5. Benefits of changing this habit: _____
   _____
   _____

6. Affirmations that will help me: _____
   _____
   _____

7. Visualize yourself doing the new behavior.

Figure 6C

are put away. (3) The things I don't want are thrown away or given away. (4) My bed is made each morning.

4. Problems my habit creates: *(1) I can't find things. (2) I'm late because I'm looking for my other shoe. (3) I don't know clean clothes from dirty. (4) It's embarrassing.*

5. Benefits of changing this habit:*(1) I can find things. (2) I'll have more time for fun. (3) It's easy to decide what to wear. (4) I feel good having a clean and organized room.*

6. Affirmations that will help me:*(1) I choose to make my bed every morning. (2) I choose to organize my room — one step at a time. (3) I choose to put my clothes where they belong. (4) I have the power to keep my room clean and organized. (5) I have the time to keep my room clean and organized.*

7. Visually rehearse cleaning and organizing your room, and performing your measurable results. See your room the way you want it to be.

Time Management Made Easy by Peter Turla and Kathleen L. Hawkins.

© 1994 by Peter Turla and Kathleen L. Hawkins. (Plume, ISBN0-452-27202-5) www.timeman.com.

Why do I procrastinate?

Do you make up excuses for not doing things? Do you say, *"I'll do it tomorrow?"* Do your personal delay tactics cause serious problems and lots of stress? If so, you're procrastinating. Everyone procrastinates to some extent, but some people procrastinate so much that they get nothing done. In her book, *Success Gems: Your Personal Motivational Success Guide,* Jewel Diamond Taylor lists the following most common reasons people procrastinate:

> Time is the scarcest resource and unless it is managed, nothing else can be managed.
>
> ~Peter F. Drucker

Desire for Perfection

Do you want to wait until you have enough money, lose a few pounds, wait until everybody approves, or wait until you're perfect and know everything?

Fear of Making a Mistake

Do you think you'll look stupid if you fail? Do you want guarantees? Are you a know-it-all? Do you let your image, ego, or pride get in the way? Are you afraid you'll mess up?

Fear of Responsibility

Why can't someone else do it for me? I don't know what to do. I don't know how to do it. It's too hard making decisions. I'm a victim.

Lack of Goals

Whatever happens, happens. I'm not sure what I want. I'll just wait and see.

Lack of Faith, Self-doubt, or Low Self-esteem

Maybe it won't work, so why try? I'm not worthy. I don't think I can do it. I'm not smart/pretty/rich enough.

Lack of Information

I don't know anybody who can help. I don't have time to read or take a class.

Associating with the Wrong People

He/she won't go with me. He/she won't let me. He/she doesn't believe in me. No one I know has been successful.

Reliance on Others to Act or Decide for You

I thought he/she would take care of it. I've never done that before. Can you do it for me?

Trapped in a Comfort Zone

It's not that bad. I'm used to it.

Fear of the Unknown

I don't know what to expect. I like being in control.

Perceive Conflict as Painful

I don't want to "rock the boat." Every time I try something new, I'm attacked or questioned. I don't want to make anyone angry at me.

Success Gems: Your Personal Motivational Success Guide by Jewel Diamond Taylor.

©1999 by Jewel Diamond Taylor. (Quiet Time Publishing, ISBN 1884743-01-3)

Organizing My Home

 Do I keep it, donate it, or trash it?

Interactive
CD-ROM

Movie

Are you a pack rat? Or disorganized? Or indifferent to clutter? Do you have piles of stuff just sitting around on every table, chair, and bookcase waiting for you to do something with them? Organize your home so that everything has a place — and then return everything to its place after you've used it. Even though it can seem like an overwhelming task, there's no need to fear organizing your home. It's as easy as putting together a puzzle. You organize one room (or piece) at a time. And, it's easy to do when you're first starting out since you don't have a houseful of stuff to organize. So, start in the room that's easiest for you — and store things in the room you'll use them in.

What do you do with all that stuff you've collected over the years? Do you keep it, donate it, or trash it? As you start organizing your home, get rid of stuff that's just adding clutter to your life. Throw stuff away — or give it away. If it's not useful or sentimental, why keep it? And never touch anything twice. To help you determine what to keep, ask yourself the following questions:

- When did I use it last?

- Does it work?

- Do I love it?

- Does it have sentimental value?

- What's the worst thing that can happen if I throw it out?

- Can I get another one if I need to?

- If I keep it, where will I store it?

How do I organize my bills?

Organizing your bills is crucial to paying them on time. Put your bills in a pile, and handle all the other mail, including junk mail, only once. Throw the junk mail and paperwork away, act on it, or file it for later use. Designate one space in your home for all your paperwork. (See "Is there an easy way to pay bills?" in Chapter 1 for more information on organizing your bills.)

For a quick and easy system, see The Ultimate Bill Paying Tablet sample on page 49.

 ## How do I organize my home?

Is there an easy way to organize my home?

Picking a place to begin is the first step to organizing your home. Start in the room that's easiest for you, and then move to the next. Sort through each drawer, then each shelf, each closet, etc., and decide what you want to keep, donate, or throw away. As you sort through things, store only those things that you use in that room. If you find something in a room that belongs in another room, just take it to that room and leave it. You'll get to it when you organize that room. (Stick with organizing only one room at a time. It's easy to lose track of what you're organizing if you jump back and forth between rooms.)

Once you have everything sorted, put like items together. You'll need to get containers to store things in — plastic bins, drawer dividers, clothes hangers, shelves, etc. Containers are a key to organizing, but don't get them until you've sorted through everything and know what you'll need. Keep a list of the sizes and types you'll need as you sort through each room — and then go buy them all at the same time.

How do I organize my bedroom?

An easy thing to do is make your bed when you get up. It requires no decision-making on your part — and it's an easy way to start your day feeling like you've already accomplished something. Organize each drawer in your dresser — one drawer at a time. When that's done, move to your closet. Organize each shelf, then the clothes rack, and then your shoes. If you have stuff under your bed, pull it out and organize it, too. (See "Is there an easy way to organize my home?" and "How do I organize my clothes?" for more tips.)

How do I organize my clothes?

When you cut down on the number of clothes you have to choose from, it actually makes finding the right outfit easier. When sorting through clothes, the rule is that if you haven't worn an item in the last two years, you never will. Give it away. Someone else would love to have it. Or throw it away. Hang as many of your clothes as possible, with all like items together: all pants together, all long-sleeved shirts together, all short-sleeved shirts, all dresses. Also hang them by work, play, and dress. For the clothes you fold, again put all like items together in your drawers. Rotate your clothes by season. Get a shoe rack for your shoes, and sort by type. Build inexpensive shelves in your closet, if needed. Also, keep a hamper or laundry basket in your closet for dirty clothes so they don't end up on the floor, the bed, the chair, or wherever. (For more information on donating clothes, see Chapter 14, "Charities and Giving Back.")

How do I organize my drawers?

Start with a single drawer. Empty everything in the drawer and lay it out so you can see it. Make the decision to keep, throw away, or donate each item. Organize the items that you want to keep by category and store together in one place. To stay organized, it is essential that all like items be stored together in the place you use them.

How do I organize my kitchen?

In the kitchen, decide what to keep, throw away, and give away. Then rearrange your cabinets to put all the items you use frequently within reach of where you stand at the counter. Store like items together. Put your glasses near the refrigerator. Spend a few dollars on a silverware organizer and put it in a drawer near your dishes. Put all pots and pans together near the stove. Sort dishes by type and store together. Organize your food cupboards and refrigerator in the same way — like items together.

Another good organizing tip is to keep a notepad and pen on your kitchen counter. When you are running low on something (shampoo, milk, cereal, socks, whatever), write it on the list. Then do your shopping once a week. And when writing a check at a store, fill out all but the amount of the check while you wait to pay the cashier. This will save you, the cashier, and the customers behind you valuable time. Also, get in the habit of returning your shopping cart at the store.

▶ Additional Information for this Chapter

Books

- *It's About Time: The Six Styles of Procrastination* by Linda Sapadin

- *The Now Habit: A Strategic Program for Overcoming Procrastination* by Neil Fiore, Ph.D.

- *Organizing from the Inside Out* by Julie Morgenstern

- *Success Gems: Your Personal Motivational Success Guide* by Jewel Diamond Taylor

- *Take Time for Your Life* by Cheryl Richardson

- *Time Management from the Inside Out* by Julie Morgenstern

- *Time Management Made Easy* by Peter Turla and Kathleen L. Hawkins

- *The Time Trap* by Alec Mackenzie

Web Links

- *www.Dayrunner.com*

- *www.FranklinCovey.com*

- *www.Palm.com*

- *www.Calendar.yahoo.com*

- *www.OfficeDepot.com*

- *www.BedBathandBeyond.com*

- *www.ContainerStore.com*

- *www.GetOrgInc.com*

- *www.Ikea.com*

Interactive CD-ROM

Click to the web from the CD-ROM!

Web Resource

- *www.LillianVernon.com*

- *www.Target.com*

- *www.JulieMorgenstern.com*

- *www.homemadesimple.com*

- *www.timeman.com*

Do I know what it takes?

Relationships are hard work. But, you can develop the skills necessary to have a healthy and happy future with the many relationships in your life: your lover, your parents, your siblings, your friends, your co-workers, your neighbors, and more. How much do you know about basic relationship skills? Answer each statement as True or False.

Interactive CD-ROM

Quiz

T F

1. Hugs stimulate endorphins, the body's natural pain suppressors.
2. Romance doesn't just happen. It has to be planned.
3. By giving a compliment, I make someone feel great & realize that my opinions matter.
4. According to Dr. Phil, I create my own experiences.
5. If I'm not comfortable with myself, I can't be comfortable with others.
6. The waitress was rude — but it's not about me.
7. My happiness is my responsibility — not someone else's.
8. If I marry for money, I'll earn every penny of it.
9. Positive relationship skills include being proactive, appreciative, and honest.
10. A draining relationship might include gossip and complaining.
11. Personal boundaries are like having a fence around my house.
12. One of the best ways to set boundaries is to learn to say "*no*."
13. Words account for only eight percent of my message.
14. How I say my words & my body language tell more about my message than my words.
15. In conversation, I should make eye contact for 5 to 10 seconds before looking away.
16. Most listeners miss 75 percent of what is told to them.
17. Listening is a learned behavior.
18. It is a sign of strength to say "*I'm sorry.*"
19. Just saying "*sorry*" is not an apology.
20. Many men don't apologize because they think it's a sign of weakness.
21. Forgiveness is a gift I give to myself.
22. The person most hurt by holding a grudge is me.
23. The key to being free of past mistakes is to learn the lesson and forget the details.
24. "*Coulda, woulda, shoulda*" will get me nowhere.
25. Conflict can be good for a relationship.
26. Feedback lets a person know how he/she affects me.
27. Life isn't perfect. I'm not perfect. My partner isn't perfect.
28. Anger is only one letter from danger.
29. Just about anyone can learn to do anything.
30. There is no "right" way to grieve.

SCORE   All answers are *True*, so if you scored …

26 to 30 points   You're a good friend! You know that relationships are give-and-take.

21 to 25 points   You're riding the fence. Make a commitment to yourself to learn the keys to a good relationship.

0 to 20 points   You must be a real challenge. Learn the lessons in this section and you'll be on your way to much happier and healthier relationships.

Figure 7A

Relationships

Relationships are hard work. But, you can develop the skills necessary to have a healthy and happy future with the many relationships in your life: your lover, your parents, your siblings, your friends, your co-workers, your neighbors, and more.

Chapter 7

 ## What are the keys to a good relationship?

What are the keys to a good relationship?

- Be committed.

- Keep dating each other, even if you get married.

- Spend time together.

- Do nothing — together.

- Share simple pleasures.

- Say *"I'm sorry."*

- Forgive yourself.

- Forgive others.

- Make and keep promises. Don't make promises you can't or won't keep.

- Take responsibility for your actions.

- Be loyal to those not present.

- Don't jump to (usually wrong) conclusions.

- Be kind.

- Express appreciation and affection.

- Look for the good in each other.

- Be grateful.

- Respect yourself.

- Respect others.

- Validate each other.

- Give compliments.

- Accept compliments.

- Share positive communication.

- Say *"please."*

- Say *"thank you."*

- Send handwritten personal thank you notes for every gift you receive.

- Get off the couch when someone enters the room — and offer a place to sit.

- Hold the door for the person behind you.

- Smile, make eye contact, and repeat the other person's name when you meet.

- Be compassionate.

- Be aware of how your actions affect others.

- Put yourself in another person's shoes.

- Learn empathy (an active process) to perceive and respond to another person's thoughts and feelings.

- Have sympathy (an involuntary feeling) to share another person's fear, grief, anger, or joy.

- Learn to cope with stress.

- Don't take conflict personally.

- Get enough sleep.

- Exercise.

- Laugh.

- Look for humor in any situation.

- Set priorities.

Are hugs good for people?

Yes. Research indicates that hugs increase the supply of oxygen to all the organs in our bodies. Even a simple touch can reduce the heart rate and lower blood pressure. Touch also stimulates the release of endorphins, the body's natural pain suppressors.

Romance just happens, doesn't it?

"If he really loved me, he would know what I like." "I shouldn't have to tell him what to do." So, don't tell. Miss out on all the fun. Keep complaining. Or, get creative. Try to teach him what makes you happy, what you find romantic. Romance has little to do with jewelry, chocolates, roses, and expensive dinners. It's really about the little things you do to tell your partner you care. If you're lacking in the romance department, check out *1,001 Ways to Be Romantic* by Gregory J.P. Godek. Romance doesn't just happen — you have to make it happen. (And, ladies, romance isn't just for you. Find out what makes him happy!)

Should I give compliments?

By giving a compliment, not only will you make someone feel great, you'll realize that your thoughts and opinions matter when you see the other person's face light up. The idea that someone values your opinions makes you value yourself more.

If someone compliments you, don't down-play it. Studies show that 70 percent of women minimize their successes by saying something like, *"Oh, it was nothing."* When you allow yourself to accept a compliment or take credit, you feel a tremendous sense of satisfaction, which motivates you to be even more successful. Plus, you'll come across as capable and self-assured. Make eye contact and say *"thank you"* with a smile. That makes both you and the person giving the compliment feel good.

What are Dr. Phil's Laws of Life?

If you're ready for a bit of honesty about your life, get a copy of *Life Strategies: Doing What Works, Doing What Matters* by Phillip C. McGraw, Ph.D. He's brutally honest — something everyone could use a dose of every now and then. Want to be responsible for your life? Learn Dr. Phil's *10 Laws of Life*:

1. You either get it, or you don't.

2. You create your own experience.

3. People do what works.

4. You cannot change what you do not acknowledge.

5. Life rewards action.

6. There is no reality, only perception.

7. Life is managed; it is not cured.

8. We teach people how to treat us.

9. There is power in forgiveness.

10. You have to name it before you can claim it.

A *Life Strategies* workbook is also available. It provides exercises and self-tests to help change your life.)

Life Strategies: Doing What Works, Doing What Matters by Phillip C. McGraw, Ph.D.
© 1999 by Phillip C. McGraw. (Hyperion, ISBN 0-7868-6548-2)

The Life Strategies Workbook: Exercises and Self-Tests To Help You Change Your Life by Phillip C. McGraw, Ph.D.
© 2000 by Phillip C. McGraw. (Hyperion, ISBN 0-7868-8514-9)

Why do I have to like myself first?

Because if you don't like yourself, you won't trust anyone else to like you. As Eleanor Roosevelt once said, *"Friendship with oneself is all-important because without it, one cannot be friends with anyone else in the world."*

> *It's surprising how many persons go through life without even recognizing that their feelings toward other people are largely determined by their feelings toward themselves.*
>
> *If you're not comfortable within yourself, you can't be comfortable with others.*
>
> ~ Sydney J. Harris

Author Cheri Huber provides a compassionate process for learning to accept yourself exactly as you are, regardless of what you were taught to believe. Her books are fun and easy to read — and full of tremendous insight into what you've been taught to believe about yourself and about life. In *There is Nothing Wrong With You*, she states, *"If you had a person in your life treating you the way you treat yourself, you would have gotten rid of them a long time ago ..."*

Spend some time by yourself and read her books:

- *Be the Person You Want to Find: Relationships and Self-Discovery*

- *The Fear Book: Facing Fear Once and For All*

- *How You Do Anything is How You Do Everything: A Workbook*

- *The Key and the Name of the Key is Willingness*

- *There Is Nothing Wrong With You*

- *There Is Nothing Wrong With You for Teens*

There Is Nothing Wrong With You by Cheri Huber.

© 1993 by Cheri Huber and June Shiver. (Keep It Simple Books, ISBN 0-9636255-0-0)

Should I take "it" personally?

When the checkout clerk is rude to you, it's not personal. It's not that she doesn't like you. She doesn't even know you. You are customer 243 on a busy day. This morning she had a fight with her husband, the dog got out, the school called because her son was in a fight at recess, and when her shift is done, she still has to do grocery shopping. She's having a bad day. It's not personal. So, don't take it personally.

In her book, *Don't Take It Personally: The Art of Dealing With Rejection*, Elayne Savage, Ph.D., provides guidance on learning to *not* take it personally:

- Ask yourself, *"Am I taking this personally?"*

- Ask yourself, *"Am I trying to read someone's mind?"*

- Ask yourself, *"Am I expecting someone to read my mind?"*

- Remind yourself that certain beliefs that seemed true in childhood are not true now.

- Make sure you're not blowing things way out of proportion or over-generalizing.

- Keep reminding yourself that you have choices.

- Empathize — put yourself in the other person's shoes.

- Practice making eye contact.

- Practice saying *"thank you"* to compliments.

- Don't assume — check things out with the other person.

- Create clear boundaries for yourself.

- Practice asking directly for what you want or need.

- Ask about the other person's needs.

- If you're uncomfortable in a situation, you can leave.

- Try rejecting rejection. Just ignore it for a change.

- Don't take it personally.

Don't Take It Personally: The Art Of Dealing With Rejection by Elayne Savage, Ph.D.

© 1997 by Elayne Savage. Reproduced with permission of New Harbinger Publications, Oakland, CA 94605.

1-800-748-6273. www.newharbinger.com. (ISBN 1-57224-077-6)

Shouldn't my partner make me happy?

One of the most common myths about relationships is that your partner is, and should be, the cause of your happiness. This leads to blaming your partner unjustly for your unhappiness. Many who do this feel perfectly justified in criticizing, blaming, or suggesting improvements — but this notion can make life miserable. Most un-

> Most people are about as happy as they make up their minds to be.
>
> ~ *Abraham Lincoln*

happy people are so involved in their relationship struggle that they fail to recognize what they truly want for themselves and that they are responsible for their own happiness.

Happiness comes from within yourself. You have to live from the inside out. Happiness is not produced by what happens to you, but by your perceptions, thoughts, and reactions to the events that happen to you. Finding happiness requires finding ways to gain control over your state of mind — the ultimate source of happiness. Try to maintain balance in your life. And know that you can't be happy all the time. If you can't feel sadness, how will you know happiness?

How do I introduce my partner?

When introducing your partner, say, *"This is Joe, my boyfriend."* If you say, *"This is my boyfriend, Joe,"* you put the description before the name, which demeans the person and implies he/she belongs to you. The description given after the name suggests that Joe is an independent person who is also your boyfriend.

What should I ask before getting married?

On a recent *Oprah* TV program, Dr. Phil McGraw said he'd met a lot of people who had a great wedding — but a lousy marriage. He recommended asking yourself the following questions before getting married:

- Why am I getting married?

- Do I know and trust my partner's personal history?

- Have we spent more time planning our wedding than planning our marriage?

- Am I investing more than I can afford to lose?

- Am I marrying for money? (If so, you'll earn every penny of it.)

What is the Autobiography in Five Short Chapters?

The *Autobiography in Five Short Chapters* was written by Portia Nelson. See the feature on page 229.

Autobiograpy in Five Short Chapters

Chapter One.
I walk down the street.
There is a deep hole in the sidewalk.
I fall in.
I am lost … I am helpless.
It isn't my fault.
It takes forever to find a way out.

Chapter Two.
I walk down the same street.
There is a deep hole in the sidewalk.
I pretend I don't see it.
I fall in again.
I can't believe I am in this same place.
But, it isn't my fault.
It still takes a long time to get out.

Chapter Three.
I walk down the same street.
There is a deep hole in the sidewalk.
I see it is there.
I still fall in … it's a habit … but,
*   my eyes are open.*
I know where I am.
It is my fault.
I get out immediately.

Chapter Four.
I walk down the same street.
There is a deep hole in the sidewalk.
I walk around it.

Chapter Five.
I walk down another street.

There's A Hole In My Sidewalk: The Romance of Self-Discovery by Portia Nelson. ©1993 by Portia Nelson.

Reproduced with permission of Beyond Words Publishing, Inc. (ISBN 0-941831-87-6)

Anything that won't help a relationship?

- Being quick to take offense.

- Holding grudges.

- Continually bringing up past mistakes.

- Avoiding commitments.

- Promising but not following through.

- Talking about others in a negative way.

- Criticizing and complaining.

- Being insincere.

- Being disrespectful.

- Putting people down.

- Acting rude.

- Never apologizing.

▶ Who's most important?

Dr. Joel and Michelle Levy of InnerWork, Seattle, Washington, offer the following thoughts:

1. Name the five wealthiest people in the world.

2. Name the last five Heisman trophy winners.

3. Name the last five winners of the Miss America contest.

4. Name 10 people who have won the Nobel or Pulitzer Prize.

5. Name the last six Academy Award winners for Best Actor and Actress.

6. Name the last decade's worth of World Series' winners.

How did you do? The point is that none of us remember the headliners of yesterday. And these are no second-rate achievers. They're the best in their fields. But, the applause dies. Awards tarnish. Achievements are forgotten. Certificates are buried with their owners. People forget.

1. List a few teachers who aided you in your journey through school.

2. Name three friends who have helped you through a difficult time.

3. Name five people who have taught you something worthwhile.

4. Think of a few people who have made you feel appreciated and special.

5. Think of five people you enjoy spending time with.

6. Name half a dozen heroes whose stories have inspired you.

Easier? The lesson? The people who make a difference in your life are not the ones with the most credentials, the most money, or the most awards. They're the ones who care. (For quotes and writings, visit *www.wisdomatwork.com*.)

 ## What are personal boundaries?

What are personal boundaries?

Personal boundaries are like having a fence around your house. Author Pia Mellody asserts that these symbolic fences serve three purposes:

1. to keep people from coming into our spaces;

2. to keep us from going into the spaces of others; and

3. to give us a sense of wholeness.

A low fence at the property line allows for a flow of energy and ideas between neighbors, yet both know where their rights begin and end. However, if one or the other builds a high wall, a barrier is created and the energy ceases to flow freely. People who build walls instead of boundaries are looking for extra protection, extra security. They don't know how to set good personal boundaries.

What are the types of boundaries?

Poor personal boundaries are often mistaken for personal insults when the boundaries are not respected — by you or by the other person. In her book, *Don't Take It Personally: The Art of Dealing with Rejection*, Elayne Savage, Ph.D. offers several types of personal boundaries that can be violated:

Physical Boundaries
Physical boundaries respect your physical space. They're violated when someone goes into your room, uses your stuff without asking, or reads your letters. They're also violated if someone touches or tickles you when you don't want him/her to or when someone hits you.

Intellectual Boundaries
Intellectual boundaries respect your ideas and thoughts. They're violated when someone tries to discount your thoughts, saying things like, *"You're imagining it."* or *"Do you really think that?"*

Emotional Boundaries
Emotional boundaries respect your feelings. They're violated when someone tries to invalidate or ignore your feelings, takes you for granted, or psychologically abuses you by criticizing, belittling, or shaming.

Social Boundaries
Social boundaries respect your choices of social contact. They're violated when someone criticizes where you go or who you choose to be with. For example, *"Why on earth would you want to go out with **her**?"* or *"Why would you want to see **that** movie?"*

Sexual Boundaries
Sexual boundaries respect your right to privacy and choosing *who* can touch you, as well as *where* and *how* they can touch you. In other words, if you have clear sexual boundaries, no one can touch you without your permission. (Some sexual boundary violations, such as stranger or date rape

are obvious, but others, such as tickling, staring, and leering can be confusing because they're not so obvious.)

Money Boundaries

Money boundaries respect money — how you earn it, spend it, save it, and how much you need to feel a sense of security. There's no question that different attitudes about money can cause relationship problems, especially if the other person's style isn't respected.

Time Boundaries

Time boundaries respect your own and others' ways of getting things done. Some are on time or early for meetings or getting projects done. Others thrive on the excitement of deadlines.

Don't Take It Personally: The Art Of Dealing With Rejection by Elayne Savage, Ph.D.

© 1997 by Elayne Savage. Reproduced with permission of New Harbinger Publications, Oakland, CA 94605.

1-800-748-6273. www.newharbinger.com. (ISBN 1-57224-077-6)

How do I set clear boundaries?

One of the best ways to set clear boundaries is to learn to say *"yes"* and *"no"* very clearly. (See "Can I learn to say 'no?'" in Chapter 6 for more information.)

Am I a good listener?

Am I a good listener?

Most of us are *not* good listeners. We listen at about 25 percent of our potential, which means we ignore, forget, distort, or misunderstand 75 percent of what we hear. Hearing is not listening. To listen effectively, you must hear and select information from the speaker, give it meaning, determine how you feel about it, and respond — all in a matter of seconds. You must also understand the speaker's purpose to know how to listen effectively. Amazingly, research shows that when you communicate, only a small percentage of your message is based on the words you say.

> The greatest motivational act one person can do for another is to listen.
>
> ~ *Roy E. Moody*

Verbal Message

Your verbal message (the words you say) accounts for only eight percent of your message.

Vocal Message
Your vocal message (the way you say the words) accounts for 37 percent of your message.

Visual Message
Your visual message (facial expressions and body language or what people see) accounts for 55 percent of your message.

Any tips for being a good listener?
Listening requires an understanding of what the person is saying. Good listening skills can be learned. The following tips can help:

- Have one conversation at a time. Concentrate on the conversation. Make eye contact and focus on the person speaking. Resist distractions.

- Let others finish talking. Don't interrupt or put words in the other person's mouth. Don't change the subject.

- Show empathy to encourage open and honest communication.

- Listen to what is said, not how it is said. Concentrate on the message, not the speaker. Recognize your own biases.

- Make sure you understand. Repeat, in your own words, what the person said, i.e., *"What you're saying is ...."*

- Know what the other person wants. Why are you talking? Is it small talk, venting, an exchange of information, or to persuade someone?

- Watch body language. Gestures, tone of voice, body posture, and facial expressions may say more than words.

- Don't let emotional "hot button" words throw you. When you hear things that make you mad or upset, try to listen with an open mind.

© University of Nebraska Cooperative Extension and the Nebraska Health and Human Services System.

Should I make eye contact?

Eye contact is very important in communication. Your eyes are the only part of your central nervous system that directly connects with another person. Good eye communication promotes trust, confidence, and respect. When talking to another person, look the person in the eyes for five to 10 seconds before looking away.

Why don't I hear others?

The Writing Lab at Purdue University devised a list of non-listeners. If you really want to listen, make sure you're *not* one of the following:

Mindreader

You hear little as you wonder, *"What is this person really thinking or feeling?"*

Rehearser

Your mental tryouts for *"Here's what I'll say next"* tune out the speaker.

Filterer

You hear only what you want to hear.

Dreamer

You drift off during a face-to-face conversation. You ask, *"What did you say?"* quite often. You are physically present, but "not really there." You are easily distracted and often change the subject without warning. (The daydreamer is the most difficult to communicate with. The best way to get a daydreamer's attention is to talk about his interests.)

Identifier

If you refer what someone says to your own experiences, you probably didn't really hear what was said because your brain is busy recalling your own experiences.

Comparer

You get sidetracked assessing the messenger and miss the message.

Derailer

You change the subject too quickly, which soon tells others you're not interested in anything they have to say.

Sparrer

You hear what's said but quickly belittle it or discount it. You listen to find fault. You listen for all the facts, but are often so critical that you miss "the big picture." You ask demanding questions and take a lot of notes. Your eye contact is limited. You find little time for small talk.

Placater

You agree with everyone and everything you hear just to be nice or to avoid conflict. You listen much more than you talk. You are often shy. You want to please others and keep communications pleasant. When you do speak, you usually keep your opinions to yourself for fear of criticism. You nod your head — but add little to the discussion. (This is *not* good listening.)

Is it okay to criticize?

Criticism is fault-finding. It eats away at the worth of another person. If kept up long enough and hard enough, it will destroy a person, a relationship, a trust. Accept that mistakes will be made — sometimes costly ones — and find ways to correct them. Instead of criticizing others, especially those who are important in your life, consider these suggestions:

- Really listen before you judge.

- Before criticizing, make sure you have a clear picture. It's easy to criticize someone based on a limited understanding of the person's motives or situation. Take time to understand the other person's reality before trying to reshape it to fit your own reality.

- Before suggesting ways to improve, focus your comments on what was done well, even if there's not much to say. Express your respect and concern for the person. Otherwise, negative feedback can come across as a personal attack instead of well-meant advice.

- Suggest ways to improve instead of attacking or criticizing. Be specific and objective. Stay focused on particular issues or behaviors. Avoid the temptation to generalize about a person, whether positive or negative.

▶ What's the difference between men and women?

Let's say a guy named Roger is attracted to a woman named Elaine. He asks her out to a movie. She accepts. They have a pretty good time. A few nights later, he asks her out to dinner, and again they enjoy themselves. They continue to see each other, and after a while, neither one of them is seeing anybody else. And then, one evening when they're driving home, a thought occurs to Elaine — and without really thinking, she says, *"Do you realize that as of tonight, we've been seeing each other for exactly six months?"*

There is silence in the car. To Elaine, it seems like a very loud silence. She thinks to herself, *"I wonder if it bothers him that I said that. Maybe he's been feeling confined by our relationship. Maybe he thinks I'm trying to push him into some kind of obligation that he doesn't want or isn't sure of."*

And Roger is thinking, *"Six months."*

And Elaine is thinking, *"But, hey, I'm not so sure I want this kind of relationship, either. Sometimes I wish I had a little more space, so I'd have time to think about whether I really want us to keep going the way we are, moving steadily toward … I mean, where are we going? Are we just going to keep seeing each other at this level of intimacy? Are we heading toward marriage? Toward children? Toward a lifetime together? Am I ready for that level of commitment? Do I really even know this person?"*

And Roger is thinking, *"… so, this means that it was …. let's see … February when we started going out … which was right after the car was in the shop … which means … lemme check the odometer … I'm way overdue for an oil change."*

And Elaine is thinking, *"He's upset. I can see it on his face. Maybe I'm reading this completely wrong. Maybe he wants more from our relationship, more intimacy, more commitment. Maybe he has sensed even before I sensed it — that I was feeling some reservations. Yes, I bet that's it. That's why he's so reluctant to say anything about his own feelings. He's afraid of being rejected."*

And Roger is thinking, *"... and I'm gonna have them look at that transmission again. I don't care what those morons say. It's still not shifting right. And they better not try to blame it on the cold weather this time. What cold weather? It's 87 degrees out and this thing is shifting like a garbage truck ... and I paid those incompetent thieves $600."*

And Elaine is thinking, *"He's angry. And I don't blame him. I'd be angry, too. I feel so guilty, putting him through this. But I can't help the way I feel. I'm just not sure."*

And Roger is thinking, *"They'll probably say it's only a 90-day warranty. That's exactly what they're gonna say, the scum."*

And Elaine is thinking, *"Maybe I'm just being idealistic, waiting for a knight to come riding up on his white horse, when I'm sitting right next to a perfectly good person — a person I enjoy being with — a person I truly care about — a person who truly seems to care about me. A person who is in pain because of my self-centered schoolgirl romantic fantasy."*

And Roger is thinking, *"Warranty? They want a warranty? I'll give them a warranty. I'll take their warranty and ..."*

"Roger," Elaine says aloud.

"What?" says Roger, startled.

"Please don't torture yourself like this," she says, her eyes brimming with tears. *"Maybe I should never have ... Oh, I feel so ... "* (She breaks down, sobbing.)

"What?" says Roger.

"I'm such a fool," Elaine sobs. *"I mean, I know there's no knight. It's silly. There's no knight and there's no horse."*

"There's no horse?" asks Roger.

"You think I'm a fool, don't you?" Elaine asks.

"No!" says Roger, glad to finally know the correct answer.

"It's just that … It's that I … I need some time," says Elaine.

There is a 15-second pause while Roger, thinking as fast as he can, tries to come up with a safe response. Finally, he comes up with one that he thinks might work. *"Yes,"* he says.

Elaine, deeply moved, touches his hand. *"Oh, Roger, do you really feel that way?"* she says.

"What way?" asks Roger.

"That way about time," says Elaine.

"Oh," says Roger. *"Yes."*

From *Dave Barry's Complete Guide to Guys* by Dave Barry

© 1995 by Dave Barry. Used by permission of Random House, Inc.

 ## Why should I apologize?

Why should I apologize?
Nothing damages a relationship more than the lack of a genuine apology when you've offended a person you care about. An apology has the power to generate forgiveness. If you accidentally bump into someone on the sidewalk, a simple *"Excuse me."* will work. If you do something that attacks another person's self-image, though, a real apology is needed.

Often, people fear that if they accept responsibility, they'll suffer a loss of respect, be shamed, or made to jump through hoops to right the wrong. Some believe that apologizing is a sign of weakness. It isn't. Apologizing is a sign of character and strength. It takes courage to admit wrongdoing. When you apologize, it clears your conscience, prevents the buildup of emotional baggage, and you feel better about yourself.

Is there a right way to apologize?

For an apology to work, the apology must match the offense and it must be done in a timely manner. Admit that you have hurt the other person and take responsibility.

Have the guts to say, *"I was wrong."* When you own up to your act, you show you understand that it violated the trust and respect between you and the other person. Demonstrate that you understand the impact your actions had. (It's important to know how your behavior affected the other person.) Say why you committed the offense. Don't make up an excuse. If something has been lost or broken, replace or mend the item. And commit to acting differently in the future.

Is there a wrong way to apologize?

If you find that you owe someone an apology, avoid the following examples. They are *not* apologies.

- *"Sorry."* (What does that mean?)

- *"I'm sorry you're upset."* (Does this mean you take no responsibility for your act and are trying to make the problem the other person's?)

- *"I'd never intentionally hurt you."* (Are you implying that the other person is too sensitive or misunderstood you?)

- *"I wouldn't have done it if you hadn't ..."* (Are you creating an excuse so you won't have to take responsibility?)

Why is it hard to say "I'm sorry?"

In a recent column, Dr. Joyce Brothers explains the importance of saying *"I'm sorry."* Most women make several apologies each day as a matter of diplomacy. Women tend to view an apology as an effort to save a relationship or resolve a personal conflict before it escalates into something serious. They tend to appreciate receiving an apology more than men do. Men, on the other hand, are more likely to associate apologizing with losing. For many men, it's a sign of weakness rather than strength. In fact, apologies can be a valuable tool for both men and women. When you say, *"I'm sorry,"* you allow the offended party to save face — which in turn allows that person to forgive and forget more easily.

What if someone owes me an apology?

If you feel you are owed an apology, but don't get one, experts suggest that you ask for one. You might say *"I found your behavior offensive"* or *"I was troubled by ...."* If you still don't receive an apology, you may want to rethink the relationship.

How do I let go of past mistakes?

Why is forgiveness a gift to myself?

When you forgive, you replace negative emotions with positive emotions, such as empathy, sympathy, and love. These positive emotions reduce the hostility and negative stress you might feel, which in turn will reduce your risk for heart problems. Forgiveness frees you to live in the present instead of in the past.

> The
> value of
> mistakes
> is to learn from
> them and then
> forget them.
> ~ *Vince Lombardi*

Does forgiving mean forgetting?

In an article entitled *Forgiveness is a Gift You Give Yourself,* Michele Weiner-Davis writes,

> Are you someone who walks around feeling angry with your loved one much of the time? Do you have a little inner voice that constantly reminds you of all of your loved one's wrongdoings? Have you become expert at remembering all the details of past injustices just so you can keep score? Lack of forgiveness imprisons you. It takes its toll on your physical and emotional health. It keeps you stuck in the deepest of relationship ruts. No matter how justified you feel about your point of view regarding your partner's in-

sensitive behavior, you're the one who's miserable. You can't feel joy because you're too busy being angry or feeling disappointed.

You hang on to your belief that, since you feel let down, you must not 'give in.' To you, giving in means forgiving, letting go, making peace. To do so would be like giving up your soul. So, you keep your distance. You interact in unenthusiastic ways, never allowing your partner to step over the emotional line you've drawn. And though the distance often feels intolerable, forgiveness is not on your short list of solutions.

I have worked with so many couples who say they want to heal their relationships. And yet, when they're offered the tools, they can't seem to move forward. These are the couples who, instead of finding effective ways to get beyond blame, continue to repeat their mantra, *'Our problems are your fault and you must pay.'* As long as they maintain this mindset, they are doomed to failure. How very sad.

If any of this strikes a cord with you (you wouldn't be reading this if it didn't), you need to internalize that *Forgiveness is a gift you give yourself.* Letting go of resentment can set you free. It can bring more love and happiness into your life. It opens the door to intimacy and connection. It makes you feel whole. Forgiving others takes strength, particularly when you feel wronged, but the courage required to forgive pales in comparison to the energy necessary to maintain a sizable grudge.

*The person most hurt by holding out or blaming is **you**, no matter what the circumstances.*

*"All this sounds good, "*you tell yourself, *"but how can I ever forget what my partner did to me?"* Good question. You don't! *Forgiveness is not the same as forgetting.* You will probably remember the particular injustice(s)

that drove you into your corner. When you forgive, the intense emotions associated with the event(s) begin to fade. You will feel happier, lighter, more loving. And these renewed positive feelings won't go unnoticed. Others will be drawn to you.

Forgiveness isn't a feeling. It's a decision. You decide that you are going to start today with a clean slate. Even if it isn't easy, you make the determination that the alternative is even harder and that you are going to do what you must to begin creating a more positive future. So promise yourself, that no matter what the reason, you will not go another day blaming your partner and feeling lonely. Make peace. Make up. (Visit *www.divorcebusting.com* for more information.)

Do I dwell on the past?

Do you allow yourself to dwell on the past, especially over mistakes made long ago? Do you realize that it is your choice to waste precious energy on something you cannot change? It's much healthier to just accept what you do, make appropriate apologies or changes, and let it go. The truth is that "crying over spilled milk" not only wastes time and diminishes self-esteem and self-confidence, it also cuts into future successes. When you obsess over past blunders, you call up the same negative emotions you experienced the first time around, which in turn re-creates the stress and distress that resulted. To lessen those emotions, go to "Can I change how I think?" If you find yourself chronically unhappy and stuck in the past, it may be time to seek professional help.

The key to being free of past failures and mistakes is to learn the lesson and forget the details. What are the payoffs that keep you stuck in the past? People repeat certain actions because they're getting something out of it. It might be comfort, soothing memories, anxiety reduction, attention, or any of a thousand motivations that reinforce behavior. Unfortunately, these payoffs aren't always good. If you can identify what keeps you stuck, you can change and move on.

What's wrong with *"coulda, woulda, shoulda"*?

"Coulda, woulda, shoulda" will get you nowhere. Berating yourself isn't going to change or improve what has already happened. Just accept it —

and move forward. You can use your energy worrying about small things — or move forward to what's really important in your life. Choose to do something now instead of wishing you *"coulda, woulda, shoulda ..."*

 ## How do I resolve conflicts?

> You cannot control anyone by yelling at them any more than you can control a car with its horn.
>
> ~ *Author Unknown*

Is conflict good for a relationship?

Conflict itself is not bad, but if it doesn't serve a purpose or solve a problem, it can cause chaos and disruption. Partners that don't have any conflict probably ignore issues that need attention. This doesn't mean partners always need to have conflict in order to have a strong relationship. It does, however, mean that a strong relationship can handle conflict and that some conflict is normal. There should be no losers with partner conflict. You want to support each other and build each other up — even through conflict. Neither partner should always get their way; nor should either partner always give in to the other. Rather, compromise and negotiation are necessary for building respect, showing love, having a caring relationship, and nurturing trust between partners. Relationships are not destroyed by working toward a mutually-agreeable solution to a conflict. They can actually be enhanced.

How do I resolve conflict?

First, don't ignore something that bothers you. Work on the issue involved before the situation becomes intolerable. Talk directly to the other person involved. Be sure there is a real problem and that you aren't just in a bad mood. Before approaching the other person, identify the specific issue or opportunity, not just the symptoms or personalities.

Be prepared to work toward a mutually-agreeable solution. Establish a common goal and stay focused on it. Look for a "win/win" solution. Is there a way you and the other person involved can both "win?" Put yourself in the other person's shoes. What do you think is going on with that person? Be willing to "own" your part of the problem. Avoid thinking that "it's not my problem." At the end of the discussion, summarize what has been decided and who will take any next steps.

Pick your battles carefully. (You remember the story of the *Little Boy who Cried Wolf?*)

If someone approaches you with an issue, be willing to work on it. If someone complains to you about another person, encourage him/her to talk directly with the other person. This approach is much more positive and discourages the perpetuation of rumors, gossip, and false information.

Am I a fair fighter?

How do you handle conflict? How do you treat each other when you fight or disagree? How often do you fight? What behaviors or patterns have you seen emerge? Are you proud of the way you handle yourself? Do you share your true feelings or do you give in too much? Do you try to bully your partner into doing the things you want done? Is there equality in your relationship and in the way you resolve conflict? Do you feel closer after you have dealt with some conflict? Do you find alternative solutions if you can't agree on something? Do you basically feel good about the decisions you make?

Life isn't perfect. You're not perfect. Your partner isn't perfect. With that in mind, practice the following guidelines when resolving conflicts:

- Allow for mistakes.

- Deal with the current situation.

- Talk rationally.

- Look at both sides.

- Allow some time to deal with the conflict or problem.

- Take time to cool down.

- Determine the main cause of the conflict.

- Have mutual respect for each other.

- Be willing to share your feelings.

- Listen to the other person.

- Ask for your partner's opinions.

- Care about your partner's feelings.

- Stand your ground for beliefs and values you hold dear — but be willing to listen to the other side.

- Fight only over the things that really matter.

- Take care of yourself.

- Get enough sleep.

- Exercise.

- Eat healthy foods.

- Have a friend or counselor to talk to.

- Be honest.

- Tackle the problem and not each other.

- Don't bring up the past.

- Don't put each other down.

- Don't de-value each other.

- No name-calling.

- No swearing.

- No yelling.

- Don't withhold discussion or affection.

- Control your temper.

- Don't get physical.

- No verbal abuse.

- Get help from a third party, if needed.

Should I give feedback?

Feedback lets a person know how he/she affects you. Used properly, it can be a helpful tool for improving behaviors. Follow these guidelines:

- Describe the other person's behavior. Don't judge it. Describe your own reaction to the behavior. Avoid "judging" language so the other person won't feel so defensive.

- Use specific terms, not general ones. Discuss a particular incident, not *"You always ... "*

- Consider the needs of the other person, as well as your own needs. Feedback can be destructive when it serves only the needs of the person who gives it and fails to consider the needs of the person who receives it.

- Discuss behavior that the other person can do something about. Frustration is only increased when a person is reminded of some shortcoming over which he/she has no control.

- Feedback is more effective when requested, rather than when it is "dumped" on someone. The person who requests feedback is more likely to appreciate it.

- Give feedback as soon as possible after the behavior has occurred. Feedback is most useful and has the greatest impact when it follows the behavior in a timely fashion. However, you may sometimes want to wait to calm down or avoid embarrassing the person in front of others.

- Check to make sure what you said is clear. After you've given your feedback, ask the other person to rephrase what you said. If it is unclear, restate it in a manner that is better understood.

Is my anger a problem?

One out of five Americans has an anger-management problem. Some of the ones we hear about everyday include domestic abuse, road rage, workplace violence, divorce, and addiction. The problem isn't anger, though. Anger is a natural human emotion. It's the mis-management of anger that causes a majority of the conflict in our personal and professional relationships. Most people can use their anger in appropriate ways in some situations — and still be out of control in others.

> Anyone can become angry — that is easy. But to be angry with the right person, to the right degree, at the right time, for the right purpose, and in the right way — this is not easy.
> ~ *Aristotle*

In a recent Harvey Mackay column, the following tips were given to help control your anger:

- Acknowledge your anger. Don't pretend it isn't there or ignore it, hoping that it will go away.

- Don't look for slights. If a co-worker doesn't acknowledge you in the hallway, it may simply mean he/she is racing to get to the bathroom. Don't take things personally. It's not about you!

- Know what is provoking you. If you have had a fight with your partner, leave your baggage at home. If you're under pressure on a project, don't take it out on a co-worker.

- Don't get angry just because someone else is. If your co-worker is mad at something or someone, it doesn't mean you have to be angry, too.

- Be aware of your anger signals. Anger reveals itself physically through a racing pulse, shortness of breath, or pacing. Read the signs before your anger gets out of control.

© Harvey Mackay. Reprinted by permission of United Feature Syndicate, Inc.

Am I responsible for what I do?

Tempers flare when people are too rushed, too stressed, or just too self-centered. However, you're responsible for what you do, no matter how you feel. According to Sydney J. Harris, *"You*

> Mackay's Moral: Anger is only one letter from danger.

have not passed that subtle line between childhood and adulthood until you move from the passive voice to the active voice — that is, until you stop saying, 'It got lost' to 'I lost it.'" If you allow someone to make you angry, they win. You control your attitude or it controls you. How people treat you is actually more a reflection of how they feel about themselves than what they think of you.

 ## Are religion and spirituality the same thing?

(Contributed by Tammy L. Young)

Religion and spirituality are personal choices. The information in this section is intended for informational purposes only. It is not included to encourage nor discourage religious beliefs.

What is religion?

Religion is the thread that connects mankind by uniting people in their desire to understand eternity and the mystery of life. It is a worldwide phenomenon that has played a part in all human culture. There are many religions throughout the world, with the four largest briefly described below:

Buddhism

Buddhism developed in India during late 500 B.C. from the teachings of a prince who became known as Gautama Buddha — the "enlightened one." Buddha taught that people should devote themselves to finding release from the suffering life. Through this release, people will gain "Nirvana," a state of perfect peace and happiness. Buddha proclaimed the Four Noble Truths:

1. Life is sorrow.

2. Cause for sorrow is craving.

3. Removing the cause of craving will end the sorrow.

4. The way that leads to the ending of sorrow is the noble Eight-Fold path.

Christianity

The Christian religion is founded on the teachings of Jesus of Nazareth, the Messiah, as foretold by prophets of the Old Testament. This was from the 4th century B.C. to 29th century A.D. Qualities taught and demonstrated by Jesus Christ are love, kindness, and tolerance. Christianity has many different orders, including Jesuits, Methodists, Mormons, Protestants, Roman Catholics, and others.

Islam

Followers of Islam are called Muslims. "Allah" in Arabic means "God," the same God that Christians and Jews worship. Muslims believe the faith of Islam began to take shape when Allah spoke to the prophet Muhammad in the year 610. Allah's messages to Muhammad were collected and became the Qur'an, the holy book of Islam. Muslims follow the Five Pillars of Islam:

1. There is only one God, and Muhammad is his messenger.

2. Prayer five times a day.

3. Charitable giving.

4. Fasting during daylight hours of Ramadan, the holy month.

5. Pilgrimage to Mecca, in Saudi Arabia, the holiest place on Earth for Muslims, at least once in your lifetime.

Judaism

Judaism began among the ancient Israelites in the Middle East. Jewish tradition traces the roots of the religion back to Abraham, who lived between 1800 and 1500 B.C. His grandson, Jacob (also called Israel), had 12 sons. They founded the 12 tribes that became Israelites. Jewish tradition says that the great lawgiver Moses received from God the first five books of the Bible. Judaism was the first religion to teach the belief in one God.

What is spirituality?

Spirituality is a belief that the spirit is associated with the mind and feelings as distinguished from the physical body. In a religious sense, one believes that his soul pertains to God and is the essential nature of a person. Some people consider themselves spiritual, but not religious. Again, it's a personal preference.

What is faith?

Faith, simply put, is about hope and trust. It's about believing. Reason has limits — faith has no limits. Faith sees the invisible, believes the incredible, and receives the impossible. Faith is believing what one cannot prove.

Can I change HOW I think?

What is NLP?

NLP, Neuro-Linguistic Programming, is about communications and language and how our brains "code" our experiences. NLP helps you understand how your brain makes distinctions so that it's easier to make changes, to learn, and to communicate effectively. *"Neuro"* refers to your mind and how you organize your mental life. *"Linguistic"* refers to language — how you use it and how it affects you. *"Programming"* refers to your sequences of repetitive behavior and how you act with purpose.

So, when an experience is sorted out at the linguistic and neurological levels, procedures and techniques can be created that allow you to change the structure of your experience and run your own brain — freeing you from old habits, fears, and limiting beliefs. NLP offers a structure of new and empowering ways of being in the world.

NLP began in the early 1970s with the work of Richard Bandler and John Grinder, who studied the language and behavior patterns of people who excelled in their fields, modeled those patterns, and taught them to others.

Do you assume the way you see things is the way they really are or the way they should be? You see the world, not as it is, but as you are — or as you are conditioned to see it. NLP offers you more choices in how you respond, feel, and communicate. If you have more options, you can make better decisions. For more information, contact these NLP trainers:

- Anchor Point Institute, (800) 544-6480, *www.nlpanchorpoint.com*

- NLP Comprehensive, (800) 233-1657, *www.nlpco.com*

- NLP Institute of California, (800) 767-6756, *www.nlpca.com*

- NLP University, (831) 336-3457, *www.nlpu.com*

- Success Skills, (800) 775-3397, *www.nlpok.com*

What are NLP pre-suppositions?

A pre-supposition is an assumption. For example, if someone asks what you're majoring in, they're pre-supposing that you attend college. Of the pre-suppositions listed below, are there any that you could use in your everyday life?

If what you're doing isn't working, do something else.
If you always do what you've always done, you will always get what you've always gotten.

The meaning of your communication is the response you get.
Communication is not about what you intend or about saying the right words — it's about creating an experience in, and getting a response from, the listener.

People always make the best choices available to them at the time.
But often there are lots of other "better" choices. NLP can make you aware of these other choices.

Just about anyone can learn to do just about anything.
If one person can do something, it is possible to model it and teach it to anyone else.

People already have all the resources they need.
What they need is access to those resources at appropriate times and places.

There is no such thing as failure, only feedback.

Anything can be accomplished if broken into small enough pieces.

We are all responsible for creating our own experiences.
Even when challenging events occur that you can't control, you're responsible for your responses. Typically, however, you have much more control than you think you have.

Can I change HOW I think?

Here's a simple NLP exercise that demonstrates how you can change your feelings and behaviors by changing *how* you think:

1. Find a comfortable chair to sit in. Lean back, close your eyes, and think of a pleasant experience you've had. Focus on the part of the

experience that was really pleasant for you. It might be something that you do often or it might be a special event.

2. Try bringing the experience closer to you. What happens? Make it bigger. Make it bright in color. Now, how do those changes make you feel about the experience?

3. Move the image far away from you. Make the image dull, gray, and small. How do those changes make you feel about the experience?

4. Put the brightness, closeness, and color back into the image the way you like so that you leave that memory as pleasant as you like.

Did your feelings change when you changed the color, brightness, distance, and size of the image? This exercise works for both pleasant and unpleasant experiences. If you have an unpleasant memory, you can adjust *how* you think about that memory by repeating the above four steps. (This might be a helpful technique if you're struggling with forgiveness.)

How does language affect me?

Try this NLP exercise:

> *Don't think about a purple cow with green polka dots.*

What did you do? Did you think about a purple cow with green polka dots? You weren't supposed to. Most people do think of the cow — and then try really hard *not* to think of it.

In order to make sense of the words, our brains have to recall an experience of the very thing that it is being asked *not* to do. Telling someone what *not* to do may actually increase the likelihood of the action. For example, *"Don't spill the milk."* may result in spilling the milk. *"Don't fall."* may result in falling. *"Don't be late."* may result in being late. Use your language in a clear and easily understood manner, such as *"Be here by nine."* instead of *"Don't be late."*

Is there an easy way to remember names?

NLP trainers Tim Hallbom and Suzi Smith developed an NLP strategy for remembering names. The strategy is based on the way people learn and recall information: through sight, sound, and touch.

Sound

Concentrate on listening to the person. Repeat the person's name to yourself three times while looking at him/her. Avoid having conversations in your head about what to say, etc.

Sight

Imagine seeing the person's name written on his/her forehead. You might even try seeing the name in your favorite color. Do this while saying the name to yourself three times.

Touch

Imagine letting your finger write the person's name on their forehead in your favorite color. Do this while you're saying it to yourself and seeing it on the person's forehead.

 ## What can I say to someone who's grieving?

> There
> is not enough
> darkness in the world
> to put out the light of
> just one candle.
>
> ~ *Author Unknown*

Is there a right way to grieve?

Grief is normal and essential — and there is no "right way" to experience it. It is an individual process and everyone's experience is different. Grief is a life-long process. There are several stages of grief that most people experience. You may not experience them in the same order or for the same amount of time as someone else. Common stages of grief include shock, confusion, denial, depression, loneliness, isolation, bargaining, anger, guilt, and acceptance. You can go from one stage to another and then back again. And you can get stuck anyplace along the way.

Keep in mind, too, that any time there's a loss in one's life, there is a grieving process. Whether you lose a loved one, a pet, a job, your health — you will experience a sense of loss. Just know that the emotions you feel are part of this process.

What are the stages of grieving?

Grief is a life-long process. There are several stages of grief that most people experience — and you may not experience them in the same order, or for the same amount of time, as someone else. Common stages of grief include shock, confusion, denial, depression, loneliness, isolation, bargaining, anger, guilt, and acceptance.

Will I ever feel joy again?

If you're struggling with the loss of a loved one, read *Awakening from Grief: Finding the Road Back to Joy*, an insightful book written by John E. Welshons. It will show you that even in sorrow, there are opportunities for joy. In his *Foreword*, he writes,

> *The losses in our lives are the hardest things we have to face … A loved one dies … A relationship ends … We lose a job, a friend, a treasured dream … A child is ill … We lose our physical health, or ability … And … Our world is turned upside down.*
>
> *We lose our bearings. We lose our joy. We lose our security. We no longer know who we are. We no longer know what our life is about. We no longer trust. We long for something to take away the pain … to change the circumstance … to bring back the one we love … to return us, and our lives, to wholeness.*
>
> *For many of us, the question is, "How do I begin again? How do I find happiness?" For others, the only real question is, "When will this pain end?"*
>
> *If we can look at the losses in our lives a little differently … if we can change our perspective just slightly … we may see that within this experience lie the seeds of a new beginning … of a new life … of a deeper experience of love and fulfillment than we ever imagined possible.*
>
> *We may see that … When our heart is broken … It is also wide open.*
>
> *We may find that … No matter how devastat-*

ed we feel ... There is still boundless joy to be found in our heart.

Awakening from Grief is about changing perception ...It is about healing the losses we have already experienced, and preparing for the inevitable losses to come. It is about learning to see the pain of loss as a gift ... A gift we didn't ask for ...

But ... Here it is. Loss is an inevitable part of being human. And our choice is either to remain in pain and bitterness ... Or ...To learn how to use this experience to grow into a richer, more fulfilling life.

In that sense, loss is a gift ... A gift that can help us uncover the extraordinary LOVE we always hoped, but never dared imagine, is within us. It is about finding JOY again."

Awakening From Grief: Finding The Road Back To Joy by John E. Welshons.

© 2000 by John E. Welshons. (Open Heart Publications, ISBN 1-928732-57-7)

Do I need professional help?

Most people work through the grieving process in a year or two, and then move on with their lives. Some people may get stuck in one phase of grief, or suffer so terribly that they cannot function. Contact your healthcare provider for professional help immediately if you experience any of the following signs:

- Thoughts of suicide.

- Continually withdrawing and avoiding others.

- Neglecting basic needs for food and rest.

- Persistence in one phase of grief.

- Insomnia or sleeping too much.

- Inability to function at a basic level.

- Inability to stay alone.

- Panic or chronic fear.

- Inability to make decisions.

- Unwillingness to talk about anything but your loss.

- Abuse or continued dependence on tranquilizers, sleeping pills, or alcohol.

What can I say to someone who's grieving?

In her book, *I Will Remember You*, Laura Dower offers several *appropriate* things to say when someone is grieving:

- I'm sorry for your pain.

- What was your relationship like?

- I'm sorry. How can I help?

- I just don't know what to say.

- I'm here if you need to talk or cry.

She also offers a list of *inappropriate* things to say:

- I understand how you feel.

- You'll get over it.

- He lived a full life.

- You must be strong.

- It was the will of God.

- Don't cry.

- You shouldn't get angry.

- Be brave.

- She is better off where she is now.

- Move on. Get on with your life.

- At least he's no longer suffering.

- Just be patient.

- Don't you think you should be over your grief by now?

- You need to be active and get out more.

- You're young. Be thankful for that.

- Quit feeling sorry for yourself.

- Why are you so upset that she died. You didn't even like her anyway.

- You're doing such a wonderful job.

- There must have been a reason.

I Will Remember You by Laura Dower. © 2001 by Laura Dower. (Scholastic, Inc., ISBN 0-439-13961-9)

What can I do for someone who's grieving?

If someone you know is recovering from a loss, stay in touch, even if it's just to say *"hello."* Don't drift away. Be the friend you were before. Bring over a meal. Offer to take care of some chores, such as grocery shopping or laundry. See a movie together. Offer to listen. When someone you know suffers a loss, your condolences do make a difference. No, you can't take the pain away, but acknowledging it — in a letter, on the phone, or in person — will help your friend know that you care and that he or she is not alone.

If you're struggling for the right words, focus on the personal. Mention anything you remember about the deceased, even something funny.

Search your memory even if you didn't know the person very well. Avoid assumptions. In other words, don't say, *"I know how you feel."* Be careful of comforting phrases that may trivialize the loss, such as, *"You'll get over this soon."* Show empathy and caring instead. If you've been out of touch, write or call anyway. Your friend needs all the love and support he or she can get. Lastly, realize it's not your job to try and explain tragedy or loss.

For a list of appropriate and inappropriate words to say, go to "What can I say if someone's grieving?"

 Additional Information for this Chapter

Books

- *Awakening from Grief: Finding the Road Back to Joy* by John E. Welshons

- *Boundaries: When to Say YES, When to Say NO, To Take Control of Your Life* by Dr. Henry Cloud and Dr. John Townsend (Workbook available)

- *The Dark Side of the Light Chasers* by Debbie Ford

- *Hope for the Flowers* by Trina Paulus

- *The Language of Letting Go* by Melody Beattie

- *Life Strategies: Doing What Works, Doing What Matters* by Phillip C. McGraw, Ph.D. (Workbook available)

- *O, the Oprah Magazine* (To subscribe, write O Magazine, PO Box 7831, Red Oak, IA 51591-2831)

- *101 Nights of Grrreat Romance* by Laura Corn

- *The Seat of the Soul* by Gary Zukav

- *There is Nothing Wrong With You* by Cheri Huber

- *Tuesdays with Morrie* by Mitch Albom

- *Why We Pick the Mates We Do* by Anne Teachworth

Web Links

- *www.oprah.com*

- *www.philmcgraw.com*

- *www.cherylrichardson.com*

- *www.about.com*

- *www.divorcebusting.com*

- *www.carycounseling.com*

- *www.nlpanchorpoint.com*

- *www.nlpca.com*

- *www.nlpco.com*

- *www.apa.org/pubinfo/anger.html*

- *www.grief-recovery.com*

- *www.1000deaths.com*

- *www.add.ca/grieving*

Lessons from Geese

Geese flying in V-formation have always been a welcome sign of spring, as well as a sign that heralds the coming of winter. Not only is this a marvelous sight, but there are some remarkable lessons that we can learn from the flight of the geese — because all that they do has significance.

1. As each goose flaps its wings, it creates an uplift for others behind it. There is 71 percent more flying range in V-formation than in flying alone.

   Lesson: People who share a common direction and sense of purpose can get there more quickly.

2. Whenever a goose flies out of formation, it feels drag and tries to get back in position.

   Lesson: It's harder to do something alone than together.

3. When the lead goose gets tired, it rotates back into formation and another goose flies at the head.

   Lesson: Shared leadership and interdependence give us each a chance to lead as well as an opportunity to rest.

4. The geese flying in the rear of the formation honk to encourage those up front to keep their speed.

   Lesson: Encouragement is motivating. We need to make sure our "honking" is encouraging — not discouraging.

5. When a goose gets sick or wounded and falls, two geese fall out and stay with it until it revives or dies. Then they catch up or join another flock.

   Lesson: We may all need help from time to time. We should stand by each other in difficult times.

~ Lessons from Geese was transcribed from a speech given by Angeles Arrien at the 1991 Organizational Developmental Network, based on the work of Milton Olson.

How much do I know about sex?

Interactive CD-ROM

Quiz

Test your Sex IQ.
Answer the following as True or False.

T   F

○ ○   1. Abstinence means choosing not to have sex.

○ ○   2. Abstinence provides 100 percent protection against pregnancy.

○ ○   3. Depo-Provera, a contraceptive injection, is a shot given every three months.

○ ○   4. Norplant, inserted in a woman's arm, can prevent pregnancy up to five years.

○ ○   5. The Pill must be taken every day at the same time to be effective.

○ ○   6. An IUD is not recommended for young adults.

○ ○   7. A male condom can only be used once.

○ ○   8. A female condom should not be used with a male condom.

○ ○   9. A diaphragm must be fitted and prescribed by a healthcare provider.

○ ○   10. A cervical cap can be worn for up to 48 hours.

○ ○   11. Vaginal spermicides are only 74 percent effective when used alone.

○ ○   12. Natural planning requires high motivation on the part of the couple.

○ ○   13. "Withdrawal" does not prevent pregnancy.

○ ○   14. The "morning-after pill" must be taken within 72 hours of unprotected sex.

○ ○   15. A vasectomy is a permanent form of contraception.

○ ○   16. One in five Americans has a sexually-transmitted disease (STD).

○ ○   17. Chlamydia can cause infertility in women.

○ ○   18. Gonorrhea can be treated and cured.

○ ○   19. Syphilis, if left untreated, can affect my heart, brain, or other vital organs.

○ ○   20. Genital herpes is not curable.

○ ○   21. Genital warts are not curable.

○ ○   22. HIV/AIDS is the most serious STD. It can kill me.

○ ○   23. If I have an STD, all my former sex partners must be told.

○ ○   24. I can get STDs from oral sex.

○ ○   25. Raising a baby for 18 years costs more than $100,000.

○ ○   26. If I'm pregnant, I have three options: keep the baby, adoption, abortion.

○ ○   27. If I give the baby up for adoption, I can choose the adoptive parents.

○ ○   28. The father of a child can be legally forced to pay child support.

○ ○   29. Whenever force is used to have sex, it's rape, even if I know the person.

○ ○   30. Hitting another person is never okay.

SCORE   The answers are all *True*, so if you scored ...

26 to 30 points   Way to go! You paid attention in Sex Education class.

16 to 25 points   You need a refresher course. Continue with this chapter.

0 to 15 points   Stay out of the back seat of the car! Read this chapter ...
and then read it again. Luck is never on your side when it comes to sex.

Figure 8A

Sex

Entering a sexual relationship involves all parts of who you are — not just your body. Your emotions, your relationships, and your future can be affected by the choices you make. Know how to keep yourself safe and how to make decisions that leave you in charge of your life.

The information in this chapter is intended for informational purposes only. It is not all-inclusive and cannot substitute for professional medical guidance and treatment.

The medical community has recently changed the term STD to STI. STD refers to sexually-transmitted diseases, while STI refers to sexually-transmitted infections. The term STD will be used throughout this chapter as a reference for both STDs and STIs.

 ## What is abstinence?

What is abstinence?

Abstinence is choosing *not* to have sex. It is a voluntary choice. You can choose to be abstinent at any time in your life — even if you've already had sex. The definition of abstinence is different for everyone. To some it means no sexual touching except kissing and hugging. To others, it means some sexual touching. And some may consider abstinence to be everything except sexual intercourse. It's a personal decision to make and should be based on what you're comfortable with.

What are the benefits of abstinence?

Abstinence is safe. There are no side effects. And it is the most fool-proof means of birth control. Abstinence provides 100 percent protection against pregnancy and STDs, including HIV/AIDS — if no semen, vaginal secretions, or blood are exchanged. Abstinence can also give you and your partner time to know and trust each other.

What type of contraception is best for me?

How do I choose a method of birth control?

Today there are many forms of contraception available to men and women. Any method of contraception can be effective in preventing pregnancy if used carefully, correctly, and con- sistently. The condom, however, is the *only* method that prevents you from getting sexually-transmitted diseases (STDs) or sexually-transmitted infections (STIs), and can be used with other methods of contraception. Contraception does not have to be a bur- den, so when choosing a method, ask yourself the following questions:

- How important is it that I definitely avoid pregnancy? (Men need to ask this, too.)

- Is it easy to use?

- How safe is it?

- How convenient is it?

- Does it fit my lifestyle and sexual habits?

- Will I use it consistently?

- What is my partner's preference?

- What is the cost?

- Do I have any health concerns that would prevent me from using this method?

- Do I want to have children in the future?

What are the hormonal methods of contraception?

Hormonal methods include injections, implants, the Pill, the Patch, the vaginal ring, and the IUD. Smoking is discouraged when using hormonal methods of contraception.

Injections

Injections, such as Depo-Provera, are a method of birth control you think about just four times a year! The injections use a synthetic hormone to prevent pregnancy in three ways:

1. it inhibits ovulation,

2. it changes the cervical mucus to help prevent sperm from reaching the egg, and

3. it changes the uterine lining to prevent the fertilized egg from implanting in the uterus. You get the injection (in your arm or buttocks) from a healthcare provider. *Depo-Provera* requires an injection once every three months. A new injection method, *Lunelle*, is now on the market. It requires a monthly injection. When taken as scheduled, injections are 99 percent effective.

Implants

Implants, such as *Norplant*, contain a hormone that is similar to one your body normally produces. Implants prevent pregnancy by preventing ovulation. Match-sized, soft rubber tubes that contain hormones are placed beneath the skin of the upper arm by a healthcare provider in a minor surgical procedure using a local anesthesia. The implants provide birth control for up to five years and can be removed when you want to stop using them or when it's time to replace them. Failures are rare, but are higher with increased body weight.

The Pill

The Pill is one of the most common methods of birth control. The Pill contains hormones that closely resemble those your body produces naturally.

When you take the Pill as prescribed (every day at the same time) your body stops releasing eggs. If there is no egg to fertilize, pregnancy cannot occur. The Pill requires a prescription from a healthcare provider. If you're taking antibiotics, the Pill does not work. Talk to your healthcare provider, consult your prescription information sheet, and use another form of birth control.

The Patch

The *Ortho Evra* contraceptive patch, a new contraceptive, delivers the same hormones as the Pill to prevent ovulation. Three patches, each worn for a week, are used during a woman's menstrual cycle. The woman has a period in the fourth week. The adhesive patch (about the size of a matchbook) can be worn on your abdomen or buttocks.

Vaginal Ring

The *NuvaRing*, a new contraceptive, is a vaginal ring that inhibits ovulation. The ring is inserted by the woman into the vagina and worn for three weeks. The woman has a period in the fourth week, when no ring is inserted. *NuvaRing* is a soft, flexible, transparent ring that is easily self-administered and provides month-long protection.

IUD

The IUD (Intra-Uterine Device) is a small, plastic device that's inserted into your uterus by a healthcare provider. Of the two types of IUDs available, one can be left in your uterus for up to 10 years. The other must be replaced every year. It isn't entirely clear how IUDs prevent pregnancy, but they seem to prevent sperm and eggs from meeting. IUDs have one of the lowest failure rates. There is a risk of pelvic inflammatory disease (PID), which can cause infertility. They work best if you're in a monogamous (one partner) relationship and are suggested for use after you've had one child. IUDs are not recommended for young adults.

What are barrier methods of contraception?

Barrier methods include the following: male condom, female condom, diaphragm, cervical cap, vaginal spermicides, and the sponge.

Male Condom

The male condom is a latex rubber sheath placed over the erect penis before penetration, preventing pregnancy by blocking the passage of sperm. Condoms also prevent direct contact with semen, infectious genital secretions, and genital lesions and discharges, which lower your chances of contracting an STD. A condom can be used only once.

Female Condom

The female condom is a lubricated polyurethane sheath shaped somewhat like the male condom. The closed end has a flexible ring and is inserted into the vagina. The open end remains outside the vagina. Female condoms can be used only once. Do *not* use a female condom with a male condom because it may slip out of place.

Diaphragm

The diaphragm is a dome-shaped rubber disk with a flexible rim that works in two ways to prevent pregnancy. Inserted properly in the vagina, it covers the cervix so sperm can't reach the uterus, while a spermicidal jelly or cream (applied to the diaphragm before insertion) kills sperm. A diaphragm must be sized by a healthcare provider to fit properly and is available by prescription only.

The diaphragm protects for six hours after it's inserted. (For intercourse after the six-hour period, or for repeated intercourse within this period, fresh spermicidal jelly or cream must be placed in the vagina with the diaphragm still in place.) The diaphragm should be left in place for at least six hours after the last intercourse. It should not, however, be left in the vagina for more than 24 hours because of the risk of toxic shock syndrome (a rare but potentially fatal infection).

Cervical Cap

The cervical cap is a soft rubber cap with a round rim that's inserted into the vagina and fits snugly around the cervix. It is used with a spermicidal jelly or cream. It protects for 48 hours and for multiple intercourse within this time. (Do not wear it for more than 48 hours because of the risk of toxic shock syndrome. Wearing the cap for more than two days may also cause an unpleasant odor or discharge in some women.) The cervical cap must be sized by a healthcare provider and is available by prescription only.

Vaginal Spermicides

Vaginal spermicides are available in cream, jelly, foam, tablet, or suppository forms. All contain a chemical that kills sperm. These can be applied to condoms and/or inserted into the vagina to kill sperm. Spermicides are best used in conjunction with other types of birth control. (The failure rate when used alone can be as high as 26 percent.)

Sponge
The sponge is not currently marketed, but may be sold again in the future. It is a disk-shaped polyurethane device that contains spermicide and is inserted into the vagina to cover the cervix.

What is natural planning?
Natural planning involves periodic abstinence (or using a barrier method of birth control) during those times in a woman's menstrual cycle when she is most likely to become pregnant.

> Natural planning requires high motivation on the part of the couple. It is not recommended for young adults.

Does "withdrawal" work?
No! Use a contraceptive!

What is the "morning-after" pill?
The morning-after pill is basically a high-dose birth control pill that prevents ovulation, or if it has already occurred, blocks implantation of a fertilized egg. It must be taken within 72 hours of having unprotected sexual intercourse and has been found to be 75 percent effective. For more information, visit *www.not-2-late.com*.

What is surgical sterilization?
Surgical sterilization is a contraceptive option intended for people who don't want children in the future. It is considered *permanent* because reversal requires major surgery that is often unsuccessful.

Female Sterilization
Called tubal ligation, female sterilization blocks the fallopian tubes so the egg can't travel to the uterus. Sterilization is done by various surgical techniques, usually under general anesthesia.

Male Sterilization
Called a vasectomy, male sterilization involves sealing, tying, or cutting a man's vas deferens, which carries sperm from the testicles to the penis. Vasectomies involve a quick operation performed in a doctor's office, and usually take less than 30 minutes to do.

Am I the "one in five" to get an STD?

The medical community has recently changed the term STD to STI. STD refers to sexually-transmitted diseases, while STI refers to sexually-transmitted infections. To lessen confusion, the term STD will be used throughout this chapter as a reference for both STDs and STIs.

> Be
> polite
> to all,
> but intimate
> with few."
>
> ~ *Thomas Jefferson*

What are STDs?

STDs are sexually-transmitted diseases that are spread through sexual contact, including vaginal, oral, and anal sex. According to the American Social Health Association, an estimated 56 million Americans have one or more sexually-transmitted diseases. That's one in five Americans. Are you going to be that "one in five?"

Chlamydia

Chlamydia is the most-frequently reported STD in America. It is also the fastest-spreading, striking more than three million men and women each year. Chlamydia infects males and females during unprotected vaginal or anal sex. If left untreated, it can cause pelvic inflammatory disease (PID) and infertility in women. In men, painful urination and discharge from the penis may occur. Chlamydia often produces no signs of infection and may be difficult to diagnose. Chlamydia can be *treated and cured* with antibiotics.

Gonorrhea

Gonorrhea, also known as "the clap," is spread by unprotected vaginal, anal, and oral sex. Men who are infected may develop painful urination and a thick, pus-like discharge from the penis. The symptoms may not be as obvious in women, although some may have a cloudy vaginal discharge and pelvic pain. Women are more likely to learn they have gonorrhea after their male sex partner is diagnosed. If left untreated, it can cause damage to heart valves, chronic infection of the genital tract, and arthritis. Gonorrhea can be *treated and cured* with antibiotics.

Syphilis

Syphilis is a treacherous disease. It begins with a painless sore at the site of infection (such as the penis, vagina, or mouth), and is often mistaken for a harmless cold sore. After the cold sore goes away, syphilis goes into hiding. Weeks or months later, a rash may appear anywhere on your body. Again, it's easy to be fooled. Untreated, the third stage of syphilis, which may not occur for years, can strike the heart, brain, or any other vital organ. It can be diagnosed with a simple blood test and can be *treated and cured* with *penicillin*.

Trichomoniasis (Trich)

Trich affects five million men and women annually. Many have no symptoms. Some have burning during urination, vaginal discharge, abdominal pain, or painful intercourse. Trich is the most common treatable and curable STD, with a single dose of the antibiotic *Flagyll*. Both sex partners should be treated for Trich.

Genital Herpes (HSV)

Genital herpes is a very serious STD and should not be taken lightly. More than 45 million people have chronic genital warts, with another one million new cases occurring each year. You can get herpes from vaginal, anal, and oral sex — and also by kissing or touching an infected area if you have a break in your skin. You may become infected and never know it or you might develop painful bumps and sores at the site of infection days or weeks after exposure. Herpes can also flare up or recur at any time throughout your life. You can contract or transmit herpes even if you have no visible sores. There is *no cure* for herpes, but there are various drugs that can reduce the duration and severity of outbreaks and delay recurrences.

Genital Warts or Human Papilloma Virus (HPV)

Genital warts cause a variety of different-looking warts in the genital and anal areas. There are already more than 20 million Americans who have genital warts and 5.5 million new cases reported each year. HPV attacks both sexes and may be hard to spot if the wart is hidden inside the vagina. Genital warts can lead to cervical cancer, so females who have them should have a Pap smear done every year for early detection. There is *no cure* for genital warts. They can be treated by lasers, freezing, or burning — but they can reappear at any time.

Hepatitis B

Hepatitis B is a viral infection of the liver and is spread primarily through infected blood. It is highly contagious but can be prevented with a vaccine. (It's the *only* STD that can be prevented with a vaccine.) There is *no treatment or cure* for Hepatitis B, and it can cause liver disease and cancer.

HIV/AIDS

HIV/AIDS is the most serious STD. It can kill you. It is caused by a virus that attacks the body's immune system and leaves a person unable to fight off many kinds of infections and cancers. There is *no cure*, but new medicines can slow the damage that causes the immune system to gradually fail and contract infections.

Symptoms may not appear for years after infection. Almost one million Americans may be infected with the HIV/AIDS virus. *Young women are the fastest-growing group contracting HIV/AIDS through unprotected sex.* HIV/AIDS is transmitted through blood, semen, and vaginal fluids during all forms of unprotected sexual intercourse (vaginal, anal, or oral) and from sharing drug needles with a person who is an HIV-carrier. It can also be passed from a mother to her unborn child.

How will I know if I have an STD?

Most people who have an STD have no symptoms, so testing is the only sure way to know. If you do have symptoms, they may appear right away — or they might not show up for weeks or months. Symptoms might come and go, and even if the symptoms do disappear, the disease may still be active. The following are possible STD symptoms:

For women

- Sores, bumps, or blisters near your genital area or mouth.

- Painful, burning, or frequent urination.

- Itching, a bad smell, or unusual discharge from your vagina.

- Burning or itching in the vaginal area.

- Redness, swelling, or soreness of the vulva.

- Pain in your lower pelvic area.

- Pain during intercourse.

- Vaginal bleeding between your periods.

● Itching, pain, or discharge from your anus.

For men

● Sores, bumps, or blisters near your genital area or mouth.

● Burning or painful urination.

● Drip or discharge from your penis.

● Itching, pain, or discharge from your anus.

If you think you have an STD, get help from a healthcare provider or STD clinic immediately. Early treatment can prevent lasting damage to your body — and can prevent it from being spread to others. Testing is fairly simple and can include the following: a urine test; a blood test; visual inspection; a specimen from an ulcer or sore; or a swab-sample from the vagina, the opening of the penis (urethra), the anal canal, or the tonsils. (Ladies, testing for STDs is not included in your annual Pap smear. Ask to have them included.)

All county health departments offer free or low-cost STD testing.

What does treatment involve?

Treatment often involves taking antibiotics for a few weeks to kill the organism that causes the STD. Some STDs cannot be cured, but treatment can relieve symptoms and may prevent further damage to your body. Take the following precautions when being treated for an STD:

● It is absolutely essential that you avoid sex until your treatment is finished.

● Take **ALL** of your medicine, even if you start feeling better or symptoms go away.

● Never take anyone else's medicine or give yours to someone else.

● If you are told to return to the clinic for a follow-up check, go!

- Tell everyone you've had sex with that they may have an STD and need to be tested.

How can I keep myself from getting an STD?

Of course, the best way to prevent STDs is to avoid having sex. If this isn't an option, practice the following:

- Before having sex, talk to your partner and agree to use condoms. *Use a condom every time you have vaginal, anal, or oral sex.* Male and female condoms are now available.

- Be prepared. Carry condoms with you … just in case.

- Limit your number of sex partners. You're more likely to get an STD if you have more than one partner. Avoid one-night stands, too.

- Get tested for STDs if you or your partner had other sexual partners. Remember, you're sleeping with everyone your partner has ever slept with.

- Refuse to have sex with anyone who won't use a condom. This person does not have your best interests at heart.

- Don't have sex when you're under the influence of alcohol or drugs. They can affect your judgment and lead to unsafe sex.

Do I have to tell my partner?

Yes! STDs have been referred to as "the gift that keeps on giving." In order to stop the spread of STDs — and to ensure the health of your partner — you *must tell* him or her — or them. You probably got the STD from someone you slept with who didn't tell you. By not telling your partner, you are potentially harming your partner and everyone he or she sleeps with. It's a vicious cycle — and overcoming the embarrassment of telling isn't as bad as letting the cycle continue and harming the health of others. Be prepared to receive a range of reactions, from support to complete rejection. Your local health department can help prepare you for this task.

Can I get STDs from oral sex?

Yes! Oral sex is not totally safe. STDs are spread through *sexual contact —*

not just sexual intercourse. Go to *www.mama-shop.com/oralsex/* for tips on safer oral sex.

Do STDs cause infertility?

Yes. While it may not seem important to you now, in a few years, you might want to marry and start a family. Many STDs can lead to infertility, tubal pregnancies, or miscarriages. Often a woman has no idea she has an STD until the infection has caused lasting damage. That's why it's so important to *wear a condom every time* you have sexual intercourse.

Where can I get more information?

For more information, call these confidential hotlines:

- National Herpes Hotline: 1-919-361-8488

- National HPV Hotline: 1-919-361-4848

- CDC* National STD Hotline: 1-800-227-8922

- CDC* National AIDS Hotline: 1-800-342-AIDS (English)

  - 1-800-344-SIDA (Spanish)

  - 1-800-AIDS-TTY (Touchtone)

You can call the HPV and Cervical Cancer Prevention Resource Center toll-free at 1-877-478-5868. Visit the American Social Health Association at *www.ashastd.org* for more information on STDs.

    * CDC is the U.S. Department of Health's Centers for Disease Control.

▶ Help! I'm pregnant!

The options in this section are neither encouraged nor discouraged. The information is provided as a service to help you make a better, more-informed decision if you should find yourself faced with an unplanned pregnancy.

What are the wrong reasons to have a child?

- Your friends are having babies.

- You think babies are cute.

- You think a baby will keep your relationship together.

- You want someone to love.

- You want someone to love you.

- Your parents want a grandchild.

- You want your family name to live on.

- Your priest, minister, rabbi, or bishop wants more church members.

How much does a baby cost?

The dollar cost to raise a child until he/she reaches 18 is estimated to be more than $100,000. And, the birth alone can be $3,000 or more (if there are no complications). If you have a baby, *at a minimum*, you have to pay for the following:

- 18 years of food.

- 18 years of clothing.

- 18 years of medical care.

- 18 years of shelter (an extra room in your home).

- 18 years of odds and ends (toys, bathroom supplies, junk food).

- 13 to 14 years of schooling.

How do I know if I'm pregnant?

When was the first day of your last menstrual period? Most women get pregnant two weeks after their last period (See "What's so special about Day 14?"), and won't know it until two weeks later when they miss their period. If your period is a week late, go to your county health department or other medical office to have a pregnancy test done. Public health centers offer pregnancy tests free of charge or for a very small fee.

Beware of so-called "crisis pregnancy centers." Most are anti-abortion and may perform pregnancy tests without medical supervision; give you incomplete or incorrect information about your options; try to frighten you with films designed to keep you from choosing abortion; or lie about the medical and emotional effects of abortion.

A urine test performed by a medical professional is the surest way to find out if you're pregnant. You can also get a home pregnancy test at a drugstore. They're simple to use, but they're not as accurate. If your test is positive, go to a medical doctor for a pelvic exam and to start pre-natal care (even if you choose not to have the baby).

For health reasons, it is important to keep track of your Last Menstrual Period (LMP). Get a small calendar to keep in your underwear or bathroom drawer. (The free ones given away at card shops work well.) Each month, circle the days of your period. If anything abnormal happens during that cycle, write that on the calendar, too.

If I'm pregnant, what are my options?

An unplanned pregnancy is one of life's most difficult experiences. Thoughts and feelings are often confusing, and there typically is a lot of fear. It's hard to know what to do or who to turn to for help and support. When an unplanned pregnancy occurs, you have three choices:

1. You can choose to have the baby and raise it yourself.

2. You can choose to have the baby and place your baby for adoption.

3. You can choose to terminate the pregnancy by having an abortion.

Whatever choice you make, see a healthcare provider as soon as possible, even if you terminate the pregnancy. (If you choose abortion, it should be done within the first twelve weeks, so don't wait to go to a healthcare provider.) Don't hide the pregnancy until the baby is born. Tell someone now so you can begin prenatal care for the baby immediately and get the emotional support you need. For more information, visit your county health department or call the following:

- Planned Parenthood at 1-800-230-PLAN

- National Birthright Hotline at 1-800-550-4900

What questions can I ask myself to help me decide?

There are no easy answers, but one thing is certain: *You do have to make a decision.* And, the longer you wait to make that decision, the fewer choices you have. To help you choose the option that is best for you, talk with your partner, your parents, or a counselor. Explore your feelings. Listen to your heart and your own voice to find the right answer for you. Trust yourself. And ask yourself the following questions to help you make your choice:

- Which choice(s) could I live with?

- Which choice(s) would be impossible for me?

- How would each choice affect my everyday life?

- What do I believe is best for me in the long run?

- What are my plans for the future? Am I willing to put school and career on hold?

- What are my spiritual and moral beliefs?

- How does the father of this baby feel about the pregnancy?

- Is the baby's father able or willing to help with the baby's needs?

- Will my family and friends be supportive? What if they're not?

- What can I afford?

- Am I ready to take care of a child 24 hours a day, seven days a week for 18 years?

- Is having a baby the best choice for me? Am I ready to be a parent?

- Will I be raising the child alone? Who will be there to help and support me?

- Can I provide for my baby's needs financially?

- Where will we live?

- Are my partner and I both financially and emotionally ready?

- Would my partner and I stay together even if I weren't pregnant?

- Am I ready to be married?

- Is raising a child with a partner the best choice for me?

- Am I prepared to be a single parent if things don't work out between us?

- Am I being pressured to keep the baby?

- Am I willing to be more dependent on other people?

- Do I know someone who is always available and trustworthy to care for my child?

- What will my life be like as a parent in one year? In five years?

- Will I still have friends and be able to go on dates?

- Will my family be against my choice of parenting? What if they are?

- How would I react to a baby who was making me angry or upset?

- Will finding a life partner be easy with a child?

- How would I feel if someone else raised my child?

- Is placing the baby for adoption the best choice for me?

- Will my family be against my choice of adoption? What if they are?

- Would I want to know the adoptive family?

- Would I want to choose the adoptive family?

- Would I want on-going contact with the adoptive family?

- Would I want someone in my family to adopt my child as his/her own?

- Is having an abortion the best choice for me?

- What are my beliefs about abortion?

- Is anyone pressuring me to choose abortion?

- Do I have strong religious beliefs against abortion?

- If I choose abortion, how will I feel about my choice in one year?

- If I choose abortion, how will I feel about my choice in five years?

- Will my family be against my choice of abortion? What if they are?

See the Pros and Cons of Pregnancy Options on page 280 to help you further examine and understand this imporant decision.

What are the real costs of raising a child?

Planning to keep and raise your baby takes a great deal of financial, emotional, and practical planning. Do you have adequate resources to care for a child? Talk with a counselor who can help you evaluate your readiness to become a parent. The worksheet on page 281 can help you.

Will I have to pay child support?

Under the Welfare Reform Act, laws now require women to name their child's father when applying for public assistance. Under Welfare Reform, each state must operate a child support enforcement program that meets federal requirements, including the following:

Pros & Cons of Pregnancy Options

Following is an example of the issues a person might face in examining pregnancy options. Use this sample to determine your own pros and cons.

Interactive CD-ROM

Print It!

Keep & Raise the Baby

Pros	*Cons*
● Maturity	● Not enough money
● Learn compromise	● Not mature enough
● Constant learning	● Might break us up
● Have a family	● Physically tired
● Baby is cute	● Emotionally tired
● Watch baby grow	● No life except baby
● Live on own	● Have to quit school
● Be married	● College has to wait

Adoption

Pros	*Cons*
● People who can't have baby could have one	● Can't go through 9 months and then give away
● Make someone happy	● Can't watch grow up
● Give baby better life with someone who's ready	● Emotionally torn

Abortion

Pros	*Cons*
● No financial strain	● Depressing
● Be ready next time	● "What if"
● No emotional strain	● Guilt

Figure 8B

Real Costs to Raise a Child

What will it really cost me to keep and raise a child? Diapers and a crib aren't the only costs you'll have. Use this example to determine your own financial, emotional, social, and spiritual costs.

Interactive CD-ROM

Print It!

Financial Costs
- Food
- Clothes
- Hospital for birth
- Medical bills for baby
- Diapers, Wipes, Powders
- Toys
- Shelter / Rent
- Car, Gas, Repair
- Car Insurance
- Car Seat
- Health Insurance
- Crib and bedding
- Stroller
- High Chair
- Changing Table
- Babysitter / daycare

Social Costs
- No life except baby
- Have to quit school
- College has to wait
- Fewer parties
- Less going to mall / shopping
- Less time with friends
- Have to depend on others
- Friends may get tired of baby
- Can't just pick up and go

Spiritual Costs
- Conflict w/ religion
- Hard to get to church
- Feel judged
- Judge myself

Emotional Costs
- Tired / Exhausted
- Frustrated
- Love
- Happiness
- Pride

Figure 8C

Reporting Newly-Hired Employees

The National New-Hire Reporting law requires employers to report all new-hires to state agencies for transmittal of information to a national directory.

Establishing Paternity

If the mother and child are receiving welfare assistance, and fail to cooperate in establishing paternity, or who the child's father is, their monthly welfare cash assistance will be reduced by at least 25 percent. That's incentive to name the "daddy." If you're not sure you're the father, DNA testing can be used. DNA, a person's genetic code, can determine if you're the father with a 99.9 percent probability. The tests cost $450 to $600 and can be completed within days. Samples for the tests are collected by mouth swabs or blood samples.

Paying Child Support

The ability to test DNA has had a significant impact on court cases regarding custody and child support. Many federal and state laws require that a mother name the child's father. The father can be legally forced to pay child support or to reimburse the state for welfare payments made to the child. Laws vary by state, but you need to know that DNA is a very exact science — and can prove that you're the father — or eliminate you as the father. Tough new penalties allow states to implement strict child support enforcement techniques. The new law expands wage garnishment, which means child support will be taken out of your paycheck before you're paid. News laws allow states to seize assets and, in some cases, to require community service. States are also empowered to revoke drivers and professional licenses for parents who owe delinquent child support.

Teen-Parent Requirements

In order to receive public assistance, unmarried minor parents (under age 18) are required to live with a responsible adult or in an adult-supervised setting and participate in educational and training activities.

What if I choose adoption?

Within the U.S., children can be adopted through public welfare agencies, private adoption agencies, and depending on the state, by independent or open adoption. You can arrange an adoption through a doctor, lawyer, or adoption agency. While laws concerning adoption vary from state to state, you are generally asked to sign "relinquishment papers" indicating that you cannot change your mind after delivery and adoption (although you may be given a limited time during which you can change your mind). Adoption is legal and binding — and few are ever reversed by the courts. If you choose adoption, you must have regular prenatal care and abstain from alcohol and drugs for the entire pregnancy. For adoption laws in your state, the National Adoption Information Clearinghouse can be reached at 1-888-251-0075 or *www.calib.com/naic*.

There are two types of adoption: closed and independent or open. In closed adoptions, the names of the birthmother and the adoptive parents are kept secret from each other. In an open adoption, the birthmother may select the adoptive parents for her child. She and the adoptive parents may choose to get to know each other. They may also choose to have an ongoing relationship. (Independent or open adoptions are not legal in some states.) The adoptive parents will often agree to pay for your hospital and medical bills until the child is born. They may even pay for your living expenses during that time. Usually the adoptive parents hire one attorney to represent them *and* you. If you choose independent adoption, get your own lawyer.

You may want your child to stay in your family. If a relative adopts your child, the adoption must be approved by the courts. In some cities and states, temporary foster care might also be available for your child if you need time to decide between adoption and parenting.

What if I choose abortion?

Abortion is a legal and safe procedure. If you choose to terminate your pregnancy, it is recommended that the abortion be done during the first 12 weeks of pregnancy (the first trimester). Abortion is a safe and relatively simple procedure that will not affect future pregnancies or reproductive health. Most abortions cost between $300 and $400.

For most abortions, vacuum aspiration is used. First, the cervix is numbed. Then the embryo or fetus is removed through a narrow tube with vacuum suction. The surgery takes about five minutes and is usually done in a clinic, doctor's office, or hospital. The procedure is done on an out-patient basis, with most women returning to normal activities the next day. Most women who've had an abortion say it feels like menstrual cramps.

You'll have to sign a form prior to the procedure that says you have been informed of your options; have been counseled about the procedure you choose, its risks, and how to care for yourself afterwards; and have chosen the abortion of your own free will. Many states also require a parent's consent if you're a minor.

You are more likely to experience serious regrets about abortion if you have strong religious feelings against it. Examine these concerns before choosing abortion.

For more information, call the National Abortion Federation hotline at 1-800-772-9100.

What is "Abandoned Baby" legislation?

According to the U.S. Department of Health and Human Services, 108 babies (that are known about) were abandoned in public places in 1998. Incidents of women delivering babies and then literally throwing them in the trash happens all across America. Sometimes the babies are found alive, but many times, they're found too late.

In most states, there is a penalty (usually a felony abandonment charge) for a woman to leave her baby unless she signs papers that would release her child for adoption. However, since many abandoned babies die from lack of care or exposure to the weather, what might have been an abandoned child prosecution often becomes a homicide case.

In response, many states are working on legislation to make it legal to leave your child at a safe place, such as a hospital, fire department, or welfare office, with no criminal charges brought against you. If you are struggling with raising a child, please call your state's Department of Health and Human Services or your county health department. (The numbers can be found in the government pages of the phone book.)

 ## What's so special about Day 14?

Of course, you've had Sex Ed. in school, but do you know about **Day 14?** It's typically the day a woman ovulates — the day she can become pregnant. (Pregnancy can occur up to seven days before and one day after Day 14, also.)

A woman has two ovaries located on each side of her uterus. Each month an egg is released by one of the ovaries and moves into the fallopian tube, which is connected to the uterus. If a woman has a regular 28-day menstrual cycle, ovulation — the release of an egg from an ovary — usually occurs 14 days before the next menstrual period. For example, if a woman has a 28-day cycle, Day 1 is the day her period starts. Ovulation occurs about Day 14. Pregnancy can occur if you have sex during or near the time of ovulation (anywhere from Days 10 to 20). Keep in mind that menstrual cycles may vary from month to month. You may have a 28-day cycle one month and a 30-day cycle the next.

When the man ejaculates during sex, his sperm are released into the vagina. They travel up through the cervix (the opening of the uterus), and out into the fallopian tubes. If a sperm meets an egg in the tube, fertilization can occur. The fertilized egg then moves through the tube into the uterus and becomes attached there to grow and develop. If you're not ready for this to happen, go to "What type of contraception is best for me?"

 ## What's the difference between love and sex?

For some young adults, sex is a form of recreation, with a new partner every time. For others, however, sex is a very personal, intimate connection with another person. With love or a committed relationship, there's emotional involvement, trust, and respect. With lust, or casual sex, there is little or no emotional involvement (at least on the part of one member of the situation). Lust is typical of one-night stands. Lust is not selective. Lust can take place with anyone. Lust leaves most people (men and women) feeling empty afterwards.

If you meet a woman, and are turned on because she has big breasts, nice hips, a pretty smile — that's lust. But if you meet that same woman, get to know her, enjoy talking to her and being around her, seeing more than just her body — that's love. Love isn't something that's rushed or that happens at "first sight." It takes time to get to know a person, and not just intimately.

Men, do you think you own women?

Why do some men become abusive?

Studies have shown that when young males leave home for the first time, they think that life means good times and lots of women. Drinking, drugs, and a new sense of freedom may trigger abusive behavior, but ingrained attitudes play a part as well. Jealousy is often a catalyst in arguments that lead to abuse. Some men also have a belief that they have a sense of "ownership" of the women they date. Abusive behavior is about power and control. It can be physical, emotional, psychological, social, economic, or sexual. Women can also be abusers. (Go to Chapter 10, "What is domestic violence?" for more information.)

Male support groups are working to change the attitudes men have about women. They're working to stop the denial, the blaming, the minimizing, and to get men to take responsibility for their own actions, behaviors, and beliefs. The following tips are things men can do to stop violence against women:

- Never hit a woman, no matter what!

- Think about the attitudes you grew up with. Were other men in your family violent to women? You don't have to keep these learned patterns. You can learn new, healthy patterns. The choice is yours.

- Learn to see women as truly equal and independent partners, rather than as possessions to be owned by you.

- Speak up. Don't be a silent bystander. If you know someone who shows abusive behavior, confront him. Silence is tolerance. Call 911.

- If you know a woman who is being abused, offer support. Ask her how the threat of violence impacts her life. Listen and learn from her.

- Control your drinking. Alcohol makes people do stupid things that they later regret.

- Find a counselor, support group, or anger-management class to help you.

Is date rape increasing?

Yes. An increasing number of rapes are being committed by men known to the victim, not by strangers.

Ladies, unless you've known a man for some time, it can be dangerous to accept an invitation to go to his room or home alone. One of the best ways for you to protect yourself is to stay away from events that involve heavy drinking. A number of date rapes have also been linked to drugs that weaken your senses and cause amnesia. Some men slip these drugs into drinks, so don't let your drink out of your sight. (Go to Chapter 11, "Are club drugs safe?" for more information.)

And, ladies, be aware of the messages you're sending. If you don't want sex, stop before things go that far. If you're being pressured into having sex, stand up, back away from the person, and say with all seriousness, *"I don't want to have sex,"* and then leave.

And, men,

- *"No"* really does mean *"No,"* even if you think she's teasing you or leading you on.

- If you cross that line, you are committing rape and can be charged.

- No one owes you sex — not for anything.

- Whenever force is used to have sex, it's rape — and rape is a crime, even if the people involved know each other and have had sex before.

So, when she says *"No,"* go for a walk or visualize something really disgusting to lessen your frustration.

Additional Information for this Chapter

Books

- *K.I.S.S. Guide to Sex* by Anne Hooper

- *101 Nights of Great Romance* by Laura Corn

- *101 Nights of Great Sex* by Laura Corn

- *Sex for Dummies* by Dr. Ruth K. Westheimer

- *Sexual Intimacy: How to Build a Lasting and Loving Relationship* by Anne Hooper

- *Surviving Teen Pregnancy: Your Choices, Dreams and Decisions* by Perry Bergman

- *The Ultimate Sex Book: A Therapist's Guide to Sexual Fulfillment* by Anne Hooper

Web Links

- *www.iwannaknow.org*

- *www.plannedparenthood.org*

- *www.allaboutsex.org*

- *www.gynpages.com*

- *www.coolnurse.com*

- *www.drcondoms.com*

- *www.itsyoursexlife.com*

- *www.rape101.com*

- *www.ncava.org*
  (National Coalition Against Violent Athletes)

- *www.ashastd.org*
  (American Social Health Association)

- *www.calib.com/naic*
  (National Adoption Information Clearinghouse)

- *www.glnh.org*
  (Gay and Lesbian National Hotline)

- *www.drizzle.com/~kathleen/wla/youth.htm*
  (Gay/Lesbian Resources)

- *www.gaylesteens.about.com/teens*

- *www.arhp.org/success/index.html*
  (Association of Reproductive Health Professionals)

Is my health my responsibility?

Your health is your responsibility — and so is your health-care. Do you know how to take care of yourself? Answer the following questions as True or False to see if you know the keys to living a long, healthy life.

Interactive CD-ROM

Quiz

True   False

True	False		
○	○	1.	My health is my responsibility.
○	○	2.	If Barbie was human, she'd have to walk on all fours due to her proportions.
○	○	3.	Women should do breast self-exams each month.
○	○	4.	PMS can cause a Jekyll-and-Hyde personality in some women.
○	○	5.	My feet contain 26 bones, 33 joints, 107 ligaments, and 19 muscles.
○	○	6.	A Pap smear is a simple test that can save a woman's life.
○	○	7.	Vaginitis is a common problem that affects up to one-third of women.
○	○	8.	Healthcare is a lifetime commitment to prevention.
○	○	9.	Testicular cancer is most common in men aged 15 to 35.
○	○	10.	Cigarettes kill more than 400,000 Americans each year.
○	○	11.	If I stop smoking, there are almost instantaneous benefits to my health.
○	○	12.	Lung cancer is now the leading cause of death among women.
○	○	13.	Dentists suggest brushing my teeth for two to three minutes twice a day.
○	○	14.	Canker sores occur outside the mouth. Cold sores occur inside the mouth.
○	○	15.	If I pierce my tongue, it could swell large enough to close my airway.
○	○	16.	I'm considered overweight if my Body Mass Index (BMI) is 32.
○	○	17.	I can get my blood pressure checked at the grocery store.
○	○	18.	An ideal cholesterol reading is below 200.
○	○	19.	Many people confuse hunger with thirst.
○	○	20.	Stress can weaken my immune system, making it easier for me to get sick.
○	○	21.	Chocolate can give me a mental boost.
○	○	22.	Pre-schoolers laugh an average of 400 times per day.
○	○	23.	Adults laugh an average of 15 times per day.
○	○	24.	The symptoms of road rage are classic signs of sleep deprivation.
○	○	25.	If I sleep with someone who snores, I lose an hour of sleep each night.
○	○	26.	Sleep apnea causes a person to repeatedly stop breathing during sleep.
○	○	27.	Up to 13 million people in the U.S. have an undiagnosed thyroid problem.
○	○	28.	Students who live on campus are three times more likely to get meningitis.
○	○	29.	I need a tetanus shot every 10 years.
○	○	30.	More than five million Americans suffer from eating disorders.
○	○	31.	Anorexia nervosa is essentially self-starvation.
○	○	32.	Bulimia nervosa is compulsive over-eating followed by self-induced vomiting.
○	○	33.	I should have a primary healthcare provider.
○	○	34.	I should make a list of my symptoms before going to the doctor.
○	○	35.	It's important that a healthcare provider pays full attention to me.

SCORE

30 to 35 points   Congratulations! You take responsibility for your health and should live a long, healthy life.

20 to 29 points   You need a mental boost. Enjoy a few chocolates while reading this chapter.

0 to 19 points   You might be a bit sleep-deprived or stressed out. Head to bed an hour earlier tonight.

Figure 9A

In this Chapter

Staying healthy means you'll have more energy for the activities you want to pursue. Be proactive in maintaining good health. Know when to go to a doctor and how to communicate your physical symptoms. Learn how to take care of yourself!

The information in this chapter is intended for informational purposes only. It is not all-inclusive and cannot substitute for professional medical guidance and treatment.

 ## What healthcare do women need?

What size did Marilyn Monroe wear?

Did you know that if store mannequins were real, they'd be too thin to menstruate? There are three billion women who don't look like supermodels and only eight who do. Marilyn Monroe was a size 14. If Barbie was a real woman, she'd have to walk on all fours due to her proportions. The average woman weighs 144 pounds and wears a size 12 or 14. One out of every four college-aged women has an eating disorder. The models in the magazines are air-brushed — not perfect! A psychological study in 1995 found that three minutes spent looking at a fashion magazine caused 70 percent of women to feel depressed, guilty, and shameful. Models 20 years ago weighed eight percent less than the average woman. Today, they weigh 23 percent less! The beauty of a woman is not in the clothes she wears, the figure she carries, or the way she combs her hair. The beauty of a woman must be seen from her eyes because that is the doorway to her heart, the place where love resides. The beauty of a woman is not in a facial mole. True beauty is reflected in her soul. It is the caring that she gives, the passion that she shows. The beauty of a woman, with passing years, only grows.

~ Author Unknown

What health checks do I need?

Because no one is "the average woman," customize these recommendations to reflect your unique health profile. The most effective health strategies are determined by basic principles that apply to everyone. Prevention isn't the only variable for good health. Early detection is important, so evaluate your family and personal health history with your healthcare provider. The following health checks are recommended for young women:

- Pap smear, with pelvic, rectal, and breast exams every one to three years based on your health history.

- Physical exam every five years (or as specified by your healthcare provider).

- Baseline cholesterol test at age 20, and if normal, every five years thereafter.

- Breast self-examination every month.

- Skin check for changes in moles every month.

- Dental exam and cleaning every six months.

- Eye exam every two to four years, even if you aren't having problems.

Am I getting enough iron?

Iron carries oxygen throughout your body. Without enough iron in your diet, you make too few blood cells to carry the oxygen adequately, causing anemia. Symptoms of anemia include looking pale and feeling tired. If you think you're iron deficient, see your healthcare provider to have your hemoglobin (blood) tested.

Iron deficiency is a real problem for menstruating women. A study published in the *Journal of American Medical Association* found an estimated 7.8 million women are iron deficient with 3.3 million of those having iron deficiency anemia. Fortunately, it is easy to prevent. To get enough iron in your diet, eat a wide variety of foods, including meat, fish, poultry, eggs, green vegetables, grains, fruits, orange juice, and tomatoes. Read food labels to identify iron-enriched and iron-fortified foods. You can also take a daily multi-vitamin that supplies 18 milligrams (mg) of iron.

Is my thyroid out of whack?

As many as 13 million people in the U.S. may have an undiagnosed thyroid problem. Your thyroid gland is one of the regulating engines of the body. It sends thyroid hormone into the bloodstream and affects everything from heart rate to skin texture. Too much thyroid hormone can make it seem as if you're jumping out of your skin. Too little can leave you sluggish. If you're not quite yourself, check with your healthcare provider for a simple blood test to determine if you have a thyroid problem.

Do I need to examine my breasts?

Yes. Breast cancer affects an estimated one in eight American women. Breast cancer kills more women than any other cancer, with an estimated 183,000 new cases occurring annually. Of these, 41,000 women die. Early detection of breast cancer is the best way to ensure survival, so perform monthly breast self-exams. About 90 percent of breast lumps are discovered by women checking their breasts at home. Alert your healthcare provider to any changes in your breasts. If treatment is needed, it's best if lumps are small and found early.

It's recommended that you do the self-exam a few days after the last day of your period (on the same day each month) when your breasts are not tender or swollen. This will help you learn the normal shape and feel of your breasts and make it easier to find any changes as soon as they occur. Get in the habit of examining your own breasts. The *MammaCare©* method (*www.mammacare.com*) has women examine a larger area than other methods — from the collarbone down to the bra line and from the underarm across to the breast bone. The method places emphasis on the upper, outer breast where nearly 50 percent of breast tumors develop. Ask your healthcare provider to demonstrate how to examine yourself each month.

If you have breast implants, you still need to do a careful breast exam each month, especially around the chest wall.

How will I know if I have PMS?

Actually, everyone around you may know before you do. Here are some signs:

- Everyone around you has an attitude problem.

- You're adding chocolate chips to your cheese omelet.

- The dryer has shrunk every last pair of your jeans.

- Your partner is suddenly agreeing to everything you say.

- You're using your cell phone to call every *"How's my driving? Call 1-800-xxx-xxxx."*

- Everyone's head looks like an invitation to batting practice.

- You're counting down the days until menopause.

- You're sure that everyone is scheming to drive you crazy.

- The Ibuprofen bottle is empty and you just bought it yesterday.

- Everyone scatters when you enter the room.

How can I relieve PMS?

If you think you're suffering from premenstrual syndrome (PMS), ask your healthcare provider to do blood tests to check your hormone levels. For some women, the 10 days to two weeks before their period brings about a Jekyll-and-Hyde personality. One day they're feeling fine, the next they're emotional, bloated, and can't eat enough chocolate and potato chips. Many women think PMS is something they have to live with. But healthcare providers and women are finding ways to make the time before your period less difficult.

PMS has been studied for more than 70 years but it is difficult to study because every woman has a different chemical makeup. More than 150 physical and mental symptoms, from breast tenderness and bloating to panic attacks and irritability, can suggest PMS. PMS is most likely caused by one, or a combination, of three things: a hormone, chemical, or nutritional imbalance. Your nutrition is believed to play a role. For instance, foods often flagged as PMS triggers are white sugar and flour, caffeine, alcohol, and fatty foods. Many PMS sufferers get relief from aspirin, anti-inflammatory drugs, or birth-control pills.

If you think you might be suffering from PMS, chart your symptoms for a few months. Write on a calendar the days you don't feel well. Include your symptoms, such as bloating, headache, and anxiety. If you find that your symptoms occur during the two weeks prior to your period, it's probably PMS. Unless your symptoms are severe, a few simple changes in diet and stress management may help. Try these suggestions to gain control of your PMS symptoms:

- Keep your blood sugar level intact by eating at least every four hours. Choose slow-burning foods, such as chicken, turkey, soy, fish, broccoli, cauliflower, and peppers. Avoid eating foods that can raise blood sugar: white flour, sugar, potatoes, and carrots.

- Skip the salt, which encourages your body to retain water. This fluid retention can cause bloating in your entire body, including your brain (which causes headaches). It can also cause breast tenderness.

- Avoid caffeine and alcohol. Soft drinks are packed with sugar and alcohol is processed into sugar by your body. Caffeine often causes breast tenderness, mood swings, and anxiety. Anger is also a side effect of drinking alcohol.

- Drink water. Drinking water will not add to your bloating. It will help your body rid itself of other fluids.

- Consider calcium. A recent study published by the *Journal of Obstetrics and Gynecology* found that women who took 1,200 milligrams (mg) daily of chewable calcium carbonate cut their PMS symptoms by almost 50 percent. Check with your healthcare provider about other possible supplements.

- Walk for 20 to 30 minutes at least three times a week.

- Take a hot bath for 20 minutes to relax.

- Check with your healthcare provider about low-dose birth control pills to regulate your menstrual cycle and keep your hormone levels steady throughout the month.

What are Kegels?

Kegels are exercises that are done to strengthen your pelvic muscles. They are easy to do. Basically, you squeeze and release your vaginal muscles. You can do Kegels anywhere: at your desk, while watching TV, in the shower. Healthcare providers suggest doing three sets a day, eight to 12 contractions each time. How do you know if you're doing them right? Test yourself while urinating. Squeeze your vaginal muscles to stop the flow of urine; then release your muscles to flow again. It's as easy as that.

Does my bra fit?

Do your straps slip? Do the cups look less than smooth? Do you frequently adjust your bra? Does your bra ride up? Does your bra feel uncomfortable? Do too-tight straps leave ridges in your shoulders? If you answered YES to any of these questions, you're wearing the wrong bra. To find a bra that's right for you, get a tape measure and measure yourself:

Band Size

Wearing your usual bra, place a soft tape measure (found in craft departments) around your rib cage just beneath your breasts. Keep the tape straight around your back. Add five inches to get your band measurement. If the number is odd, round up to the next even number (32, 34, 36, etc.). Stand straight and relax. Don't inhale or expand your rib cage.

Cup Size

Hold the tape measure around the fullest part of your breasts, over the nipples. Keep the tape straight, but don't pull it tight. The difference between this measurement and the band size will be your cup size (for example, a difference of one inch is an "A" cup):

Difference	Cup Size
0 inches	AA
1 inch	A
2 inches	B
3 inches	C
4 inches	D
5 inches	DD
6 inches	DDD

Many women settle for a bra that's okay — but not as well-fitted as it could be. The most important consideration in finding a bra that fits is comfort, but you should also consider the following: While putting the bra on, bend over and allow your breasts to fall naturally into the cups. Stand slowly and adjust the bra. The center of the bra should lie flat against your breastbone. Be sure there are no gaps. Make sure the bra cups are smooth with no wrinkles. Turn to the side and look in the mirror. Does the bra ride up on your back? If it does, then it doesn't fit correctly. The back of the bra should rest comfortably against the middle of your back.

Most department stores have a professional bra-fitter in the lingerie department. Don't be embarrassed to get a fitting. Keep in mind that bras are like shoes, no two fit alike. You have to try them on.

Do I need a sports bra?

Consider the size of your breasts and your activity level. The larger your breasts and the higher the impact of your sport, the more support you'll need. Sports bras are available in two basic styles:

Over-the-Head Compression

This type of bra gives support by compressing your breasts to your chest. It provides adequate support if you have A- or B-sized breasts and your sports activities are low impact, such as walking, cycling, or golf. Racer-back, cross, or x-shaped bras offer less support but offer more room to breathe.

Traditional-Looking Bra with Cups

This type of bra is good if you are a C-cup or larger and your activities are high-impact, such as jogging, running, or basketball. Find one with wider sides, back, and straps.

Do I take my feet for granted?

If you're like most people, you take your feet for granted. Did you know that your feet each contain 26 bones, 33 joints, 107 ligaments, and 19 muscles, plus numerous tendons, nerves, and blood vessels? Women experience foot problems at four times the rate of men, and most often because of shoes that don't fit right. Fortunately, almost any style is "in style" these days, so select shoes with wide toe space, flexible soles, and heels no more than two inches high. According to the *Mayo Clinic's Women's Health-Source*, you should do the following when shopping for shoes:

- Buy shoes for fit, not size. Sizes vary among brands and styles.

- Shop for shoes at the end of the day when your feet are their largest.

- Have both feet measured and fit the shoe to the larger foot.

- Choose a shoe that conforms as closely as possible to the shape of your foot.

- Ensure no wrinkles are on the top of the shoe near your toes when you bend your foot.

- Check that the ball of your foot fits comfortably into the widest part of the shoe.

- Aim for a relatively snug fit around the heel with a minimum amount of slippage.

- Don't buy shoes that fit too tight. They may not stretch to fit.

- Select shoes made of soft materials, such as suede or leather.

- Stand up with the new shoes on. There should be about a one-half inch space from your longest toe to the end of each shoe.

● Walk around the store in the new shoes for a few minutes. If they aren't completely comfortable, don't buy them.

 What is a Pap smear?

What is a Pap smear?

A Pap smear is a simple test that can save your life. Since women have been getting Pap tests, deaths from cervical cancer have dropped by about 70 percent. Forty years ago, 20,000 women died each year from this cancer. Today that number is closer to 5,000 — although that figure could be lower if more women had the test done on a regular basis. Of those who die of cervical cancer each year, 50 percent haven't had a Pap test done in five or more years. If you should develop cervical cancer, your chances for a cure are as high as 90 percent — if discovered early. The Pap smear detects changes in the cells of the cervix (the opening of a woman's uterus). These changes could lead to cancer. The Pap smear helps find these changes early so they can be treated before they become serious.

Do I need to have a Pap smear?

If you're female, a Pap smear should be a part of your lifetime health plan. You should have your first Pap smear when you become sexually-active, begin taking birth control pills, or turn 18. Pap smears are typically done annually, but check with your healthcare provider to determine the best schedule for you.

Your Pap smear should also include a breast and pelvic exam. It is recommended that a rectal exam be done at this time, too. You'll need to provide medical, menstrual, and sexual history. Even if it's embarrassing, be honest.

How is a Pap smear done?

Pap smears, while slightly uncomfortable, are easy to do and take only a few minutes. Your gynecologist or healthcare provider will insert a speculum (a metal or plastic device that gently opens the vaginal canal) into your vagina so the cervix can be seen. A small brush and scraper will be used to remove cells from your cervix. (You won't feel any pain.) The cells are then smeared onto a glass slide and sent to a lab. A specially-trained lab technician examines the slide for abnormal cells. All abnormal cells are further reviewed by a pathologist who makes the final diagnosis.

Even if your Pap test shows some abnormalities, it doesn't necessarily mean you have cervical cancer. You may have a yeast infection or an STD. Your healthcare provider will work with you to prepare a treatment plan based on any findings. Will it hurt? You might feel some discomfort, but if it hurts, say *"Ouch."* Your discomfort will either tell the healthcare provider to be a bit gentler — or signal something that needs attention.

Several methods for screening cells are now available. They include *PAP-NET, AutoPap,* and *ThinPrep.* The *PAPNET* and *AutoPap* methods rescreen slides and use a computer program to detect abnormal cells on the manual screening. With the *ThinPrep* method, the cells that are removed from your cervix with a swab are rinsed in a preservative solution. A machine then filters the cells and applies a thin, even layer of cells on a slide to be screened. Ask your healthcare provider for more information.

Are STD/STI tests part of the Pap?

Your annual Pap smear should also include a breast and pelvic exam. It is recommended that a rectal exam be done at this time, too. You will need to provide medical, menstrual, and sexual history. Even though it may seem embarrassing, be honest. Your healthcare provider can't help you if you're not honest. If you need or want any STD/STI (sexually-transmitted diseases/infections) tests done, you must ask your healthcare provider for them. They are *not* part of the Pap smear.

Is the Pap smear foolproof?

False-negative results can occur five to 10 percent of the time. This means that in one of every 10 to 20 cases of cervical cancer, no abnormality is identified on the Pap smear. The flip side of this is that 90 to 95 percent of the time, significant abnormalities are accurately detected. The most common cause of a false-negative Pap smear is "sample failure," which means that no abnormal cells are present on the slide. False-positives can also occur, showing a problem when there isn't one.

The results of your Pap test are most often classified by a system developed by the National Cancer Institute. The classification of the cells helps healthcare providers plan treatment. If your test results are anything but "normal," your healthcare provider will discuss further testing and/or a treatment plan with you. Although abnormal cells can be missed, cervical cancer takes several years to develop, so they're likely to be detected on your next exam while the cancer is still in its early, most-treatable stages.

Only a very small number of women with abnormal Pap test results have cancer. If you don't receive test results, follow-up with your healthcare provider. Some healthcare providers use the "no news is good news" approach. Don't make the same assumption. Call to find out for sure or ask that the results be mailed to you.

When's the best time to get a Pap smear?

The best time to have a Pap smear is between 10 and 20 days after the first day of your menstrual cycle. Avoid intercourse, douching*, tampons, or use of any vaginal medicines or spermicidal foams, creams, or jellies for two days prior to your Pap test because they may wash away or hide abnormal cells.

It is suggested that women have an annual exam. Current guidelines suggest that you have your initial Pap smear when you first begin having sexual relations or at age 18 if you're not sexually-active. You should continue to get a Pap smear every year for the rest of your life; however, after three consecutive years of a normal test, your healthcare provider may suggest less frequent testing. Discuss this with your healthcare provider.

* You should *never* douche.

What are five things a healthcare provider should never do?

1. He/she should never pass judgment on your sex life by making rude comments or berating you for having multiple partners.

2. He/she should never make inappropriate and/or sexual comments about your body parts.

3. He/she should never touch you in a sexual or suggestive way.

4. He/she should never discuss your personal history or diagnosis in the hallway or where other people can hear it.

5. He/she should never ask the nurse to leave the room during the pelvic exam/Pap test.

Am I at risk for cervical cancer?

If you're considered "high risk" for cervical cancer, you may want to have a Pap smear done at least once a year. What makes you high risk? Do any of the following apply to you?

- You became sexually-active as a teenager.

- You have had multiple sex partners or your partner has had multiple partners.

- You have more than one sexual partner now.

- You have a history of sexually-transmitted diseases.

- You have a history of abnormal Pap smears.

- You have a family history of cervical cancer.

- You had a diagnosis of cervical cancer or a pre-cancerous Pap test.

- You are infected with HPV (Human Papilloma Virus).

- You smoke cigarettes.

 ## What is vaginitis?

What is vaginitis?

Vaginitis is a common problem that affects up to one-third of women at some point in their lives. It can occur whether you're sexually-active or not. It includes yeast infections, bacterial vaginosis, and some STDs. Vaginitis is rarely a serious threat to a woman's health, but it can be annoying and uncomfortable. It usually does not go away without treatment.

Vaginitis causes redness, swelling, and irritation of the outer genital area and discharge from the vagina. One of the most common signs of vaginitis is an abnormal vaginal discharge that causes itching and burning or has an unpleasant odor. If you have these symptoms, visit your healthcare provider.

What causes vaginitis?

Vaginitis can result from anything that causes a change in the normal environment of the vagina, including the following:

- Infections (such as bacteria and viruses, including those acquired through sex).

- Certain medications (such as antibiotics used to treat infections).

- Irritating chemicals (such as those in douches) or objects that irritate the vaginal walls (such as forgotten tampons).

- Some types of health problems (such as diabetes).

- Changes in the body's normal hormonal balance.

- Allergic reactions to chemicals or perfumes in soaps, bubble baths, deodorant tampons or pads, or latex condoms.

- Leaving contraceptives (such as the diaphragm or cervical cap) in the vagina too long.

What are the types of vaginal Infections?

The three types of infections include yeast, bacterial, and STDs/STIs.

Yeast Infections

Sometimes called candidiasis, yeast infections are the most common type of vaginal infection. They are caused by a fungus that is normally found in the vagina. Changes in the normal vagina can promote the growth of the fungus. The use of certain antibiotics can increase the risk of repeated yeast infections. Bacteria are killed by the antibiotics, and the yeast is then allowed to over-grow.

Symptoms

The most common signs of a yeast infection are redness, itching, and burning of the vagina and vulva. The vaginal discharge is usually white and without odor. It may have a cheesy or curd-like texture.

Treatment

Yeast infections are most often treated by placing tablets or creams into the vagina. You can now buy over-the-counter treatments, but you should see your healthcare provider if this is the first time you've had a vaginal infection, the symptoms don't go away after treatment, the vaginal discharge is yellow or green or has a bad odor, or there is a chance that it's an STD.

A note on over-the-counter yeast treatments

A recent study found that 75 percent of women had used over-the-counter medications for yeast infections in the past year, but only one-third of those women actually had a yeast infection. The wrong medicine won't heal you and could make your infection worse or cause complications. If you're not absolutely sure you have a yeast infection, see your healthcare provider first.

Bacterial Vaginosis

The bacteria causing this infection are found in the normal vagina. Unlike yeast infections, though, bacterial vaginosis is thought to be caused by an overgrowth of a number of different organisms. It is not known if this infection can be passed to your partner during sex, so you and your partner should be treated.

Symptoms

The main symptom is an increased vaginal discharge that is usually thin, watery and grayish white or yellow. There is often a strong "fishy" odor. (This may be more noticeable after sex.) There may also be a mild burning or irritation.

Treatment

Antibiotics are usually prescribed by a healthcare provider.

Trichomonoiasis and STDs

See Chapter 8, "What are STDs?"

What can I do to prevent vaginitis?

There are a number of things you can do in your daily life to try to keep from getting vaginitis:

- Avoid spreading bacteria from the rectum to the vagina. After a bowel movement, wipe from front to back, away from the vagina.

- Clean the outer genital area thoroughly and keep it as dry as possible. (Some women use a blow dryer after showering.)

- Avoid irritating agents such as harsh soaps and scented toilet paper. (A good soap to use is *Cetaphil*.)

- Avoid feminine hygiene sprays, douches, and scented or deodorant tampons. It is better to let the vagina cleanse itself in its own natural way. An unpleasant odor should not be merely covered up with these products because it could be a sign of infection that should prompt you to see a healthcare provider. Avoid using talcum powder. It acts as food for yeast. Avoid hanging out in a wet bathing suit.

- Clean diaphragms, cervical caps, and spermicide applicators well after each use.

- Avoid tight jeans or slacks, panties or pantyhose without a cotton crotch, or other clothing that can trap moisture.

- Use condoms during sex. Also keep in mind that men carry natural yeast in their mouths, so if you're infected often and have oral sex often, your partner should see a healthcare provider. He may have an oral yeast infection that can be treated with antifungal mouthwash.

- Check with your healthcare provider about preventing yeast infections if you are prescribed antibiotics for another type of infection.

- Cut down on your intake of sweets and fruits. Yeast can flourish when blood-sugar levels are high.

 ## What healthcare do men need?

Do I take better care of my car?

Do you pay attention to your health? You're young. You're strong. You're in shape. What's to worry about, right? Wrong. Healthcare is a lifetime of prevention. Don't wait until you're 40 … or 50 … or 60. Research suggests that macho attitudes and avoiding medical attention contribute to the widening gap between male and female life expectancy. Did you know that women tend to outlive men by six years? Did you know that women also visit their healthcare provider more often — on a preventive basis?

Your own preventive checkups are like automobile checkups. Are you proud of the way you maintain your car or truck? You know all about car maintenance — tune-ups, oil changes, and such. Taking care of your car means regular maintenance — and taking care of *you* means regular maintenance.

What health checks do I need?

Prevention is the key to good health. The following health checks are recommended for young men:

- Testicular self-exam every month.

- Physical exam every five years (or as recommended by your health-care provider).

- Baseline cholesterol test at age 20, and if normal, every five years thereafter.

- Blood pressure check every year.

- Skin check for changes in moles every month.

- Dental exam and cleaning every six months.

- Eye exam every two to four years, even if you aren't having problems.

How do I manage my own healthcare?

Team up with a healthcare provider. Find one you like and feel comfortable discussing things with. It's best to have one healthcare provider that you see for most health concerns. Eat healthy foods. Exercise. Set up a regular routine that you can stick with. You're much better off doing moderate activity regularly than knocking yourself out every now and then.

Limit the amount of alcohol you drink. Moderation is the key. Some studies suggest one drink a day is generally healthful. (One drink is defined as 12 ounces of beer, five ounces of wine, or 1.5 ounces of liquor.) If you have more than one drink a day, see Chapter 11, "What do I need to know about alcohol?"

If you smoke, quit! No amount of smoking is healthy. See "Will my health improve if I quit?"

If you use recreational drugs, stop. They're also not healthy. See Chapter 11, "What are the straight facts on drugs?"

Learn coping skills for stress and aggression. Do you wear your seatbelt? Do you get speeding tickets? Do you allow anger to affect your driving? What do these questions have to do with health? They show a pattern of exhibiting aggressive and risky behaviors. If you have trouble controlling your anger, help is available. Talk to your healthcare provider.

What is testicular cancer?

Testicular cancer is a disease in which cells become malignant (or cancerous) in one or both testicles. *Testicular cancer is the most common cancer in young men between the ages of 15 and 35.* Any man can get testicular cancer, but it is most common in Caucasian men. (The testicles produce and store sperm, and are also the body's main source of male hormones. These hormones control the development of the reproductive organs and male characteristics.)

What are the risk factors for testicular cancer?

The causes of testicular cancer are not known. Studies, however, show that several factors increase a man's chances of developing it:

Undescended Testicle

Normally the testicles descend into the scrotum before birth. Men who have had a testicle that didn't move down into the scrotum are at greater risk for developing this cancer. (This is true even if surgery was performed to place the testicle in the scrotum.)

Abnormal Testicular Development

Men whose testicles didn't develop normally are at higher risk.

Klinefelter's Syndrome

Men with Klinefelter's Syndrome (a sex chromosome disorder that may be characterized by low levels of male hormones) are at greater risk of developing this cancer.

History of Testicular Cancer

Men who have previously had testicular cancer are at an increased risk of developing cancer in the other testicle.

How will I know if I have testicular cancer?

Most testicular cancers are found by men themselves, sometimes in the shower, sometimes doing a self-check. If you notice anything unusual about your testicles, talk with your healthcare provider. (Again, it's just anatomy to a healthcare provider.) When testicular cancer is found early, the treatment can be less aggressive and may cause fewer side effects. If you notice any of the following symptoms, see your healthcare provider immediately:

- A painless lump or swelling in either testicle. It is typically the size of a pea, but can be as large as a marble or an egg.

- Any enlargement of a testicle or change in the way it feels.

- A feeling of heaviness in the scrotum.

- A dull ache in the lower abdomen or the groin (the area where your thigh meets your abdomen).

- A sudden collection of fluid in the scrotum.

- Pain or discomfort in a testicle or in your scrotum.

- Enlargement or tenderness of the breasts.

These symptoms can be caused by cancer — or by other conditions. Only your healthcare provider, preferably a urologist, can determine what it is and how to treat it.

Is there a self-exam I can do?

Beginning at age 15, you should do a monthly self-exam of your testicles to detect testicular cancer at an early and very curable stage. Perform the exam after a warm bath or shower. (Heat relaxes the scrotum, making it easier to spot anything abnormal.) The National Cancer Institute recommends following these steps every month:

1. Stand in front of a mirror. Check for any swelling on the scrotal skin.

2. Examine each testicle with both hands. Place your index and middle fingers under the testicle with the thumbs placed on top. Roll the testicle gently between the thumbs and fingers. You shouldn't feel

any pain doing this exam. Don't be alarmed if one testicle seems slightly larger than the other. That's normal.

3. Find the epididymis (the soft, tubelike structure behind the testicle that collects and carries sperm). If you're familiar with this structure, you won't mistake it for a suspicious lump. Cancerous lumps usually are found on the sides of the testicle but can also show up on the front. Lumps on the epididymis and free-floating lumps in the scrotum (seemingly not attached to anything) are not cancerous.

If you find a lump, see a healthcare provider, preferably a urologist, right away. The abnormality may be cancer. It may just be an infection. But if it is testicular cancer, it will spread if it is not stopped by treatment. Waiting and hoping will *not* fix it — or make it go away.

How is testicular cancer treated?
Testicular cancer is often completely curable if found and treated early. Most men with testicular cancer can be cured with surgery, radiation, and/or chemotherapy. The side effects depend on the type of treatment and may be different for each person. Early treatment is best, so check your testicles in the shower — and if you find anything, visit your healthcare provider.

How do I get rid of athlete's foot?
Athlete's foot and jock itch are both caused by a fungus. To prevent athletes' foot, apply an anti-fungal powder to your feet and in your shoes. (Don't use talcum powder. It acts as food for athlete's foot.) Wear light-colored socks and open shoes. To prevent jock itch, dry your "privates" thoroughly after showers. To treat, try drugstore remedies like *Lamisil* and *Tinactin*.

 ## What if I'm embarrassed to go to the doctor?

Interactive CD-ROM

Movie

What if I'm embarrassed to go to the doctor?
No need to be. Doctors and other healthcare providers see thousands of body parts in all shapes and sizes. From your provider's point of view, your "private parts" are not sexual — they're just anatomy. You may feel more comfortable with a healthcare provider of your same sex.

What do I tell the doctor?

Before going to the healthcare provider, make a list of everything you want to discuss. Mention the most important issues first, even if they're the most embarrassing. Know your symptoms before you get to the healthcare provider's office. Keep a diary of how you've been feeling, listing symptoms, times of day, what activities you were doing, etc. Be prepared to answer the following questions about your symptoms:

- What do your symptoms feel like?

- How long have you had them?

- Does anything trigger the symptoms?

- Does anything make it feel better or worse?

- Is there a family history of the problem?

What if my doctor doesn't pay attention?

You are responsible for your health, so question your healthcare provider. Try not to be intimidated by or fearful of healthcare providers. Ask questions. Make sure the provider explains everything clearly. If you don't understand something, keep asking until you do. It's important that the healthcare provider pays full attention to you, so if the healthcare provider asks the same questions repeatedly, cuts you off when you're trying to answer, ignores you, or brushes off your questions, get his/her attention before proceeding. If you feel your concerns are not being addressed, get a second opinion or find a different healthcare provider.

How do I choose a doctor?

It's always a good idea to have a primary healthcare provider so that you can both keep track of your medical history as you grow older. But how do you find a good one? Ask for recommendations from family, friends, or co-workers. Check the healthcare provider's credentials. Use your local library to check the *American Medical Association's Directory of Physicians in the U.S.* or the *Directory of Medical Specialists*, which lists dates and details of a healthcare provider's background. Is he/she affiliated with a major respected hospital? Is he/she board certified?

Schedule a get-acquainted visit to determine how easy the primary care provider is to talk with and whether your approaches to healthcare are in sync with the healthcare provider's. Don't wait until you're sick to have this meeting. If you're not satisfied with this healthcare provider, keep looking. You have a right to change healthcare providers. (Keep in mind, though, that if you have health insurance, there may be a limited number of healthcare providers to choose from.)

 ## Was I born to be fat?

Was I born to be fat?

No. A study conducted by the Centers for Disease Control found that 53 percent of a person's health is related to lifestyle; 10 percent is based on the quality of medical care; and 19 percent is from the environment. The remaining 18 percent? Heredity. So, 82 percent of your weight problem is based on things within your control. Here are some easy ways to shed a few pounds without even trying:

- Cut back on soft drinks. They're empty calories full of sugar.

- Order smaller portions or eat half and take the rest home for lunch tomorrow.

- Stop "super-sizing" your meals. Never order anything other than a "small" size.

- Eat slowly. Take time to enjoy the taste and texture of your food.

- Buy single-servings of snack foods (like the six-cookie packages of Oreos).

- Use smaller-sized dishes at home.

What's my BMI?

BMI is your Body Mass Index. The BMI, developed by a panel of obesity experts, describes body weight relative to height. See the chart on page 313 to determine your BMI.

You're considered overweight if your BMI is 25 to 29.9. You're considered obese if you have a BMI of 30 and above. The panel's assessment of weight also includes having a waist circumference greater than 35 inches for women and 40 inches for men.

BMI can't distinguish heavier lean tissue (such as bone and muscle) from fat, so if you're very muscular, you may have a high BMI without health risks. A fitness professional or medical professional can use a special tool (calipers) to pinch folds of skin to measure underlying fat.

Why can't I just diet?

If you want to reduce your body fat, you have to improve your diet and work out to get stronger and add muscle. One big plus of regular exercise is that, as your body adds muscle, it burns more daily calories to maintain that muscle than it does to maintain fat. Another plus is that muscle is denser than fat. A pound of muscle takes up much less space on your body than a pound of fat. That's why your clothes fit more loosely.

People who lose weight by dieting alone and gauge their success by what they see on the scale have a much smaller chance of long-term success. (The scale is a poor indicator of overall fitness.)

Can I make fitness a part of my daily life?

Staying active is the key to maintaining vitality throughout your life. When fitness is your goal, you'll find success easier and more rewarding. If you focus on weight loss or body sculpting, you'll end up frustrated because you won't see results fast enough. Fitness is about health — physical, mental, and nutritional. Getting fit is a challenge. You must form habits to get in shape and stay that way. Start exercising three times a week at a pace that keeps you moving but is not so strenuous that you can't hold a normal conversation. Practice weight-bearing exercises, such as running, walking, aerobics, or weight-lifting. It can help slow bone loss.

Set realistic and specific goals. Examples are to exercise three times a week for 90 days, to increase my time on the track from 20 to 30 minutes in two months, to lose one inch by a specific date. Make exercise a part of your daily life. You eat everyday. You breathe everyday. You drink water everyday. These things keep you healthy. So, add, "You exercise everyday" to the list. Try to do at least 10 minutes of some form of exercise everyday.

What's my BMI?

To determine your BMI...

1. Multiply your weight in pounds by .45.

2. Multiply your height in inches by .025.

3. Square the answer from Step 2.

4. Divide the answer from Step 1 by the answer from Step 3.

For Example:

Let's say you are 150 pounds and 5'6" tall...

1. 150 x .45 = 68   (your weight in pounds x .45)
2. 66 x .025 = 1.65   (your height in inches x .025)
3. 1.65 x 1.65 = 2.72   (square the answer [1.65] from Step 2)
4. 68 ÷ 2.72 = **25 BMI**   (divide the answer from Step 1 [68] by
                              the answer from Step 3 [2.72])

For most women, 18 to 22 percent body fat is a healthy range.

For men, 19 to 24 percent body fat is a healthy range.

Figure 9B

Find a gym that's within 10 minutes of your home or work — or you won't make the effort to get there.

Pick a fitness method that works for you. If you're a social person, pick an exercise class. If you're solitary, running, swimming, or hiking might be preferred. Keep in mind, however, that too much of one activity can cause injuries and burnout. Add variety and discover under-used muscles while resting over-used ones. Use the buddy system. Exercising with a friend, trainer, or club can help you stay motivated — and it won't seem like exercise. It'll be fun!

Do I have to drink eight glasses of water a day?

Yes! Water helps prevent minor aches and pains, as well as diseases. If you exercise or are battling a cold, you need even more water. Drinking enough water can prevent headaches, weight gain, kidney stones, even cancer. If the idea of 64 ounces of water a day seems overwhelming, grab two one-quart bottles from your local grocery and drink them each day. Refill them for the next day. And the next.

Many confuse hunger with thirst. So, if you're between meals and feeling hungry, drink a glass of water before you reach for that candy bar. Don't wait until you're thirsty to drink water.

Is my blood pressure normal?

Your blood pressure is calculated with two numbers: a systolic rate and a diastolic rate. As an example, it is read as 135 over 85. Normal systolic rate is 135 or lower. Normal diastolic rate is 85 or lower. A blood pressure check is simple: A healthcare provider (or even a machine in your grocery store) places a cuff around your upper arm, pumps air into the cuff, and then reads the measurements as the air is let out. Your blood pressure should be checked at least every two years.

Is my cholesterol below 200?

A blood cholesterol test measures the total amount of cholesterol in your blood. The HDL, or "good" cholesterol, cleanses your arteries, while the LDL, the "bad" cholesterol, builds up and clogs arteries. An ideal cholesterol reading is below 200. The following are the latest guidelines to help you read your test results:

Risk	Total Cholesterol	HDL/good	LDL/bad
Healthy	below 200	above 35	below 130
Borderline	200-239	n/a	130-159
High	above 239	less than 35	above 159

It is recommended that you have a cholesterol test done when you're 20, and then once every five years. If your test scores in the borderline or high-risk categories, get retested; and if necessary, work with your healthcare provider to make changes in your food and fitness plan. Eating an unhealthy diet, being a couch potato, and gaining weight can make cholesterol rise.

 ## Is stress making me sick?

Is stress making me sick?

Scientists have long suspected that stress can weaken your immune system, which makes it easier for you to become sick. Stress can take a toll on your health. Those who suffer from chronic stress, such as an on-going conflict with relatives or co-workers, can increase the odds of catching a cold by as much as five times. A stressful day can leave your stomach in turmoil, with cramping, diarrhea, or constipation. Those who suffer from headaches, particularly migraines, often find that their headache strikes or gets worse during times of stress, anger, fear, or disappointment.

When you're stressed, cuts, scrapes, and bruises can take longer to heal. A number of skin problems may also be a result of stress. Acne can become worse. People even lose their hair after a very stressful event. Stress has long been linked to heart disease. New research now suggests that even a little stress can damage your heart. It is also common for people who are highly stressed to develop fat around their middles, which increases their risk of heart attack.

How can I reduce stress?

First, put your problems into perspective. Before you let something upset you, ask yourself these questions,

- *"Will this matter tomorrow?"*

- *"Will this matter a year from now?"*

If not, don't fret over it. Here are some tips that can help you reduce stress:

- Maintain a healthy diet. Avoid caffeine (coffee, tea, and sodas) at least six hours before you go to bed.

- Exercise. Aerobic activity reduces stress and the risk of depression. Take a 10- to 20- minute walk to clear your head.

- Get eight hours of sleep every night. It can help relieve tension and improve your mood, not to mention making you more clear-headed.

- Learn to relax. Calm your mind and body. Try yoga. Check out *www.yogasite.com* and *www.yogazone.com.*

- Find support — a friend, colleague, or mental healthcare provider — to confide in.

- Learn time management skills. (See Chapter 6, "Time Management.")

- Visit your healthcare provider if you're feeling depressed or anxious.

- Live in the moment. Stop anticipating life — and live it.

- Accept imperfection. No one is perfect, not even you.

- Put yourself at the top of the list. If you don't take care of yourself, how can you take care of anything else? Take 30 minutes each day just for you to do whatever you want.

- Be quiet with yourself for at least five minutes a day.

- Take responsibility for your emotions. There is only one person who gives you your problems — and that's you! You create your own feelings and responses to situations. If you're feeling stressed, what can *you* do to change your situation?

- Pay attention to your feelings and conflicts. Don't blame someone. Do you find yourself saying, *"My boss ruined my day."* or *"She pushes my buttons."* or *"If he wouldn't have ..."* Start using the word *"I"* to begin your sentences. This helps you regain control over your life.

- Don't take things personally.

- Change your attitude. A positive mind leads to a healthy body.

- You cannot control anyone but you.

- Use positive statements when talking to yourself. *"I can handle this."* or *"Something good will come out of this."*

Can chocolate help?

Wonderful news ... YES! Chocolate is a perfect blend of ingredients that stimulate feel-good endorphins and boost calming serotonin in the brain. It contains *phenylethylamine*, a chemical in the brain that's released when two people fall in love. It also contains *theobromine* and *magnesium*, which help increase brain function. The caffeine in chocolate (about six milligrams per ounce) may also give you a mental boost.

Stressed spelled backwards is 'desserts!'

Keep in mind that a little chocolate goes a long way. For the perfect dose, keep a supply of **Dove Dark Chocolate Promises** (or milk chocolate, if you prefer). One or two are enough to satisfy your craving. (And they have a little note of inspiration on the inside of the wrapper!)

Am I laughing enough?

Research has found that pre-schoolers laugh an average of 400 times a day — and adults laugh an average of 15 times a day. Is it time to lighten up? Laughter has long been called "the best medicine." Laughing relaxes muscles and eases tension. It boosts your immune system, eases pain, and reduces stress hormones. No one knows why laughter has the effects it does, but one theory is that it releases more endorphins that make you feel good.

The first studies of the effect of humor on the body were conducted in the

U.S. in the 1930s. It wasn't until 1979, however, that humor research got a real boost when the editor of *Saturday Review*, Norman Cousins, developed a painful and potentially-crippling arthritis. Cousins watched videos of *Candid Camera, the Marx Brothers*, and the *Three Stooges*. And, although healthcare providers gave him little chance of recovery, within eight days, Cousins' pain began to subside and he returned to work. He documented his recovery in the book, *Anatomy of an Illness,* and founded the Humor Research Task Force.

Will writing in a journal help?

Yes. Studies have shown that people who express their emotions on paper feel less anxiety and depression. They also find that it helps them understand issues before trying to communicate with others. Start by writing down your reactions to this section. Simply describe how you're feeling. As you write, deeper thoughts and connections to past events will emerge. Just continue writing. Once you get started, write whenever you feel like it — between classes at school, on lunch breaks, over morning coffee. Don't worry about using correct grammar or punctuation. (This isn't an English class — and you won't be graded.) As you write, look for recurring themes in your journal to help you figure out the source(s) of your stress. Once you figure it out, take action. Oh, and guys, journals aren't just for girls! (Refer to Chapter 5, "How do I set goals?" to help you take action.)

 Am I getting enough sleep?

Am I getting enough sleep?

Adults need eight hours of sleep each night, yet the National Sleep Foundation says that 40 percent of Americans report feeling so sleepy during the day that it interferes with their activities. Inadequate sleep can make you cranky and irritable. It impairs your motor skills and your ability to think, concentrate, remember, make decisions, and be creative. It can make you more likely to become easily upset and act out. (The symptoms of road rage are classic signs of sleep deprivation.) It's also a major reason that car accidents are the second leading cause of death in young people.

> It is a common experience that a problem difficult at night is resolved in the morning after the committee of sleep has worked on it."
> ~ *John Steinbeck*

Should I take a nap?

If you're not getting enough sleep, these tips may help:

- Establish a routine. Although this may seem unrealistic with your schedule, try to keep a regular bedtime and get up at the same time everyday, regardless of what time you fell asleep or how long you slept. Try not to vary your times by more than an hour, even on weekends.

- Relax before you go to bed. Take a warm shower or bath, listen to soothing music, read a book.

- Avoid alcohol. While it may help you temporarily relax, it actually lightens sleep or wakes you up as it leaves your system.

- Don't drink soda, coffee, or tea that contains caffeine after 5 p.m.

- Keep your bedroom cool and dark.

- Don't use your bedroom for other activities, such as work, studying, or watching TV.

- Take a 15-minute nap during the day.

- Exercise regularly, but don't exercise within four hours of bedtime or your increased adrenaline levels will keep you awake longer.

- Finish a big meal at least three hours before bedtime.

- Reflect on your successes for the day … and look forward to something positive happening tomorrow.

- If you don't fall asleep within 30 minutes, get up and do something non-stimulating until you feel sleepy.

- Visualize yourself waking up alert, cheerful, and in a positive state of mind.

What if I wake up in the middle of the night?

If you wake up, don't toss and turn. Get up and do some light reading in another room. You might also try writing down things that are bothering you. (These might be what's keeping you awake.) Don't start working, cleaning, or paying your bills. It wakes your brain up. Go back to bed when you feel sleepy.

Do I have sleep apnea?

Up to nine percent of adult males and four percent of adult females have some form of sleep apnea. Sleep apnea causes a person to repeatedly stop breathing during sleep. Most sleep disorders are treatable, so if you think you have a sleep disorder, such as sleep apnea or insomnia, visit your healthcare provider.

Am I too old to get a cavity?

(Contributed by Robert L. Bell, D.D.S.)

Am I too old to get a cavity?

Many adults think cavities are just for kids, but cavities are an adult problem, too. Tooth decay occurs when bacterial plaque on the tooth's surface dissolves the outer enamel and makes its way into the tooth. Certain foods, such as candy, cookies, breads, crackers, and cereals, cause acid to form and decay your teeth.

Just floss the teeth you want to keep.

The best way to prevent tooth decay is to brush your teeth twice a day and to floss between your teeth once a day. Dentists suggest brushing your teeth for two to three minutes. (Most people brush for only 45 seconds!) To brush long enough, sing a song (to yourself), count to 300, or buy an inexpensive egg timer to put on your bathroom counter. Use a toothpaste that contains fluoride, which also helps protect your teeth from decay.

Replace your toothbrush every three months or when the bristles look splayed, matted, or begin to stiffen. Use a toothpaste with a flavor you like so you'll brush longer. Use a mouth rinse that contains fluoride. When choosing any dental product, look for the American Dental Association (ADA) Seal of Acceptance. Visit your dentist twice a year for cleanings. Eat a balanced diet. And, no matter how tired you are, always brush your teeth before you go to bed.

Do I have gum disease?

Gum disease is a major cause of tooth loss in adults. Because it's usually painless, you may not know you have it. In the early stages, called gingivitis, the gums can become red, swollen, and bleed easily. Gingivitis can be healed by brushing and flossing daily. In the more advanced stages, called periodontitis, the gums and bones that support your teeth can become seriously damaged, causing your teeth to become loose, fall out, or have to be removed by a dentist.

If you notice any of the following signs of gum disease, see your dentist immediately:

- Gums that bleed when you brush your teeth.

- Red, swollen, or tender gums.

- Gums that have pulled away from your teeth.

- Bad breath that doesn't go away.

- Pus between your teeth and gums.

- Loose teeth.

- A change in the way your teeth fit together when you bite.

What is TMJ?

Do you cringe when you eat, drink, or laugh? If so, you could be one of the 10 million Americans with temporo-mandibular joint disease, better known as TMJ. TMJ is a painful jaw condition that can cause limited jaw movement; radiating pain in the face, neck, or shoulders; a painful clicking of the jaw joint; headaches; blurred vision; numbness in the hands and fingers; and more. If you suspect TMJ, visit a dentist who is experienced in treating TMJ.

TMJ usually goes away with little or no treatment. Medications or surgery can help, but recent studies show that the following steps can be up to 97 percent effective in relieving symptoms:

- Eat soft foods.

- Apply heat or ice packs.

- Avoid extreme jaw movements, like singing aloud or chewing gum.

- Yawn. Although yawning may be the last thing you want to do when your jaw hurts, research shows that if you open your mouth as wide as you can, hold it for five seconds, then close it slowly, you should feel less jaw pain within two weeks. Do five sets of five repetitions, four times a day. Within three weeks, work your way up to five sets of fifteen repetitions, four times a day. Yawning relaxes the muscles surrounding the jaw joint.

- Listen to music. Are you stressed? Stress, anger, and depression can aggravate TMJ by causing muscle tension in your jaw. Try relaxing to your favorite music for 20 minutes a day. Studies show it can reduce your pain by as much as one-third.

- Take your vitamins. Take a daily multi-vitamin that contains calcium, phosphorus, iodine, zinc, magnesium, and copper. These minerals build healthy bones and muscles (even into adulthood). TMJ has been linked to a deficiency of these minerals.

For ladies taking the Pill, researchers at the University of Washington discovered that women taking oral contraceptives had a 20 percent increase in their risk of developing TMJ. Although researchers are not sure why, they believe the link is estrogen. Talk to your healthcare provider. You may be able to use a lower-dose estrogen Pill.

What causes bad breath?
Bad breath (halitosis) can be caused by several things:

1. the foods you eat (such as garlic and onions);

2. infrequent eating by dieters; and

3. food particles that stay in your mouth collecting bacteria if you don't brush and floss daily.

Persistent bad breath is a warning sign of periodontal disease. Visit *www.breathcure.com* for more information.

Do I have a canker sore or a cold sore?

Canker sores occur outside the mouth. Canker sores, small ulcers with a white or gray base and a red border, are very common and often recur. You can have more than one canker sore at a time. Canker sores usually heal in a week or two. Treat with an over-the-counter topical anesthetic.

Cold sores usually occur inside the mouth. Cold sores, also known as fever blisters or herpes simplex, are composed of groups of painful, fluid-filled blisters that often appear around the lips. They are usually caused by herpes virus type 1 and are very contagious. Cold sores usually heal in a week. Treat with an over-the-counter topical anesthetic. If you have frequent cold sores, your healthcare provider may prescribe anti-viral drugs to help reduce these kinds of viral infections.

Do I need to have my wisdom teeth pulled?

Wisdom teeth are a valuable asset when they're healthy and properly positioned. Problems, however, often develop that require them to be removed. If your jaw isn't large enough to accommodate wisdom teeth, they can become impacted (unable to come in or misaligned). Wisdom teeth may grow sideways, emerge only part way from the gum, or remain trapped beneath the gum and bone.

Dentists generally recommend extracting (pulling) your wisdom teeth when:

1. wisdom teeth only partially erupt, leaving an opening for bacteria to enter around the tooth, which can cause infection;

2. there is a chance that the poorly-aligned wisdom teeth will damage adjacent teeth; or

3. a cyst (fluid-filled sac) forms, destroying surrounding structures such as bone and tooth roots.

Is oral piercing dangerous?

Infection is common in oral piercings because your mouth contains millions of bacteria. Your tongue, a popular piercing site in the mouth, could swell large enough to close off your airway. Piercing can also cause uncontrollable bleeding or nerve damage. You can choke on the studs, barbells, or hoops that come loose in your mouth and contact with the jewelry can chip or crack your teeth. If you feel you need to get your tongue (or any other body part) pierced, find a clean, reputable business to do the piercing.

 ## Can I commit to quit smoking?

Can cigarettes kill me?

Cigarettes alone kill more than 400,000 Americans each year — more than AIDS, alcohol, car accidents, murders, suicides, illegal drugs, and fires combined. Those who breathe your "second-hand" smoke are also at risk. Why do so many people smoke when they know cigarettes can kill? Because the health consequences seem so far in the future. (Lung cancer can take years to develop.) And because cigarettes are addictive.

Seventy percent of adult smokers *want* to quit completely, but because the nicotine in cigarettes is an addictive drug, quitting can be difficult. For some, nicotine is as addictive as heroine or cocaine — and even if you only smoke a few cigarettes a day, you'll crave cigarettes when you try to stop. Smoking among 10th-grade girls in high school is now 25 percent higher than it was in 1991 and more than 80 percent of smokers start using cigarettes before the age of 18. Each day, almost 3,000 youngsters become regular smokers — of which an estimated 1,000 of them will die from smoking-related illnesses.

Cigarette smoke contains more than 4,000 chemical compounds that pass through your mouth and into your lungs each time you take a puff. The three main ingredients that harm your body are tar, carbon monoxide, and nicotine. A few of the other chemicals present in cigarettes include:

- arsenic (a poison);

- hydrogen cyanide (a gas used in executions);

- ammonia (a cleaning agent); and

- formaldehyde (a gas that, when dissolved in water, is used as a preservative for dead specimens. Remember that frog in biology?)

Cigars and smokeless tobacco (chew) are not safe alternatives to cigarette smoking. They, too, can be addictive and can cause serious health effects, such as cancer of the mouth.

How much money does it cost me to smoke?

Do you have any idea how much money you spend on cigarettes each year? You may be surprised — and horrified! Enter the following information:

_____ # of packs I smoke per day

x $ _____ price I pay per pack

x   365 days

= $ _____ I spend per year on cigarettes.

Wow! Just think of the things you could buy with that money — things that don't harm your health… a new car, a trip to Hawaii, three semesters of college, several months of rent, a new computer, a to-die-for stereo, and more.

How will my health improve if I quit?

When you stop smoking, there are almost instantaneous benefits to your health. According to a 1990 U.S. surgeon general's report, the health benefits listed on page 326 can occur. (Keep in mind that these are estimates and will vary depending on how long and how much you have smoked, your age when you started and stopped, and your overall health.)

Are there certain risks for women?

Lung cancer is now the leading cause of death among women, killing more women than breast and ovarian cancer combined. Lung cancer is fatal within five years of diagnosis for 86 percent of its victims.

Almost one in four American women smoke. That's 23 million women! Researchers are finding the effects of tobacco seem to be far worse for women than for men. In 1999, scientists at the University of Pittsburgh discovered a gene that accelerates lung-cancer growth is more active in females. This finding might explain why women are one and one-half times more likely than men to develop lung cancer, even when they smoke fewer cigarettes over a shorter period of time.

How will my health improve if I quit?

When you stop smoking, there are almost instantaneous benefits to your health. According to a 1990 U.S. Surgeon General's report, the following health benefits can occur. (Keep in mind that these are estimates and will vary depending on how long and how much you have smoked, your age when you started and stopped, and your overall health.)

Immediately following your last puff
Your pulse rate and blood pressure, which are abnormally elevated during smoking, start returning to normal. Blood levels of carbon monoxide, a potent carcinogen inhaled during smoking, begin to decrease.

A few days after you quit
Your senses of taste and smell become sharper as nerve endings re-grow. Breathing is less difficult as greater amounts of oxygen reach your lungs and you may begin to feel more energetic.

Within a year after you quit
Cilia, tiny hair-like filaments that sweep impurities out of the lungs and stop functioning when you smoke, start to regenerate. Coughing, sinus congestion, fatigue, and shortness of breath diminish.

After five smoke-free years
Your risk of developing mouth, esophageal, or bladder cancer drops by 50 percent. Lung infections, such as bronchitis and pneumonia, are far less frequent. The lung cancer death rate for the average pack-a-day smoker decreases from 137 deaths per 100,000 to 72 deaths per 100,000.

After 10 to 15 years
The lung cancer death rate drops to 12 deaths per 100,000, almost the same rate as non-smokers. Your likelihood of dying prematurely, especially from a stroke or heart attack, is about the same as for a person who has never smoked. Your chances of developing other cancers, such as those of the mouth, larynx, esophagus, bladder, kidney, and pancreas, will decline significantly. Compared with a person who continues to smoke, your risk of getting lung cancer will drop by 50 to 70 percent — and will continue to fall if you remain tobacco-free.

Figure 9C

Research suggests that the nicotine in cigarettes has a somewhat different physical effect on women, easing stress and anxiety levels much more profoundly than it does for men. It's also been discovered that nicotine-replacement therapies (patches, gums, nasal inhalers) aren't as effective in women. If they're not working for you, ask your healthcare provider about *Zyban*, an anti-smoking pill that also inhibits weight gain after you quit smoking.

If you're pregnant, please quit smoking today. You can severely endanger your unborn child's health.

What are my options?

Most people who quit smoking for three months never smoke again. There are now medical aids, nicotine replacement products, to help you quit smoking. Like cigarettes, the products deliver nicotine into the blood to relieve some of the withdrawal symptoms, but they don't contain the tar and carbon monoxide that are largely responsible for the dangerous health problems associated with cigarettes.

Studies show that nicotine replacement therapies can double your chances of quitting. Choose the method that appeals to you — and try a different method if the first one doesn't work. You don't have to quit cold turkey — these products can help you: nicotine gum, inhalers, patches, and nasal sprays. The newest option is *Zyban*, an anti-smoking pill that contains no nicotine.

Nicotine Gum
Nicotine is absorbed through the lining of your mouth.

Nicotine Inhaler
A plastic cylinder containing a cartridge that emits nicotine when you puff on it. It delivers nicotine into the mouth, not the lungs, and enters your body much more slowly than nicotine in cigarettes.

Nicotine Patch
Delivers nicotine through the skin in different strengths over different lengths of time.

Nicotine Nasal Spray
Delivers nicotine through the lining of the nose when you squirt it directly into each nostril.

Zyban

The newest option available is an anti-smoking pill, *Zyban*, that seems to reduce nicotine withdrawal symptoms and the urge to smoke. *Zyban* has one thing that sets it apart: it contains no nicotine. (Available only through a healthcare provider.)

Some people have found hypnosis and acupuncture helpful in quitting, but these methods have not been proven to work.

How do I manage withdrawal symptoms?

As with other addictive drugs, you can experience withdrawal when you get less nicotine than you're used to. When you quit smoking, you may *temporarily* experience irritability, frustration, anger, anxiety, difficulty concentrating, restlessness, and cravings for tobacco. The list below offers suggestions to help you manage temporary symptoms:

Bad Breath

Brush and floss your teeth more often. Drink lots of water.

Constipation, Gas, Stomach Pain

Drink plenty of liquids and add roughage to your diet. Go for walks.

Cough, Dry Mouth/Throat, Nasal Drip

Sip ice water. Drink plenty of liquids. Try cough drops, chewing gum, or hard sugarless candy.

Craving a Cigarette

Wait out the urge. It will only last a few minutes. Exercise, stay busy, and drink water.

Dizziness

Get fresh air. Go for a walk. Change positions when getting up.

Fatigue

Get extra sleep. Exercise. Take naps.

Headaches

Take a warm bath or shower. Do more physical activities. Cut down on caffeinated beverages like coffee and soft drinks.

Hunger and/or Cravings

Drink water or low-calorie drinks. Keep low-calorie snacks on hand. Chew a toothpick or sugar-free gum, or munch on raw vegetables.

Insomnia

Take a hot, relaxing bath. Avoid caffeine after 5 p.m. Try relaxing at bedtime with a glass of warm milk, deep breathing, and relaxation techniques.

Irritability, Grouchiness, Tension

Breathe deep, take walks, exercise, use relaxation techniques, chew nicotine gum, and cut down on coffee and soft drinks.

Tightness in the Chest

Try deep breathing and relaxation methods. Wait it out.

(Source: Saskatchewan Lung Association)

Any tips that can help me quit?

A smoker's entire day is filled with cues that trigger the desire for a cigarette: the first cup of coffee, sitting down to check e-mails, finishing a meal, a break between classes. Smokers get used to lighting up in certain situations. If you're serious about quitting, drugs alone won't work. You must also change your "smoking" situations. So, set a date to quit and then change your smoking routine:

- Change to a less desirable brand of cigarettes.

- Buy one pack at a time.

- Discard your lighter. Use matches instead.

- Carry your cigarettes in a different place.

- Smoke with the opposite hand.

- Throw away all your cigarettes and ashtrays in your home, car, and workplace.

- Inhale less of each cigarette and smoke less of each cigarette.

- Smoke fewer cigarettes each day. If necessary, count out a limit to smoke each day. When you've smoked your limit for the day, wait until the next day to smoke again.

- Delay lighting up. The craving will go away.

- Find a support system, whether it's a formal stop-smoking program or informal support from your friends. Try to find a buddy who'll quit with you.

- Spend time around non-smokers.

- Don't drink alcohol while trying to quit. It's one of the most common smoking triggers.

- As a distraction from thoughts of smoking, take time for a fun activity.

- Exercise. It'll keep your mind off smoking and will help you feel better physically.

- Get information. Quit-smoking programs, self-help materials, and hotlines are available throughout the U.S. Call the American Lung Association at 1-800-LUNGSA or log onto *www.lungusa.org* for help to quit.

What are my top 10 reasons to quit?

When you make the decision to stop smoking, commit to use whatever means it takes. Make a list of your Top 10 reasons to quit smoking. See page 331.

What does it feels like to have emphysema?

Next time you get a cup of coffee, take the plastic straw coffee stirrer (with hollow ends) and put it in your mouth. Pinch your nose closed and breathe through the straw for one minute. Do you feel panicky? Can you imagine breathing like that for a full day? How about a year? Ten years? Keep smoking and you may find out.

Are bidis safe to smoke?

Bidis produce three times the nicotine and carbon monoxide and five times the tar of regular cigarettes. Bidis also don't burn as easily as ciga-

My Top 10 Reasons
to Quit Smoking

List your top 10 reasons to quit smoking. Writing them down, committing to a quitting date, and listing a reward will encourage and inspire you.

1. _____

2. _____

3. _____

4. _____

5. _____

6. _____

7. _____

8. _____

9. _____

10. _____

My date to quit smoking: _____

My reward after being smoke-free for one month: _____
_____
_____

Figure 9D

rettes, so you have to inhale more deeply and frequently to keep the bidi from going out. Bidi smokers have been found to have twice the risk of lung cancer as cigarette smokers, and five times the risk of lung cancer as non-smokers.

 ## Any other good health tidbits?

Why am I always tired?

Do you feel tired a lot? You might be causing your own fatigue. Here are some common energy drainers:

- You don't exercise. You can boost your energy just by walking 20 to 30 minutes two or three times a week.

- You go for long periods without eating. When you skip food for more than three and a half hours, your blood sugar drops and you start to drag. Try snacking on fruit and low-fat yogurt.

- You don't get enough sleep. If you think you gain time by losing sleep, you're wrong. It catches up with you by making you less efficient and more prone to anxiety and depression.

- You get dehydrated. Drink eight glasses of water each day. Your energy will boost after a day or two.

- Your roommate snores. A recent Mayo Clinic study found that if you sleep with someone (not necessarily in the same room) who snores, you lose one hour of sleep each night. The snorer's problem may be curable, so send him/her to a sleep specialist. In the meantime, turn a fan on in your room at night for white (background) noise.

- You're not getting enough iron. A common problem among young women is iron deficiency, especially chronic dieters and vegetarians. To get more iron in your diet, eat meat, chicken, dried peas and beans, and enriched breads and grains. While there are iron supplements on the market, have your healthcare provider do a hemoglobin (blood) test first. Too much iron can be harmful.

Is it a cold or the flu?

No one wants to spend time and money at the doctor's office only to be told, *"You have a cold. Stay home, get plenty of rest, eat soup, and drink lots of fluids."* So, how do you know if you have a cold or the flu? See page 334.

To prevent yourself from getting the flu, wash your hands (sing the *Happy Birthday* song twice while washing) using warm water and soap to avoid picking up the virus from other people, and drink plenty of water or caffeine-free drinks to keep your body hydrated. Get a flu shot in October or early November. It can lower your risk of getting the flu by 70 to 90 percent. Cost is about $20, although some clinics offer free shots. Check your county health department or a local clinic.

If I have ADD or ADHD, can I manage it?

Attention Deficit Disorder (ADD) and Attention Deficit Hyperactivity Disorder (ADHD) affect many children — and even some adults. If you have any of the following characteristics, you might want to check with your healthcare provider: over-activity, inattentiveness, distractibility, restlessness, impulsiveness, uncooperativeness, and disorganization. There are many resources available to help you manage ADD and ADHD into your adult life. Two excellent books are *Driven to Distraction* and *Answers to Distraction* by Edward M. Hallowell, M.D. and John J. Ratey, M.D.

Have I had a meningitis vaccine?

Before you head off to college, make sure you have a meningococcal vaccine. A study in a recent issue of the *Journal of American Medical Association* found that college students who lived on campus were three times more likely to catch this deadly infection than students who lived off campus. The vaccine is about $60, although some clinics offer free vaccines. Contact your county health department or local clinic.

When was my last tetanus shot?

If you haven't had a tetanus shot within the last 10 years, get one. Tetanus happens when bacteria invade an open wound and cause lockjaw, muscle spasms, difficulty swallowing, headache, and fever. Clean all wounds thoroughly because dirt and dead tissue promote the growth of bacteria.

What are eating disorders?

According to the National Institute of Mental Health, more than five million Americans suffer from eating disorders such as anorexia nervosa and

Is it a cold or the flu?

Symptoms	Cold	Flu
Fever	Rare	102° – 104° for 3 to 4 days
Headache	Rare	Common
General aches & pains	Slight	Common, often severe
Fatigue, weakness	Mild	Can last for 2 to 3 weeks
Extreme exhaustion	Never	Early and common
Stuffy nose	Common	Sometimes
Sneezing	Common	Sometimes
Sore throat	Common	Sometimes
Chest discomfort/ Cough	Mild to moderate; hacking cough	Common, can be severe
Complications	Sinus congestion or earache	Bronchitis, pneumonia
Prevention	None	Vaccinations, anti-viral drugs
Treatment	Over-the-counter medicines, rest, lots of water and Gatorade, and good hand-washing	Anti-viral drugs, over-the-counter medicines, rest, lots of water and Gatorade, and good hand-washing

Figure 9E

bulimia nervosa. These disorders are physically and emotionally destructive. They're not illnesses, but coping mechanisms — faulty coping mechanisms. They can cause serious health problems, from mood swings to osteoporosis, kidney failure, heart failure, and even death.

The National Eating Disorders Screening Program estimates that 1,000 women die each year from anorexia nervosa. Eating disorders aren't just "girl" problems anymore, though. They're on the rise among teenage boys — with devastating health effects. Conservative estimates suggest that one sufferer in 10 is male, although some experts put the number as high as one in six.

Anorexia nervosa

Anorexia nervosa is essentially self-starvation, a refusal to maintain a minimally normal body weight. Anorexia can be life-threatening. People with anorexia are usually extremely thin. The main symptoms of anorexia include weight loss (sometimes severe), refusal to maintain body weight at or above a minimally-normal weight, intense fear of gaining weight, disturbance in the body image you hold of yourself, menstrual changes or no menstruation at all. Secondary signs include fatigue, depression, anxiety, sleeplessness, and avoiding other people.

Bulimia nervosa

Bulimia nervosa involves repeated episodes of compulsive overeating usually followed by self-induced vomiting, abuse of laxatives or diuretics, fasting, or excessive exercise. People of normal weight may have this condition. The main symptoms of bulimia include recurrent episodes of binge eating, feeling that eating behaviors can't be controlled, eating more food in a binge episode than in a normal meal or snack, following a binge by efforts to prevent weight gain, and unhealthy focus on body shape and weight. Secondary signs include cyclical weight loss and gain of more than 10 pounds, dehydration, fatigue, depression, anxiety, damaged teeth and gums from the acid in vomit, swollen cheeks from regular vomiting, and unexplained and persistent diarrhea.

Denial is often a part of eating disorders — but if you, or someone you know, avoids meals, heads for the bathroom after eating, is losing weight, exercises excessively, or seems withdrawn, get help. The longer the disorder goes on, the harder it is to recover. Treatment can include nutrition education, psychotherapy, family counseling, prescribed medications, or hospitalization. Contact a healthcare provider or call the National Anorexia Hotline at 1-847-831-3438 to find a support group or referrals in your area.

 ## Do I need health insurance?

Do I need health insurance?

Going without personal medical insurance is risky. You may feel perfectly fine today, but you could be sick or injured tomorrow. Not having health insurance could mean financial ruin. Unfortunately, there are no cheap choices. If you do buy health insurance, it's expensive. If you don't, and you get sick or hurt, healthcare will be very expensive. If your employer offers health insurance, take it. If you're currently insured on your parent's policy, check to see how long you'll be covered. Some policies only cover dependents until they reach the age of 18 (or 22 if you go to college). Some schools also offer group insurance policies for students.

What are my insurance options?

The most common options are traditional fee-for-service plans and managed-care plans. These are offered through health maintenance organizations (HMOs) and preferred provider organizations (PPOs).

Fee-for-Service

Fee-for-service plans generally allow you to visit a healthcare provider or hospital of your choice. Either you or your healthcare provider will send the bill to the insurance company, which will pay a portion of your covered expenses (usually 80 percent) after you've met your annual deductible. You pay the remaining 20 percent, or the co-payment, up to the maximum out-of-pocket sum specified by your policy.

HMO

An HMO provides health services through a network of healthcare providers and hospitals. The HMO pays these providers a fixed payment (regardless of the amount of services provided). In addition to the plan's premium, enrollees (you) pay a modest fee — usually between $5 and $20 — each time you use the services of the HMO providers. Most HMOs ask you to choose a healthcare provider to be your primary care physician (PCP) to take care of most of your medical needs. You are normally required to use the plan's network of providers to receive benefits and must get a referral from your primary care physician to see a specialist.

PPO

A PPO consists of physicians, dentists, hospitals, and other facilities contracted with insurance companies, employers and other organizations to provide services to members in specific groups. Services are offered at a discount, but members are not strictly limited to using the services of PPO providers. Members can use healthcare providers outside the plan, but they must pay any additional costs.

 ## Additional Information for this Chapter

Books

- *Heal Your Body: The Mental Causes for Physical Illness and the Metaphysical Way to Overcome Them* by Louise L. Hay

- *How to Sleep Soundly Tonight* by Barbara L. Heller

- *No More Sleepless Nights Workbook* by Peter Hauri, Murray Jarman, and Shirley Linde

Web Links

- *www.healthfinder.gov*

- *www.cancer.org*

- *www.laughterremedy.com*

- *www.justmove.org*

- *www.mayohealth.org*

- *www.medscape.com*

- *www.shapeup.org*

- *www.intelihealth.com*

- *www.4woman.gov*

Interactive CD-ROM

Click to the web from the CD-ROM!

Web Resource

- *www.webmd.com*

- *www.breathcure.com*

- *www.bcrfcure.org* (Breast Cancer Research Foundation)

- *www.nlm.nih.gov* (National Library of Medicine/ National Institutes of Health)

- *www.mammacare.com*

Am I aware of my own personal safety?

Crime can happen to anyone, at any time, anywhere. Safety depends less on where you are than on what precautions you've taken. To prevent crime, you need to be aware of your surroundings and the people in them. How aware are you of crime? Answer True or False for each statement.

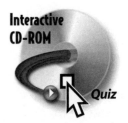

Interactive CD-ROM

Quiz

True	False		
○	○	1.	Most crimes occur in broad daylight, when I least expect it.
○	○	2.	People are often attacked in places that seem safe — homes, offices, cars.
○	○	3.	I am ultimately responsible for my own personal safety.
○	○	4.	The typical burglar is a young male who lives within two miles of me.
○	○	5.	Sliding patio doors provide easy access for burglars.
○	○	6.	Criminals have been known to impersonate repairmen and salesmen.
○	○	7.	If I live alone, it isn't safe to put my full name on my mailbox.
○	○	8.	I should leave a TV or radio on at night when I'm not home.
○	○	9.	I shouldn't get in a stranger's car, even if he threatens me with a gun.
○	○	10.	On elevators, I should stand near the control panel.
○	○	11.	I should keep my gas tank at least half full.
○	○	12.	If someone demands my car or money, I should let them have it.
○	○	13.	I should never pick up hitchhikers, no matter how harmless they seem.
○	○	14.	Rape is an act of violence. It is not motivated by sexual desire.
○	○	15.	Most women are raped by someone they know.
○	○	16.	The typical rapist is clean-cut and honest-looking.
○	○	17.	Date rape is a serious crime.
○	○	18.	Thirty percent of all violent crime is domestic in nature.
○	○	19.	It is abusive to humiliate my girlfriend/boyfriend in front of others.
○	○	20.	A pencil makes a good weapon when fending off an attacker.
○	○	21.	If my checkbook is stolen, I should close my account.
○	○	22.	My Social Security number is the key to identity theft.
○	○	23.	If my credit card is stolen, I am responsible for fixing my credit rating.
○	○	24.	Call 911 for an emergency or if I think a police officer is needed.
○	○	25.	It's against the law to make false 911 calls.

Give yourself one point for each True answer, zero points for each False answer.

_____ **YOUR SCORE**

All answers are true. If you scored less than 25, study this chapter to learn more about personal safety. It's your responsibility to be aware of your surroundings and the people in them.

Personal Safety

Chapter 10

There are many steps you can take to make sure you stay safe. Most are simple precautions that can make a big difference in your life. Lower the odds that you'll be a victim of crime. Take action! Stay safe!

 ## What can I do to make my home secure?

When do most burglaries occur?

More than 6.5 million burglaries are estimated to occur each year — in one of every 12 homes. That's 720 burglaries every hour, one every five seconds. No matter where you live, your home could be targeted by a burglar. More than 75 percent of home burglaries are made through doors, with more than half made through the front door during the daylight. The most likely times for home burglaries are 10:30 a.m. to noon and 1:30 p.m. to 3 p.m. (although

Interactive CD-ROM

Movie

nighttime burglaries have increased in recent years). Less than 10 percent of all stolen property is returned to the victim.

Who is the typical burglar?

You may not recognize the typical burglar. He's often one of the neighborhood kids, a young male who usually lives within a mile or two of his targets. He is usually an opportunist — and an amateur — but that doesn't mean he can't find his way into your home. He selects homes he can enter quickly and quietly — and exit with little risk of being noticed.

How do I make doors and windows safe?

Install a *wide-angle peephole* in your door so you can see visitors without opening the door. Many burglars look for unlocked doors and windows, so lock everything before you leave. Put a *deadbolt lock* on all exterior doors — and lock it as soon as you enter (and exit) your home. Never rely on a chain lock as a security device.

Interactive
CD-ROM

Movie

Sliding patio doors are very hard to secure. Install a folding bar on the inside of your home that fits firmly against the back edge of the sliding door or use a piece of wood (2" x 4" preferably) that's long enough to wedge into the bottom track to keep the door from sliding. During the summer, don't leave fans in unprotected, raised windows during the night or while you're gone. (Check with your landlord before installing any hardware.)

Do criminals impersonate repairmen?

Yes. It is common for criminals to claim they are salesmen or repairmen to gain entry into a home. Don't let an attacker get into your home. He then has a private, relatively soundproof place to attack you. There are countless cases where an attacker gains access to his victim by simply knocking on the door. Ask to see an I.D. or call the company the person claims to work for before allowing the person inside your home. If you don't have a peephole, get one — and use it. Don't let any stranger into your home when you're alone — no matter what the reason, even if the person claims it's an emergency. Offer to make a phone call while the person waits outside.

Is there a safe message to put on my answering machine?

Don't give criminals the impression that you're not home — or that you live alone. If you live alone, use only your last name and initials on mail boxes and in phone directories. Record your answering machine or voice mail to play a message similar to this: *"Hi. You've reached (your phone number). Sorry we can't take your call right now. Please leave your name, number, and a brief message. Thank you."* If you're female and live alone, you might have a male friend record your message and use *"we"* instead of *"I"* in your message.

Is my yard safe?

When working outside, don't leave doors on the opposite side of the house unlocked. Don't hide your house key under a rock or doormat. Burglars know the most well-known hiding places. Instead, give a spare key to a trusted neighbor, relative, or friend. Trim your bushes so a burglar won't have a place to hide.

How do I stay safe at night?

During the night, burglars look for homes that are unoccupied and dark. Keep entrances well-lit to expose a burglar. Leave interior lights, radios, and televisions on to create the illusion that someone is home. When you come home, have your house key out and ready to use as you approach your door. If you find a door or window open or signs of forced entry, don't go in. Go to the nearest phone and call the police. If you live in an apartment, avoid being in the laundry room or garage alone, especially at night.

 ## What safety measures can I take when walking?

- Be alert to your surroundings and the people around you. Trust your instincts.

- Walk confidently (with your chin up) at a steady pace on the side of the street facing traffic.

- Stay in well-lit areas as much as possible.

- Avoid doorways, bushes, and alleys.

- Walk a different route occasionally.

- Wear clothes and shoes that allow you to run, if necessary.

- Don't walk alone at night and always avoid areas where there are few people.

- Don't wear headphones. They make you less aware of what's going on around you, and they make you look like an easy target. If you must wear them, play at a low volume and keep your head up.

- Carry identification and always have two quarters for the phone or carry a cell phone.

- Be alert to people hanging out at stopping points, stop lights or signs, and intersections.

- Know where you're going and the safest way to get there. Tell a friend when you leave and when you expect to arrive.

- If you feel you're being followed, walk into a store or knock on a house door. If followed by a car, turn around and walk in the opposite direction.

- Be careful when people stop you to ask for directions. Always reply from a distance, and never get too close to the car.

- Don't get into an attacker's car if he pulls a gun and orders you to. Most attackers don't want to shoot you; they want to take you to a deserted place and torture you. Don't get in the car. Run screaming. The attacker will probably just move on to an easier target.

- If you're in trouble, attract help any way you can. Scream, yell for help, yell *"fire."* Wear a whistle around your neck and blow it if you're in danger. Consider carrying pepper spray.

- On elevators, stand near the control panel. If attacked, you can hit the alarm button. If you feel uncomfortable, don't get into an empty elevator with a stranger. If you become uncomfortable for any reason, get off the elevator on the next floor.

What safety measures can I take while driving?

- Keep your car in good repair with the gas tank at least half full.

- Always lock your car. Make this a habit when getting in and out. Never leave valuables in your car, or hide them out of sight. Keep your windows rolled up.

- Lock your doors while driving. In numerous cases, an attacker simply walked up to a woman's car while she was at a traffic light and jumped in with his gun or knife drawn.

- Travel on well-lit and busy streets.

- If you have a flat tire, drive on it until you reach a safe, well-lit, and well-traveled area.

- If you're being followed, don't go home. Go to the nearest police department, fire station, or emergency room and honk your horn. Or drive to an open gas station, grocery store, or other business where you can safely call the police. Don't leave your car unless you are certain you can get inside the building safely. Try to obtain the license tag number and description of the car following you.

- If someone demands your car, money, jewelry, or other property, give it to them. Property can be replaced. You cannot.

- Never pick up hitchhikers, no matter how harmless they seem.

- If you have to leave your keys with a mechanic or parking attendant, give your ignition key only. Remove it from your key ring. Keep your house keys and all other keys with you.

- Park in well-lit areas and lock the doors, even if you'll only be gone for a short time.

- When you return to your car, have the key ready and check inside your car before getting in.

- Be alert in parking garages, regardless of the time of day. Get in your car and leave as quickly as possible. Try not to go alone.

- Be alert in parking lots. If you go to a grocery store at night, don't be shy about asking for an escort to your car. Too many women are abducted from, or even raped in, parking lots.

- Avoid parking next to vans and trucks whenever possible. Attackers can hide easily in vans, and both vans and trucks can obstruct other people's view of you. If someone attacks you, it's possible that no one else could see it.

- If you see another motorist in trouble, don't stop. Help by going to a telephone or using your cell phone to call the police. Don't stop to assist a stranger whose car is broken down. It may be an attacker portraying himself/herself as a victim. Some women have even acted as if they are alone with a stranded car, only to have a man/men jump out from behind the car when someone stops to help.

- Don't pull over if a man drives alongside you pointing at your car, pretending something is wrong. If this happens, drive to the nearest well-lit and populated gas station and look the car over yourself (or ask an attendant). Never pull over.

- When using public transportation at night, use well-lit, busy stops. Avoid isolated stations or bus stops. Stay alert. Don't doze or daydream. Stay near other passengers. If someone bothers you, make a loud noise, scream, or say, *"Leave me alone."* If that doesn't work, hit the emergency signal on the bus or train. Sit in an aisle seat, near the driver. Notice who gets off at your stop. If you sense danger, stay on the bus or train, or walk or run towards people.

 How can I reduce my risk of being raped?

What is rape?

Rape is an act of violence. Rape is not a sexual act. It isn't about lust or love. It isn't something that happens in the heat of the moment. It is sexual violence that's directed mostly at women. It's an act of anger and power and control. Rape is the fastest growing crime in the country, and the most seriously under-reported. As many as 10 rapes occur for every one rape reported. Over 70 percent of all rapes are planned.

Rape can happen to anyone — children, teens, mothers, grandmothers, the rich, the poor. Women do not cause rape — and they are not raped because they dress seductively. In fact, police believe that in the stranger-rape situation, rapists tend to prey on people who look frightened, easily intimidated, or seem to be daydreaming.

Who is the typical rapist?

There is no typical rapist. Attackers come from all age groups; races; and social, economic, and cultural backgrounds. Rapists are not "dirty old men." Most sex offenders don't look like monsters. Only a few attackers actually look scary. Don't trust a stranger, though, just because he's clean-cut and honest-looking. Over half of rapists are under 25 years old and three out of five are married, leading otherwise normal sex lives. In fact, many rapes are committed by a seemingly "nice guy" whom the victim knows quite well.

What is date rape?

Date rape is rape that occurs in a social situation and is committed by someone you know. The rapist could be anyone you go out with — an acquaintance, classmate, co-worker, boss, ex-husband, family member, or neighbor. He could even be your boyfriend or fiancé. If you have made it clear that you are unwilling or do not want to "make love," then it is rape if you are forced. It is also rape for someone to have sex with you if you are drunk, drugged, or unconscious, and have not given permission. Date rape is a serious crime — and is no less serious just because you know your attacker.

What behaviors increase the tendency of rape?

Sex Role Stereotypes
Some people believe that men should be sexually aggressive, women sexually passive.

Poor Communication
The potential for a rape can be increased when two people don't have a clear idea of the other's sexual expectations and intentions.

Mixed Messages

If a man believes that a woman really means *"yes"* when she says *"no"* (the playing "hard-to-get" theory), a man may rationalize rape by not believing she really means *"no."*

Learned Violence

Violence is often seen as an acceptable way for a man to solve problems, so some men feel it's okay to use force to get what they want from a woman.

Are there tips for safer dating?

Watch for behaviors or attitudes that may signal trouble. For example, if you are out with a man, does he show a lack of respect for your feelings, ideas, and/or point of view? Does he want to make all the decisions? Does he act overly-jealous if you talk to anyone else? Does he get angry if you try to pay for any of the expenses on the date? Does he pressure you to drink? (Keep in mind that women can also have these characteristics.) If you sense something is wrong, get away as soon as possible. It's best to be cautious.

Be independent. Don't let your date make all the decisions about where you go and what you do. Don't be solely dependent on him for transportation. Always have quarters for the phone or some money for cab fare. Meet him on the first date. Don't have him pick you up at your apartment.

Be wary of alcohol and other drugs. It's much easier to be in control if you aren't under the influence. Be aware of how much your date drinks. And, make your sexual limits known. Make it clear that *"no"* means *"no."*

What if I'm raped?

Stay as calm as possible. Think rationally and evaluate your resources and options. Try to escape. If you can't run, it is your choice to attack or tolerate, depending on your judgment in the situation. (Take a self-defense class to learn basic ways to protect yourself.) Go with your instincts. You may decide to run, scream, kick, hit, bite, head-butt, poke eyes, kick in the groin, or try anything else you can think of to protect yourself.

The decision to report the rape is yours. (Keep in mind that reporting attacks is an important part of ending violence against women.) Go to a hospital emergency room or doctor immediately for treatment of any injuries. Don't bathe, shower, douche, clean under your fingernails, comb your hair, or change your clothes before you go. You might destroy valuable evidence. Make sure you're checked for risks of pregnancy and sexually-transmitted diseases (STDs).

Talk to someone you trust about what happened. Call a Rape Crisis line. See a counselor who's trained to help deal with fears and painful feelings that may linger after the attack. Many common feelings include numbness, guilt, confusion, mistrust, shock, shame, anger, sadness, fear, depression, helplessness, and grief.

 # What is domestic violence?

What is domestic violence?

Domestic violence includes behaviors used by one person in a relationship to control the other — and it is a crime. One of every four women in the United States will suffer some kind of violence at the hands of her husband, boyfriend, lover, or relative. Very few will tell anyone. They share feelings of helplessness, isolation, guilt, fear, and shame. All hope it won't happen again, but it does.

> When angry, count to ten before you speak. If very angry, a hundred.
>
> *~ Thomas Jefferson*

Abuse is never a one-time event.

Abusers are not easy to spot. There is no "typical" abuser. In public, most appear to be friendly and loving towards their significant other — and only abuse behind closed doors. They also try to hide the abuse by causing injuries that can be hidden and don't need a doctor's attention. Domestic violence sometimes results in permanent disability, accidental death, or even murder. Abusers have learned to abuse to get what they want — and that is to control the victim.

Are you abused?

Does the person you're with…

- have to know where you are all the time?

- constantly accuse you of being unfaithful?

- discourage your relationships with family and friends?

- prevent you from working or attending school?

- criticize you for little things?

- anger easily when drinking or on drugs?

- control all finances and force you to account in detail for money you spend?

- humiliate you in front of others?

- destroy personal property or sentimental items?

- hit, punch, slap, kick, push, choke, or bite you?

- use, or threaten to use, a weapon against you?

- threaten to hurt you? Or a family member? Or a pet?

- threaten suicide to get you to do something?

- force you to have sex or do sexual acts you don't want to do?

If you find yourself saying *"yes,"* it's time to get help. You don't deserve to be hit, threatened, beaten, or criticized. Nothing you say or do justifies being abused.

Part of the abuser's power comes from your secrecy. Learn to think independently. Try to plan for the future and set goals for yourself. Get help from family and friends. Find a support group or counselor. Call the police. Go to a battered women's shelter or call a crisis hotline in your community. If you think you're in danger, leave immediately.

If you're physically abused, get medical attention from your doctor or an emergency room. Ask the staff to photograph your injuries and keep detailed records in case you decide to take legal action. Contact your local family court for information about a personal protection order that does not involve criminal charges or penalties.

Are you an abuser?

Do you…

- have to know where your significant other is all the time?

- constantly accuse your significant other of cheating on you?

- discourage your significant other from having relationships with family and friends?

- prevent your significant other from working or attending school?

- criticize your significant other for little things?

- anger easily when drinking or on drugs?

- control finances and force your significant other to account in detail for money spent?

- humiliate your significant other in front of others?

- destroy personal property or sentimental items that belong to your significant other?

- hit, punch, slap, kick, push, choke, or bite your significant other?

- use, or threaten to use, a weapon against your significant other?

- threaten to hurt your significant other? Or a family member? Or a pet?

- threaten suicide to get your significant other to do something?

- force your significant other to have sex against her/his will or to do sexual acts that she/he doesn't want to do?

If you find yourself saying *"yes,"* it's time to get help. Don't ignore the problem. You break the law when you physically hurt someone, so take responsibility for your actions and get help. Many communities offer anger management classes and other types of counseling and support groups. Call a domestic violence hotline or health center for information. Accept the fact that your violent behavior will destroy your relationships. Violence is a learned behavior … but it can be un-learned. If you answered *"yes"* to these questions, call to get help today.

Any statistics on domestic violence?

Here are some staggering statistics on domestic violence:

- A woman is beaten every 15 seconds in the United States.

- 92 percent of all domestic violence is committed against women.

- 63 percent of the young men between the ages of 11 and 20 who are serving time for homicide have killed their mother's abuser.

- 50 percent of men who abuse their female partners also abuse their children.

- 40 percent of teenage girls aged 14 to 17 report knowing someone their age who has been hit or beaten by a boyfriend.

- 33 percent of female murder victims are killed by their male partners.

- 30 percent of all violent crime is domestic in nature.

- 30 percent of female murder victims were slain by their husbands or boyfriends in 1996.

- 25 percent of battered women are pregnant.

- Family violence costs the U.S. from $5 to $10 billion annually in medical expenses, police and court costs, shelters and foster care, sick leave, absenteeism, and non-productivity.

- Domestic violence is the leading cause of injury to women aged 15 to 44 — more than car accidents, muggings, and rapes combined.

- A child's exposure to the father abusing the mother is the strongest risk factor for transmitting violent behavior from one generation to the next.

How can I defend myself?

There are many ways to defend yourself if you are being attacked. Your brain is your most powerful weapon, so think self-defense. Take a course in self-defense. Even if you never use the skills you learn, taking the course will give you more confidence and boost your self-esteem. Your confidence alone can make you a less-inviting target. If you're attacked, you could try any of the following:

- Burst into tears.

- Shout loudly in the attacker's face.

- Kick the attacker in the groin.

- Stand there and talk calmly to the attacker to gain time to decide what to do next.

- Turn and run.

- Pick your nose very thoroughly. (Even attackers find this disgusting!)

- Throw up (or pretend you're going to be sick).

- Poke the attacker in the eyes. (Keys and fingers work well for this.)

- Scratch the attacker's face.

- Pull the attacker's hair.

- Bite the attacker.

- Use a weapon (hairbrush, umbrella, book, pen or pencil, nail file, etc.).

- Give in.

- Or anything else you can think of to protect yourself.

See the diagram on page 352 for more ways to defend yourself.

Can I defend myself?

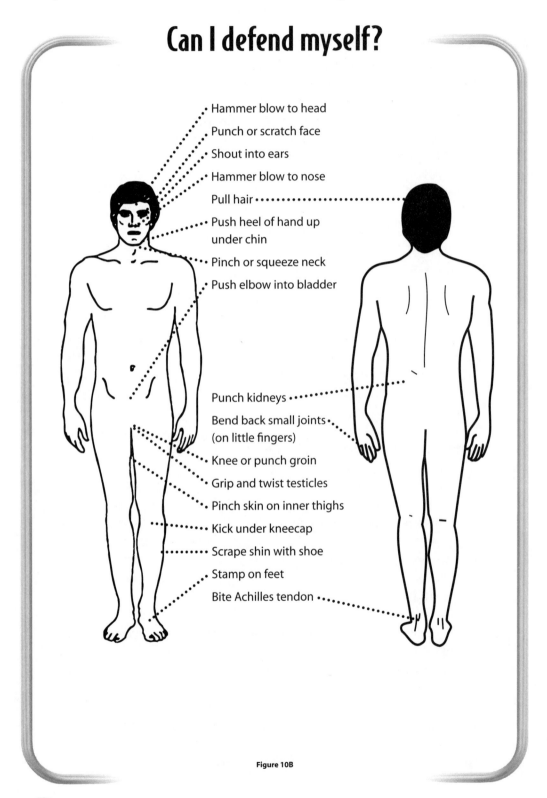

Hammer blow to head

Punch or scratch face

Shout into ears

Hammer blow to nose

Pull hair

Push heel of hand up under chin

Pinch or squeeze neck

Push elbow into bladder

Punch kidneys

Bend back small joints (on little fingers)

Knee or punch groin

Grip and twist testicles

Pinch skin on inner thighs

Kick under kneecap

Scrape shin with shoe

Stamp on feet

Bite Achilles tendon

Figure 10B

How does someone steal my identity?

How does someone steal my identity?

Identity theft occurs when a criminal uses your personal information to take on your identity. Identity thieves get your personal information through a variety of means. They steal your purse or wallet (even at work). They steal your mail. They rummage through your trash looking for personal data. They illegally obtain your credit report posing as a landlord, employer, or someone who may have a legitimate need (and legal right) to the information. They get your business and personal records at work. They find personal information in your home. They get information from the Internet. They also "buy" personal information from "inside sources," such as store employees.

What if someone steals my Social Security number?

If your Social Security number is stolen, someone has access to steal your identity. If your state allows Social Security numbers to be used for your driver's license number, opt to have a random number given to you. Do not use your Social Security number. The Social Security Administration also recommends that you do not carry your card with you.

It is illegal for another person to use your Social Security number. The Identity Theft and Assumption Deterrence Act of 1998 makes it a felony to use or transfer the identity of another person. Under this Act, a Social Security number is considered a means of identification. If your number is stolen, however, the Social Security Administration will not change it unless you can document that you are being disadvantaged because of the misuse. Social Security recommends that you periodically check your records by calling 1-800-772-1213. You can download an application on the Internet at *www.ssa.gov* or stop by your local Social Security office.

If someone uses your Social Security number to obtain credit, the Social Security office cannot fix your credit rating. You'll need to work with each credit reporting agency and creditor to remove inaccurate information. It is recommended that you continue checking your credit report annually.

The three major credit reporting agencies that you should contact include Equifax, Experian, and TransUnion. To reach them, call the following numbers:

	Report fraud	Order credit report	Web address
Equifax	1-800-525-6285	1-800-685-1111	*www.equifax.com*
Experion	1-888-397-3742	1-800-397-3742	*www.experian.com*
TransUnion	1-800-680-7289	1-800-916-8800	*www.tuc.com*

You should also contact:

- Social Security Administration's Fraud Hotline: 1-800-269-0271

- Federal Trade Commission's ID Theft Hotline: 1-877-IDTHEFT (438-4338)

What if my purse or wallet is stolen?

If your purse or wallet is stolen, notify your bank immediately. If your checkbook is stolen and you know the exact check numbers, you can stop payment on those checks. Otherwise, close your account, along with any ATM or debit cards, and open a new account. You must also notify any credit card companies and cancel your credit cards immediately. Most criminals know they have a limited time to act and will quickly pass many checks, often before you even realize they're stolen.

Getting a purse or wallet stolen can create some major problems for you. Credit card fraud and check forgery can mean a lot of buying power for thieves — it can also mean a lot of headaches for you. Never assume you're safe. Many purse thefts happen because people assume their purse is safe. Always lock up your purse or wallet at work. (Or leave it at home.) Carry only a small amount of cash and your driver's license. If you have credit cards, carry only those that you think you'll need. Criminals may also have access to your home, so you may want to change the locks on your home. If your driver's license is stolen, get a new one (without your Social Security number on it).

 ## What should I know about calling 911?

Call 911 for an emergency or if you think a police officer is necessary. (The call-taker has the authority to determine if an officer will be dispatched.) If you just need information, call a police administrative number found in your phone book.

Calls to 911 will be answered immediately if there are enough call-takers available to take the call. If the number of incoming calls is greater than the number of call-takers working, you will hear a recorded message. Don't hang up! Follow the instructions given on the recording.

Calls to 911 are answered by the police department. Calls for fire or ambulance must be transferred to those agencies. The caller must remain on the line and wait to be connected. The caller will hear another phone ringing when the call is transferred and may hear a recording if their lines are busy. Do not hang up!

It's against the law to make false 911 calls, and the police department will prosecute.

If you hear a recording when you call 911, or if you call 911 by mistake, do not hang up. If you don't stay on the line, a call-taker will try to call you back. If your line is busy, the call-taker must contact the operator to break the line and then re-dial your number. If you have called back and are talking to another call-taker, two call-takers are now tied up on the same call and are not available to answer other incoming calls.

All 911 calls that require an officer to be dispatched are assigned a level of priority:

1. Is the crime in progress?

2. Is anyone injured?

3. Does anyone have weapons?

4. Has any property been lost? If your call is a low priority, it may be several hours before an officer is available for dispatch.

It is difficult to pinpoint where cellular phone calls are made from, so if you're calling 911 from a cellular phone, give the call-taker your location.

Calling 911 from a pay phone is free. Dialing 0 (zero) to call an operator will delay your call.

Violent Crime
Victim Characteristics
(Murder, Rape, Sexual Assault, and Assault)

The FBI's Uniform Crime Reports show that in 1999, murder victims were ...

- 63% were under age 35

- 12% were under age 18

- 50% were white

- 47% were black

- 3% were Asian, Pacific Islander, or Native Americans

- 75% were male

According to the U.S. Department of Justice, Bureau of Justice Statistics, in 2000:

- Persons aged 12 to 24 were victims of violent crime more than all other ages.

- Persons aged 16 to 19 were raped or sexually assaulted more than all other ages.

- Persons aged 16 to 19 were about twice as likely to be robbed as persons aged 25 to 34 and about 10 times as likely as persons age 65 or older.

- Per every 1,000 persons in that racial group, 35 blacks, 27 whites, and 21 persons of other races sustained a violent crime.

- Hispanics and non-Hispanics were victims of overall violent crime at similar rates.

- Non-Hispanics were more likely to be raped or sexually assaulted than Hispanics.

- Hispanics were more likely to be robbed than non-Hispanics.

- Males were victimized at rates 42% higher than females, with the exception of rape and sexual assault.

- Persons in households with incomes less than $7,500 annually had the highest rate of violence (60 per 1,000 persons).

- Persons in households earning more than $75,000 annually were victims of violent crime and aggravated assault at rates about a third of those with lower incomes.

- Persons who never married were victims of violent crime at more than 4 times the rate of married persons and more than 6 times the rate of widowed persons.

Figure 10C

Additional Information for this Chapter

Web links

- www.domesticviolence.org

- www.realworldsafety.com

- www.consumer.gov/idtheft/

- www.selfdefenseproducts.com

- www.tri-countycouncil.org/dvhome/dvfacts.html

- www.ftc.gov/bcp/conline/pubs/credit/idtheft.htm

- www.consumer.gov/idtheft/

- www.ssa.gov/pubs/idtheft.htm

- www.walking.about.com

Do I have a problem?

Alcohol and drug problems can affect anyone, regardless of age, sex, race, marital status, place of residence, income level, or lifestyle. Most people do everything possible to deny to themselves that they have an alcohol or drug problem. They also do their utmost to hide it from everyone else. There are certain warning signs that may indicate if you have a problem drinking alcohol or using drugs. Check each statement that applies to you.

Interactive CD-ROM

Quiz

I may have a problem with alcohol or drugs if ...

○ I drink or use drugs because I have problems.

○ I drink until intoxicated.

○ I drive a car while intoxicated or on drugs.

○ I drink or use drugs to relax.

○ I drink or use drugs when I get mad at other people.

○ I drink or use drugs to build self-confidence.

○ I get defensive when someone says I use too much alcohol or drugs.

○ I hang out with a crowd that drinks heavily or uses a lot of drugs.

○ I feel guilty or bummed out after using alcohol or drugs.

○ I drink or use drugs until my supply is gone.

○ I prefer to drink alone, rather than with others.

○ I begin to drink in the morning, before work or school.

○ I've stolen money or sold something to pay for alcohol or drugs.

○ I get drunk when I drink, even when I don't mean to.

○ I think it's cool to be able to hold my liquor.

○ I believe that, in order to have fun, I have to drink or use drugs.

○ I've gotten into trouble with the law because of alcohol or drugs.

○ I take sexual risks while under the influence of alcohol or drugs.

○ I feel run-down, tired, hopeless, depressed, or even suicidal.

○ I've been suspended from school or fired from work because of alcohol or drugs.

○ I use more alcohol or drugs to get the same effect I got with smaller amounts.

○ I've woken up and wondered what happened the night before.

○ Someone in my family has a problem with alcohol or drugs.

○ I think it's okay to break the law when it stands in the way of personal needs.

○ I buy alcohol or drugs before I pay for living expenses.

_____**TOTAL SCORE**

4 or more   You may be at risk for developing alcoholism and/or dependence on drugs.

6 or more   You should seek professional help immediately or call the National Council on Alcoholism and Drug Dependence Hope Line at 1-800-NCA-CALL. Someone can be reached 24 hours a day, seven days a week.

This test was adapted from a test by the National Council on Alcoholism and Drug Dependence. It is not meant to be used to diagnose a problem with alcohol or other drugs. Its purpose is for identification of a possible problem.

Figure 11A

Alcohol and Drugs

Do you have a problem with alcohol or drugs? You say you're not an alcoholic or a drug addict, so no problem. Right? Wrong! Alcohol and drugs may seem to lessen your anxiety — but they can change your life forever. Thousands die or are seriously injured each year in alcohol- or drug-related accidents. Don't be a statistic. Know the facts about how these substances affect you and your ability to make decisions — and how you can get help for yourself or someone you care about.

Chapter 11

The information in this chapter is intended for informational purposes only. It is not all-inclusive and cannot substitute for professional medical guidance and treatment.

 ## Why do people use alcohol and drugs?

Why do people use alcohol and drugs?

There are several main reasons people use alcohol and drugs:

To Feel Grown Up

To Take Risks and Rebel

Risk-taking is part of growing up. That's how one learns the limits of independence. Alcohol and drugs may give young people a chance to prove they can "handle it." Some people take more risks than others. There are also some people who really want to rebel against society by engaging in anti-social behavior, juvenile delinquency, treating others poorly, and so on. When you're young, you feel immortal. You don't believe you are physically in much danger in the world. You must take risks to learn your own boundaries — but leave the alcohol, tobacco, and drugs out of it.

To Fit In and Belong

Sometimes people turn to alcohol, tobacco, or drugs to feel like they fit in — to overcome anxiety or awkward social moments, change their personality, or give themselves courage to talk to other people. Wanting to fit in and belong is one of the most natural parts of growing up. It is important. In fact, it may be *the* most important part of growing up.

To Relax and Feel Good

Some people repress their feelings and choose to comfort themselves through alcohol, tobacco, or drugs. Others say that alcohol and drugs help them unwind and relax.

To Satisfy Their Curiosity

To Escape From Reality

Are you unhappy? Do you feel like your life is out of control? Do you have a lot of problems that you don't know how to resolve? Do you think that alcohol and drugs can take you away — or make your problems go away? The only thing they can do is *increase* your problems. They are not an escape from reality — but an entrance into a life that can only cycle dangerously out of control.

Because They've Become Addicted

An alcoholic is a person who suffers from a disease that has no known cure. Alcoholism is a physical compulsion combined with a mental obsession to drink. Because it is an illness, an alcoholic must learn to avoid alcohol completely in order to lead a normal life. Alcoholism is a heath problem. It's not a question of too little willpower or of moral weakness. One thing alcoholics tend to have in common is that, as time passes, the drinking gets worse unless they commit to being sober.

Everybody's doing drugs, aren't they?

"Everybody does it. I guess I will, too." *Wrong.*

● Over 86 percent of teens have *never* tried marijuana.

- Over 98 percent have *never* used cocaine.

- Over 99.5 percent have *never* used crack.

How can I make the right decisions?

Learn to make the right decisions for yourself about alcohol and drugs. To help you make wise decisions, ask yourself the following questions:

- What am I trying to decide?

- What do I know about it?

- How do I know my information is correct?

- Who told me about it?

- Do I need to know more before going ahead?

- What are the good effects of this decision?

- What are the bad effects of this decision?

- Am I willing to take responsibility for this decision?

Is drinking a healthy way to deal with stress?

People sometimes develop unhealthy ways of dealing with stress. How many times have you heard someone say, *"Boy, I could use a drink,"* as a reliever for stress? How can you tell if you're stressed? Some signs of stress include the following:

Low self-esteem • little energy • short attention span • often sleepy • extremely hyperactive • often depressed • inactive • often misbehaves • angers easily • fights frequently • frustrates easily • uses profanity • says bad things about self • refuses to do what he/she is told • walks unsteadily • cries easily • sulks • detached and unresponsive • doesn't communicate • changes in eating habits • mood swings • rejection of authority • change in appearance and personal hygiene • change in personality • abusive to others • grades fall in school • frequently sick • low energy • seems confused • abusive • suspicious of others • abusing alcohol or drugs • unable to sleep • worries constantly • inability to make quick decisions • overwhelmed •

fearful • poor eating habits • constant complaining • tension headaches • desire to be alone more often • rejection of advice and assistance • sleeping more • irritable or short-tempered.

(Go to Chapter 9, "Is stress making me sick?" for information on how to handle stress.)

What do I need to know about alcohol?

What do I need to know about alcohol?

Alcohol is a drug. Purchase or public consumption of alcohol is illegal for anyone under the age of 21 in the United States. Alcohol is a "psycho-active" or mind-altering drug. It can alter moods, cause changes in the body, and become habit-forming. Alcohol is a downer because it depresses the central nervous system. That's why drinking too much causes slowed reactions, slurred speech, and sometimes even unconsciousness or passing out. Alcohol works first on the part of the brain that controls inhibitions. As people lose their inhibitions, they may talk more, get rowdy, or do foolish things. After several drinks, they may feel "high," but their nervous system is actually slowing down.

Drinking alcohol is a part of many people's social lives, but it can have serious effects on your life. Roughly one in eight American adult drinkers is an alcoholic or experiences problems due to the use of alcohol. The cost to society is estimated in excess of $166 billion each year.

A person does not have to be an alcoholic to have problems with alcohol. Every year, for example, people lose their lives in alcohol-related traffic accidents, drownings, and suicides. (Thirty-eight percent of drownings are alcohol-related.)

Alcohol abuse can lead to serious physical problems, such as damage to the brain, pancreas, and kidneys; high blood pressure, heart attacks, and strokes; alcoholic hepatitis and cirrhosis of the liver; stomach ulcers and irritable colon; premature aging; and a host of other disorders.

Alcohol also causes impotence and infertility. In pregnant women, it is absorbed into the mother's bloodstream and passes to the growing baby. A baby born to a woman who drinks during pregnancy may have severe physical and mental abnormalities.

Alcoholism is a disease — just like diabetes or high blood pressure. It can make people do things that later bring remorse or embarrassment. Even with just one or two drinks, your judgment becomes impaired — putting you more at risk for driving while drunk, riding with a drunk driver, having unsafe sex, and becoming violent.

Does my drinking affect my family?

Alcoholism usually has strong negative effects on marriages and family relationships. Alcohol is associated with a substantial proportion of violence. Perpetrators of crimes are often under the influence of alcohol. Alcohol is a key factor in …

- 68 percent of manslaughters

- 62 percent of assaults

- 54 percent of murders and attempted murders

- 48 percent of robberies

- 44 percent of burglaries

How can I drink in moderation?

Know your limits. Make a plan to have a set number of drinks — and stop when you reach that number (or before). Eat before you drink and while you're drinking. Food slows down alcohol absorption. Drink slowly. Don't gulp. Alternate alcoholic drinks with non-alcoholic drinks. Drink plenty of water. Avoid drinking games.

Know what you're drinking. How strong is the drink? How hard and how soon will the alcohol "hit" you? Keep track of how much you've had.

Be honest with yourself. If you know you're drunk, don't drive.

What affects my BAC?

BAC, Blood Alcohol Concentration, is the ratio of alcohol to blood in your

How do drinks add up?

Whether you drink a 12-ounce can of beer, a shot of brandy, or a half-ounce glass of wine, the amount of pure alcohol per drink is about the same: one-half ounce. The following shows what happens when you drink:

One or more drinks
The judgment center of your brain is affected.

Three or four drinks
The motor section of your brain is affected.

Five or six drinks
Your emotions are affected. (Whatever emotion you felt before drinking now will be enhanced. You may go from happy to highly excited or from sad to depressed.)

Six to 10 drinks
Your body will attempt to protect itself by either vomiting or passing out. Blackouts can occur at this level, creating alcohol-related amnesia.

More than 10 drinks
Involuntary muscles are affected. Because alcohol is a depressant, the lungs and heart may shut down and lead to coma or death.

Figure 11B

What's my Blood Alcohol Concentration?

When you drink, the alcohol is absorbed into your bloodstream where it quickly travels to every organ in your body, including your brain. To determine how intoxicated you are, the ratio of alcohol to blood in your bloodstream is measured. This is your Blood Alcohol Concentration, or BAC. The more you drink, the more alcohol is absorbed in your bloodstream. The higher your BAC, the drunker you are. Here's what happens when your BAC reaches each range:

BAC .02%   Alcohol slows down your nervous system right away so you get more relaxed. Your reaction time is impaired as soon as you start drinking.

BAC .04%   Your reaction time continues to slow down. You relax more and develop a "buzz."

BAC .06%   Your brain's ability to process information and make judgments is greatly impaired.

BAC .08%   Your motor coordination is greatly reduced. You may feel nauseous and throw up.

BAC .10%   Your judgment and motor coordination are visibly sloppy.

BAC .15% to .25%   You have a high risk of blackouts and injuries.

BAC .25% to .35%   You can pass out. You risk death.

BAC .35% to .45%   This is a lethal dose for most people.

Figure 11C

bloodstream. The chart on page 365 shows how it relates to intoxication. Following are four main factors that affect your BAC:

- Your weight. If two men drink at the same rate, the man who weighs less will get more intoxicated. (The same applies to women.)

- Your gender. If a man and a woman of the same weight drink at the same rate, the woman will get intoxicated faster.

- How fast you drink. The faster you drink, the faster your BAC will go up.

- How much you drink.

If I'm pregnant, is it safe to drink alcohol?

No. Alcohol absorbed into a mother's bloodstream during pregnancy passes to the growing baby. A baby born to a woman who drinks alcohol during pregnancy may have physical and mental abnormalities.

Do I have tolerance to alcohol?

Tolerance means that, over time, you have to drink more to get the same effect. If you've built up tolerance, you may not know how impaired you really are — which can lead to bad judgment calls, such as driving while under the influence. If you have a tolerance to alcohol, you may be dependent on it. If you have tolerance built up, you may not show the same effects as someone with no tolerance, but your BAC is still the same, regardless of the effects you experience. Your BAC, or Blood Alcohol Concentration, is the ratio of alcohol to blood in your bloodstream. The higher your BAC, the drunker you are.

What is binge drinking?

Binge drinking is defined as consuming five or more drinks in a row for males and four or more drinks in a row for females. The heaviest alcohol consumption is by 18 to 21 year-old drinkers in the United States. However, within this age group, binge drinking is more prevalent among college students than non-students.

According to the National Clearinghouse for Alcohol and Drug Information, more than 60 percent of college men and almost 50 percent of college women who are frequent binge drinkers report that they drink and drive.

How many drinks can I have in an hour?

Once your BAC reaches the .05% to .06% range, the negative effects of alcohol become drastically worse. Use the following chart as a guideline to keep your BAC below warning range:

| | | If you drink for | | |
| | | 1 hour | 2 hours | 3 hours |
Gender	Weight	you should have no more than		
Male	120	2 drinks	2 drinks	3 drinks
Male	140	2 drinks	3 drinks	4 drinks
Male	160	3 drinks	3 drinks	4 drinks
Male	180	3 drinks	4 drinks	5 drinks
Male	200	4 drinks	4 drinks	5 drinks
Female	100	1 drink	2 drinks	2 drinks
Female	120	2 drinks	2 drinks	2 drinks
Female	140	2 drinks	2 drinks	3 drinks
Female	160	2 drinks	3 drinks	3 drinks
Female	180	3 drinks	3 drinks	4 drinks

* A drink is a 12-ounce beer, a 4-ounce glass of wine, a 10-ounce wine cooler, or a 1-ounce shot of liquor.

Spread the drinks over the time period, not all at the beginning or end.

This information does not convey that any drinking is safe.

Figure 11D

By comparison, drinking and driving has been reported by 20 percent of college men and 13 percent of college women who don't binge drink.

Frequent binge drinkers are eight times more likely than non-binge drinkers to miss a class, fall behind in schoolwork, get hurt or injured, have trouble with authorities, have hangovers, and damage property.

Binge drinking during college may be associated with mental health disorders such as compulsiveness, depression, or anxiety.

In a national study, 91 percent of women and 78 percent of men who were frequent binge drinkers considered themselves to be moderate or light drinkers. They did not perceive themselves as problem drinkers.

Among men, research indicates that greater alcohol use is related to greater sexual aggression. Binge drinkers appear to engage in more unplanned sexual activity and to abandon safe sex techniques more often than those who don't binge drink.

Students living on campuses with higher proportions of binge drinkers experience more incidents of assault and unwanted sexual advances.

About 10.4 million adolescents aged 12 to 20 reported drinking alcohol. Of those, 5.1 million were binge drinkers and included 2.3 million heavy drinkers who binged at least five times a month.

Students who live in fraternity or sorority houses are the heaviest drinkers, with 86 percent of fraternity residents and 80 percent of sorority residents reporting binge drinking.

Can I get alcohol poisoning if I binge drink?

Alcohol poisoning is a severe and potentially fatal physical reaction to an alcohol overdose. It is the most serious consequence of binge drinking. When excessive amounts of alcohol are consumed, the brain is deprived of oxygen. The struggle to deal with an overdose of alcohol and lack of oxygen will eventually cause the brain to shut down the voluntary functions that regulate breathing and heart rate. If a person consumes large quantities of alcohol in a short period of time, symptoms of alcohol poisoning include vomiting; unconsciousness; cold, clammy, pale, or bluish skin; and slow or irregular breathing (less than eight breaths per minute or 10 or more per second).

Will black coffee get rid of my hangover?

No. Nothing but time will get rid of a hangover. You can't reduce the effects of alcohol by taking a cold shower, drinking black coffee, exercising, fresh air, or vomiting. Your body (your liver) has to burn off the alcohol — at a rate of .016 of blood alcohol per hour.

Can I use a fake ID?

Is the crime worth the fine? Advertised as "novelty" items, falsified identification or "fake IDs" are *not* toys. Nor is their use just fun and games. In fact, it's a crime, punishable by law. Violations vary by state, and may include altering one's own ID; using someone else's ID (either stolen or borrowed); applying for an ID using another person's birth certificate; creating one's own fake ID; and purchasing an ID from a counterfeiter (including Internet sites). If you create and/or sell fake IDs, that's a felony.

Age identification policies exist for outlets that sell or serve alcohol or tobacco. Servers, clerks, and managers of establishments face the risk of criminal and civil liability if they serve or sell to an underage person. Checking IDs decreases the potential liability a server or seller could face for selling to an underage person. A new device called ID-Check is now available. It looks like a small fax machine and reads magnetic strips or bar codes on the back of driver's licenses and state ID cards. It can also read military ID cards.

Does alcoholism affect children?

Alcoholism affects the entire family. About 43 percent of the U.S. population, or 76 million people, have been exposed to alcoholism in their families. Almost one in five adult Americans lived with an alcoholic while growing up. There are an estimated 26.8 million children of alcoholics in the U.S., with almost 11 million under the age of 18.

Each member of the family may be affected differently. They usually have higher levels of conflict within the family. Studies of family violence frequently document high rates of alcohol and other drug involvement. Children of alcoholics are more likely to be targets of physical abuse and to witness family violence. State welfare records have indicated that substance abuse is one of the top two problems of families in 81 percent of reported cases.

Children of alcoholics exhibit symptoms of depression and anxiety more than children of non-alcoholics. They tend to have lower self-esteem. They are also at risk for disruptive behavioral problems and are more likely to be sensation-seeking, aggressive, and impulsive. They experience greater physical and mental health problems and have higher healthcare costs.

Children of alcoholics often have difficulties in school and at work. They score lower on tests measuring verbal ability. Their ability to express themselves may be impaired, which can limit their school performance, peer relationships, ability to develop and sustain intimate relationships, and hamper performance on job interviews. Low verbal scores, however, do not imply any intellectual impairment.

There is strong scientific evidence showing that alcoholism tends to run in families. Genetic factors play a major role in the development of alcoholism. Children of alcoholics are four times more likely to develop alcoholism and other drug abuse than children of non-alcoholics. Almost one-third of any sample of alcoholics has at least one parent who also was or is an alcoholic.

Children of alcoholics are more likely to marry into families in which alcoholism is prevalent.

What happens when these children grow up?

 ## What if I get stopped for drinking and driving?

Do one in 10 drivers drink?

About three in 10 Americans will be involved in an alcohol-related accident in their lifetimes. According to the National Highway Traffic Safety Administration, someone dies in an alcohol-related traffic accident every 33 minutes. On

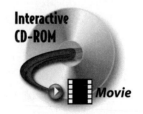

Interactive CD-ROM

Movie

any given weekend evening, one in 10 drivers on America's roads has been drinking. In 1999, almost 16,000 people were killed in alcohol-related accidents, representing 40 percent of all traffic fatalities. For each death from an alcohol-related accident, 19 people are hospitalized and 300 receive injuries requiring medical attention. Alcohol-related crashes cost $45 billion per year.

Sixty percent of all deaths in the 15 to 24 age group happen in alcohol-related car accidents.

If you're worried about being caught driving drunk … you should be more worried about being caught *dead*. As a drunk driver, you're four times more likely to crash and be killed or injured than to be arrested for exceeding the legal limits of driving while intoxicated.

What's a drunk driver?

In most states, the law says a drunk driver is one whose Blood Alcohol Concentration (BAC) as measured by blood sample or breath test is .08% or higher. Drivers may also be considered to be under the influence if their ability to operate a vehicle is impaired by illegal or prescription drugs.

What happens if I get stopped?

When a police officer stops you, if he/she thinks you've been drinking, he/she may ask you to take some field sobriety tests(such as walking heel to toe or standing on one leg). These tests will help the officer decide if you should have a chemical test of your breath, blood, or urine. The result of the chemical test is known as your Blood Alcohol Concentration (BAC) level. If you refuse to take the BAC test, you might automatically lose your license for a specified period of time. (This varies by state.)

What's a designated driver?

A designated driver is a person in the group who agrees to drive — and stays sober. If you're the designated driver, take it seriously. Your friends' lives are in your hands. If a drunk friend is insistent on driving, do whatever it takes to stop him or her. It's better to risk a friendship than to risk a life.

What is being done to decrease drunk driving?

Drunk driving is no longer socially acceptable. It's a serious crime. Federal law recently enacted a national drunk driving standard that lowers the legally-drunk Blood Alcohol Concentration (BAC) limit to .08 (from .10).

States must comply in order to receive federal transportation funds. You could face criminal penalties if convicted of driving while under the influence of alcohol or drugs. Your license could be suspended or permanently revoked (taken away). You could receive jail time and have to pay a hefty fine, attend and pay for alcohol-management classes, and pay for a psychological profile.

In many states, if you have three convictions in a five-year-period, the third one is a felony. And, unlike speeding tickets that only stay on your driving record for a few years, all DUI convictions throughout a person's lifetime may be taken into account. Many states are now sharing this information with each other.

Every state in the nation has raised the drinking age to 21. Programs implemented in many states include laws placing increased liability on bars, parents, and others caught giving beer to minors or continuing to give/sell alcohol to those who've already had enough. A "SafeRides" program has been implemented so that drunken teens can call for rides.

Several cities are also incorporating "mock accidents" for high school students. For example, several communities in California participate in a program called "Every 15 Minutes." Drama students portray accident victims. The police and highway patrol, fire department, paramedics, hospitals, helicopter transport, and coroners participate. Every 15 minutes* during the day, a student is selected as a victim. Their faces are painted white to identify them as the victim and they are not allowed to be spoken to for the rest of the day. This real-life exercise gives students a wake-up call about drinking and driving — and its consequences.

Some states are also using an ignition interlock device for repeat offenders. This device requires a driver to blow through a tube to determine his/her BAC. If the person has been drinking, the device won't allow the car to start. In addition, many states now implement a program where first-time offenders (or those refusing to take a breathalyzer test) are forced to face a panel of family members who've lost loved ones in accidents caused by drunk drivers.

---

* When the program first began, someone died due to a drunk driver every 15 minutes in the U.S. Currently, one person dies every 33 minutes due to a drunk driver.

What if I'm throwing a party?

Interactive
CD-ROM

Movie

If you're throwing a party, be a friend first, then a host or hostess. Never force drinks on your guests. If they say, *"no,"* don't insist. Provide non-alcoholic drinks for those who don't want alcohol. Offer coffee, water, or soft drinks for the "one for the road." Close "the bar" at least one hour before the end of the party. Never let a guest drive away from your party under the influence. Ask someone to drive the person home, call a cab, or let him or her crash on the couch.

 ## Are club drugs safe?

What is Ecstasy?

Ecstasy is a synthetic drug that has amphetamine-like and hallucinogenic properties. Use of the drug Ecstasy has surged among young people who say it's harmless — but law enforcement and health professionals worry users are fooling themselves about its dangers.

After a pill is swallowed, it usually takes from 20 minutes to an hour to take effect, with a "high" that lasts three to six hours. After Ecstasy enters the bloodstream, it aims for brain cells that release serotonin, a chemical that helps regulate body temperature. In a normal brain, only a small amount of serotonin is released at one time. Ecstasy releases serotonin all at once, which can short-circuit the body's ability to control its temperature. This leads to overheating — the drug's biggest short-term danger. Ecstasy users have been hospitalized with temperatures reaching 110 degrees.

Recent studies indicate that Ecstasy causes permanent brain damage in the areas critical to thought and memory. It may alter motor skills, giving the user the appearance of suffering from Parkinson's disease. Users who develop an acne-like rash and continue to use the drug are at increased risk of severe liver damage. Ecstasy also causes users to grind through the enamel on their teeth.

If, after reading this, you still choose to use Ecstasy, experts recommend using extreme caution. They suggest you stay hydrated by drinking plenty of water to avoid severe and sometimes deadly overheating; avoid "stacking" or taking more than one tablet in a night; and be cautious of what you're really taking. (Ecstasy pills aren't always pure.)

Ecstasy goes by different names: E, X, XTC, Love Drug, Hug Drug, Lover's Speed, Clarity, Disco Biscuits, or MDMA.

What is liquid Ecstasy?

Also known as GHB or Liquid X, but quite different from Ecstasy, this odorless, colorless, and tasteless liquid induces a state of dazed relaxation not unlike that caused by alcohol. Undetectable in a drink, it has been linked to incidents of date rape. It is sometimes used by bodybuilders for its alleged anabolic effects.

Its pleasurable effects are often followed by headache, nausea, vomiting, fever, muscle rigidity, drowsiness, overdoses, slowing of respiration. If combined with alcohol or in an overdose, seizures, cardiac arrest, coma, and even death can occur.

What are roofies?

Roofies are a potent, widely-distributed sedative that have been cited in date rape cases. A small amount in a drink leaves a person sleepy, uncoordinated, and unable to remember what happened. Taken with alcohol, roofies (like liquid Ecstasy) can be fatal.

What is ketamine?

Ketamine is a tasteless, odorless depressant. It is often used to commit sexual assaults due to its ability to sedate and intoxicate unsuspecting victims. It's a tranquilizer most often used on animals, but has recently been found at parties. It produces hallucinatory effects similar to those of PCP and LSD and can be produced as a liquid or powder. The effects of ketamine last only an hour or so, yet the user's senses, judgment, and coordination can be affected for up to 24 hours after the initial use of the drug.

How can I prevent my drink from being spiked?

Take your beverage with you or ask someone you trust to watch it. At a bar or restaurant, accept drinks only from a bartender or server — and never from someone you don't know. At a party, bring your own beverage and accept only sealed drinks.

If you think you've been drugged, go to a hospital or healthcare provider within 24 hours. Ask to be checked for date rape drugs. Don't leave the party by yourself. Have several friends go with you.

 ## What are the straight facts on drugs?

What are cocaine and crack cocaine?

Cocaine and crack cocaine are highly addictive. Even first-time users may experience seizures or heart attacks, which can be fatal. This addiction can erode physical and mental health and can become so strong that these drugs dominate all aspects of an addict's life. Some users spend hundreds or thousands of dollars on cocaine and crack each week and will do anything to support their habit. Many turn to drug selling, prostitution, or other crimes.

Cocaine is a white powder that comes from the leaves of the South American coca plant. Cocaine is either "snorted" through the nasal passages or injected intravenously. Cocaine belongs to a class of drugs known as stimulants, which tend to give a temporary illusion of limitless power and energy that leave the user feeling depressed, edgy, and craving more.

Crack is a form of cocaine that has been chemically altered so that it can be smoked. Crack is a drug dealer's dream. It's the most potent form of one of the most addictive drugs — and can leave a person seriously addicted after just one use. Smoking crack produces a high, with feelings of invincibility, that lasts only about 10 or 15 minutes, at most. This period is followed by a severe crash, with overwhelming feelings of depression and dependency. Out of desperation to get out of this condition, the user has an intense craving for more crack — and the cycle continues.

Cocaine and crack are highly addictive. Even first-time users may experience seizures or heart attacks, which can be fatal. This addiction can erode physical and mental health and can become so strong that these drugs dominate all aspects of an addict's life. Some users spend hundreds or thousands of dollars on cocaine and crack each week and will do anything to support their habit. Many turn to drug selling, prostitution, or other crimes.

The physical risks associated with using any amount of cocaine and crack include increases in blood pressure, heart rate, breathing rate, and body temperature; heart attacks, strokes, and respiratory failure; hepatitis or AIDS through shared needles; brain seizure; inability to function sexually; and reduction of the body's ability to resist and combat infection.

The psychological risks include violent, erratic, or paranoid behavior; hallucinations and "coke bugs" — a sensation of imaginary insects crawling over the skin; confusion; anxiety; depression; loss of interest in food; "cocaine psychosis" — losing touch with reality; and loss of interest in friends, family, sports, hobbies, and other activities.

What are depressants?

Depressants include sleeping pills, tranquilizers, and barbituates. They are illegal unless prescribed by a healthcare provider. They cause many effects, including anxiety, depression, insomnia, irregular menstruation, impaired judgment, and suicide.

Depressants include sleeping pills, tranquilizers, and barbituates. They are illegal unless prescribed by a healthcare provider.

Psychological effects include reduced pain; feeling of well-being; lowered inhibitions; anxiety; depression; restlessness; and psychotic episodes.

Physical effects include chronic fatigue; insomnia; changes in eyesight; irregular menstruation; suicide; dependence requiring more of the drug to get the same effect; slowed pulse; lowered blood pressure; poor concentration or confusion; impaired coordination; impaired memory; impaired judgment; and respiratory/breathing problems. Barbituates also have these effects: sedation or drowsiness; unusual excitement; fever; irritability; poor judgment; slurred speech; and dizziness.

What are hallucinogens?

Hallucinogenic drugs distort the perception of objective reality making the senses of direction, distance, and time become disoriented. These drugs can produce unpredictable, erratic, and violent behavior in users that sometimes leads to serious injuries and death.

Hallucinogenic drugs are substances that distort the perception of objective reality. The most well-known hallucinogens include PCP, angel dust, love boat, LSD (or acid), mescaline and peyote, and "magic" mushrooms. Under the influence of hallucinogens, the senses of direction, distance, and time become disoriented. These drugs can produce unpredictable, erratic, and violent behavior in users that sometimes leads to serious injuries and death. The effects of hallucinogens can last for 12 hours. And everyone reacts differently to hallucinogens — so there's no way to predict if you can avoid a "bad trip."

The physical risks associated with using hallucinogens include increased heart rate and blood pressure; sleeplessness; tremors; lack of muscular coordination; sparse, mangled, and incoherent speech; decreased awareness of touch and pain that can result in self-inflicted injuries; convulsions; coma; and heart and lung failure.

The psychological risks associated with using hallucinogens include a sense of distance and estrangement; depression; anxiety; paranoia; violent behavior; confusion; suspicion; loss of control; flashbacks; behavior similar to schizophrenic psychosis; and catatonic syndrome where the user becomes mute, lethargic, disoriented, and makes meaningless repetitive movements.

What are inhalants?

Inhalants are a diverse group of chemicals that are found in consumer products such as aerosols and cleaning supplies. They are sniffed or huffed to give the user an immediate head rush or high. Inhalant use can cause a number of physical and emotional problems — and even a one-time use can result in death. Long-term use of inhalants has been associated with irreversible brain damage.

Inhalants are a diverse group of chemicals that are found in consumer products such as aerosols and cleaning supplies. They are sniffed or huffed to give the user an immediate head rush or high. Inhalant use can cause a number of physical and emotional problems — and even a one-time use can result in death. Long-term use of inhalants has been associated with irreversible brain damage.

Possible effects of using inhalants include headache; muscle weakness; abdominal pain; visual hallucinations; severe mood swings; numbness and tingling of hands and feet; decrease or loss of sense of smell; nausea; nosebleeds; violent behavior; irregular heartbeat; sudden death; suffocation; liver, lung, and kidney impairment; irreversible brain damage; nervous system damage; dangerous chemical imbalances in the body; and involuntary passing of urine and feces.

What is marijuana?

Marijuana is the most widely used illicit drug in the United States and tends to be the first illegal drug teens use. Marijuana blocks the messages going to your brain and alters your perceptions and emotions, vision, hearing, and coordination. It is extremely addictive on both a psychological and physical level.

Marijuana is a dangerous and understated drug. It is more than five times more harmful to lungs than cigarettes, containing over 400 harmful chemicals. It is approximately seven to 10 times stronger today than it was in the 1960s. Some people may conclude that it is safe to smoke it for "recreation" given the current publicity about marijuana's alleged medical uses.

Potential short-term health risks of using marijuana include sleepiness; increased hunger; difficulty keeping track of time; impaired or reduced short-term memory; reduced ability to perform tasks requiring concentration and coordination (such as driving a car); increased heart rate; potential cardiac dangers for those with pre-existing heart disease; bloodshot eyes; dry mouth and throat; decreased social inhibitions; paranoia; and hallucinations.

Marijuana kills brain cells. Other potential long-term health risks of using marijuana include enhanced cancer risk; increased risk of infertility in men and women; diminished or extinguished sexual pleasure; impotency; disruption of the normal menstrual cycle; and psychological dependence requiring more of the drug to get the same effect. Marijuana also decreases testosterone levels for men and increases testosterone levels in women. (Testosterone is a male hormone that controls hair and beard growth, development of the penis, muscle mass, and voice changes at puberty.)

"Second-hand" marijuana smoke can produce a "contact high" when near others who are smoking because the smoke is in everyone's breathing area. It can also endanger your lungs and respiratory system.

What is methamphetamine?

Methamphetamine ("meth") is produced in underground "labs." The people making the drug have no scientific background and manufacture it dangerously. There's no way to know how strong the meth is on the street or what is actually in it. (Doctors have reported cases of people whose throats were severely burned by meth that was cut with Drano.)

Meth's affect on the body is similar to that of the natural chemical adrenaline, but with deadly side effects. Once in the body, meth quickly affects the central nervous system, speeding up the heart and increasing blood pressure uncontrollably. While the high from one hit of crack lasts about 15 to 20 minutes, a meth high can last for hours. Smoking the rock form, ICE, can produce a high for up to 24 hours.

Meth is highly addictive. It causes the brain to release dopamine, a natural chemical that makes you feel good and is vital to normal brain functioning. After a while, meth's presence in the brain forces neurons to destroy extra dopamine, as well as the brain's ability to produce dopamine. Prolonged use of meth results in a permanent altering of the brain's natural chemistry. Translation: brain damage. The body also builds up a tolerance for meth. This means that a user will need more of the drug each time to reach the same high.

With prolonged use, meth leads to bingeing — consuming the drug continuously for three or more days without sleep. The user is then driven into a severe depression, followed by worsening paranoia, belligerence, and aggression — a period known as "tweaking." Finally, collapsing from exhaustion, the user awakens days later to repeat the cycle. Chronic abuse of meth can kill you. It produces a reaction more severe than crack cocaine, with sleepless binges that can last up to 14 days and end with intolerable crashes.

Short-term side effects include a false sense of well-being; convulsions, twitching, and jerking; aggressive behavior; increased heart rate; increased muscle tension; grinding of teeth; stimulation of the adrenal gland; constriction of blood vessels; rise in blood pressure; impaired speech; dry, itchy skin; loss of appetite; hallucinations; acne and sores; paranoia; and insomnia.

Long-term effects include malnutrition; liver damage; brain damage; severe weight loss; fatal kidney and lung disorders; insomnia; permanent psychological problems; lowered resistance to illness; stroke; coma; and death.

If you or someone you know uses meth, get help. Quitting meth is a slow and difficult process. The addict needs the assistance of a drug treatment program and/or facility.

What are narcotics?

Narcotics include heroin, morphine, codeine, Demerol, Percodan, Methadone, and Talwin. They are illegal unless prescribed by a healthcare provider. They can cause lethargy; drowsiness; euphoria; nausea; constipation; constricted pupils; and slowed breathing. Potential health risks include HIV/AIDS; heart or respiratory problems; mood swings; chronic constipation; tremors; toxic psychosis; and a high potential for addiction.

What are stimulants?

Stimulants increase alertness and physical activity. Some people use them to counteract the drowsiness or "down" feeling caused by sleeping pills or alcohol. This up/down cycle is extremely hard on the body and is very dangerous. Potential consequences include weight loss; nutritional deficiency; chronic sleep problems; high blood pressure; paranoia; anxiety or nervousness; decreased emotional control; severe depression; violent behavior; and death from heart failure or suicide.

Stimulants include amphetamine, methamphetamine, cocaine, and even caffeine. Symptoms of use include excitability; tremors; insomnia; sweating; dry mouth and lips; bad breath; dilated pupils; weight loss; paranoia; and hallucinations.

Is alcohol a drug?

Yes. Before you take that first drink, think about the effects alcohol can have on your life. Short-term risks include impaired judgment, car crashes, unwanted pregnancy, and criminal involvement. Long-term risks include mental health problems, sadness and anxiety, paranoia, and possible suicide. Legal problems can include suspended driver's license, fines, imprisonment — even vehicular manslaughter. Financial problems include loss of employment, damage to personal property, and the expense of alcohol abuse.

Physical health risks include increased risk of heart disease, nervous disorders, cancer, weight gain, bad breath, and malnutrition. Family problems include violence, disruption of home life, and alienation of parents/partners/children. School behavior problems include poor grades, missing classes, and suspension. Alcoholism can cause liver damage, severe withdrawal symptoms, and death.

Is caffeine a drug?

Yes. Caffeine may be the world's most popular drug. It's a white, bitter, crystal-like substance found in coffee, tea, cocoa, and soft drinks. It's also found in some products such as aspirin, non-prescription cough and cold remedies, diet pills, and some street drugs. As with all drugs, the effects vary depending on the amount taken and the individual. When a person drinks two cups of coffee (150 to 300 milligrams of caffeine), the effects begin in 15 to 30 minutes. The person's metabolism, body temperature, and blood pressure may increase. Other effects include increased urine production, higher blood sugar levels, hand tremors, a loss of coordination, decreased appetite, and delayed sleep.

Is tobacco a drug?

Cigarette smoking is perhaps the most devastating and preventable cause of disease and premature death. Cigarettes are highly addictive. One-third of young people who are "just experimenting" end up addicted by the age of 20. (Go to Chapter 9, "Can I commit to quit smoking?" for more information.)

Are anabolic steroids safe?

Some people think that anabolic steroids are safe for weight training — but they're not. The list of side effects or adverse reactions from long-term use of steroids is extensive. People who use steroids are aware of the possible side effects or adverse reactions, but they figure that most of the problems will be in the future — and the future is a long way off. Actually, that's not so. Acne, sexual function problems, rashes, and the infamous uncontrollable "roid rages" are among possible immediate consequences.

The argument is that anabolic steroids help a person recover from injuries. There is very little evidence to support that claim. Anabolic steroids can cause hypertension; blood clotting; cholesterol changes; liver cysts and cancer; kidney cancer; hostility and aggression; and acne. In men, it can cause prostate cancer; reduced sperm production; shrunken testicles; and breast enlargement. In women, it can cause menstrual irregularities and development of beards and other masculine characteristics.

Do alcohol and drugs contribute to suicides?

Authorities agree that many suicides are not reported, but the National Center for Health Statistics records between 25,000 and 30,000 self-inflicted deaths in the U.S. annually. For every death from suicide, experts estimate eight other suicide attempts are made. Suicide is now the second leading cause of death among persons 15 to 24 years of age.

No cause-and-effect relationship between the use of alcohol and/or other drugs and suicide has been established, but such use often is a contributing factor. Research indicates several possible explanations. Drinking, use of other drugs, or both, may reduce inhibitions and impair the judgment of someone contemplating suicide, making the act more likely. Use of alcohol or other drugs may also aggravate other risk factors for suicide, such as depression. (Alcohol is a depressant. So if you're already depressed, it can be deadly.)

Recent studies suggest that...

High rates of alcohol use have been found among suicide victims who use firearms. Alcohol tends to be associated with impulsive, rather than premeditated, suicides. (Go to Chapter 12, "What is Erek's story?")

Between 20% and 35% of suicide victims had a history of alcohol abuse or were drinking shortly before their suicides.

In one study of youth suicides, alcohol and drug abuse was the most common characteristic of those who attempted suicide. Fully 70% of these young people frequently used alcohol and/or other drugs.

Nearly 24% of suicide victims in another study had Blood Alcohol Concentrations (BACs) of .10 or greater. The legal level for intoxication in most jurisdictions is now .08.

A study of 100,000 deaths found positive BACs in 35% of suicide deaths.

 ## How do I say "No" to drugs?

Find creative ways to refuse alcohol, tobacco, and drugs. Use humor — and practice your refusals. You might say, *"No, thanks."* or *"I gotta go."* and then walk away. If you're more outgoing, you might say, *"What? Are you*

talking to me? Forget it." or *"No, I don't do drugs."* Use language that feels comfortable for you. Come up with a response that doesn't insult someone, especially if there is danger or violence involved.

Establish a clear position for yourself about alcohol and drugs. Refuse both subtle and direct offers. Don't give in to peer pressure. While you may temporarily feel like part of the crowd, true friendship doesn't depend on whether you go along with everything everyone else does.

 ## How can I get help?

How can I get help?

You *can* learn to take charge of your life and live healthy and drug-free. Contact a qualified alcohol and drug professional or mental health professional who can give you further advice.

You can get help for yourself, a friend, or a loved one from numerous organizations, treatment centers, referral centers, and hotlines throughout the country. There are various kinds of treatment services and centers. No single treatment is appropriate for all individuals. Many treatment programs focus on counseling and support groups. Recovery from alcohol and drug addiction can be a long-term process and frequently requires multiple episodes of treatment. And treatment does not have to be voluntary to be effective.

Each community has its own resources. Some common referral sources that are often listed in the phone book include the following:

- Community Drug Hotlines
- Alcoholics Anonymous (A.A.)

- Local Emergency Health Clinics
- Narcotics Anonymous (N.A.)

- Community Treatment Centers
- Al-Anon/Alateen

- County Health Departments
- Hospitals

Many symptoms of alcohol or drug abuse, such as sudden mood changes, difficulty in getting along with others, poor job or school performance, irritability, and depression, might be explained by other causes. It can be hard to determine the cause of these problems.

While you, your friend, or your loved one may be hesitant to seek help, know that treatment programs for people with alcohol and drug abuse problems offer organized and structured services with individual, group, and family therapy. Research shows that when appropriate treatment is given, and when clients follow their prescribed program, treatment can work. (Some people may go through treatment several times before they are in full recovery.)

What is A.A.?

Alcoholics Anonymous®, A.A., is an informal society of more than 2 million recovered alcoholics around the world. These men and women meet in local groups, which range in size from a handful in some locations to many hundreds in larger communities. Currently, women make up 35 percent of the total membership. The only requirement for membership is a desire to stop drinking. A.A. is supported through contributions. There are no dues or fees. It is not allied with a religious or political organization. Al-Anon helps family members, friends, and loved ones recover from the effects of living with a problem drinker. Alateen is for teens who have an alcoholic in their lives and is sponsored by an Al-Anon member.

> **Alcoholics Anonymous**
> PO Box 459
> Grand Central Station
> New York, NY 10163
> (212) 870-3400
>
> **Al-Anon Family Group HQ, Inc.**
> PO Box 862
> Midtown Station
> New York, NY 10018
> 1-800-356-9996
>
> **Alateen**
> 1600 Corp. Landing Pkwy
> Virginia Beach, VA 23454-5617
> 1-800-356-9996

www.alcoholics-anonymous.org
www.al-anon.alateen.org

Who attends A.A. meetings?

More than 97,000 local A.A. groups meet worldwide. There is probably a group that meets near your home. Most groups hold one or more meetings each week. Members discuss their own drinking experiences before finding A.A. and explain how A.A. principles led them to sobriety and a new outlook on life. Members share their stories — happy and sad. A.A is not just for "skid-row bums." It's for people of all races, ages, income levels, occupations, and so on. The common thread is a desire to be sober. Meetings are generally filled with laughter and a general atmosphere of goodwill and warmth. Members take the sobriety seriously. Part of the recovery process is laughing over the things that once brought tears.

What are the 12 Steps?

The *12 Steps of Alcoholics Anonymous* are a suggested "spiritual" recovery program, but it is up to the individual to decide if, when, and how the steps will be used.

1. We admitted we were powerless over alcohol — that our lives had become unmanageable.

2. Came to believe that a Power greater than ourselves could restore us to sanity.

3. Made a decision to turn our will and our lives over to the care of God *as we understood him.*

4. Made a searching and fearless moral inventory of ourselves.

5. Admitted to God, to ourselves, and to another human being the exact nature of our wrongs.

6. Were entirely ready to have God remove all these defects of character.

7. Humbly asked Him to remove our shortcomings.

8. Made a list of all persons we harmed, and became willing to make amends to them all.

9. Made direct amends to such people wherever possible, except when to do so would injure them or others.

10. Continued to take personal inventory and when we were wrong, promptly admitted it.

11. Sought through prayer and meditation to improve our conscious contact with God, *as we understood Him,* praying only for knowledge of His will for us and the power to carry that out.

12. Having had a spiritual awakening as the result of these steps, we tried to carry this message to alcoholics, and to practice these principles in all our affairs.

If you use alcohol, drink moderately and refrain from drinking for celebrations and holidays. Learn other ways to celebrate. Try to deal with stress without tossing down a few drinks. Try exercise, talking with a friend, or deep breathing. Allow yourself a "time out" from your regular routine.

What is intervention?

Intervention means that you interfere in the affairs of someone else. It has been said that people who drink only hurt themselves. That's just not true. They also hurt their families, friends, fellow workers, and others. If you feel you need to intervene, wait until the person is not under the influence and calmly and rationally confront him/her with your evidence or concerns. Be firm but not accusatory. Be prepared for the user to lie and for the possibility that you might have to seek outside help to deal with the problem. Your doctor, hospital, local mental health or substance abuse counselor, or the *Yellow Pages* can all be helpful resources for drug abuse information and can refer you to treatment programs in your area.

Intervening to help a family member or friend who has an alcohol or drug problem can be difficult and hurtful. The person with the problem will most likely deny the problem and try to put you on the defensive. He/she may say something like, *"I thought you were my friend ... and you're calling me a drunk?"* In such cases, what you *don't* do is as important as what you should do:

- Don't cover up or make excuses for the person.

- Don't take over his/her responsibilities, leaving the person with no sense of importance or dignity.

- Don't argue with the person when he/she is drunk or high.

- Don't hide alcohol or drugs (or dump alcohol) or shelter the person from situations where alcohol is present.

- Don't accept responsibility for the person's actions or guilt for his/her drinking.

What you can do is learn about the illness and sources of treatment; guide the person to treatment; and support the person during treatment and after. Doing this requires effort, patience, and most importantly, genuine concern. Don't label people as bad or good — only their behavior. Illicit drug use, for instance, is bad behavior, but a drug user is not a bad person.

What are the legal implications?

When alcohol or drugs are used by minors on your property, you are subject to both criminal charges and civil lawsuits for monetary damages (both actual and punitive). It is also illegal to purchase alcoholic beverages for a minor (anyone under the age of 21). If you're under the age of 21, it is illegal for you to possess, consume, obtain, or purchase alcohol.

The use of alcohol and drugs is not only harmful to your health, but also to your freedom. If you use, sell, or even possess them, you are breaking the law and could be imprisoned for long-term sentences and fined thousands of dollars.

Know the law. Methamphetamines, marijuana, hallucinogens, crack, cocaine, and many other substances are illegal. Depending on where you are caught, and with what, you could face high fines and jail time. Alcohol is illegal to buy or possess if you're under 21. It's also illegal to drive with it in your system.

Get the facts. One drink can make you fail a breath test. In some states, people under age 21 who are found to have any amount of alcohol in their systems can lose their driver's license, be subject to heavy fines, and/or have their cars permanently taken away.

 ## Personal Stories to Share

What if the designated driver is a passenger?

(Contributed by Diana Halstead)

As I sit thinking about this article, I am consumed with so many feelings — anger, helplessness, despair, and a great sorrow. Thinking back over my last 11 years, I wonder what I can say that might make a difference in your lives.

Perhaps if you were to see a picture of a car, going too fast, driven by a drunk driver with a passenger who was the designated driver but instead chose to ride … I wonder … will this make a difference? What can I say that will make a difference to you? Will you then speak up the next time you're with a friend who is too intoxicated to drive?

On September 13, 1990, my life changed forever — my two sons, Byron and Derek Hurney, were killed in a drunk-driving accident.

I believe sorrow is the strongest feeling that I continue to experience. When the phone rings, I still want it to be the boys. I want to hear about their days and their lives — or even just to hear their voices. I was not so fortunate to have a video camera when they were growing up so their voices are also lost. They are buried in another state, so even vacations are spent visiting the cemetery.

Maybe you're thinking to yourself that the boys are not there, so why go so far? The need to be near them is sometimes so great that it consumes my whole life. I go to their graves to fulfill the loneliness that remains in my heart. It is there that I can carry on that one-sided conversation with them, since all that comes from the ground is silence.

Our family goes through the motions of living — but sometimes I wonder how happy we truly are. When I hear the news that a drunk driver killed a child, my heart breaks for that family as I know what kind of lives they will be living and how they will exist from that point on.

If you get nothing else from this, think about the lives you leave behind ... The joy that they will no longer have ... The family that is no longer complete ... The emptiness that everyday brings them.

No second chances?

(Contributed by Morgan Chilson)

When all is said and done, it's the little things that rock your soul ... The missed phone call ... your last opportunity to talk to him ... because you went to buy a lottery ticket ... Wondering if he felt the impact of the crash ... if his eyes were open ... if he knew he was dying ...

Photo by Barb Rollings

Barb Rollings tells the story of her son's death now without crying. But for the first year after his death, she suffered from bouts of uncontrollable crying. The sight of a white baseball cap in the mall was enough to bring a flow of tears that threatened to flood her very existence.

Jason Patrick Dunegan died on June 5, 1999 — his 21st birthday. He died because he chose to get in a car with someone who was drunk. He died because no one watched out for him — not the waitress who served him, not the bartender who mixed the drinks, not his boss who charged the drinks to the company's credit card.

It means a lot to Barb that her son kept his promise to her that he wouldn't drink and drive. She just wishes he had carried it one step further and not gotten in the car with the friend he'd been drinking with.

"Looking back, it's still difficult to this day. When you go through something like that, it is such a shock and a devastation that the first year, you're in a fog. You truly don't know what's happened. It's just such an unthinkable thing that you think won't ever happen and when it does, you're just literally thrown for a loop."

Two years later, the events of that last weekend still replay in sharp focus through Barb's mind. She recalls the events in her words:

"It was Jason's 21st birthday. His boss decided to take him and another fellow that he worked with out to celebrate. (The other fellow was only 19 and underage at the time.) Jason's boss bought all the drinks — and they served them for three hours. The servers sang 'Happy Birthday' to Jason. He called home around 8:30 that evening — and I just missed his call because I had run up the street to get a lottery ticket. Charlotte, his sister, talked to him. Charlotte asked him, 'You're not driving, are you?' And he said, 'Oh, no, no, no. I know I've had too much to drink.' When it came time to leave, Jason knew he couldn't drive, so the other boy that was with him said he'd drive.

"Within 15 minutes after they left, the driver lost control of

his car, hit a telephone pole at 80 miles an hour, and killed Jason instantly."

(The coroner's report revealed Jason hadn't eaten — not one ounce of food was in his stomach.)

> *"Jason's name was misspelled by one letter on his driver's license when he moved so they couldn't find his family. (He lived in an apartment by himself.) He was killed at 9:30 the night of his birthday but it wasn't until ten 'til two the next morning that I got the call. I knew something was wrong. I was the only one still awake and my heart wasn't beating right. I remember lying there thinking, 'This is the first birthday in 21 years that I've not talked to him.' I waited and waited for him to call back … and when he didn't call back, I kept trying to convince myself that he was okay. This was his special birthday and I should just let him be. He's almost grown now.*

> *"I was holding my chest when the phone rang. 'Is this Barbara Rollings? You have a son, Jason?' (Because it had been so many hours, the police told me over the phone.)"*

Those words preceded the worst news that Barb has ever gotten — and probably will ever get.

> *"When you have the time to reflect back on something like that, you think about all the different stages in your children's lives — from the time you first bring them home … to when they sit up by themselves … to being able to walk … and then it's the first day of school … and the first dance … and the first date … Then they get their license … and you want to take them back because the danger of things that are out there come close to home."*

Barb can't fix what happened in her life. There's no way she will ever fill the emptiness left by Jason's death. She does try to save other families from dealing with the pain she has felt by speaking to groups, trying to impress upon young people the feelings of those left behind.

> *"It can happen in a moment. Jason's life was ended. He doesn't get a second chance. For the survivors left behind, it's like being given a life sentence. We don't have a choice. We don't get a pardon. We have to serve it as long as we live without him."*

The grief never stops.

Note: The bartender, a server, and Jason's boss were all cited with serving alcohol to a minor, misdemeanor charges. The driver of the car, who was seriously injured and in a coma for a short while, was convicted of vehicular manslaughter and is serving time in jail as of October 2001.

Anything but Ecstasy

(Contributed by Lynn Smith)

I hear a lot of people talking about Ecstasy — calling it a fun, harmless drug. All I can think is, *"If they only knew … "*

I grew up in a small, rural town in Pennsylvania. It's one of those places where everyone knows your name, what you did, what you ate, and so on. They certainly knew me. I was a straight-A student involved in many school activities. I was one of the popular kids, liked by all the different crowds. I was on the homecoming court and regularly cast in school theater productions.

Drugs never played a part in my life. They were never a question. I was too involved and focused on other things.

I always dreamed of moving to New York City to study acting and pursue a career in theater. My dream came true when my mom brought me to the

City to attend acting school. As you can imagine, it was quite a change from home. I was exposed to new people, new ideas, and a completely new way of life — a way of life that exposed me to drugs. Most of the people I met and spent time with in acting school had already been doing drugs for years. I guess I felt that by using drugs, I would become a part of their world and it would deepen my friendships with them.

My introduction to drugs was very casual. I dropped my first pill among close friends in a chill environment, not in a back alley with "scary drug dealers," although I would meet some in the months ahead. I tried pot and then cocaine. One drug led to the next — like stepping stones across dark waters.

But it was Ecstasy that changed my life forever.

I remember the feeling I had the first time I did Ecstasy: complete and utter bliss. I could feel the pulse of the universe; I let every breath, touch, and molecule move my soul. It was as if I had unlocked some sort of secret world — as if I'd found heaven. And even though it was a chemical, it didn't feel any less real.

At first, going to school and holding down two jobs to stay afloat left little time for partying. But, as time went by, things changed. I graduated, had a steady job, made more new friends — and began to use drugs, especially Ecstasy, more frequently. As I did, I actually started to look down on those who did not. I surrounded myself only with those who did.

Looking back on my old friends, I see how we were all so similar — not just in our drug use, but in a deeper sense. We were all broken in some way — feeling sad, hurt, and alone — whether it was from a difficult childhood, a broken heart, or feelings of insecurity. We were a crowd of lost souls wanting so badly to be a part of something.

I had gone from a girl who never used drugs to a woman who couldn't imagine life without them.

Fortunately, at least as I saw it, all my friends did Ecstasy. And since my boyfriend sold it, I rarely paid for anything. My weekends were spent popping pills and dancing at one of the many clubs in New York City. It didn't really matter where I was — clubs, bars, apartments — anywhere, anytime became a good place and a good time to use. My weekends began on Thursday and ran until Sunday.

I had come to New York dreaming of a career in the theater. Drugs didn't rob me of that dream, but they did make me willing to forget about it. It wasn't that I stopped getting parts because I was using drugs — I just stopped auditioning. Sometimes I stopped eating and sleeping. I worked only two days a week to support my habit. The rest of the time was spent getting high, almost always on Ecstasy. The utter bliss of my first Ecstasy experience was a distant memory. Of course, I never could recapture that first high, no matter how much Ecstasy I took.

In five months, I went from living somewhat responsibly while pursuing my dream to a person who didn't care about a thing … and the higher I got, the deeper I sank into a dark, lonely place. When I did sleep, I had nightmares and panic attacks. I had pasty skin, a throbbing head, and the beginnings of paranoia. I ignored it all, thinking it was normal …

… until the night I thought I was dying.

On this night, I was sitting on the couch with my boyfriend and roommates. We were watching a movie. I was feeling normal when suddenly I felt as if I needed to jump out of my skin. Racing thoughts, horrible images, and hallucinations crept through my mind. I thought I was seeing the devil. I repeatedly asked my friends if I was dead. I was pacing frantically back and forth, incapable of relaxing or understanding anything that was going on around me. On top of all this, I felt as if I was having a heart attack. The worst part was those moments when I could see myself — and what I had become.

Somehow, I managed to pick up the phone and call my mom in the middle of the night — telling her to come get me. She did, pulling me out of my apartment the next morning.

I didn't know who I was or where I was as my mom drove me back to a hospital in Pennsylvania. I spent most of the drive curled up in the back seat while my younger sister tried to keep me calm. I think she and my mom were afraid I'd jump out of the moving car at any moment — and given my state of mind at the time, I can't say I blame them.

When we finally got to the hospital, I was committed to the psychiatric ward — where I spent the next 14 days in a state of extreme confusion. This is what Ecstasy gave me — but it didn't stop there …

While I was in the hospital, my doctors performed something called a "neuro-spec scan" of my brain. I couldn't believe my eyes when I saw the results. The scan showed several dark splotches on the image of my brain. My doctors told me those were areas that carry out memory functions — areas where the activity of my brain had been changed in some way. Because I used other drugs, the doctors couldn't say that my heavy Ecstasy abuse was solely responsible for this. But this much I know for sure: There's nothing in my medical history that could have contributed to this.

Since I saw that scan, my life has been an uphill crawl — filled with doctors, therapists, meetings, and a lot of soul-searching. I have been placed on several medications — anti-depressants, anti-psychotics, and mood stabilizers — all to help me live with the chemical imbalance caused by my drug abuse.

Looking back, it all happened so fast. And worst of all, I know I did this to myself.

I hear people say Ecstasy is a harmless, happy drug. There's nothing "happy" about the way that "harmless" drug chipped away at my life. Ecstasy took my strength, my motivation, my dreams, my friends, my apartment, my money — and most of all, my sanity. I worry about my future and my health every day.

I have many mountains ahead of me — but I plan to keep climbing because I'm one of the lucky ones. I've been given a second chance — and that's not something that everyone gets.

Temptation of a Pretty Poison

Numbness, tingling
It starts at my toes and
Works its way up to my head.

Projecting the self
I'd like to be
Sexy, talkative, mysterious
Carefree.

One pill has dissolved
Chills surge through my core
Before it wears off
I swallow one more.

My skin's not my own
So many faces to see
Before I know it
I'm on to number three.

Sweat pours off my brow
The world is my stage
Lashing and dancing
Unleashing my rage.

Four, five,
And six (on a bet)
But usually after three
I try to forget.

The music has faded
There is no one around
The lights are too bright
My thumping heart,
 the only sound.

Open the door
Shield my eyes from the sun
Knees are throbbing
A cab, not one.

My clothes tell a story
Of where I have been
My mind racing with emptiness
My soul dirty with sin.

I get home to my cave
And shed my night skin.
Clenched eyes while awake
The drug always wins.

~Lynn Smith

God, where's Ray?

Why does Mommy cry when she looks at me? I went to my room for my puppy and Mommy cried. She picked me up and held me close. I like Mommy to hold me close in her lap.

My mommy smells nice. I wish my puppy, Magic, smelled like that. Then she could come to bed with me at night and keep me warm.

God, why doesn't Ray come home anymore? I heard Mommy and Daddy tell him to get out. Why did they do that to my brother? I guess it's because he can't walk straight all the time.

Mommy says Ray has stars in his eyes. I like stars, don't you?

Is something wrong with my brother? Daddy says I can't see him anymore.

Ray sometimes comes to the park to see me and Magic play. Sometimes he makes me sit down and promise never to "blow grass" or "punch holes in my arms."

What does he mean by that? I like to watch the grass blow through my fingers. But I wouldn't like to punch holes in my arms. That would hurt and it wouldn't look pretty.

God, why does Mommy have a black dress on? She doesn't look good with puffy eyes — like I get when she spanks me.

Daddy's crying, too. What's in the big box? Is it for me?

Why are they putting it into the ground?

God, where's Ray?

~ Author Unknown

What's the harm in a pizza, a party, and a moonlight ride?

Jenny was so happy about the house they had found.
For once in her life, it was on the right side of town.
She unpacked her things with such great ease
As she watched her new curtains blow in the breeze.
How wonderful it was to have her own room.
School would be starting — she'd have friends over soon.
There'd be sleepovers and parties. She was so happy.
It's just the way she wanted her life to be.

On the first day of school, everything went great.
She made new friends and even got a date!
She thought, *"I want to be popular and I'm going to be,*
Because I just got a date with the star of the team!"
To be known in this school you have to have clout
And dating this guy would sure help her out.
There was only one problem stopping her fate …
Her parents had said she was too young to date.

"Well, I just won't tell them the entire truth.
They won't know the difference. What's there to lose?"
Jenny asked to stay with her friends that night.
Her parents frowned, but said, *"All right."*
Excited, she got ready for the big event,
But as she rushed around like she had no sense.
She began to feel guilty about all the lies.
But what's a pizza, a party, and a moonlight ride?

Well, the pizza was good, and the party was great.
But the moonlight ride would have to wait.
For Jeff was half-drunk by this time,
But he kissed her and said that he was just fine.
Then the room filled with smoke and Jeff took a puff.
Jenny couldn't believe he was smoking that stuff.

continued...

Now Jeff was ready to ride to "the Point."
But only after he'd smoked another joint.
They jumped in the car for the moonlight ride,
Not thinking that he was too drunk to drive.
They finally made it to "the Point" at last,
And Jeff started trying to make a pass.
A pass is not what Jenny wanted at all.
(And by a pass, I don't mean "playing football.")

"Perhaps my parents were right … Maybe I am too young.
Boy, how could I ever, ever be so dumb?"
With all of her might, she pushed Jeff away.
"Please take me home, I don't want to stay."

Jeff cranked up the engine and floored the gas.
In a matter of seconds, they were driving too fast.
As Jeff drove on in a fit of wild anger,
Jenny knew that her life was in real danger.
She begged and pleaded for him to slow down,
But he just got faster as they neared the town.

"Just let me get home. I'll confess that I lied.
I really went out for a moonlight ride."
Then all of a sudden, she saw a big flash.
"Oh, God. Please help us! We're going to crash!"
She doesn't remember the force of impact.
Just that everything all of a sudden went black.
She felt someone remove her from the twisted rubble.
And heard, *"Call an ambulance. These kids are in trouble."*

Voices she heard … a few words at best.
But she knew there were two cars involved in the wreck.
She wondered to herself if Jeff was alright.
And if the people in the other car were alive.

continued…

She awoke in a hospital to faces so sad.
"You've been in a wreck and it looks pretty bad."
These voices echoed inside her head
As they gently told her that Jeff was dead.
They said, *"Jenny, we've done all we can do,*
"But it looks as if we'll lose you, too."

"But the people in the other car?" Jenny cried.
"We're sorry, Jenny. They also died."
Jenny prayed, *"God, forgive me for what I have done.*
I only wanted to have just one night of fun."

"Tell those people's families, I've made their lives dim
And I wish I could return their loved ones to them.
Tell Mom and Dad I'm sorry I lied
And that it's my fault so many have died.
Oh, nurse, won't you please tell them that for me?"

The nurse just stood there — she never agreed.
But took Jenny's hand with tears in her eyes.
And a few moments later Jenny died.

A man asked the nurse, *"Why didn't you do your best*
To bid that young girl her one last request?"
She looked at the man with eyes so sad,
"Because the people in the other car were her mom and dad."

This story is sad and unpleasant but true,
So young people take heed. It could have been you.

~Author Unkown

Additional Information for this Chapter

Books

- *Codependent No More* by Melody Beattie

- *Beyond Codependence* by Melody Beattie

Web Links

- *www.freevibe.com*

- *www.whitehousedrugpolicy.gov*

- *www.health.org*

- *www.alcoholics-anonymous.org*

- *www.al-anon.alateen.org*

- *www.drugfreeamerica.org*

- *www.factsontap.org*

- *www.clubdrugs.org*

- *www.tobaccofree.org*

- *www.drughelp.org*

- *www.expage.com/mazelia77*

- *www.themeadows.org*

- *www.lastcall.org*

Interactive CD-ROM

Click to the web from the CD-ROM!

Web Resource

- *www.badd.org*
  (Boaters Against Drunk Driving)

- *www.itsnotanaccident.com*

- *www.add.ca/grieving*

- *www.drmike-hypnosis.com/recipe*
  (non-alcoholic drink recipes)

- *www.geocities.com/ missnmiss.coa.html*
  (Children of Alcoholics)

- *www.acde.org*
  (American Council for Drug Education)

- *www.ncadd.org*
  (National Council on Alcoholism and Drug Dependence)

Am I depressed?

Growing up can be tough. Life gets complicated and demanding. Deep down, you're not quite sure of who you are, or what you want to be, or whether the choices you make each day are the right choices. Sometimes the changes and pressures you're facing threaten to overwhelm you. So, it isn't surprising that you might feel down or discouraged at times. But what about those times when your outlook on life stays down for weeks and begins to affect your relationships? If you're feeling like this, you might be suffering from depression. Check the following symptoms that you've had for more than two weeks:

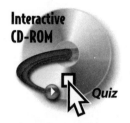

Interactive
CD-ROM

Quiz

Do I express feelings of...
○ sadness or emptiness?
○ nervousness or anxiety?
○ hopelessness or pessimism?
○ helplessness, worthlessness, or guilt?

Do I seem...
○ unable to make decisions?
○ unable to concentrate and remember?
○ to have lost interest or pleasure in ordinary activities?
○ to have more problems with school, work, and/or family?

Do I complain of...
○ being tired, having no energy and drive, or seeming "slowed down?"
○ sleeping more or less than usual?
○ eating more or less than usual? Am I losing or gaining weight?
○ headaches, stomach aches, or backaches?
○ chronic aches and pains in joints and muscles?

Has my behavior changed suddenly so that...
○ I'm restless and more irritable?
○ I want to be alone most of the time?
○ I've started cutting classes, skipping work, or dropping other activities?
○ I'm drinking heavily or taking drugs?

Do I feel like...
○ no one loves me?
○ life isn't worth living?
○ my family would be better off without me?
○ there's nothing I can do to make things better?

Have I talked about...
○ death?
○ suicide?

Have I attempted suicide?
○ Yes
○ No

If you checked five or more items, you may be suffering from depression. Don't assume you can take care of the problem. Please get help immediately. Treatment may save your life. Symptoms of depression are present in almost 70 percent of people who commit suicide. Read "What is Erek's story?" to see what depression can do.

Adapted from "What to do when a friend is depressed..." (National Institute of Mental Health's (NIMH) publication No. 01-3824).

Figure 12A

Depression & Suicide Prevention

Feeling depressed can alter the way you view everything in your life. With all the changes of entering adulthood, feeling overwhelmed sometimes is expected. But consistent depressed feelings can lead to serious problems — and there are many people willing to help you deal with depression before it changes your life. Know when to seek help.

The information in this chapter is intended for informational purposes only.

It is not all-inclusive and cannot substitute for professional medical care or counseling.

 What is depression?

What is depression?

Depression is a brain disorder that affects your thoughts, moods, feelings, behaviors, and physical health. Depression is more than the "blues" or the "blahs." It's more than the normal everyday ups and downs. It's more than "all in your head." It's more than "having a bad day." If you're feeling down, and have for more than a few weeks, you may be clinically depressed. Clinical depression is a serious health problem that affects the total person. In addition to feelings, it can change behavior, physical health and appearance, academic or work performance, social activity, and the ability to handle everyday decisions and pressures.

> *Whatever else it may be, depression is a box of lies. The person trapped in this darkness often is unable to see past its murk to future happiness or even to past joys. They believe, erroneously, that they have always been unhappy, and therefore, always will be."*

~ Richard Paul Evans in *The Carousel*

The Carousel by Richard Paul Evans. ©2000 by Richard Paul Evans. (Simon & Schuster, ISBN 0-684-86891-1)

Depression isn't the same as a passing blue mood. It's not a sign of personal weakness or a condition that can be willed or wished away. People with a depressive illness cannot merely "pull themselves together" and get better. Appropriate treatment can help most people who suffer from depression. Without treatment, though, symptoms can last for weeks, months, or years — and can lead to suicide.

According to the National Institute of Mental Health (NIMH), in any given one-year period, almost 10 percent of the population, or about 18.8 million American adults, suffer from a depressive illness. Depression can strike men, women and children of any age and of any ethnic or socio-economic background. The economic cost is high, but the cost in human suffering cannot be estimated.

Depression can take many forms and is often disguised as poor health or a bad attitude. One of four people seeking medical care for physical problems is actually suffering from some kind of mental disorder. Depressive disorders often co-occur with anxiety disorders and substance abuse. They often interfere with normal functioning and cause pain and suffering not only to people who have a disorder, but also to those who care about them.

Are women more likely to be depressed?

Women experience depression almost twice as often as men. Many hormonal factors may contribute to the increased rate of depression in women, particularly such factors as menstrual cycle changes, pregnancy, miscarriage, postpartum phase, pre-menopause, and menopause. Ten to 20 percent of women experience postpartum depression after giving birth. Many women also face additional stresses such as responsibilities both at work and home, single parenthood, and caring for children and/or aging parents.

Does depression disguise itself as anger in men?

Men do suffer from depression, but they're less likely to admit to depression and doctors are less likely to suspect it. The rate of suicide in men, however, is four times that of women (although more women attempt it). Men's depression is often masked by alcohol or drugs, or by the socially-acceptable habit of working excessively long hours. Depression typically shows up in men as being irritable, angry, and discouraged.

 ## What are the three major types of depression?

What is major depression?

According to the National Institute of Mental Health, major depressive disorder is the leading cause of disability in the U.S. and affects 9.9 million adults. Major depression is a combination of symptoms that interfere with the ability to work, study, sleep, eat, and enjoy once pleasurable activities. A disabling episode of depression may occur only once in a lifetime, but more commonly occurs several times. Major depression is a significant predictor of suicide and is a widely under-recognized and under-treated medical illness.

What is dysthymia?

A less severe type of depression, dysthymia involves long-term, chronic symptoms that do not disable, but keep you from functioning well or from feeling good. Many people with dysthymia also experience major depressive episodes at some time in their lives.

What is bipolar disorder?

Bipolar disorders (manic-depression) affect 2.3 million American adults. Men and women are equally likely to develop bipolar disorder. The average age for onset is in the early 20s. It's characterized by cycling mood changes: severe highs (mania) to lows (depression). Sometimes the mood switches are dramatic and rapid, but most often they are gradual. When in the depressed cycle, an individual can have any or all of the symptoms of a depressive disorder. When in the manic cycle, an individual may be overactive, over-talkative, and have a great deal of energy. Mania often affects thinking, judgment, and social behavior in ways that cause serious problems and embarrassment.

Symptoms can include abnormal or excessive elation, unusual irritability, decreased need for sleep, grandiose notions, increased talking, racing thoughts, increased sexual desire, increased energy, poor judgment, and inappropriate social behavior. Severity and number of symptoms varies with individuals.

 ## What are the symptoms of depression?

Refer to the "Am I depressed?" quiz at the beginning of this chapter for a list of symptoms.

Not everyone who is depressed experiences every symptom. Some people experience a few symptoms, some many. Severity of symptoms varies with individuals and also varies over time.

 ## What causes depression?

What causes depression?

The exact causes of depression are not yet known. No one is sure why some people get depressed and others don't. Sometimes depression happens because of a stressful event — but other times, it seems to happen for no reason at all. Doctors believe there are biological and emotional factors that may increase the likelihood that a person will develop a depressive disorder. Very often, a combination of factors is involved in the onset of a depressive disorder, including the following:

Genetics

Research over the past decade strongly suggests a genetic link to depressive disorders, which means that depression can run in families. However, not everyone who has a relative with depression will develop it. Depression can also occur in people who have no family history of depression.

Changes in Brain Function

Depression is often associated with changes in brain structures or brain function. Modern brain imaging technologies are revealing that in depression, neural circuits responsible for the regulation of moods, thinking, sleep, appetite, and behavior fail to function properly, and that critical chemicals used by nerve cells to communicate (neurotransmitters) are out of balance. A lack of one such chemical, serotonin, may contribute to depression.

Difficult Life Experiences

Difficult life experiences can trigger a depressive episode. Triggers can include the following:

- Death of a parent, loved one, pet (even if it occurred when you were younger).

- Break-up with a boyfriend or girlfriend.

- Failure in school or sports.

- Run-in with the law.

- Financial difficulties.

- Being bullied, harassed, assaulted, teased, or ridiculed.

- Struggling with sexuality, pressure to be sexually-active.

- Parents' divorce or parental conflict.

- Abusive parent(s) or chemically-dependent parent(s).

- Difficult relationship(s) with family, peers, co-workers, teachers.

- Failure to meet your own expectations of achievement.

- A loved one who is depressed. (Depression can be contagious.)

Low Self-Esteem

People who have low self-esteem, who consistently view themselves and the world with pessimism, or who are readily overwhelmed by stress are prone to depression. Whether this represents a psychological predisposition or an early form of the illness is not clear.

Alcohol and Drugs

Alcohol is a depressant. It can increase the severity of depression — and can lead to suicide. Depression may also be a side effect of certain medications, including birth control pills, steroids, sleeping pills, and tranquilizers. For more information, go to Chapter 11, "Alcohol & Drugs".

Medical Illnesses

Medical illnesses can cause depressive illnesses, making the sick person unable and/or unwilling to care for his or her physical needs, thus prolonging the recovery period.

Social Conditioning

Some believe that if children (especially girls) are taught to be helpless, they can become overwhelmed and depressed later in life when confronted with adult problems. This "learned helplessness" theory has shown that when children became discouraged or are punished for showing initiative, they usually become passive and shun responsibility. This leads to a perception that things are beyond their control and promotes feelings of helplessness and hopelessness — signs of depression.

Is depression my fault?

Depression is no one's fault. It's not a sign of personal weakness or a character flaw. Depression is a medical condition that can be managed with medicine, therapy, or a combination of the two.

 ## Can depression be treated?

Depression is treatable. The first step to getting appropriate treatment for depression is a visit to your healthcare provider for a physical examination. Certain medications, as well as some medical conditions (such as a viral infection), can cause the same symptoms as depression. Once a physical cause for depression is ruled out, a psychological evaluation should be done by your healthcare provider or by referral to a mental health professional. The psychological evaluation should include the following:

- A complete history of symptoms. When did the symptoms start? How long have they lasted? How severe are they? Have you had them before? If so, were they treated? How were they treated?

- A family history. Have other family members had a depressive illness?

- A history of alcohol and/or drug use.

- Do you have thoughts of death or suicide?

- Has your speech or memory been affected?

Treatment will depend on the outcome of the physical and psychological evaluations. A variety of antidepressant medications and psychotherapies can be used to treat depressive disorders. Most do best with a combined treatment: medication to gain relatively quick symptom relief and psychotherapy to learn more effective ways to deal with life's problems, including depression.

 ## What are the myths about depression?

Myths about depression often separate people from effective treatments now available. Common myths include the following:

Myth: People who claim to be depressed are weak and just need to pull themselves together. There's nothing anyone else can do to help.

Fact: Depression is not a weakness, but a serious health disorder. People who are depressed need professional treatment. For many people, a combination of psychotherapy and medication is beneficial. A trained therapist or counselor can help them learn more positive ways to think about themselves, change behaviors, cope with problems, or handle relationships. A physician can prescribe medications to help relieve the symptoms of depression.

Myth: Talking about depression only makes it worse.

Fact: Talking through feelings may help a friend recognize the need for professional help. By showing friendship and concern and giving uncritical support, you can encourage your friend to talk to his or her parents or another trusted adult about getting treatment. If your friend is reluctant to ask for help, you talk to someone who can help.

Myth: It's normal for teenagers to be moody. Teens don't suffer from "real" depression.

Fact: Depression can affect people at any age or of any race, ethnic, or economic group.

Myth: Telling an adult that a friend might be depressed is betraying a trust. If someone wants help, he or she will get it.

Fact: Depression, which saps energy and self-esteem, interferes with a person's ability or desire to get help. And many parents may not understand the seriousness of depression or of thoughts of death or suicide. It's an act of true friendship to share your concerns with a trusted adult.

 ## Do I have an anxiety disorder?

Anxiety disorders are serious medical illnesses that affect almost 19 million American adults. These disorders fill people's lives with overwhelming anxiety and fear. Unlike the relatively mild, brief anxiety caused by a stressful event (such as a class presentation or a first date), anxiety disorders are chronic, relentless, and can grow progressively worse if not treated. Effective treatments for anxiety disorders are available. Each anxiety disorder has its own distinct features — but they are all bound together by one common theme: excessive, irrational fear and dread.

Panic Attacks

If you're having a panic attack, you may experience sweating, fast heartbeat, shortness of breath, inability to breathe, faintness, tingling hands, hot or cold flashes, and the fear of dying, going crazy, or losing control. These symptoms are always experienced with a tremendous and uncontrollable terror without any clear cause. Untreated, this disorder can become very disabling.

Social Phobia

Social phobia involves overwhelming anxiety and excessive self-consciousness in everyday social settings. People with social phobias have a persistent, intense, and chronic fear of being watched and judged by others and being embarrassed or humiliated by their own actions. While many realize their fear is excessive or unreasonable, they're unable to overcome it. They often worry for days or weeks in advance of a dreaded situation. Substance abuse or dependence may develop in individuals who attempt to "self-medicate" their social phobia by drinking or using drugs.

Specific Phobias

A specific phobia is an intense fear of something that poses little or no actual danger. Some of the more common specific phobias include closed-in places, heights, escalators, tunnels, highway driving, water, flying, and dogs. Such phobias aren't just extreme fear, they're irrational fear of a particular thing. These phobias often bring on panic attacks or severe anxiety.

Post-Traumatic Stress Disorder

Post-traumatic stress disorder (PTSD) is a debilitating condition that can develop following a terrifying or traumatic event. Victims of PTSD frequently suffer from the following symptoms, which may not occur until long after the upsetting event that caused them: re-living the shocking event ("flashbacks"); severe nightmares; deadening of emotion and disregard for people and surroundings; hyper-vigilance and over-reaction; anxiety; depression; sudden outbursts of grief, anger, or fear; inability to sleep; lack of attention; and guilt feelings ("survivor's guilt"). PTSD is often accompanied by depression, substance abuse, or one or more other anxiety disorders.

Obsessive-Compulsive Disorder

OCD involves anxious thoughts or rituals you feel you can't control. If you have OCD, you may have persistent, unwelcome thoughts or images or feel an urgent need to engage in certain rituals. For example, you may be obsessed with germs or dirt, so you wash your hands over and over. The disturbing thoughts or images are called obsessions; the rituals that you perform to try to prevent or get rid of them are called compulsions.

Generalized Anxiety Disorder

Generalized anxiety disorder (GAD) is much more than normal anxiety people experience day to day. It's chronic and fills one's day with exaggerated worry and tension, even though there is little or nothing to provoke it. Having this disorder means always anticipating disaster, often worrying excessively about health, money, family, or work. Worries are often accompanied by physical symptoms: fatigue, headaches, muscle tension, muscle aches, difficulty swallowing, trembling, twitching, irritability, sweating, and hot flashes. They seem unable to relax and tend to have difficulty concentrating.

What are the statistics on suicide?

What are the statistics on suicide?

According to the National Institute of Mental Health,

> Suicide is a permanent solution to a temporary problem.

- Every 100 minutes, someone under age 24 will kill himself or herself.

- Suicide is the second-leading cause of death among 15 to 24 year olds.

- More teenagers and young adults die from suicide than from cancer, heart disease, AIDS, birth defects, stroke, pneumonia and influenza, and chronic lung disease — combined.

- From 1952 to 1995, the incidence of suicide among adolescents and young adults nearly tripled.

- More than 30,000 Americans die from suicide every year.

- Suicide is the eighth-leading cause of death in the United States.

- Every 17 minutes, another life is lost to suicide.

- Every day, 86 Americans take their own life.

- More than 90 percent of those who kill themselves have a diagnosable mental disorder.

- Seventy percent are depressed. Many also have a substance abuse disorder.

- For every two victims of homicide in the U.S., three people take their own lives.

- Men commit suicide four times more than women do.

- There are twice as many deaths due to suicide than to HIV/AIDS.

● Suicide by firearms is the most common method for both men and women, accounting for 58 percent of all suicides.

What are the statistics on attempted suicides?

No annual national data on attempted suicides is available, however, reliable scientific research has found that...

● Every day, over 1,500 Americans attempt suicide.

● 4.5 million Americans attempt suicide each year.

● There are an estimated 8 to 25 attempted suicides to one completed suicide.

● Almost twice as many women as men attempt suicide.

● Gays and lesbians are three times more likely to attempt suicide.

● Many who make suicide attempts never seek professional help following the attempt.

● The strongest risk factors for attempted suicide in adults are depression, alcohol abuse, cocaine use, and separation or divorce.

Why do people commit suicide?

Why do people commit suicide?

People are not trying to end their lives. They're trying to end their pain. Would it surprise you to know that many people think about committing suicide at some time in their lives? Most decide to live, though, because they realize that the crisis is only temporary — and death is permanent. On the other hand, people who are experiencing a crisis sometimes perceive their problem as inescapable and feel an utter loss of control. The act of suicide is very often a desperate, final

> When life becomes confusing and just plain hard to bear, it doesn't matter what your age if you think there's no one to care."
>
> ~ *Joan R. Miller*

effort of control over the symptoms of depression. When people are severely depressed, their brains selectively retrieve memories that are dark and sad. This is a symptom of the illness — and is not who the person really is.

According to the American Association of Suicidology, these are some of the feelings and things suicidal people experience. They ...

- can't stop the pain.

- can't think clearly.

- can't make decisions.

- can't see any way out.

- can't sleep, eat, or work.

- can't get out of depression.

- can't make the sadness go away.

- can't see a future without pain.

- can't see themselves as worthwhile.

- can't get someone's attention.

- can't seem to get control of their lives.

Suicide is not about death. It's about ending pain. If you experience any of these feelings, please get help! And if someone you know shows these symptoms, offer help!

What are the risk factors?
Suicidal behavior is complex. Some risk factors vary with age, gender, and ethnic group, and may even change over time. The risk factors for suicide frequently occur in combination. Research has shown that more than 90 percent of people who kill themselves have depression or another diagnosable mental or substance abuse disorder. In addition, research indicates that alterations in neurotransmitters, such as serotonin, are associated

with the risk for suicide. Diminished levels of this brain chemical have been found in people with depression, impulsive disorders, a history of violent suicide attempts, and in post-mortem brains of suicide victims.

Adverse life events in combination with other risk factors, such as depression, may lead to suicide. However, *suicide and suicidal behavior are not normal responses to stress.* Many people have one or more risk factors and are not suicidal. Aside from depression, other risk factors can include the following:

- Prior suicide attempt(s).

- Family history of suicide.

- Family history of mental disorder, substance abuse, or suicide.

- Exposure to suicidal behavior of others (family members, peers, and the media).

- Unusual stress.

- Consumption of alcohol and/or drugs.

- Victim of violence (physical, sexual, domestic, or child abuse; or being bullied).

- Breakup of a romance.

- Poor parent/child communications.

- Failing school.

- Spent time in jail or prison.

- Feel socially isolated.

- Firearms in the home.

- Have a medical condition.

- Frequent moves.

It's also estimated that a teen in the U.S. takes his or her own life every five hours because he or she is gay, lesbian, bisexual, or transgender, and cannot deal with the added stresses that society puts upon them. According to a U.S. Department of Health and Human Services study, these youth are two to three times more likely to attempt suicide and commit up to 30 percent of teen suicides.

What are the warning signs?

According to the American Association of Suicidology, there is no typical suicide victim. It happens to young and old, rich and poor. There are, however, some common warning signs. A person might be suicidal if he or she…

- Talks about committing suicide.

- Is depressed.

- Lacks self-esteem.

- Increases his or her use of alcohol or drugs.

- Experiences drastic changes in behavior.

- Has trouble eating or sleeping.

- Withdraws from friends and/or social activities.

- Loses interest in work, school, hobbies, etc.

- Has attempted suicide before.

- Takes unnecessary risks.

- Has had recent severe losses.

- Loses interest in his or her personal appearance.

- Is cheerful after a long period of sadness.

- Gives away prized possessions.

● Prepares for death by making out a will and final arrangements.

● Is preoccupied with death and dying.

Some suicides do occur, however, with no warning signs.

What role does depression play?

It's estimated that about 60 percent of people who commit suicide have had a mood disorder (major depression, bipolar disorder, dysthymia). Younger persons who kill themselves often have a substance abuse disorder in addition to being depressed. Although the majority of people who have depression do not die by suicide, having major depression does increase suicide risk compared to people without depression. The risk of death by suicide may, in part, be related to the severity of depression.

What role does alcohol play?

A number of recent national surveys have shown a link between alcohol and other drug use and suicidal behavior. A review of minimum-age drinking laws and suicides among those aged 18 to 20 found that lower minimum-age drinking laws were associated with higher youth suicide rates. In a large study following adults who drink alcohol, suicide ideation was reported among persons with depression. In another survey, persons who reported that they had made a suicide attempt during their lifetimes were more likely to have had a depressive disorder, and many also had an alcohol and/or substance abuse disorder. In a study of all non-traffic injury deaths associated with alcohol intoxication, over 20 percent were suicides.

In studies that examine risk factors among people who have completed suicide, substance use and abuse occurs more frequently among youth and adults. For particular groups at risk, such as American Indians and Alaskan Natives, depression and alcohol use and abuse are the most common risk factors for completed suicide. (See Chapter 11, "Do alcohol and drugs contribute to suicides?" for more information.)

Do suicide victims go to hell?

According to Sue Chance in *Stronger Than Death*, neither the *Old Testament* nor the *New Testament* directly forbids suicide. The Christian prohibition on suicide dates back to the 4th century and was proclaimed by St. Augustine, who was simply concerned about the declining number of Christians who were seeking martyrdom or were religious zealots bent on getting into heaven "without passing GO." St. Augustine didn't say a word about those who committed suicide because of physical or emotional suffering, old age, altruism toward others, personal honor, illness — the reasons which explain 99.9 percent of today's suicides. So, in that illiterate society, the word of an authority was given the same credibility as the written word and soon became confused with it.

Michael Hall, Ph.D. adds further insight into the subject. He says, *"The whole issue [of whether or not a suicide victim goes to hell] comes down to 'response-ability.' God only holds 'response-able' those who truly have the ability to respond. Infants don't. Children don't. People in the midst of an emotional crisis don't. We can indeed lose — permanently or temporarily — the ability to respond. Such describes the nature of despair — when one suffers from a 'broken spirit.'"*

What should I do if I'm feeling suicidal?

What should I do if I'm feeling suicidal?
Call someone. Stay with someone until you can get help. Know that if you make it through the day (or the night), you'll be okay. Please get professional help. You are not alone in this world. Others truly do care about you.

Silence
is
the
enemy.

John Edwards, Crossing Over

- National Suicide Hotline: 1-800-SUICIDE (1-800-784-2433)

- National Crisis Helpline: 1-800-999-9999

The American Association of Suicidology offers this information:

If you're unable to think of solutions other than suicide, know that other solutions do exist. You're just currently unable to see them. Suicidal crises are almost always temporary and although it may seem like your unhappiness will never end, it's important to realize that crises usually have time limits.

Solutions are found, feelings change, unexpected positive events occur.

Suicide is sometimes referred to as a *"permanent solution to a temporary problem."* Don't let this temporary problem rob you of better times to come. Give yourself some time. It might help to imagine yourself five years from now, knowing that you've survived this problem. Ask yourself these questions:

> **There will be a time when you believe everything is finished. That will be the beginning.**
> ~ *Louis L'Amour*

"Will this matter a year from now?"
"Will this matter five years from now?"

No problem is worth dying for…

Avoid alcohol and drugs. Most deaths by suicide result from sudden, uncontrolled impulses. Alcohol and drugs contribute to such impulses. (They also interfere with the effectiveness of medications prescribed for depressive disorders.)

Check the yellow pages under *Mental Health, Health, Social Services, Suicide Prevention, Crisis Intervention Services, Hotlines, Hospitals,* or *Physicians* for local phone numbers and addresses. In times of crisis, an emergency room doctor at a hospital may be able to provide temporary help for an emotional problem, and will be able to tell you where and how to get further help.

How can I help someone who's suicidal?

If someone is suicidal, don't leave the person alone! Take emergency steps if needed, such as calling 911. Limit the person's access to firearms, large amounts of medication, or other lethal means of committing suicide. The American Association of Suicidology offers some ways to be helpful to someone who is threatening suicide:

- Be direct. Talk openly and matter-of-factly about suicide.

- Be willing to listen.

- Get involved. Be available. Show interest and support.

- Don't dare him or her to do it.

- Don't act shocked. This will put distance between you.

- Don't be sworn to secrecy. Seek support.

- Offer hope that alternatives are available, but don't offer glib reassurances.

- Take action. Remove means, such as guns or pills.

- Try to maintain as normal a relationship as possible.

- Acknowledge that the person is suffering.

- Get help from persons or agencies specializing in crisis intervention and suicide prevention.

- Be non-judgmental. Don't debate whether suicide is right or wrong or whether feelings are good or bad. Don't lecture on the value of life.

If a person talks about suicide, take it seriously. People who are suicidal make such comments for a variety of reasons — and it's extremely important to take these remarks seriously and to help that person seek a mental health evaluation and treatment. Don't accuse the depressed person of faking illness or of laziness. Don't expect him or her to "snap out of it." Don't criticize, pick on, or blame the person for his or her depressed behavior. And don't say anything you think might worsen the person's current poor self-image.

Should I talk about depression and suicide?

Yes! If someone is contemplating suicide, talking about it will usually be a welcome relief. It can give the person a chance to talk about his or her feelings.

Talking can also provide much-needed education about depression and suicide. More than 30,000 people take their own lives each year — yet suicide is still a "hush-hush" topic. Depression is widespread today, and without treatment, can lead to suicide. A depressed person works very hard to keep the signs hidden. The mental health care field in the U.S. is changing. The stigma of having a mental disorder is fading. The stigma of getting help — therapy, counseling, medications — is fading. Clinical depression is an illness, but unless people talk about it, it will stay a deep, dark secret — and it will continue to take lives.

 ## What are the myths about suicide?

In *Some Facts About Suicide*, E.S. Schneidman and N.L. Farberow share common myths about suicide:

Myth: Suicide happens without warning.
Fact: Of any 10 persons who kill themselves, eight have given definite warning of their suicidal intentions.

Myth: Suidical people are fully intent on dying.
Fact: Most suicidal people are undecided about living or dying. They gamble with death, leaving it to others to save them.

Myth: Once a person is suicidal, he or she is suicidal forever.
Fact: Individuals who wish to kill themselves are "suicidal" only for a limited period of time.

Myth: Improvement following a suicidal crisis means that the suicidal risk is over.
Fact: Most suicides occur within about three months following the beginning of "improvement," when the individual has the energy to put his morbid thoughts and feelings into effect.

Myth: Suicide strikes much more often among the rich, or conversely, it occurs almost exclusively among the poor.
Fact: Suicide is neither the rich man's disease nor the poor man's curse. Suicide is very "democratic" and is represented proportionally among all levels of society.

Myth: Suicide is inherited or "runs in the family."
Fact: Suicide does not run in families, although depression (a leading cause of suicide) may run in families.

How do suicide survivors "get over it?"

How do suicide survivors "get over it?"
They don't.

> A man's dying is more the survivors' affair than his own.
> ~ *Thomas Mann*

One never "gets over it." Suicide survivors learn to live with it ... knowing that the grief can strike at any time for the rest of their lives ... knowing that they'll get angry every now and then ... at their loved one who took his or her life ... at themselves for not doing more ... at the unanswered questions ... at the *"What ifs"* ... and the *"If onlys"* ... on holidays and anniversaries ... when memories are triggered ... The death — the suicide — the tragic loss of their loved one — becomes a part of them, a part of their lives.

It has been said that the person who completes suicide dies once. Those left behind die a thousand deaths — trying to relive those terrible moments and to understand. Why?

In his book, *The Carousel*, Richard Paul Evans writes, *"Suicide wears a heavier cloak. It is a psychological land mine, killing, maiming, and scarring not just the hapless who tripped it, but all those in its vicinity."* Survivors often suffer from several mental disorders following a suicide, including depression, post-traumatic stress disorder, and illnesses that have a psychological basis. Feelings of suicide are not uncommon for a suicide survivor. However, you must differentiate between your own feelings of suicide and thinking about the suicide of your loved one. If thoughts of suicide persist, please seek medical help. You know first-hand the devastation a suicide causes. Don't leave that pain to those who love you ... and know that your pain will lessen.

Survivors of all deaths experience some guilt at being alive when their loved one is dead, but survivors of suicide are especially prone to guilt feelings. It's human nature to assume that you could have done something to prevent the suicide if you'd only known the pain your loved one was feeling. (See Chapter 7, "What can I say to someone who's grieving?" for more information about grieving.)

The Carousel by Richard Paul Evans. ©2000 by Richard Paul Evans. (Simon & Schuster, ISBN 0-684-86891-1)

How do survivors deal with the stigma of suicide?
Compounding the tragedy of loss of life, suicide evokes complicated and

uncomfortable reactions in most people. Too often, the victim is blamed and the surviving family members and friends are stigmatized. These reactions add to the survivor's burden of hurt, intensify the isolation, and keep suicide in secrecy.

> *We believe that suicide occurs in all types of families: the functional and the dysfunctional, the very good, the not so good, and the just good enough.*
>
> ~ Edward Dunne and Karen Dunne
>
> *Maxim in Suicide and Its Aftermath: Understanding and Counseling the Survivors*

In an excerpt from *The Healing of Sorrow* by Norman Vincent Peale, he writes,

> In many ways, this [suicide] seems the most tragic form of death. Certainly it can entail more shock and grief for those who are left behind than another. And often, the stigma of suicide is what rests most heavily on those left behind. Suicide is often judged to be essentially a selfish act. Perhaps it is. But the Bible warns us not to judge, if we ourselves hope to escape judgment. And I believe this is one area where that Biblical command especially should be heeded. Nor do we know how many valiant battles such a person may have fought and won before he loses that one particular battle. And is it fair that all the good acts and impulses of such a person should be forgotten or blotted out by his final tragic act?
>
> I think our reaction should be one of love and pity, not of condemnation. Perhaps the person was not thinking clearly in his final moments; perhaps he was so driven by emotional whirlwinds that he was incapable of thinking at all. This is terribly sad ... but surely it is understandable. All of us have had moments when we lost control of ourselves, flashes of temper, or irritation, of selfishness that we later regret. Each one of us, probably, has a final breaking point — or would if our faith did not sustain us. Life puts more pressure on some of us than it does on others. When I see in the

paper, as I do all too often, that dark despair has rolled over some lonely soul, so much so that for him life seemed unendurable, my reaction is not one of condemnation. It is, rather, *"There but for the grace of God ...."*

And my heart goes out to those who are left behind, because I know that they suffer terribly. Children, in particular, are left under a cloud of "differentness," all the more terrifying because it can never be fully explained or lifted. The immediate family of the victim is left wide open to tidal waves of guilt, *"What did I fail to do that I should have done? What did I do that was wrong?"* To such grieving persons, I can only say, *"Lift up your heads and your hearts, surely you did your best. And surely the loved one who is gone did his best, for as long as he could."*

The Healing of Sorrow: Understanding and Help for The Bereaved by Norman Vincent Peale.

©1966 by Norman Vincent Peale. (Doubleday)

What about sibling survivors?

Sibling survivors are often considered the "forgotten mourners." Because the parents are the primary mourners, siblings are often pushed aside. Parents are so consumed in their own grief that they're unable to help their surviving children. And, in many cases, the surviving children must take on the role of comforting the parents.

Suicide leaves a huge hole in a sibling's life. As children, siblings spend more time with each other than they do with their parents. They play with their siblings. They learn from their siblings. They conspire with their siblings. They confide in their siblings. So, when a sibling dies, everything is thrown out of balance.

Unfortunately, there isn't much help available for grieving siblings. Michelle Linn-Gust, however, recently published a book entitled, *Do They Have Bad Days in Heaven? Surviving the Suicide Loss of a Sibling*. Her book was written following the suicide of her sister. When asked about the title of her book, she replied, *"Before Denise [her sister] died, I never questioned whether there were bad days in heaven. Everything in heaven was perfect. But I often wonder if, when she looks down on us, she is sorry or sad. I know she didn't know the pain that she was going to cause. And I wonder if she does wish that she were still here. So, maybe she does have some bad days in heaven."* For more information on her book, visit *www.siblingsurvivors.com*.

Do They Have Bad Days in Heaven? Surviving the Suicide Loss of a Sibling by Michelle Linn-Gust. ©2001 by Michelle Linn-Gust.

What are 25 suggestions for survivors?

Hundreds of books have been written about loss and grief, yet few have addressed the aftermath of suicide for survivors. Because grieving is an individual journey, there are no answers, only suggestions from those who have lived through — and beyond — the event. Iris M. Bolton, executive director of The Link Counseling Center's National Resource Center for Suicide Prevention and Aftercare (*www.thelink.org*), has compiled this list of 25 suggestions for survivors:

1. Know you can survive. You may not think so, but you can.

2. Struggle with "why" it happened until you no longer need to know "why" or until you're satisfied with partial answers.

3. Know you may feel overwhelmed by the intensity of your feelings, but all your feelings are normal.

4. Anger, guilt, confusion, and forgetfulness are common responses. You're not crazy; you're in mourning.

5. Be aware that you may feel appropriate anger at the person, at the world, at God, or at yourself. It's okay to express it.

6. You may feel guilty for what you think you did or didn't do. Guilt can turn into regret, through forgiving.

7. Having suicidal thoughts is common. It doesn't mean that you will act on those thoughts.

8. Remember to take one moment or one day at a time.

9. Find a good listener with whom to share. Call someone if you need to talk.

10. Don't be afraid to cry. Tears are healing.

11. Give yourself time to heal.

12. Remember, the choice wasn't yours. No one is the sole influence of another's life.

13. Expect setbacks. If emotions return like a tidal wave, you may only be experiencing a remnant of grief, an unfinished piece.

14. Try to put off major decisions.

15. Give yourself permission to get professional help.

16. Be aware of the pain of your family and friends.

17. Be patient with yourself and with others who may not understand.

18. Set your own limits and learn to say *"no."*

19. Steer clear of people who want to tell you what or how to feel.

20. Know that there are support groups that can be helpful, such as *Compassionate Friends* or *Survivors of Suicide*. If not, ask a professional to help start one.

21. Call on your personal faith to help you through.

22. It's common to experience physical reactions to your grief (headaches, loss of appetite, inability to sleep).

23. Be willing to laugh with others and at yourself. It's healing.

24. Wear out your questions, anger, guilt, or other feelings until you can let them go. Letting go doesn't mean forgetting.

25. Know that you'll never be the same again, but you can survive, and even go beyond surviving.

What is Erek's story?

This section is written from the perspective of Erek's aunt. First names of Erek's friends have been used, not to blame or embarrass, but to help you understand about depression and suicide. By telling Erek's story, it is hoped that if you or a friend are in trouble … you'll be able to get help — before it's too late.

Interactive CD-ROM

Movie

Erek's Life

As Erek's aunt, I struggle with writing this section because I can't bear to use the word *"was."*

Erek … was my nephew … was my best friend … was a son … was a big brother … was a grandson … was a cousin … was a friend … was a U.S. Marine … was an Eagle Scout … was a fraternity brother … was a college student … was a dog lover … was a truck lover … was a pickle lover … was a music lover … was adventurous … was an athlete … was hard-working … was dedicated … was compassionate … was very proud … was kind and thoughtful and generous … was always there when anyone needed a shoulder to lean on … was a sushi lover …. was a sound sleeper … was a smoker … was a social drinker … was an outdoor lover … was patriotic, even when it wasn't so popular to be … was a volunteer … was so many things to so many people …

And Erek was depressed … and he was drunk … and he was only 20 years old when he took his own life.

Erek's Death

The events leading up to Erek's death began on June 26, 1999, at 2:33 a.m. He and his high school buddies went to an outdoor weekend music festival, the Country Stampede. They were drinking. Almost everyone at the Stampede was drinking. When Klint needed a ride to his car so it wouldn't get towed, the group decided Erek should drive since he was the "least drunk" of them all. While driving to Klint's car, a woman driving in the opposite direction reached down to her passenger floor to get her purse, swerved across the center line, and hit Erek head-on. While the officers at the scene stated that it was the other driver's fault, they gave Erek a breathalyzer test. His blood alcohol content was .097. (The legal limit in Kansas is .08, with .02 for minors under age 21.) Erek was 19 — and in an effort to help his friend, had just gotten a DUI and totaled his truck.

Erek was devastated. He had talked with a recruiter about becoming an officer in the U.S. Marine Corps and was supposed to sign papers that next week. In the months that followed, Erek had to come up with $6,792 to pay the following: $1,500 to an attorney for a diversion; $295 for court costs; $175 for a Drug/Alcohol Psychological Evaluation; and $4,822 to get his truck repaired.

Unfortunately, his friends all went off to their own colleges and didn't offer to help Erek pay for any of this. When I asked one friend, after Erek's death, why they didn't offer to help, he said they thought Erek had inherited money from his Grandma Edna. (She passed away the previous February while Erek was at boot camp.) Erek felt betrayed by his friends at the time — but was too proud to call and ask for their help. Instead, he worked at a lumber yard part-time making $7 an hour and used every penny he made with the Marine Corps Reserves to pay for these expenses. He didn't have any time or money left over for fun.

This DUI didn't end when Erek paid the money. Following the accident on June 26th, he had to drive four hours round-trip for the following activities:

- July 23rd — hire attorney to file Diversion

- September 3rd — Drug/Alcohol Psychological Evaluation (which stated that the *"probability [of an] alcohol-related offense will repeat,"* but no further help was offered)

- September 10th — Diversion Status Hearing

- September 28th — Alcohol/Drug Information School

- September 30th — Alcohol/Drug Information School

- October 5th — Alcohol/Drug Information School

- October 7th — Alcohol/Drug Information School

- November 8th — Driver's License Hearing

In August, Erek started his second semester at the University of Kansas (KU). While he was trying to complete all of the above so he could attend Marine Corps officers' school that next summer, he was also trying to complete college and fraternity requirements.

Erek's truck was in the shop until October 26th. He hated borrowing his dad's truck during that time. He wanted so much to be independent. He locked the keys in the truck on several occasions — but I thought he was just stressed from school, work, and the diversion. I got him a spare set of keys, and we laughed about the incidents. I didn't realize these were the beginning signs of his depression.

After Thanksgiving, he really became depressed. He didn't do as well on finals as he thought he would. He couldn't believe he'd done so bad since he knew the information. (Loss of memory is another sign of depression.) When grade cards came out, he had a GPA of 2.29. He needed a 2.3 to stay in the fraternity. He was worried that he might not get to stay in the fraternity. He also thought his girlfriend had broken up with him — when, in fact, she had just been terminated from a job and was depressed herself.

Erek stayed at the fraternity house after finals were over. Most of the guys went home for Christmas. So, there were only a few guys living there and he wasn't working out since his workout partner was home for the holidays. The weather was also dreary and cold during December. That must have added to his depression.

Erek spent a lot of time at my house. We lived 20 miles apart. I noticed changes in his behavior around Thanksgiving time … and really started worrying following finals. He seemed so sad. I tried to get him to talk to me — but he just wasn't ready. One afternoon, about a week before he died, he was walking in my dining room, and I thought to myself, *"Erek, you're scaring me. I don't know how to help you."* But, I didn't say it out loud. I knew he was really depressed, but I didn't think he would go to a doctor. I also knew that if I could get him to a doctor, they would give him anti-depressants — and I thought that would end his military career. (The military tends to have very out-dated guidelines about depression. Most believe that if you take anti-depressants, you won't be an officer. I also knew that if he went to a doctor and didn't tell the military, he could be called in for a random drug test in the Reserves — which could end his enlisted career. I didn't want to be responsible for ending his dream …)

The last time I saw him was on December 23rd. He came over to write his essay about why he wanted to be a Marine Corps officer. Instead of helping him write his essay, I asked if he wanted to do some last minute Christmas shopping. While in the car, he called himself *"a loser."* I was so shocked. I told him he wasn't … but I didn't really address it because there was another person present at the time. I thought we'd talk about it when we were alone. When he went to leave later that night, he gave me his usual "good-bye hug" — but he held on for a long time. He was so sad … And I was so tired … In my mind, I debated on making him sit down and talk with me now … but it was late and he had to work at 7 a.m. It was Christmas Eve the next day, and he was the only one scheduled to work. I didn't want to teach him to be irresponsible … so we agreed that he would come back on Sunday. I'd help him write his essay and then we'd come up with a plan for whatever was bothering him.

I couldn't stop worrying about him the next day. He was going home (to his dad's) after work. He'd have dinner with his dad's family and then go to a party at Todd's house. I thought about calling his dad and his friends to tell them that he was depressed. I wanted to tell his friends not to let him drink and drive. But, I didn't. Todd only lived two houses down the street — so Erek wouldn't be driving. And I thought Erek would be mad at me if I told everyone he was depressed.

I'm not sure of all the details of that night … but Erek's friend, Klint, wanted a ride home early in the morning. (Klint's dad had driven him into town so he wouldn't drive drunk.) Davey was the designated driver, but apparently Erek insisted on driving. No one thought Erek was very drunk … so Erek got behind the wheel.

After dropping Klint off, Erek, Davey, and Todd headed back to town. At 5:30 Christmas morning, a police officer stopped Erek for driving seven miles over the speed limit. The officer apparently smelled alcohol and gave Erek a breathalyzer test. Erek's blood alcohol content was .14 — almost twice the legal limit. After spending the evening with Erek, Todd and Davey knew he was in trouble. They told the police officer not to give Erek the ticket because it would ruin his military career. They said that Erek wouldn't make it through the night. The police officer laughed and said a few hours in jail would do him good. And then he gave Erek four tickets and took him to jail. Merry Christmas!

(Erek's diversion/probation ended on December 28th. He was going to sign his officer papers the first week of January.)

When Erek got his first DUI in June, he had to stay in jail for eight hours. Christmas morning, however, a bondsman brought him home after just two hours in jail. Erek came in the house, mumbled something to his dad, and went to his room. His dad thought he'd let him "sleep it off …"

The shotguns were always kept at Grandma Edna's house … until she died and her house was sold. No one thought there were any shells in the house, though, so it is unsure where Erek found the shell … or what he was thinking … or if he waited for someone to call …

The doctors think Erek passed out, woke up in a drunken haze, walked across the hall to his dad's room, got the shotgun, went back to his room, stuck the barrel in his mouth … and pulled the trigger. He was dead by noon.

The Aftermath

If you learn anything from this book and CD-ROM, let it be this:

> *Suicide is not the answer. It does not end the*
> *pain. It begins a lifetime of guilt, pain, and*
> *sorrow for all who love you.*

It is Christmas Day, Saturday. And my world is spiraling out of control … Everyone is being so brave, trying so hard to maintain a sense of normalcy.

We're supposed to meet at Grandma's for Christmas at noon. Later that afternoon, we decide that we need to open gifts for Alisa, Luke, and Paul. (Alisa, Erek's cousin, is 16 at the time. Luke and Paul, Erek's brothers, are 14 and 12.) We always go around the room, one at a time, to open gifts. When it is my turn, I can't open the gifts Erek got me. I want to save them for when I am by myself. We're all opening gifts … and trying to pretend … and we can't … and it's awful … and it can't be real … and where's Erek? He's supposed to be here, too.

I want to go to the hospital. I want to go sit with him … but I know it's only his body now. I feel so empty, so numb … I want to beg his forgiveness. But I'm terrified. I don't know what he looks like. His dad found him … and I want to ask … but I don't … The paramedics tried to resuscitate him … and I don't know what damage has been done … and I'm not brave enough … and I hate that he's in the hospital all by himself … and I tell myself that his spirit is gone … so it's okay if I don't go sit with him …

I try to be brave as long as I can … and then I go sit on my mom's bed and cry. Luke comes and sits beside me. He puts his arm around me and says, *"Don't cry, Sally. God needed him more than we did."*

The day after Christmas, Sunday, we plan Erek's funeral … not his graduation, not his wedding … his funeral. No one can believe this … Not Erek … Erek loved life. He truly did. He wasn't a quitter. He gave 200 percent to everything. He's a Marine. He has so much going for him. This can't be true. Please, please … someone wake me from this nightmare …

Erek's parents pick out his casket. It is beautiful — blue in color with mountains and fir trees etched on the sides. Engraved on the top are the Marine Corps and Eagle Scout emblems. Erek would like it …

I have to go home that evening and find 40 pictures so a video can be made of Erek's life to show at the memorial service. How do you sum up someone's life in 40 pictures? I can't look Erek in the eyes in the photos … I can look at his stomach or his legs, but I can't bring myself to look him in the eyes … I feel as though I've let him down …

I don't know what happened to Monday …

Tuesday afternoon, the family is allowed to "view" Erek's body. Erek's parents, my brother, and I are there when they bring out the casket. Erek's parents step up to the casket … and my brother starts to … I grab his arm and make him wait. This is their child lying in a box … They need to be with Erek first …

Erek is dressed in his Marine dress blues. And he looks so handsome. (There was no damage to the front of his head …) I want him to wake up … but I know he won't. He is so cold … He has his white uniform gloves on, so I can't even see his hands. (I held his hand when we went to his DUI hearing … and now I'll never be able to see his hands again …) I keep touching his heart and silently ask him to forgive me … My heart is in such pain, I think it's going to burst … How can this be Erek lying here? How can his life be over? This isn't how life is supposed to work. He's supposed to grow old, get married, have kids … PLEASE, PLEASE, WAKE ME UP. I don't like this dream …

It's 7 p.m. and the room is full. His fraternity brothers take up a whole row at the back of the room. They're all dressed in suits, looking so handsome — and so sad. They're in shock, too. Not Erek. Erek would never do this. They say, *"He seemed fine when we saw him a few weeks ago."*

Erek's friends are devastated … especially those that were with him that night. I know they're all blaming themselves like I am blaming myself … and I just keep repeating, *"It was Erek's decision."* But I know it wasn't. I know how depressed he was. I know — and I didn't tell anyone. I know Erek would never hurt me like this. He would never hurt his family or his friends like this. Oh, how sad he must have been to think this was the only choice he could make. How do I live with the thought of Erek being so sad?

A very distant relative says, *"I don't know why these kids do this today. Don't they realize that this is a permanent solution to a temporary problem?"* And I want to scream at her … *"You don't even know Erek. How dare you make judgments? How can you think that Erek took his life just because he got a ticket? How stupid can YOU be?"*

On Wednesday morning before the funeral, I go back to the funeral home where Erek has been "resting." I can't bear to leave him. The funeral director says it's time to go to the church. I can't leave. I can't leave Erek. Please make this not be true … Please! I'll do anything … Please just make this not be true … I watch as they crank the casket lid shut … and I don't realize until I'm at the church that they're not going to open it again … I'll never get to see Erek again …

There aren't enough seats in the church for everyone. People are standing everywhere … and Erek's in the center … in a box … with the lid closed … Klint reads a eulogy he wrote for Erek. It is perfect. Jay reads the poem, *"The Dash Between the Lines."* The rest is a blur … I can't breathe … I can't stop crying … I can't make the pain stop … I can't bring Erek back … Why, God? Why did you take Erek?

Erek's gravesite is about 10 blocks from the church. The day is sunny and bright. And I wonder why the last three weeks couldn't have been sunny and bright instead of dark and dreary … When the hearse starts to leave the church, everyone falls in line behind it and walks to Erek's gravesite. It is quite a site. It warms my heart … and, oh, how I wish Erek knew all these people would have helped him …

Military honors are bestowed upon Erek. An American flag is draped over his casket. *Taps* are played and guns go off. And each time a gun goes off, I picture Erek sitting on his bed … and I jump … and it's as if each one of those shots is fired right into my heart … The Marines fold the flag and hand it to Mark, Erek's dad. He holds it to his heart and won't let go.

They don't lower Erek's casket into the grave because they've "squeezed" him in between his Grandma Edna and another couple already buried there. The funeral director is afraid one of the graves might collapse … So, we just stand there … No one knows what to do … and no one wants to believe. We are all so much in shock … And this is it … We can't turn the clock back … We can't undo yesterday … We can't bring Erek back … So, I walk up to the casket, lay my hand on it, and say, *"Goodbye, Erek. I love you."* Then I step back. One by one, every person there does the same thing. Some kiss their fingers before they touch the casket. It is touching and heartbreaking at the same time …

Everyone walks back to the church for lunch. I wait. Again, I can't bear to leave Erek. I am alone with him. They are all gone. Please, please, just bring him back. Bert, who was like a second mom to Erek, waits to walk back with me. Erek would like that we've become friends …

When we get back to the reception hall, people are eating and chatting …

How can they eat? I haven't eaten since Friday. I've lost 11 pounds. (Thank you, Erek!) The thought of food makes me want to wretch … I just want to crawl in a hole and die … but I can't. I have to be strong.

We go to my parent's house after the funeral … and no one knows what to do. We've sat and stared at each other all week … so I start telling stories about Erek … about our road trip to Orlando and Atlanta last June … about our trip to San Diego for his Marine graduation … about funny things he did … funny things he said … and then everyone else starts remembering … and sharing stories … and laughing … and crying … and then his dad walks in the door holding the flag and our hearts break even more …

And then everyone goes home …

The first week is a blur. It is so surreal. It is as if I am outside my body watching myself go through the motions … and I am so amazed that the rest of the world is still going on. What's wrong with them? Don't they get it? Erek is dead. No, wait. This is a nightmare. It isn't real. Erek can't be dead … I just saw him … He's only 20 years old … Please wake me …

The second week begins with New Year's Eve … It's the new millennium. What's wrong with the world? How can they celebrate? Don't they get it? Erek's dead. (I have to keep telling myself this because it just can't be true …) At midnight, my husband brings me a glass of wine to toast the new year. I appreciate his gesture, but I just snap at him, *"What's there to celebrate. Erek's dead."* I feel so bad for hurting his feelings … but I can't make myself apologize … I can't make myself do anything …

The third week, I can't breathe.

The fourth week, I can't breathe. And I hate myself for letting Erek down … I tell people that he was depressed, but no one believes me … They say, *"Not Erek. Erek wouldn't get depressed."* (Like he had a choice … *"No, I'm not going to be depressed today."* That's like saying, *"No, I'm not going to need glasses today."* or *"No, I'm not going to be 5'10" today."* or *"No, I'm not going to have brown eyes today."* Depression isn't something you can just wish away. Why don't people get that?) I want to scream, *"How would you know if he was depressed? He was away at college. When was the last time you saw him?"*

I want to scream at his friends, *"Why didn't you tell someone? Why didn't you stay with him? Why'd you let him drive? Why didn't you help him when he got the first DUI?"*

I want to scream at the police officer, *"Why didn't you listen to his friends? Why didn't you just make them park the truck and give them a ride home on Christmas morning? Why did you give Erek four tickets? Why didn't you make him stay in jail for eight hours? Why did you let the bondsman drive him home? Why didn't you call his parents? What is wrong with you?"*

I want to scream at myself, *"Why didn't I help him? Why didn't I make him stay? Why didn't I take him to a doctor? Why didn't I tell someone? Why didn't I save his life? Why? Why? Why?"*

I want to scream at God, *"Why did you take Erek? Why didn't you take me instead?"* And then I want to ask God why he didn't take Erek when he had the head-on collision. Why'd he make Erek suffer the last few months of his life? Why'd he take Erek when he was so sad? If he'd taken him in the accident, at least Erek would have been happy …

I want to scream at the world that Erek is not going to hell.

I want to scream that Erek is not a quitter.

I want to scream that Erek is not thoughtless or inconsiderate for hurting those he left behind.

I want to scream because I can't believe people are saying these things to me …

I want to scream at those who think Erek got himself into a situation he couldn't handle … *"How do you know what he can handle? Where were you for the past six months when he needed your help? And, knowing Erek, how can you even consider the possibility that he would quit?"*

I want to scream because people are so stupid about depression and suicide …

I want to scream because I can't bear to live my life without Erek in it …

I want to scream because each rare moment of joy is followed by mountains of guilt …

I want to scream loud enough to bring him back … but when I open my mouth to scream, no sound comes out …

By the fifth week, I want to die. I really want to die. I can't deal with the pain. I can't deal with the guilt. I can't even breathe. I can't stop crying. I can't stop asking Erek to forgive me for not helping him. I can't stop wishing that I'd asked him to stay that last night … that I made him talk to me … that I'd called to tell people that he was depressed … that I'd called him Christmas morning … that his Grandma Edna hadn't died in February because the guns were always at her house … that Erek hadn't found a shotgun shell … there weren't supposed to be any in the house … the guns were supposed to be safe … that his friends had told someone … that the police hadn't laughed … that they'd kept him in jail for eight hours like they did in June … that I could have just one night back … that I could give my life for his …

This is how I spend the next nine months. I exist. I breathe. I don't function. I make it to the couch and turn on the TV, but I don't remember a thing I watch. My brother is staying with us, so when he and my husband come home, I have to sit up on the couch, smile a bit, nod my head, and pretend to be handling "it." But, I'm not … I can't stand the pretending anymore. I am not okay … and I can't pretend to be … I scream at my brother and make him move out. I know I've hurt his feelings, but I just can't help myself … I want to be alone … I want to crawl in a hole … I don't want to be sociable with anyone … I want to die …

It isn't until September that I ask for help. I am ashamed of myself for not being able to admit to myself that I, too, am depressed. How could I be depressed? There's nothing wrong with me? After all that I have learned about depression since Erek's death, I am still unwilling to admit that I am depressed, too. I start seeing a counselor and take two anti-depressants a day. And little by little, I learn to live with this new title that has been given me: suicide survivor.

● ● ●

As I write this, it has been almost two years since Erek died. And it doesn't get much easier. Some days seem as though it just happened, some as though it never happened and I'm still having a bad dream, and yet others as though it was forever ago. We will spend the rest of our lives second-guessing things we said, things we didn't say; things we did, things we didn't do. We will continue to experience all the stages of grief — even when we think we're doing okay. We will have good days and bad days, good moments and bad moments. We will try to move from *"What if …?"* to *"What now …?"*

I watch as others who love Erek try to cope with this tragedy:

His parents who have to overcome the social stigma that it's the parents' fault if a child commits suicide; who can't seem to get past the pain; who feel as though they've failed their child; who have to be brave because they have two sons who need for them to be okay. His dad knows he'll die of a broken heart …

His brothers who try to be brave for everyone. They are the forgotten survivors. I watch them and my heart breaks that this tragedy has become a part of who they are. I watch them try to comfort their parents, their grandparents, me. I wonder how this event will change how they define themselves. Is Luke now the oldest? Do they have two brothers — or just one? Do they have to defend Erek? Do they have to defend their parents?

His cousin, Alisa, who looked up to Erek. She had major anxiety and panic attacks after Erek died. She was 16 — and was afraid to grow up. Erek was so strong … and if this happened to him, how would she ever survive?

His grandparents who have aged tremendously since Erek's death.

His friends who struggle to grow up without Erek. They were childhood buddies … bonded for life. And they all struggle. Many have come close to suicide themselves in the past two years.

His girlfriend, Amberay, who was afraid to get too close. Erek thought she was the most beautiful girl!

His recruiter who thought that maybe it was his fault for enlisting Erek in the Marine Corps … Being a Marine was Erek's proudest accomplishment!

The police officer who arrested Erek. He moved away after Erek's death. And I struggle with forgiving him … as I do with forgiving myself. I read that policemen have a very high rate of suicide … and I hope this will not be his fate.

And all who knew Erek. He touched so many lives. This nightmare has become a reality for everyone who knew and loved him. We are all different. Our lives are all different. We will spend the rest of our lives struggling between joy and guilt. Every bit of happiness will be twinged with a bit of sorrow … We will miss him. We will rejoice him. We will share his stories in an effort to save your life — because one thing I know for sure is that Erek did not want to die. He just wanted his pain to stop.

If you find yourself feeling this way, please, please call someone and ask for help. When you take your life, your pain stops — but it only begins for those you leave behind.

Erek's Eulogy

Photo by Don Brent

Erek Doperalski was the most unique person that I have ever known. To his family, he was a loving son. To his friends, he was a pillar, one of those guys that adds a whole new element to any situation. He was always a gentleman around the ladies, and although he was no Don Juan, what he lacked in grace, he easily made up for in gentleness and kindness.

continued...

His life affected many people, as was evident by the entire community's reaction to his passing. There will never be another person like him again, and that is part of what makes this so hard.

Erek was many things: he was a wrestler, a football player, a rugby player, a fraternity member, an Eagle Scout, and a United States Marine. He attacked every one of these things with a zeal and determination that sometimes left all of us in the dust.

Erek's unique tastes and habits were another part of what made him so special. Erek was the only man in the world who would actually skip school so he could cut firewood in 20 degree temperatures for fun. Erek is also the only person I have ever heard of to pour pickle juice on his ice cream. His love of pickles is legendary.

Erek and I had a friendship that was forged in the trials and tribulations of growing up and boot camp. Our friendship was such that we did not have to maintain daily contact to stay close. In my eyes, this is just one of those times where I won't see him for awhile. I look forward to sitting down with him in heaven to "smoke and joke," as our drill instructor would say. I know he is watching us right now and I just want him to know how much we all miss him. So, Erek, until next time, goodbye and Semper Fi."

~Private First Class Klint Janulis,
United States Marine Corps

Additional Information for this Chapter

Books

- *After a Suicide: Young People Speak Up* by Susan Kuklin

- *The Beast: A Journey Through Depression* by Tracy Thompson

- *Behind the Smile: My Journey out of Postpartum Depression* by Marie Osmond

- *The Carousel* by Richard Paul Evans

- *The Depression Book: Depression as an Opportunity for Spiritual Growth* by Cheri Huber

- *Do They Have Bad Days in Heaven? Surviving the Suicide Loss of a Sibling* by Michelle Linn-Gust

- *I Will Remember You: A Guidebook Through Grief for Teens* by Laura Dower

- *I'm Too Blessed to be Depressed* by Joanna Campbell-Slan

- *Night Falls Fast: Understanding Suicide* by Kay Redfield Jamison

- *No One Saw My Pain: Why Teens Kill Themselves* by Andrew Slaby and Lili Frank Garfinkle

- *No Time to Say Goodbye: Surviving the Suicide of a Loved One* by Carla Fine

- *The Noonday Demon: An Atlas of Depression* by Andrew Solomon

- *An Unquiet Mind: A Memoir of Moods and Madness* by Kay Redfield Jamison

- *When Nothing Else Matters: A Survival Guide for Depressed Teens* by Bev Cobain, R.N.C.

Associations and Hotlines

- American Association of Suicidology
  1-800-SUICIDE
  www.suicidology.org

- American Foundation for Suicide Prevention
  1-888-333-2377
  www.afsp.org

- Anxiety Disorders Association of America
  1-301-231-9350
  www.adaa.org

- Boys Town
  Crisis Hotline: 1-800-448-3000
  1-800-545-5771
  www.boystown.org

- National Center for PTSD
  1-802-296-5132
  www.ncptsd.org

- National Depressive and Manic Depressive Association
  1-800-826-3632
  www.ndmda.org

- National Foundation for Depressive Illness, Inc.
  1-800-239-1265
  www.depression.org

- National Institute of Mental Health
  1-301-443-4513
  TTY: 1-301-443-8431
  1-888-88-ANXIETY

- Depression brochures:
  1-800-421-4211
  www.nimh.nih.gov

● National Mental Health Association
1-800-969-6642
TTY: 1-800-433-5959
www.nmha.org

● Obsessive Compulsive (OC) Foundation
1-203-315-2190
www.ocfoundation.org

● Suicide Awareness — Voices of Education (SA/VE)
1-612-946-7998
www.save.org

● Suicide Prevention Advocacy Network (SPAN)
1-888-649-1366
http://spanusa.org

Web Links

● *www.1000deaths.com*

● *www.compassionatefriends.org/*

● *www.yellowribbon.org*

● *www.depressionet.com*

● *www.jaredstory.com*

● *www.ugotafriend.com*

● *www.depressioncentral.com*

● *www.tearsofacop.com*

● *www.have-a-heart.com/*

● *www.siblingsurvivors.com*

● *www.befrienders.org*

**Interactive
CD-ROM**

Click to the web from the CD-ROM!

Web Resource

● *www.paxil.com*

● *www.mentalhealth.com*

● *www.menninger.edu*

● *www.webhealing.com*

● *www.mentalhealthscreening.org*

● *www.road2healing.com*

● *www.beforetheirtime.com*

Am I ready for a pet?

Interactive CD-ROM

Quiz

Take this quiz to help you decide if now is the best time for you to adopt a pet. Check the following events that have either occurred in your life in the past six months or that you think might occur in the next six months:

- ○ Graduation from high school or college
- ○ Start college, technical or trade school
- ○ Move out of parent's(s') home for first time
- ○ Move back in with parent(s)
- ○ New roommate(s)
- ○ First job or new job
- ○ Longer hours or increased responsibility at work
- ○ Financial concerns
- ○ Break up with boyfriend or girlfriend
- ○ Significant changes in daily routine

- ○ Limited leisure or free time
- ○ Frequent travel (school, sports, work, leisure, etc.)
- ○ Significant health problems for yourself
- ○ Significant health problems of family member(s)
- ○ Death of a family member
- ○ Death or disappearance of a family pet
- ○ Pet(s) given away or taken to animal shelter
- ○ Disagreement with family member(s) or roommate(s) about having a pet

_____ Add 1 point for every pet you currently have (1 aquarium = 1 pet)
_____ **TOTAL SCORE**

0 to 3 points   Your life seems fairly stable. Now is probably a reasonable time to adopt a pet.

4 to 6 points   You have a lot of responsibilities right now. Although adopting a pet may still work for you, a small mammal, an adult cat, or a well-trained adult dog would probably be more appropriate than a kitten, a puppy, or an active breed of dog.

7 to 10 points   Let's think twice about this. With all the changes and responsibilities in your life right now, you may not have time to care for a new pet. It would probably be better for both you and the pet if you wait until your life settles down a bit.

11+ points   STOP! DO NOT PASS GO! Acquiring a pet now is not a wise decision. Why not consider a pet rock instead? (Visit *www.califmall.com/ST_PetRock.html* to order your own pet rock.)

Adapted from *Is this the best time to adopt a pet?* © Dumb Friends League and Humane Society of the United States.

Figure 13A

Pet Care

Whether it's dogs, cats, birds, hamsters, fish, or rats, pets are our best friends. They give us the gifts of better health, less stress, and unbeatable companionship. They are great listeners. They know when we're sad. And loyal? They invented it. Most importantly, pets give us unconditional love. But, they're also a big responsibility.

This chapter will focus on the most popular pets — cats and dogs.

 ## Can I commit to care for my pet for its entire life?

Can I commit to care for my pet for its entire life?

Interactive CD-ROM

Movie

If not, don't get a pet. Pets should never be an impulse buy. Pets can live for 10 to 20 years. Are you willing to take care of your pet for that long ... or is this a passing phase? You're responsible for providing your pet's daily needs, such as feeding and watering, cleaning up "messes" or a litter box, petting, grooming, exercising and walking, and bathing. If you have a busy schedule, the care of your pet can become lost in your daily shuffle.

How much time do I spend at home on an average day?

If you're away from your home more than six hours a day, kittens, puppies, and dogs may not be a good choice for you. Kittens and puppies need a lot of physical and emotional involvement — as well as a lot of training. And dogs need to be let out. Most adult pets can fit into your schedule, but they also need time to learn what is expected — and they need physical and emotional involvement, too. You might consider getting an adult cat (or two) instead.

Can I afford the on-going expense of owning a pet?

Reality is that pets do cost money to own. Can you afford to purchase your pet? Can you afford to spay or neuter your pet? What about shots and medical care for your pet? Cat food or dog food? Cat litter? Toys and supplies? And can you afford these expenses for the life of your pet? These things must be considered **before** you bring a pet home.

Do I have the time to train a pet?

It takes time to teach basic manners to an animal. Do you have the time, money, and commitment for obedience training? Dogs, especially, need to be trained — and puppies take even more time to train.

Interactive CD-ROM

Movie

Am I willing to spay or neuter my pet?

Spaying (for females) and neutering (for males) is the surgical removal of an animal's reproductive organs — and is essential for your pet's long-term health and happiness. Both procedures are routine, requiring only one day at a veterinarian's office. (For more information, see "Should I spay or neuter my pet?")

If I'm renting, am I allowed to have a pet?

The top two reasons given by pet owners for taking their pets to animal shelters are "Moving" and "Landlord won't allow," so check your rental agreement **before** you get a pet. Some landlords do not allow pets of any kind. Some allow certain kinds or sizes of pets. Some landlords also demand a "pet deposit" if you do have a pet ... just in case the pet does any damage that needs to be repaired when you move out. Go to *www.rentwithpets.org* for more information.

Am I willing to provide I.D. and tags for my pet?

Your pet needs to wear a collar with at least two tags:

1. his identification and owner information and

2. proof of a rabies vaccination (provided by your veterinarian).

Am I willing to obey animal laws in my area?

Do you need to license your pet? Does your pet need specific vaccinations? Your local Animal Control agency can tell you if any laws apply to you and your pet. For licensing information, look in the government or yellow pages of your phone book under *Animals, Animal Control, Police,* or *Animal Shelters.* Do any of the following pet laws apply to your neighborhood?

- Vaccinating your pet (especially for rabies).

- Licensing your pet (and wearing its identification tag at all times).

- Restraining your pet (i.e., on a leash, in a fenced yard, etc.). What happens if your pet is found running loose by an Animal Control officer? Will you have to pay an expensive fine to get your pet back?

- Excessive barking may get you a nuisance fine. If your dog barks a lot, see a veterinarian for possible medical problems, such as separation anxiety.

- You might not be allowed to own certain types of pets in your area. Many areas also have a limit on the number of pets you can own.

- You cannot "dump" your pet. It's against the law — and you'll be fined. Pets cannot survive on their own.

- You cannot be cruel to your pet, or any other animal. (See "What is animal cruelty?" for more information.)

▶ What's the right pet for me?

Why do I want a pet?

Ask yourself this question **before** you get a pet. If you want a pet just because you think it's "the thing" to do, you're making a big mistake for both you and the animal. Have a good answer to this question before getting a pet.

What kind of pet do I want?

Do I want a dog or a cat or a rat or a hamster or a parakeet? Or something else? What size do I want? What color? Long-haired or short-haired? Purebred or mixed? Active dog or lap cat? Cuddly and affectionate or independent? Or does it matter?

What age should my pet be?

Many people assume that kittens and puppies are the only "right" age for a new pet, but sometimes an older pet is a better choice. A pet of any age can bond with a person who loves and cares for him, giving as much to the relationship as he receives in return. The following are important differences between the needs and abilities of kittens and puppies and those of adult cats and dogs:

Birth to Six Months Old

The first six months of life are vital to the development of kittens and puppies and require a lot of your time, care, and energy. Animals learn many of their most important skills from their mother and litter mates during the first 10 to 12 weeks of life. During the next three months, they'll need a lot of care from you. Baby animals that are not properly taught and cared for during this time find it difficult to develop proper social skills.

Six to 16 Months Old

Kittens and puppies are considered "teenagers" or young adults at this age. They're still growing and developing, but are beginning to show the direction that their individual personalities will take. They're high-energy at this stage and will test your patience at every turn.

17+ Months Old

These pets are considered grown-up — "cats" and "dogs." If you don't have the time to care for an animal during its growing-up stages, perhaps an adult cat or dog that is already trained would be a better choice for you.

Adapted from *Selecting the Right Pet for You.* © Dumb Friends League and Humane Society of the United States.

What about physical and personality traits?

By the time a cat or dog is six months old, physical traits will be clear. As for personality traits, all animals are different. Some animals have general personality traits: retrievers like to have things in their mouths, terriers like to dig, and Siamese cats tend to be very talkative. However, an animal's personality is based on both inherited and learned traits — and that combination is what makes each animal unique. These traits can be predicted to a limited degree as babies; however, it's hazardous to make too many assumptions about an animal's individual personality based solely on what traits his or her breed is expected to have.

How large is too large?

A large dog may not be happy in a small apartment — and kittens and puppies do grow up. Unfortunately, thousands of cats and dogs are abandoned or left at shelters because owners didn't consider how large they would grow to be. By the time cats or dogs are six or seven months old, you can usually tell what size they'll be when fully-grown. If you're renting, check the pet policies in your rental agreement or lease for size limitations.

Photo by Morgan Rothenberger

 ## Should I adopt from a shelter?

Should I adopt from a shelter?

Yes! Shelters have pets of all kinds, from new kittens and puppies to older cats and dogs. Some have been lost, some abandoned, some unwanted. All are waiting for a chance to love and be loved. They're remarkably adaptable, with an endless abil-

Interactive CD-ROM

Movie

ity to love. They cost much less than buying from a pet store or breeder. And where else can you find so many breeds, ages, and personalities under one roof?

If the shelter doesn't have the animal you want, ask shelter personnel to refer you to other sources in your community that have the animal's best interests at heart.

Are animals in shelters healthy and well-adjusted?

Most shelters screen all animals for serious health problems. No animal, no matter where you adopt him from, can be completely free of health and behavioral problems. Animals are just like people — no one is completely flawless.

Do shelters have purebred animals?

Up to 25 percent of all dogs at shelters are purebred. Purebred simply means that the parents and ancestors are all members of the same breed. Purchasing a purebred is no guarantee of health and temperament. They are no better or worse than mixed breeds.

How do I find a shelter in my area?

Look in the yellow pages of your phone book under *Animal Shelter, Humane Society, Animal Control,* or *Pets.* Municipal animal care agencies are often listed in the government pages of your phone book. You can also find more information about pet adoption on the following websites: *www.petfinder.org* and *www.petshelter.net.*

Is it difficult to adopt from a shelter?

Every shelter has its own policies — but all are concerned about the animal's care for its lifetime. An adoption counselor will work with you during the adoption process to ensure the right personality and lifestyle match for you and your prospective pet. Before adopting a pet, you should spend time with the animal in a room away from the other animals at the shelter to give you a better idea of the animal's personality.

Is it expensive to adopt from a shelter?

Most shelters charge from $40 to $100 to adopt animals. Dogs usually cost more than cats because they are more expensive to care for. The adoption fee is typically used to pay for the care of all the animals that reside in a shelter — not just the one you adopt. It's a small price to pay to help so many. Most shelters require adopted pets to be spayed or neutered within a certain amount of time, and may require a deposit that will be refunded when you provide a receipt from a veterinarian.

 ## Should I spay or neuter my pet?

What is spaying and neutering?

Spaying and neutering refers to the surgical removal of an animal's reproductive organs. It simply means that a female can't get pregnant — and a male can't get a female pregnant. Female spaying consists of removing the ovaries and uterus. Male neutering involves the removal of the testicles. Both are routine operations, performed while the animal is under anesthesia. The procedure requires one day at a veterinarian's office, with most animals bouncing back in a day or so. Following surgery, your pet may act disoriented or even "drunk" for a short period of time while the anesthesia wears off. Keep your pet confined in a kennel or bathroom until the anesthesia wears off.

Should I spay or neuter my pet?

Yes! The following advantages explain why:

- Longer life expectancy for your pet.

- Eliminates the risk of infections and disease of the reproductive organs.

- Reduces the urge to roam, which reduces the chances of your pet getting hit by a car, disappearing, being picked up by an animal control officer, etc.

- Usually prevents cats and dogs from spraying or marking territory.

- Eliminates the risk of complications from pregnancy.

- No heat cycles. No crying, howling, or frantic efforts to get outside. No unwelcome visits by male cats or dogs. Reduces the risk of injury from fights over females in heat.

- Greatly reduces the chance of mammary cancer, especially if the pet is spayed before her first heat cycle. (The risk is seven times greater in unspayed cats and dogs.)

- Eliminates the risk of testicular tumors and reduces the risk of prostate disease.

- Dogs are less aggressive and easier to train.

- Dogs are less likely to bite someone, which reduces the chance for legal action. (You, as your dog's owner, are legally responsible if your dog bites someone.)

- Helps control the pet population by reducing deaths of unwanted kittens and puppies.

And for those of you who think that a dog isn't "manly" after being neutered, get over it! Pets don't have any concept of sexual identity or ego. A dog's personality is not formed solely by his sex hormones, but more by his genetics and environment. So, your dog will be just as "manly" after surgery as he was before.

How old should my pet be to spay or neuter?
Cats and dogs are usually altered between three and six months of age. Neutering is best done by six months of age — before the dog develops any bad habits, but even older dogs (and cats) can benefit from the procedure.

Why is spaying and neutering so important?
Because there are too many pets, and too few responsible pet owners. Aside from the health benefits offered your pet, spaying and neutering also reduces the extremely serious problem of pet over-population. According to the Humane Society of the United States (HSUS),

> *several million cats and dogs are put to death each year*
> in this country because no one will adopt them; and

> *almost 70,000 kittens and puppies are born each day*
> (as opposed to only 10,000 humans).

A large number of the eight million animals that are euthanized, or "put to sleep," are from unwanted litters of kittens and puppies that have been abandoned or left at animal shelters. Spaying and neutering can prevent these senseless deaths.

Should my pet have "just one litter?"

If you think letting your pet have "just one litter" won't cause pet over-population, think again. If not neutered, there is no limit to the number of offspring male cats and dogs can produce. If a female is not spayed, all of the kittens or puppies in that "just one litter" could be having litters of their own.

The following statistics from the Humane Society of the United States (HSUS) put "just one litter" into perspective and show why it's so important to spay and neuter:

Cats

3 = the average number of litters a fertile cat can produce in one year.

4 to 6 = the average number of kittens in an average litter.

420,000 = the number of cats one female cat and her offspring can theoretically produce in seven years from "just one litter!"

Dogs

2 = the average number of litters a fertile dog can produce in one year.

6 to 10 = the average number of puppies in an average litter.

67,000 = the number of dogs one female dog and her offspring can theoretically produce in six years from "just one litter!"

What are the myths about spaying and neutering?

Myth: I don't need to neuter my male because he isn't the one having kittens or puppies. Only females need to be fixed.

Fact: This is the most-believed myth — and the most ridiculous. It takes two to tango! Immaculate conception doesn't explain how cats and dogs get pregnant.

Myth: I can't afford the surgery. It's too expensive.
Fact: The one-time cost of surgery is small compared to the cost of raising litters of kittens or puppies, medical treatment from fights and disease, new carpeting from spraying, dog bites, or euthanizing unwanted kittens and puppies. If you can't afford to spay or neuter a pet, you might want to wait to become a pet owner.

Myth: It's better to let my female have one litter before she is spayed.
Fact: Veterinarians believe it is best to spay your cat or dog before her first heat cycle. (See the statistics in the "Should my pet have just one litter?" section.)

Myth: Spaying and neutering will cause my pet to have personality changes.
Fact: Spaying or neutering does not alter a pet's personality. Pets may simply be a bit calmer and better-behaved after surgery since they won't have reproductive cycles or hormonal changes.

Myth: My pet will become fat and lazy after being spayed or neutered.
Fact: It is true that there is a tendency for weight gain — but most fat pets are usually overfed and under-exercised. (That's an owner problem, not a pet problem.)

Myth: My dog won't be a good watchdog if I neuter him.
Fact: If he was a good watchdog *before* the surgery, he will be a good watchdog *after* the surgery.

 ## What health care does my pet need?

What should I feed my pet?
Dry food is the most economical ... but you get what you pay for. If you buy the most inexpensive pet food, it won't be the highest quality.

Many veterinarians advise that you don't give any animal bones to your pet. Besides cracking teeth, bones can splinter and harm your pet's intestines — and they can choke your pet.

Keep your trash stored out of your pet's reach. Some pets will eat plastic wrap and tin foil because of the food left on it, which can cause serious medical problems.

In pets, bloat is a life-threatening emergency. It can result from eating a large meal within two hours of exercise, eating quickly, changes in diet, eating gas-producing foods (like hot dogs and hamburgers), or from stress. Symptoms include pacing, panting, drooling, enlarged stomach, and signs of distress. If your pet shows signs of bloat, contact your veterinarian immediately.

What if my pet is fat?

Pets are like people — if they take in more calories than they burn off, they'll get fat. An overweight pet can have serious health problems, such as high blood pressure, diabetes, heart and respiratory disease, and arthritis. Is your pet overweight? Put a hand on each side of his rib cage. You should be able to feel his ribs with gentle pressure. If you have to push any harder, your pet is overweight. See your veterinarian about a weight loss program.

What if my pet has behavioral problems?

Check with your veterinarian to determine if the problem is health-related. Also, find a good trainer to teach both you and your pet. Train your pet so you can get rid of the problem, not the pet. And don't punish your pet. Training and punishing are not the same.

How do I find a good veterinarian?

Ask for a recommendation from friends who have pets or from the place you got your pet. Or look in the *Yellow Pages*. Be involved in your pet's care by finding a pet doctor who is knowledgeable, treats your pet well, and will let you comfort your pet in the office. And if you don't like the one you found, look for another. Keep your veterinarian's name and phone number in a convenient location in case of an emergency.

What vaccinations does my pet need?

Many diseases can be prevented by vaccinating your pet. Most veterinarians keep computerized shot records, and will send you reminders when necessary. (See the sections on "Just Cats" and "Just Dogs" for a list of vaccinations.)

Is heartworm serious?

Heartworm is transmitted by mosquitoes and can kill your pet. It is more common in dogs, but can occur in cats. Have your veterinarian test your pet annually and provide preventive medications for your pet. These can be given monthly in the form of liquids, chewable tablets, or pills. There is also an injection that lasts six months.

Does my pet need dental care?

Yes! Your pet needs an annual dental exam and/or cleaning by your veterinarian. More than 85 percent of cats and dogs older than four years have some form of periodontal disease, a painful swelling of the gums. If left unchecked, bacteria in your pet's mouth can enter the bloodstream, causing serious problems. (See "Just Cats" and "Just Dogs" for warning signs.)

Is my medicine safe for my pet?

"People medicines" are for people only. This includes prescription medicines and over-the-counter medicines, such as aspirin. Only give your pet medicine that is prescribed to him by your veterinarian.

How do I get rid of fleas?

Fleas are the worst pests for you and your pet. Some pets have allergic reactions to flea bites that cause redness and itching. Fleas also carry the common tapeworm larvae, which is ingested when your pet licks its fur. To control fleas, you must treat both your pet and your home. Check with your veterinarian first.

How do I know if my pet has fleas?

If your pet has fleas, you may notice the following: tiny red or red-brown shapes jumping or moving around in your pet's fur; black or brown specks ("flea dirt") in your pet's fur, especially around his tail; your pet scratching or biting himself intensely; and flea dirt or eggs on your pet's bedding.

Flea products used on cats **MUST** be labeled as **SAFE FOR CATS.**

How do I get rid of fleas on my pet?

During flea season, purchase flea/tick drops, such as *Frontline* or *Advantage*, from your veterinarian. (Over-the-counter flea drops are not recommended.) Apply the drops to your pet's skin monthly to kill fleas on con-tact and prevent eggs from developing. Most drops have to be applied monthly. (If you use flea/tick drops, you won't need flea collars, powders, sprays, or shampoos.) You must also treat your home.

How do I get rid of fleas in my home?

If you have fleas in your home, use a spray that will kill adult fleas and keep immature fleas and eggs from developing. Ask your veterinarian for rec-ommendations and read the label carefully. Some sprays require pets to be out of the area during spraying and for several hours after. Also, clean your pet's bedding and vacuum all carpeting and furniture thoroughly.

How do I remove ticks from my pet?

A tick's bite can pass potentially life-threatening diseases to your pet — and to you. Ticks can usually be prevented by applying flea/tick drops to your pet monthly. If you find a tick on your pet, remove it immediately. Wear latex gloves. Saturate a cotton ball or paper towel with tick spray, mineral oil, or petrole-um jelly and hold it over the tick. When the tick starts to back out of the skin, grab the entire tick with a pair of tweezers. If you can't remove the tick's head, have your veterinarian do it. Flush the tick down the toilet. Apply a disinfec-tant, such as alcohol, or an antibiotic ointment to the site of the tick bite.

If you're bitten by a tick, watch for signs of infection. If a red ring appears around the bite within three days, see your doctor. You may have been bitten by a Deer tick, a carrier of Lyme Disease (which causes arthritis-like symptoms).

What if my pet eats something poisonous?

Call your veterinarian or an emergency animal clinic immediately. Keep your pet inside when bug and grass sprays and insecticides are being sprayed in your yard or neighborhood. Keep pets off sprayed grass for 24 hours or wipe the paws clean with a wet cloth so poison isn't ingested.

What grooming does my pet need?

Groom your pet regularly for his comfort and good health. Start grooming when you bring your pet home so he'll get used to it. Brush your pet daily to improve the appearance of his coat, reduce matting, stimulate circulation, and check for fleas and ticks. Cats and dogs can be bathed occasionally using a pet shampoo. In hot weather, long-haired cats and dogs do better with their fur trimmed. Brush your pet's teeth weekly with pet toothpaste. (Don't use human toothpaste. It has soap in it.) Trim your dog's toenails as needed.

What if my pet is hit by a car?

If a pet is hit by a car, caution is needed because a pet may bite from pain. For cats, slide the injured cat onto a large towel and wrap the towel around its body. For dogs, wrap a belt or cloth around the dog's mouth. Be sure the dog can breathe normally. Call your veterinarian to make sure he's in and will be prepared for the emergency.

 ## How do I make my home safe for my pet?

What household items need to be pet-proofed?

Keep the following household items out of your pet's reach:

- Items that poison pets, such as cleansers, bug sprays, and medications. Rat poisons are the most common source of pet poisoning.

- Candles that can burn your pet if brushed against, or that can burn your house down if knocked over.

- Items that strangle or choke pets, including small balls, sewing thread, needles, socks, pantyhose, bones, pennies, string, ribbon, rubber bands, dental floss, and any other small item that an animal might put in its mouth.

- Never leave your pet unattended on a balcony.

What if my pet has an "accident?"

If your pet has an accident on the carpet, dab the spot with a dry paper towel and then use a cleaner that removes pet stains and odors. If your pet isn't feeling his normal self, keep him on tile or other hard surfaces. And never rub an animal's nose in his mess. That teaches him nothing — except to fear you. If your pet has repeated accidents, talk to your veterinarian about possible medical causes. If medical causes are ruled out, discuss effective house-**training** (not house-breaking) methods with your veterinarian.

Are houseplants poisonous?

Cats and dogs can become extremely ill or even die from eating poisonous plants. Make sure all your houseplants are pet-safe. You can get a list of deadly plants from your veterinarian or local humane shelter.

Who takes care of my pet if something happens to me?

Plan for your pet's future if something happens to you. Who will care for your pet? Be sure to ask the person you choose.

Should I prepare for natural disasters?

If you have to evacuate, take your pet with you. If it's not safe for you to stay in the area, it's not safe for your pet. Don't allow your pet to roam loose after a disaster.

How do I order a free "Save My Pet" sticker?

Want to let emergency personnel know your pet needs rescued? Order a free "Save My Pet" sticker at *www.onmyown.com* or send a self-addressed, stamped envelope to:

Interactive CD-ROM

Click to the web from the CD-ROM!

Web Resource

> **Pet Sticker**
> PO Box 44
> Tecumseh, KS 66542.

If you move, remember to remove the sticker from your door or window. You don't want emergency personnel to risk their lives for pets that no longer live in the home.

(Actual size is 3^1/$_2$" x 4^1/$_2$". Allow 4-6 weeks for delivery.)

IN CASE OF EMERGENCY PLEASE

SAVE MY PET!

\# of pets in my home:
_____ CATS _____ DOGS
_____ Other (specify)_____

Vet's Name:_____
Vet's Phone #:_____

"On My Own" ISBN 0-9711500-0-1
©2001 Silly Goose Productions, LLC
P.O. Box 44 • Tecumseh, KS 66542 • www.sillygoose2.com

How do I summer-proof my pet?

Give your pet plenty of water.

Pets drink more water when it's warm, so check the dish frequently (even indoors) to prevent dehydration. Clean your pet's food and water bowls at least once a week.

Keep your pet out of the sun — and in the shade.

Pets can get sunburns and skin cancers (especially those with short fur and light coloring), so cover them when in the sun. Keep your pet in a shaded area. For dogs confined to a yard during the day, provide shade and a child's wading pool. When it's really hot outdoors, bring your pet in and leave the air conditioner on. If you're uncomfortable outside, so is your pet.

Walk your pet when it's cool outside.

Pets can burn their paws on hot pavement, so walk in the early morning or late evening when it's cooler outside. Bring water for him to drink. Walk through a few sprinklers. Cats and dogs don't sweat like humans, so over-exercising in hot weather can cause heat stroke. Watch for signs of staring, staggering, weakness, and vomiting. If your pet becomes overheated, get him out of the sun immediately, run water over him, and fan him. If he gets worse, take him to a veterinarian.

Never leave your pet in a car.

Never, ever leave your pet in a car — even with the windows rolled down. Thousands of cats and dogs die each year from being left in cars. The temperature inside a shaded car can rise to over 105 degrees within minutes. Leave your pet at home. If you must bring your pet along, have someone stay in the car with your pet with the air conditioner running. Thousands of pets are also stolen each year while left in cars.

Don't give your dog a ride in the back of your truck.

Dogs can't hold on the way humans can and any sudden stop or start can toss your pet on the street. If tied in the back of a truck, your dog could jump out and hang himself. Dogs can get sand and grit in their eyes that can cause permanent damage. The same is true for dogs that stick their heads out of rolled-down windows. If you must travel with your pet in the back of your truck, put him in a crate and tie the crate securely to the walls of the truck so it won't slide around. (It is illegal in some areas to transport a pet in the back of an open pickup truck.)

Practice water safety with your pet.

Many pets drown each year in the backyard pool. If you have a pool, teach your dog how to get out of it. If you take your dog boating, consider a doggie life vest. Don't take your animal to the lake or beach unless you provide a shaded spot for him to lie in and bring plenty of fresh water for him to drink. (Do not give him salt water to drink.) Hose your pet down after he has been swimming in any water.

How do I winter-proof my pet?

Give your pet lots of food and water.

Outdoor dogs need more food in the winter because it takes more energy to stay warm. Make sure your pet's water is fresh and not frozen by checking several times a day.

Keep your pet indoors when temperatures and windchills are cold.

Dogs and cats cannot withstand winter's bitter cold and numbing wetness any more than you can. Short-haired, very young, or very old dogs (and cats) should never be left outdoors when it's cold — and should wear a sweater when let out to walk.

Provide an adequate doghouse and protection.

Your dog needs a draft-free doghouse that is large enough for him to sit and lie down comfortably but small enough to hold in his body heat. (For more information, see the "Just Dogs" section.)

Keep thawing chemicals off your pet's paws.

Salts and chemicals that melt ice and snow can burn the pads of your pet's feet. Use melting chemicals that are pet-friendly or wipe your pet's paws with a wet cloth before he licks them and burns his mouth.

Keep antifreeze away from your pet.

Antifreeze is a poison. It tastes sweet — but it can kill pets. Parked cars can drip antifreeze, so wipe up any spots on the pavement. Never let an animal lick an area where cars have been parked.

Check for cats before starting your car.

Cats are attracted to parked cars with warm engines. To avoid injury, bang on the hood of your car to scare away any cats or stray animals before you start your engine.

 ## How do I holiday-proof my pet?

Be careful when giving a pet as a gift.
A pet can be a wonderful gift, but give one only if you know the person you're giving it to **wants** the pet and **can take care of** the pet. It's preferable to never give a pet as a gift. Instead, give a gift certificate from your local animal shelter.

Keep chocolate away from pets.
Chocolate can kill pets. Just one ounce of unsweetened chocolate can kill a small dog. So, don't leave chocolate of any kind lying around — not even a half-eaten candy bar.

Keep Christmas tree decorations out of reach.
Hang the decorations on your tree above "pet level" — high enough so your pet can't get them. Tree decorations are a real hazard for pets because they can eat the ornaments, balls, and tinsel. They can also get cut if the balls fall off and break. Cats and dogs often eat tinsel, too, which can cause major digestive problems.

Keep your pet safe on Halloween.
Keep your pet inside, away from wayward youth who might scare or harm him. Keep your pet away from flames in candles and pumpkins.

Keep your pet away from fireworks.
The loud noise can scare your pet — and hurt his ears.

 ## What if my pet gets lost?

How can I prevent my pet from getting lost?
It's your responsibility to keep your pet safe. Don't leave doors and windows open. Pets can sneak out when you're not looking. Keep screens on windows. Contrary to myth, cats cannot fall from high places and land on

their feet. Many injuries to city-dwelling cats are fall-related. Small dogs can also fall out of windows. Make sure your pet wears an identification tag to enable him to be returned to you if lost.

Electronic microchips (the size of a grain of rice) can be inserted under your pet's skin. Most animal shelters have equipment to scan the chips. Microchips should only be used as a backup to your pet's I.D. tags.

Never let your animal run loose — it's a good way for your pet to be injured, lost, stolen, or killed. And you may have to pay an expensive fine.

If lost, how do I find my pet?

If your pet gets lost, check the following:

Your Home
Check your house or apartment in the ventilation areas, behind the washer and dryer, or any other place a pet might get trapped.

Your Neighborhood
Post signs with your pet's picture, name, date and location where he was lost, and your contact information.

Your Local Veterinary Clinics
Your pet may have been hurt and taken there.

Your Local Animal Shelter
If an Animal Control officer picked up your pet, he was taken to a local shelter. Continue checking daily. Many shelters, unfortunately, can't hold pets for a long period of time.

Your Newspaper's Lost & Found Section
Place a lost pet ad in your local newspaper. Check the "Found" section. (Most "Lost & Found" ads are free of charge.)

When placing an ad or hanging flyers, don't give out all the identifying information about your pet. Some people are running pet-recovery scams — demanding that you pay money to get your pet back. They usually don't have the pet — and you're out the money. And don't give up your search. Animals have been lost for months — only to find their way home again.

What if someone is cruel to an animal?

What is animal cruelty?

Laws vary by city and state; however, according to the American Society for the Prevention of Cruelty to Animals (ASPCA), animal cruelty is any of the following:

- Beating or hitting an animal.

- Kicking an animal with force.

- Encouraging aggression between animals.

- Failure to provide food or water to an animal.

- Failure to provide veterinary care when an animal is injured or sick.

- Failure to provide shelter to an animal.

- Leaving an animal in a car or tied outside in very hot or cold weather.

- Abandoning an animal.

What if someone is cruel to an animal?

Animal cruelty is against the law! As of June 2001, cruelty to animals is a felony offense in 27 states. Evidence of animal neglect and abuse is showing up every day in animal shelters — and in courts. To report animal cruelty or neglect in your community, call your local law enforcement agency, humane society, or animal shelter. You can choose to remain anonymous if you wish, although giving your name will enable follow-up if necessary.

Just Cats

 How do I keep my cat healthy?

Should I keep my cat indoors?

Yes. The average life span for indoor cats is 13 years (though some live past 20 years). The average life span for outdoor cats is less than three years.

What vaccinations does my cat need?

Most cats require vaccinations that only veterinarians know how to pronounce — so here's their shortened version:

FDCVR or FVRCP with leukemia and rabies
(as indicated by your veterinarian).

What weekly checks does my cat need?

You should check your cat's eyes, ears, and mouth weekly. If anything seems unhealthy, or if you pet seems to be in pain, check with your veterinarian.

If your cat has any redness or discharge from his eyes, or if your cat squints, he may have an eye infection.

If there's too much wax in your cat's ears, clean them with a cotton ball or Q-tip. Don't stick the Q-tip into your cat's eardrums. Use it only on the parts of the ears you can see. If your cat's ears have a foul odor, or if he's scratching, rubbing, shaking his head, or tilting his head to one side, he may have ear mites, allergies, or other traumas to the ear.

If any of the following symptoms are present, your cat may have periodontal disease: bad breath (one of the first signs of dental disease); red and swollen gums; tenderness when his mouth or gums are touched; difficulty with eating or drinking; or loose or missing teeth.

What if my cat throws up hairballs?

When your cat grooms himself, hair is in-gested. The hair can get stuck in your cat's stomach, forcing him to throw up. To help decrease the amount of hair ingested, brush your cat daily. You can also put a drop of Vase-line on a paw to be licked off or give a cat laxative (purchased from your veterinari-an or pet supply store) to your cat. The cat laxative tastes good and seems like a treat to many cats.

> Dogs come when they're called. Cats take a message and get back to you.
> *~ Mary Bly*

What if my cat swallows string?

Take your cat to a veterinarian immediately. The string can get caught under your cat's tongue or in his intestines. Don't let your cat play with string or string-like toys without your supervision. Don't leave needles, thread, yarn, shoelaces, ribbon, tinsel, or any other string-like articles lying around for your cat to find.

What if my cat won't use the litter box?

If your cat begins to use places other than the litter box, just clean up the mess — and then move the box to a different location, use a different kind of litter, and clean the box more often. Talk to your veterinarian. Your cat may have a bladder infection or a problem with the litter. Don't punish your cat for not using the litter box — and don't rub his nose in it. Those tech-niques don't work!

What kind of litter box should I use?

There are many types of boxes on the market now, so pick the one that works for you and your cat. Scoop the litter daily — even if it doesn't "smell" like you need to. Place your litter box in an area that is conven-ient for your cat and allows your cat to have some privacy. Don't put it near appliances that make noise or in a cold basement. If you place it in a clos-et or bathroom, use some sort of door stop so your cat won't get locked in or out. And keep the box away from food and water bowls.

Does my cat like a certain kind of litter?

There are a variety of litters on the market, so pick the one that works best for both you and your cat. Some cats won't use the litter box if they don't like the litter. Fill the box with two inches of litter; and clean according to the type of litter used.

Clumping Litter

Most cat owners prefer the clumping litter that you can scoop out daily. Clumping litter is great when you have more than one cat. It's handy to find a small trash can with a seal-tight lid to put the daily clumps in. Line the trash can with a plastic bag — and then dump as often as needed. Scoop clumps daily — and clean the box once a month with soap and water. Then refill with new litter. Avoid litter that is "flushable."

Clay Litter

If you use a clay litter, dump the entire litter box as needed to maintain a clean box. If it smells bad, your cat won't go near it. Clay litter is inexpensive, but dusty. Clean the box with soap and water at least once a month, then refill with new litter.

Why is my cat shredding the furniture?

Why is my cat shredding the furniture?

Scratching is normal for cats. It removes the dead outer layers of their claws, and it helps them mark their territory by leaving a visual mark and a scent. (Cats have scent glands in their paws.) They also scratch to stretch their bodies and flex their feet and claws — and simply to work off excess energy. You can train your cat to scratch acceptable surfaces. The following can help:

> The ancient Egyptians worshipped cats as Gods. Cats have never forgotten this.
>
> *~ Author Unknown*

- Play with your cat. Lots of interactive play will work off excess energy.

- Provide objects that are appealing and convenient for your cat to scratch (from your cat's point of view). What are the objects your cat is scratching? Where are they located? Are they soft or rough? Are they wide or thin? What height are they?

- For those items you don't want scratched, place similar objects (rope-wrapped posts, corrugated cardboard, etc.) near the object your cat has been clawing. Once your cat is consistently scratching the new object, move it three inches a day to a more appropriate location.

- Scratching posts can be purchased at a pet store or made from scraps.

- Place something your cat won't like, such as double-side tape or sandpaper, on the objects you don't want scratched.

- Don't punish your cat. Provide him with an alternative object to scratch.

Should I have my cat de-clawed?

Ask your veterinarian. If your cat is scratching the furniture, refer to "What if my cat is shredding the furniture?" before de-clawing your cat. Have only the front claws removed. Never de-claw a cat that will be outdoors. If you de-claw your cat, a good time to do it is when you spay or neuter so the cat is only under anesthesia once.

Is catnip safe?

Catnip is a completely safe, harmless, and non-addictive natural herb that stimulates play and exercise. It also aids digestion. And many cats love it! Catnip has a substance in the leaves called *nepetalactone* that causes cats to act rather silly — rolling, rubbing, leaping, and purring. You can use catnip in your cat's toys, on a cat scratcher, or just sprinkled on the floor.

What if my cat bites me?

Cat bites can easily become a medical emergency. Do not ignore a bite. If a cat's bite breaks the skin, see your doctor immediately to get antibiotics. The bacteria in a cat's mouth can spread from the bite wound into your bloodstream and cause serious harm to you. Also, if two (or more) animals are fighting, don't try to break up the fight with your hands. Throw a blanket over them.

What if I'm allergic to cats?

Cat hair doesn't cause an allergic reaction — a protein on a cat's fur does. It flakes off and floats through the air when a cat washes himself. If you're allergic to cats, the following can help:

- Know that it isn't just the cat. Dust mites, pollen, and other nuisances can cause symptoms.

- Make your bedroom a **cat-free zone**. Restrict your cat to certain areas of your home.

- Get rid of allergen traps such as upholstered furniture and rugs. If you have carpet, use an allergen-proof vacuum cleaner with a HEPA filter and steam clean it occasionally. (Carpet can have up to 100 times the amount of cat allergens as hardwood floors.)

- Get some fresh air. Open windows to ventilate your home.

- Wipe the dander away with new products that remove dander and saliva from your cat.

- Bathing your cat might help.

- Check with your doctor for possible allergy remedies.

Dogs
have masters.
Cats
have staff.

~Author Unknown

A Cat's Prayer

Now hear this! You may live in this dwelling with me, but keep in mind that your sole purpose for existing is to care for me. I pray God keeps you able to do so. Feed me well and promptly, so that I may then find a quiet place to lie down and stare at you. If that place happens to be on top of the TV, do not keep trying to dislodge me even though my tail is hanging in the middle of the picture. I expect full run of the premises, including the kitchen table. I sniff your food only to see if I would prefer it to mine. Brush me twice a week. Pet me as often as you wish, but I can do without the idiotic statements you utter as you do so. When I bump my head against your leg or cheek, it means I accept you as part of my environment. Keep in mind that if I thought the lady next door would feed me better, I'd be out of here in a minute. If you're looking for loyalty, get a dog.

~Author Unknown

Just Dogs

 ## How do I keep my dog healthy?

What vaccinations does my dog need?
Your dog needs to be checked annually for heartworm because it can kill him. Consult your veterinarian for other vaccinations your dog might need.

What should I check on my dog's body?
Run your hands over your dog to see if there are any ticks, fleas, cuts, bruises, or lumps. Apply flea and tick drops during flea season in your area. If there are cuts, bruises, or lumps, consult your veterinarian about it.

Your dog should not have abnormal tearing, redness, or discharge in his eyes.

Look for any cuts, redness, swelling, or discharge in your dog's ears.

Check your dog's mouth for dental disease warning signs: bad breath (one of the first signs of dental disease); red and swollen gums; tenderness when his mouth or gums are touched; difficulty eating or drinking; or loose or missing teeth. Your dog needs an annual dental exam and/or cleaning.

If anything seems unhealthy, check with your veterinarian.

 ## Am I responsible if my dog bites someone?

Am I responsible if my dog bites someone?
Yes! An estimated 4.7 million people are bitten by dogs each year in the United States. (Almost 2,500 are postmen!) Children are the most common to be bitten, with the most severe bites. Some dogs who have attacked and killed people have been humanely put to death and the dog's owner(s) have been convicted of serious criminal charges.

Things We Can Learn From A Dog

Never pass up the opportunity to go for a joyride.
When loved ones come home, always run to greet them.
When it's in your best interest, practice obedience.
Let others know when they've invaded your territory.
Take naps and stretch before rising.
If what you want lies buried, dig until you find it.
Avoid biting when a simple growl will do.
On hot days, drink lots of water and lay under a shady tree.
When you're happy, dance around and wag your entire body.
Thrive on attention and let people touch you.
Delight in the simple joy of a long walk.
Run, romp, and play daily.
Never pretend to be something you're not.
Be loyal.
Eat with gusto and enthusiasm. Stop when you've had enough.
When someone is having a bad day, be silent, sit close by, and nuzzle them gently.
Allow the experience of fresh air and the wind in your face to be pure ecstasy.
No matter how often you're scolded, don't buy into the guilt thing and pout ...
Run right back and make friends.

~ Author Unknown

Photo by Elaine Toland

How can I help prevent my dog from biting someone?

The following tips can help ensure that your dog doesn't bite someone: spay or neuter your dog; train and socialize your dog to be comfortable around people; don't play "attack" games with your dog; be cautious if you don't know how your dog will react to a situation; seek professional training if your dog growls, nips, or bites someone; and don't get an aggressive dog for a pet. For more information, go to *www.nodogbites.org*.

How can I prevent myself from being bitten by a dog?

When approaching a dog you don't know, use caution. If possible, don't approach a dog you don't know, especially if the dog is confined behind a fence, in a car, or on a chain. Be careful when running or bicycling by a dog because a dog's instinct is to chase his prey. And let sleeping dogs lie. Dogs bite from behind, so when approached by a strange or aggressive dog, do the following:

1. Face the dog. Don't stare at him. (He may think you're a threat.) Don't speak to him.

2. Stand still with your hands at your sides.

3. Don't run, but back away slowly.

If you're knocked to the ground by a dog, curl into a ball and cover your face and ears with your hands. Lie still and be quiet until the dog goes away. If you are attacked by a dog, try to put something (jacket, purse, book, etc.) between you and the dog that can serve as a barrier to lessen your injuries. Seek medical attention if you are bitten. Serious infections, even death, can result if bites are left untreated. Report the dog bite to the police as soon as possible.

Interactive CD-ROM

Movie

 ### What should I know about dog collars?

Have your puppy wear a collar as soon as you get him — but continue to check the fitting of the collar as your puppy grows. Puppies need to have a bigger collar several times before they are full-grown. To be sure a collar fits, slip your fingers under the collar. Do this often. Your fingers should fit with a bit of room to spare. If the collar is too tight, adjust it or get a bigger one. Unfortunately, veterinarians have had to surgically remove ingrown collars because the owner's haven't paid attention. Training or choke collars should never be left on dogs that are left in a crate or are unsupervised because dogs can easily choke themselves to death. If you must tie your dog, always use a collar with a buckle — and put identification tags on the collar.

▶ How do I train my dog?

Many dogs spend their days alone, and get bored, lonely, or frustrated. Because of this, undesirable or destructive behavior might result. This behavior can include digging holes in the yard, barking non-stop, and chewing up everything in sight. An unhappy dog creates a mess during the day, which in turn creates an unhappy owner. A dog can also be so full of energy that he becomes uncontrollable when the owner comes home.

Training teaches your dog what is expected of him, and it strengthens the bond between you and your dog. Dogs are more relaxed and happier when you direct their behavior — rather than making them guess what you want. Behavioral problems can also be health-related. Your pet needs a complete medical exam by a veterinarian once a year. And, keep in mind that pet behavioral problems can also be owner-related. You and your dog both need to be trained!

A little boy and his dog sat together — the little boy's arm around his dog and the dog's paw on the little boy's knee.

Between them — a big, dirt-covered soup bone. The dad happened upon the two of them and asked the little boy about that big, dirty soup bone. The son said, "My dog gave it to me, and it's the best present I ever got."

"Why is that?" the father asked.

"Because he gave all that he had ... and he even gift-wrapped it," the boy said, as he rubbed the dirt off the bone.

~ Author Unknown

It would take an entire book to teach you how to train your dog. Find a book or video (at a store or library) written specifically for that. A good book is the *HSUS Complete Guide to Dog Care*. Another good book is *Preventing Dog Problems: Pure and Simple*. And find a good trainer. Ask your local shelter, veterinarian, or check the *Yellow Pages*. Your dog needs to learn the following commands: sit, down, stand, leave it, stay, how to come when called, and how to walk on a loose leash. If you and your dog can learn these simple commands, you're well on your way to having a very well-behaved companion.

How do I dog-proof my home?

That's easy. Pick up after yourself. Dogs will chew on almost any personal item left on the floor or accessible on furniture. Pick up your clothes and shoes, put the garbage in a container or cupboard the dog can't get into, and cover your couch with sheets. Don't leave small items that can be ingested (such as a string, ribbon, rubber bands, pantyhose, socks, or coins) lying around.

 What if my dog has to "go" while I'm away?

Can't my dog "hold it" all day?

No. Dogs were not built to "hold it" all day — just as you weren't. If you can't make it home during the day to let your dog out, limit your dog to a cozy, well-lit space with a tile floor. Put your dog's bed and some toys in the room. A window would be nice, too. If necessary, purchase an adjustable dog gate at a pet store. Products like doggy doors (for cat litter-type boxes) and absorbent mats that you just throw away are also available. Consider moving closer to work or school so you can go home during your break or lunch hour to walk your dog. Or, you might ask a friend, neighbor, or pet sitter to provide mid-day relief for your dog while you're away.

Should I punish my dog for having an "accident" in the house?

Don't punish your dog for going to the bathroom in the house. Rubbing his nose in it doesn't help. He won't understand. And you'll do more harm than good by making your dog fear you. Just clean up the mess. If, however, you catch your dog in the act, make a loud noise to interrupt him. Then take him to an appropriate spot outdoors. Praise him when he's done.

 What if I have to leave my dog outside?

What if I have to leave my dog outside?

Make sure your dog's in a securely-fenced yard so he won't stray. Provide a doghouse and fresh food and water. Dogs need exercise, care, and companionship, so if you must leave your dog outside, be sure to pay a lot of attention to him. Don't just pat him on the head when you get home from work. Take him for a walk. Play with him.

Many people leave their dogs outside because there is a behavior problem inside. Solve the behavior problem so your dog can be safe indoors. Dogs are not outdoors enjoying the fresh air and getting lots of exercise. Actually, the dog is probably bored, frustrated, and lonely — which may create more behavioral problems (such as digging, escaping, barking, etc.).

What kind of doghouse does my dog need?

If you have to keep your dog outside, his doghouse should meet the following:

- Because your dog's body heat warms his doghouse, it needs to be wide enough for him to turn around in and long enough for him to stretch out without any part of his body touching the sides. (If the doghouse is too large, your dog won't be able to stay warm.) If your dog stays in a garage or shed, he still needs the correct-sized doghouse inside.

- The doghouse needs to be well-insulated, with the floor several inches above ground.

- The roof should be slanted so that rain and snow won't collect on it; and hinged to allow for easy cleaning and to spray for fleas and ticks.

- In summer, keep the doghouse well-ventilated and place it in a shady location.

- In winter, place the doghouse where sun can reach it during the day and face it away from the wind. Put a piece of heavy carpet over the doorway to prevent drafts.

- Straw or cedar chips can be put on the floor to keep your dog warm and comfortable. Put a rug or blanket on top of that. Wash your dog's bedding often. Shredded newspaper can be used, but the ink can rub off on your dog's fur.

How do I install a ground dog trolley?

If you have to tie your dog up, use a "ground dog trolley." This allows your dog a great deal of freedom without getting tangled up. Use a leather or nylon harness, **not** a choke collar. The trolleys are easy to install, so check with your local pet store or home improvement store for instructions and supplies.

A Dog's Prayer

Treat me kindly, my beloved master, for no heart in the world is more grateful for kindness than the loving heart of me. Do not break my spirit with a stick, for though I lick your hand between the blows, your patience and understanding will more quickly teach me the things you would have me do. Speak to me often, for your voice is the world's sweetest music, as you must know by the fierce wagging of my tail when your footstep falls upon my waiting ear.

When it is cold and wet, please take me inside, for I am now a domesticated animal, no longer used to bitter elements. And I ask no greater glory than the privilege of sitting at your feet beside the hearth. Though had you no home, I would rather follow you through ice and snow than rest upon the softest pillow in the warmest home in all the land, for you are my God, and I am your devoted worshipper.

Keep my pan filled with fresh water, for although I should not reproach you were it dry, I cannot tell you when I suffer thirst. Feed me clean food, that I may be well, to romp and play and do your bidding, to walk by your side and stand ready, willing, and able to protect you with my life should your life be in danger.

And, beloved master, should the Great Master see fit to deprive me of my health or sight, do not turn me away from you. Rather, hold me gently in your arms as skilled hands grant me the merciful boon of eternal rest ... and I will leave you knowing with the last breath I draw, my fate was ever safest in your hands.

~Author Unknown

Photo by Morgan Rothenberger

Additional Information for this Chapter

Books

- *Cats for Dummies* by Gina Spadafori and Paul D. Pion, DVM, DACVIM

- *Dog Training for Dummies* by Jack Volhard and Wendy Volhard

- *HSUS Complete Guide to Dog Care*

- *Preventing Dog Problems: Pure and Simple* by Mark Katz and Dru Katz, DVM

Web Links

- *www.DrsFosterSmith.com*

- *www.PetSmart.com*

- *www.AWOLPet.com*

- *www.Cattoys.com*

- *www.Allpets.com*

- *www.PounceCat.com*

- *www.Dogleash.com*

- *www.ScienceDiet.com*

- *www.4yourcat.com*

- *www.morganthedog.com*

- *www.ASPCA.org*

- *www.HSUS.org*

- *www.digitaldog.com*

- *www.Everclean.com*

- *www.Frontline.com*

- *www.Nofleas.com*

- *www.dog.com*

- *www.PlanetUrine.com*

- *www.Nofleas.com*

- *www.AmericasPetTags.com*

- *www.rentwithpets.org*

- *www.petfinder.org*

- *www.petshelter.net*

- *www.onmyown.com*

- *www.agirlsworld.com* (Spay Now online interactive game)

- *www.califmall.com/ST_PetRock.html* (to order a Pet Rock)

Screensavers
Download the following screensavers from the CD-ROM:

- Bob the Boxer

- "I Want Out" Cats

How can I give back?

Interactive CD-ROM

Quiz

The wonderful thing about charities and giving back is that there truly is "something for everyone." What do you know about helping others?

True   False

○   ○   1. Giving back is about helping people.
○   ○   2. The best things in life are free.
○   ○   3. I don't need hours of spare time to make a difference.
○   ○   4. Donating old clothes to a homeless shelter is an act of giving back.
○   ○   5. Planting a tree is an act of giving back.
○   ○   6. Teaching a senior citizen to use the Internet is an act of giving back.
○   ○   7. Reading to a young child is an act of giving back.
○   ○   8. Donating $5 from each paycheck is an act of giving back.
○   ○   9. The possibilities for volunteering are endless.
○   ○   10. One man's trash is another man's treasure.
○   ○   11. My old cell phone can be donated to help a victim of domestic violence.
○   ○   12. Donations should be made by check or money order only, not cash.
○   ○   13. Tax-exempt means that an organization doesn't have to pay taxes.
○   ○   14. Blood donations help 4.5 million people each year.
○   ○   15. Blood can be donated once every eight weeks.
○   ○   16. The gift of life is given when a deceased person's organs are donated.
○   ○   17. Family members must be told of my decision to donate.
○   ○   18. The green ribbon signifies awareness for organ donations.
○   ○   19. There are charities for sports-lovers.
○   ○   20. If I receive a gift in the mail from an organization, I don't have to pay for it or return it.

All of the answers are true. Keep reading for more ways to help **you** find a way to **give back**.

Charities and Giving Back

Chapter 14

When people help others, they feel good about themselves, too. Giving back through charitable work is a generous act of un-selfishness. Usually, you can find volunteer work doing something you enjoy. If you like building things, check out Habitat for Humanity. Love animals? Shelters need lots of volunteers. Give a few dollars a month to a charity you believe in. There are many opportunities in life to reach out and lend a hand.

How can I give back to my community?

What's in it for me?

Giving back is about people helping people. Lives are changed as a result of your gift — whether it's the gift of your time, your talent, your money, or your treasures. There's magic in a smile you get from someone you help. Volunteering is about helping others — it's the glue that holds a com-

Interactive
CD-ROM

Movie

munity together. When you help someone, you get so much back. The act of giving teaches not only you, the giver, but also the receiver. Compassion, pride, and self-esteem are great rewards for everyone involved. Didn't someone once say that the best things in life are free?

One of the great things about volunteering is that you can do things that you might never be hired to do. Volunteering offers great work experience for your résumé and makes you look more well-rounded to employers. You'll learn things that may lead to the career of your dreams. You'll meet different people and make new friends. Volunteering helps you understand that your own problems are not as difficult as you thought. Everyone has their own personal tragedies, but when you start volunteering, you may realize your hardships aren't as tough as you once thought.

Discover the joy of giving by making a difference in your community. Get involved, even if it's just mowing your 80-year-old neighbor's lawn. Each of us has something to give, so give freely and without expecting anything in return. The rewards will be better than you can imagine!

 ## Do I have an hour to spare?

> Every day, an old man walked the beach with a pail, picking up starfish that had been washed in by the tide, and throwing them back into the sea.
>
> One day a young boy stopped the old man and asked, *"Why do you throw the starfish back? It doesn't matter. They will only wash up on the shore again tomorrow."*
>
> The old man picked a starfish out of his pail, threw it as far as he could into the sea, and replied, *"It matters to this one."*
>
> ~ Author Unknown

Do you have a spare hour or two to share your talents and skills? If you can make a little time, you can make a tremendous difference. You don't have to spend a lot of time volunteering to make a significant impact. It costs so little to bring happiness to someone else. Here are a few ideas:

Donate old clothes and household items to charity. Mow a lawn, rake leaves, walk a dog, or run errands for an elderly or disabled neighbor. Plant a garden or tree for others to enjoy. Make a care package with mittens and warm clothes for a child at a homeless shelter. Read books or tutor children. Visit sick children in hospitals. Work at a horse farm that helps disabled children. Teach an elderly friend how to use the Internet. Pick up trash you see lying on a sidewalk. Start a peer-counseling program to tackle tough issues like suicide and violence. Spend a Sunday afternoon at a senior citizens' home. Walk dogs, socialize cats, or clean kennels at an animal shelter. Bake cookies for families staying at a Ronald McDonald House. Do "virtual volunteering" on the Internet. The possibilities are endless.

You can even take a few minutes to thank our veterans. Every day, almost 187,000 veterans are treated in Veteran's Administration Medical Centers (VAMC) across America. Write letters to them or spend an afternoon visiting. Oh, the stories they can tell. To locate a Veteran's hospital near you, look under *Veteran's Administration* in the government pages of the phone book, call 1-800-827-1000, or check the website, *www.va.gov* and click on "Health Benefits and Services."

What "stuff" can I donate?

Someone once said, *"One man's trash is another man's treasure."* It is so true. Clean your closets and donate the clothes you haven't worn in two years to the Rescue Mission, Salvation Army, Goodwill, or some other organization in your community.

> No one is useless in this world who lightens the burden of it for anyone else.
>
> ~ *Charles Dickens*

Stuffed animals and toys can be donated to local hospitals, police, and fire stations to comfort traumatized children, and children in orphanages and homeless shelters. The Marine Corps Toys for Tots program collects toys for children whose parent(s) can't afford Christmas. You can even donate your old musical instrument to your school for a child who can't afford one.

Give a can of food to your local food bank or Rescue Mission. Donate cat litter, dog food, old blankets and towels, even newspapers, to the animal shelter. Donate old paperbacks to prisons, homeless shelters, or libraries. Donate your old computer to a needy organization. Donate your old cell phone to help domestic violence victims. Donate old furniture to thrift shops that help the needy.

(When you start itemizing your income taxes, you may qualify for a tax break on these donations. Order Pub. 561 from the IRS at *www.irs.gov.*)

What if I don't have any money to donate?

> No man
> was ever
> honored for what
> he received. Honor
> has been awarded for
> what he gave."
> ~ *Calvin Coolidge*

What if I don't have any money?

So, you can't keep up with Microsoft's Bill Gates and the $5 billion in stock he donated to support education and health care programs (in 1999). That's okay. Donating money is a personal decision — based in part on your income. Mr. Gates obviously makes more money than anyone reading this section. He may have even sent a few of you to college. His donation was earmarked to finance 1,000 college scholarships for minority students each year for the next 20 years! That's what giving is all about — giving what you have to help someone else.

Most financial experts suggest you donate 10 percent of your income to charity. That may seem like a lot of money when you're just starting out and don't have much to spare, but don't wait until you land that great, high-paying job. Start donating now. Give five percent of your income — even if that's only $5. Increase the amount as your income increases. Make the amount you give large enough for you to feel good about giving, but not so much that you can't afford to pay your bills. And, each time you make a donation, be grateful that you can.

How often should I give?

Give when you get paid. If you get paid weekly, give weekly. If you get paid monthly, give monthly on the first of each month. Pick a charity and write a check to that charity each month — even if it's only for a few dollars. Whatever frequency and amount you choose, stick to it. Treat it as a celebration! Be proud that you are able to give back.

Should I give cash for a donation?

Don't give cash. Pay by check and make it out to the organization, not an individual. Keep records of your donations (receipts, cancelled checks, and bank statements). Plan your giving. Each year, pick the charity or charities that you want to give to, then say *"No, thank you."* to any others that ask for donations. And don't feel pressured to give money on the spot. Don't allow a "runner" to pick up a contribution. Don't believe promises that your donation will give you "special treatment." Be wary of organizations that tell you "all the money" is going to the charity.

What does "tax-exempt" mean?

"Tax-exempt" simply means that an organization doesn't have to pay taxes. "Tax-deductible" means the donor (you) can deduct contributions to the organization on your federal income tax return if you itemize deductions. (When your paycheck is higher in a few years, you'll want to learn more about "itemizing deductions.")

How do I donate blood?

Are blood donations really needed?

The need for blood is great. On any given day, approximately 40,000 units of red blood cells are needed by accident victims, people undergoing surgery, and patients receiving treatments for leukemia, cancer, or other diseases. Each year in the United States, there are almost 14 million units of blood donated by nearly eight million volunteer blood donors. That equates to almost 27 million units of blood transfused to 4.5 million patients each year.

Is it healthy for me to donate blood?

Adult males have about 12 pints of blood in their bodies. Adult females have about nine pints. Your body replenishes the fluid lost from donation in 24 hours. The red blood cells that are lost are generally replaced in a few weeks. Blood can be donated once every eight weeks.

Am I eligible to donate blood?

Most blood donors are volunteers and must pass certain criteria, including the following:

1. You must be at least 17 years of age (although some states permit persons younger than 17 to donate blood with a parent's consent);

2. You must be in good health;

3. You must weigh at least 110 pounds; and

4. You must pass the physical and health history examination prior to donation.

Where can I donate blood?

Donating blood is easy, safe, and convenient. To provide easy access, bloodmobiles travel to businesses, high schools, colleges, churches, and community organizations. You can also donate at your community blood center, hospital-based donor center, or the Red Cross. (Check the Yellow Pages under *Blood Banks and Centers*.) Some work places offer blood drives. Call 1-800-GIVE-LIFE for more information.

How do I donate blood?

When you donate blood, you'll be asked to do the following:

- Read educational materials about blood donation and acknowledge in writing that you have read and understand the materials.

- Provide a detailed health history of questions that protect the health of both you and the recipient.

- Have a physical examination that includes checking your blood pressure, pulse, and temperature. A few drops of blood are also taken from your finger or earlobe to ensure you're not anemic (lacking in red blood cells).

- Donate blood, if you pass the above steps. It takes 20 minutes to draw your blood. Typically, one pint of blood is drawn. After it is collected, you are escorted to an observation area for light refreshments and a brief rest period. Your blood is sent to a laboratory for testing and preparation.

The entire process takes about an hour. You may be disqualified from donating blood during any part of the process. You can also choose to leave at any point without donating.

What are blood types?

What's your type? According to the American Association of Blood Banks, the percentage of people who have different blood types in the U.S. are as follows:

38%	Type O Rh-positive	**7%**	Type O Rh-negative
34%	Type A Rh-positive	**6%**	Type A Rh-negative
3%	Type AB Rh-postive	**1%**	Type AB Rh-negative
9%	Type B Rh-positive	**2%**	Type B Rh-negative

People with Type O blood are known as "universal donors" because, in an emergency, anyone can receive Type O red blood cells. People with Type AB blood can receive red blood cells of any ABO type, and are known as "universal recipients."

 ## How do I sign up to be an organ donor?

What is the "gift of life?"

The gift of life is given when your organs and tissues are donated upon your death to someone in need. Did you know that one donor can potentially benefit as many as 50 people? Many organs and tissues can be donated to help others live: eyes, heart, bones, lungs, liver, pancreas, kidney, ligaments, and tendons. Organ donation is a very personal decision, but it must be shared with your family. If something should happen to you, your family will make the final decision, regardless of whether you've signed a donor card or not.

Even if you've signed an organ donor card, you'll receive excellent care in an emergency room. Doctor's don't look at a driver's license before they start treating! And they receive no pay for finding organs that can be trans-

January 5, 2000

Dear Mr. Doperalski:

On behalf of the Midwest Transplant Network, I would like to extend my most sincere sympathy to you and your family on the death of your son, Erek. I hope you can take some comfort in knowing that others' lives may be improved. I would like to share with you the results of your decision to donate.

Our tissue recovery staff recovered grafts of bone and its connective tendons. These grafts will be used in sports medicine reconstructive surgery to repair damaged knee and ankle injuries. These grafts will enable those patients to continue to pursue the activities they love.

Erek's heart was recovered for heart valve transplantation. These valves will provide two individuals with a replacement for their own defective valves. Children under age fifteen are most often the recipients of valve transplants. These children have typically been born with a heart valve defect.

Vein grafts were recovered. They are used for patients undergoing cardiac bypass surgery or those whose circulation within their legs is so poor that, without a vein graft transplant, they might face amputation.

Also, we notified the eye bank of your wish to donate corneal tissue for transplantation. Corneal transplantation literally gives those who are blind the ability to see again

It is only through your generosity that these recipients and their families have a second chance for a healthier future. Your gift will always be remembered. Again, thank you for your decision to donate. If I can be of assistance to you, please do not hesitate to contact me at (785) 625-9149.

Sincerely,

Lisa M. Long, BS
Hospital Services Coordinator

Enclosure

Figure 14B

planted. All identities are confidential. Recipients will not know who do-nated the tissue they receive. Selection is not based on race or ethnic reli-gion, but rather on the medical need of the recipient. There is no cost to you or your family. All costs related to donation are paid for by the agency recovering the organs.

Organ donation is accepted by all religions except one — the gypsies. All other religions have made exceptions to their doctrines to encourage organ donation. Organ and tissue donation does not interfere with a tradi-tional or open-casket funeral. The donor's body is handled with respect and dignity by people specifically trained for tissue recovery.

Call 1-888-4-TISSUE for more information or visit the United Network for Organ Sharing at *www.unos.org*.

What are the facts about organ donation?

- A person can donate all body parts possible (corneas, skin, long bones, internal organs, etc.) and still have an open-casket funeral.

- One body can supply organs to 50 people.

- Even if you've signed your organ donation card, you'll still receive excellent care in the emergency room. Doctors don't look at a dri-ver's license before they start treating! And they receive no pay for finding organs that can be transplanted.

- Organ donation is accepted by all religions except one — the gypsies. All other religions have made exceptions to their doctrines to en-courage organ donation.

- Third World countries sell organs. There are reports that prisoners on death row in China have been executed prematurely to supply organs. It is against the law to sell organs in the United States. All the wild stories that circulate about people waking up in a bathtub full of ice and missing one kidney are untrue. That only happens in the movies.

How do I become a donor?

The use of donated organs and tissues is ultimately a medical decision, but

How do I become a donor?

The use of donated organs and tissues is ultimately a medical decision, but if something should happen to you and your organs are healthy, you can become a donor. Becoming a donor is an easy two-step process: (1) Sign a donor card and/or your driver's license; and (2) Share your decision with your family because next of kin is always asked to consent. Print this donor card from the CD-ROM and sign it in the presence of a witness. Keep it in your purse or wallet. (You can also let your physician and/or clergy know of your wishes.)

Interactive CD-ROM

Print It!

The Promise of a Lifetime Donor Card

I,_____am committed to saving lives through organ and tissue donation. I have spoken to my family about organ and tissue donation and they have signed this card promising to honor my wishes to become a donor if the time comes.

_____
Donor Name   Date

_____
Family/Next of Kin Witness   Date

_____
Family/Next of Kin Witness   Date

This is not a legally-binding contract.

Fold ➤   **◄ Fold**

The Promise of a Lifetime

By donating tissue, your gift will last a lifetime.

In fact, one person can help 50 people who are suffering or dying for want or need of transplants of organs and bone, skin, or other tissue.

Please take a few minutes to sign a donation card and discuss your decision with your family or next of kin.

Figure 14C

if something should happen to you and your organs are healthy, you can become a donor. Becoming a donor is an easy two-step process: (1) Sign a donor card and/or your driver's license; and (2) Share your decision with your family because next of kin is always asked to consent. Print the donor card on the CD-ROM and sign it in the presence of a witness. Keep it in your purse or wallet. (You can also let your physician and/or clergy know of your wishes.)

How do I tell my family?

It takes less than a minute to tell your family you want to donate organs if you should die. Sign the back of your driver's license or a donor card, and then have a quick conversation with your family. Many people think it has to be a big, serious conversation — and put off letting their families know about their decision. Over dinner, say, *"I signed the back of my driver's license because I'd like to donate my organs if I die. Please make sure my wishes are carried through if anything should happen to me."*

If your relatives don't know that you want to donate, *their decision* is what doctors will adhere to — even if you've signed your driver's license.

How have transplants affected the Klein family?

(Contributed by Morgan Chilson)

Linda Klein-Cheatham's life changed forever when she was 11 years old. Her sister, Peggi Klein-Moore, was just 9. Doctors discovered they have a genetic disease that often causes kidney failure. At a young age, Linda and Peggi learned to deal with the realities of having a life-threatening disease — and what a gift life is. As they grew older, they learned another indisputable fact: eight people in their immediate family would be dead if it weren't for organ donations. Linda is one of those eight.

The two sisters discovered that, like other members of their family, they suffer from polycystic kidney disease. A kidney disorder, the disease passes genetically through a family. Linda's family has traced it to her grandfather, which is as far back as medical records go. *"He died in his early 30s of, among other things, kidney failure,"* Linda said. *"Three of his four kids had kidney problems. In my mother's generation, four of six children had it."*

"In my generation, there are four kids, and all four of us have it," Linda said. *"Three of us have had kidney transplants. The fourth child, Peggi, suffered with liver problems. Instead of having a transplant, she had half of her liver removed."*

This disease has changed the Klein family's attitudes about life. *"We're very happy people. You learn not to sweat the small stuff and focus on the people who are important to you,"* Linda said. This disease has also changed what they do with their free time. Linda, in particular, is extremely active in educating the public about organ donation.

On the news, you often see heroes — people who go to extraordinary measures to save someone's life. Linda's family knows of eight heroes: they donated a kidney — ensuring that eight people in their family still get out of bed every morning. These heroes gave the ultimate gift — an organ donation. *"I love every one of the donors, even though I've never met some of them,"* Linda said. *"My donor is Peggi's best friend. My brother's donor is his father-in-law. But my mother's and my sister's kidneys came from unknown donors. It doesn't matter. They're still very special people because they either gave a piece of themselves while they were alive or their grieving families gave something of their loved one."*

Linda and Peggi race a Porsche Boxster with organ donation information plastered all over it. Linda says even driving it to the grocery store gets people talking about organ donation. Both sisters and their family members wear green ribbon pins to signify organ donation — and they take every opportunity to explain the importance of organ donation.

Those family members who have received kidney transplants include the following:

- Linda Cheatham — a kidney from Robin Ward (her "adopted" sister) in 1990.

- Annamae Evers (Linda's mom) — a kidney from a donor family in 1990.

- Patricia Klein (Linda's sister) — a kidney from a donor family in 1995.

- Craig Klein (Linda's brother) — a kidney from Dave Babel (his father-in-law) in 2000.

- Teresa Pfeiffer (Linda's aunt) — a kidney from her brother, Leo Beck, in 1976, and re-transplanted in 1990 with a kidney from her son, Mike Pfeiffer.

Photo courtesy of Peggi Moore

- Ken Pfeiffer (Linda's cousin) — a kidney from her sister, Sharon Mc-Carville, in 2001.

- Paul Klein (Linda's cousin) — a kidney from a donor family in 1989.

- Donald Beck (Linda's cousin) — a kidney from a donor family in 1989.

Anyone with questions about organ donation may e-mail Linda at *linda@cheatham-cpa.com* or visit the United Network for Organ Sharing website at *www.unos.org*. To learn more about the kidney disease the Klein family has inherited, visit *www.pkdcure.org*.

What types of charities are there?

You name it, there's a charity for it. Are you interested in people, animals, health, children, education, the arts, the environment, breast cancer research, hunger relief, tree planting and urban forestry, endangered species, children's literacy, public land conservation, adoption, stray cats, books, computers and technology, disabled people, safety, broadcasting, crisis support, gay rights, justice, politics, or sports? The possibilities for getting involved are endless. Pick a charity to get involved with that focuses on issues that you're passionate about. What do you like doing? Search the Internet, your library, or your phone book for a charity you'd like to be involved in — and make the call to get involved!

How do I know if a charity is bogus?

Don't all charities work for good causes?

Not necessarily. Some charities, unfortunately, work to put money in the pockets of a few people — but not the ones they claim to be helping. Not all charities are what they claim to be. Bogus appeals come in the mail, in person, and over the telephone. What is the charity's full name and address? Is the charity licensed by state and local authorities? Does the name look impressive or closely resemble the name of a well-known organization? Do pitches for your money clearly identify the charity and its programs? Never give cash, instead write a check payable to the official name of the charity (not an individual). Ask questions of the charity before giving your money to its cause.

If you get a request for a donation in the mail, beware of appeals that bring tears to your eyes but tell you nothing about the charity, what it's doing to resolve the problem, or what your donation is used for. Don't respond to any appeals that are in the form of an invoice or bill. This is illegal, and you are under no obligation to pay unless you accept the offer. It's also against the law to demand payment for merchandise you didn't order. For instance, if you receive address labels, stamps, greeting cards, pens, t-shirts, or other trinkets in the mail with an appeal for a donation, you are under no obligation to pay or to return the merchandise.

Donating to local charities is a good way to ensure your donations are used to your satisfaction.

How do I check on a charity?

Before making a donation, call your local Better Business Bureau or visit *www.give.org*. To inquire about national charities, contact the following:

National Charities Information Bureau
19 Union Square West
New York, NY 10003
www.give.org

Council of Better Business Bureaus, Inc.
Philanthropic Advisory Service
4200 Wilson Blvd., Suite 800
Arlington, VA 22203-1838
703-276-0100
www.bbb.org

American Institute of Philanthropy
4579 Laclede Avenue, Dept. 15
St. Louis, MO 64108
212-929-6300
www.nonprofits.org

If you suspect a charity fraud, contact your local attorney general. Also contact the Federal Trade Commission's Consumer Response Center at 1-877-FTC-HELP or complete an on-line complaint form at *www.ftc.gov.*

 ## Additional Information for this Chapter

Books

- *The Giving Tree* by Shel Silverstein

- *Heaven on Earth* by Danny Seo

- *The Rainbow Fish* by Marcus Pfister

- *Start Something: You Can Make a Difference* by Earl Woods and the Tiger Woods Foundation

> It is one of the most beautiful compensations of life that no man can sincerely try to help another without helping himself.
>
> *~ Ralph Waldo Emerson*

Web Links

- *www.give.org*

- *www.americaspromise.org*

- *www.volunteers.com*

- *www.irs.gov*

- *www.givingback.org/ GIVINGBACK/*

- *www.idealist.org*

- *www.youthventure.org/home.asp*

- *www.startsomething.target.com*

- www.unitedway.com

- www.shareyourlife.org

- www.child.net/volunteer.htm

- www.redcross.org

- www.glassslipperproject.org

- www.trioweb.org

- www.nonprofits.org

- www.unos.org

- www.transweb.org

- www.trio-ncac.org

- www.donateaphone.com

- www.bbb.org
  (Better Business Bureau)

- www.va.gov

- www.kidneywdc.org

- www.passitonforlife.org

- www.organdonor.gov

- www.pkdcure.org

- www.thankscompany.com

- www.FreeStockPhotos.com

- www.usaaedfoundation.org

- www.mybloodyourblood.org

- www.SERVEnet.org

A Rainy Night in New Orleans

It was a rainy night in New Orleans.
At a bus station in the town,
I watched a young girl weeping
As her baggage was taken down.

It seems she'd lost her ticket
Changing buses in the night.
She begged them not to leave her there
With no sign of help in sight.

The bus driver had a face of stone
And his heart was surely the same.
"Losing your ticket's like losing cash
   money," he said
And left her in the rain.

Then a young man stood up
And blocked the driver's way.
He would not let the driver pass
Before he said what he had to say.

"How can you leave that girl out there?
Have you no God to fear?
You know she had a ticket.
You can't just leave her here.

"You can't put her out in a city
Where she doesn't have a friend.
Yes, you'll meet your schedule,
But she might meet her end."

The driver showed no sign
That he heard or even cared
About the young girl's problem
Or how her travels fared.

So the young man said,
"For her fare I'll pay.
I'll give her a little money
To help her on her way."

He went and bought the ticket
And helped her to her place.
He helped her put her baggage
In the overhead luggage space.

"How can I repay you," she said.
"The kindness you've shown tonight?
We're stangers who won't meet again.
A mere 'thank you' doesn't seem right."

He said, "What goes around comes around.
This I've learned with time.
What you give, you always get back.
What you sow, you reap in kind.

"Always be helpful to others
And give what you can spare.
For by being kind to strangers,
We help angels unaware."

~ Author Unknown

Am I ready to own a car?

Owning a car is a big responsibility — and a big expense. Answer the following statements as True or False to determine how much you know about car ownership, maintenance, and safe driving.

Interactive CD-ROM

Quiz

True   False

○	○	1.	If I lease a car, I can drive it as many miles as I want with no penalties.
○	○	2.	If I buy a car "As Is," the dealer will fix any major problems the car has.
○	○	3.	If I test-drive a car I want to buy, I don't need to have a mechanic inspect it.
○	○	4.	I don't have to pay sales tax when I buy a car from an individual.
○	○	5.	If I total my car in a wreck, I don't have to finish paying off the loan.
○	○	6.	Females pay more for insurance than males.
○	○	7.	Insurance companies don't offer discounts on car insurance.
○	○	8.	If I have an accident in a parking lot, I don't need to get the other driver's insurance information.
○	○	9.	If I see a leak under my car, it's probably just the air conditioning and is nothing to be concerned about.
○	○	10.	Screeching brakes are normal as cars age and don't need to be checked by a mechanic.
○	○	11.	More people are killed by violent crimes than in traffic accidents.
○	○	12.	It is just as safe to drive with friends in the car as it is to drive alone.
○	○	13.	I have to slow down for emergency vehicles, but I don't have to stop.
○	○	14.	"Blind spots" are places in the road where you can't see on-coming traffic.
○	○	15.	Few accidents occur because the other car was in the driver's "blind spot."
○	○	16.	I should drive beside or close behind semi trucks to block the wind and increase my gas mileage.
○	○	17.	Being tired does not make me an unsafe driver.
○	○	18.	People are killed by trains only at crossings with no control lights, gates, or bells.
○	○	19.	If a tire blows out, I should immediately step on the brakes.
○	○	20.	If I begin hydroplaning, I should immediately step on the brakes.
○	○	21.	If I'm the driver, I can't be charged with homicide or manslaughter if someone dies in an accident that was my fault.
○	○	22.	If another driver cuts me off, it isn't road rage if I make a rude hand gesture.
○	○	23.	Most car thefts occur in business districts and parking lots.
○	○	24.	I just need to keep the outside of my car windows clean in the winter.
○	○	25.	If I have an accident, the police will contact my insurance company.

SCORE   All answers are false, so if you scored …

26 to 30 points   You passed driver's ed. Good luck on being a car owner.
16 to 25 points   Were you sleeping in class? Or did you miss that day? Read the chapter!
0 to 15 points   You better take the bus! And read the chapter if you want to own a car.

Car
Ownership

Sure, you've been driving since you were 16 years old. But were you always paying insurance? And what do all those abbreviations on that insurance form really mean, anyway? When's the last time you changed your oil or rotated your tires? There's a lot more to owning and operating a vehicle than remembering to put gas in the tank. Make sure you know the basics in car maintenance!

Chapter 15

(The word "car" is used in this section, but implies any type of vehicle: car,

truck, SUV, motorcycle.)

 ## How do I buy a car?

Should I buy a new or used car?

Almost 75 percent of all cars purchased each year are used. Before you start shopping for a car, you need to do some homework. Spending a little time now may save you a lot of money later. Think about your driving habits, your needs, and your budget. Learn about car models, options, and

Should I buy or lease a car?

Buying or leasing a car is a personal — and financial — choice. The following chart shows the differences between buying and leasing:

	Buying	Leasing
Ownership	You own the vehicle and get to keep it at the end of the financing term (when the loan is paid off).	You do not own the vehicle. You get to use it but you must return it at the end of the lease unless you choose to buy it.
Up-front Costs	Include the cash price or a down-payment, taxes, registration and other fees, and charges.	May include the first month's payment, a refundable security deposit, a capitalized cost reduction (like a down-payment), taxes, registration and other fees/charges.
Monthly Payments	Monthly loan payments are usually higher than monthly lease payments because you are paying for the entire purchase price of the car, plus interest and other finance charges, taxes, and fees.	Monthly lease payments are usually lower than monthly loan payments because you are paying only for the car's depreciation during the lease term, plus rent charges (like interest), taxes, and fees.
Early Termination	You are responsible for any pay-off amount if you end the loan early.	You are responsible for any early termination charges if you end the lease early.
Vehicle Return	You may have to sell or trade the car when you decide you want a different car.	You may return the car at lease end, pay any end-of-lease costs, and walk away.
Future Value	You have the risk of the car's market value when you trade or sell it.	The lessor has the risk of future market value of the car.
Mileage	You may drive as many miles as you want, but higher mileage will lower the car's trade-in or resale value.	Most leases limit the number of miles you may drive (often 12,000 to 15,000 miles per year). You can negotiate a higher mileage limit and pay a higher monthly payment. You will likely have to pay charges for exceeding those limits if you return the car.
Excess Wear	There are no limits for excessive wear to the car, but excessive wear will lower the car's trade-in or resale value.	Most leases limit wear to the car during the lease term. You will likely have to pay extra charges for exceeding those limits if you return the car.
End of Term	At the end of the loan term (usually 36 to 72 months / 3 to 6 years), you have no further loan payments and the car belongs to you.	At the end of the lease (typically 2 to 4 years), you may have a new payment either to finance the purchase of the existing car or to lease another.

Figure 15B

prices by reading newspaper ads, checking out books at the library, or searching the Internet. Once you've narrowed your car choices, research the frequency of repair and maintenance costs on the models you're interested in. This information can be found in consumer magazines or you can call the U.S. Department of Transportation's Auto Safety Hotline at 1-800-424-9393 to get information on recalls. You should also look in the *Kelley Blue Book* or *Edmund's* to find out a car's current value. Visit *www.kbb.com* or *www.edmunds.com*.

What is a Buyer's Guide?

The Federal Trade Commission's "Used Car Rule" requires dealers to post a **Buyer's Guide** in every used car they offer for sale. The Buyer's Guide must state the following:

- Whether the vehicle is being sold "As Is" or with a warranty.

- What percentage of repair costs a dealer will pay under warranty, if one is given.

- What major mechanical and electrical systems are on the car (including some of the major problems you should look out for).

You have a right to see this warranty before you buy a car. Review it carefully to determine what is covered. When you buy a car from a dealer, get the original (or a copy) of the Buyer's Guide that was posted in your vehicle. The guide *must* have any negotiated changes in warranty coverage that you and the dealer made. It also becomes part of your sales contract and over-rides any contrary provisions. For example, if the Buyer's Guide says the car comes with a warranty and the contract says the car is sold "As Is," the dealer must give you the warranty described in the guide.

What does "As Is" mean on a used car?

"As Is" means there is *no* warranty. The box on the Buyer's Guide that says "As Is — No Warranty must be checked. If the box is checked but the dealer promises to repair the vehicle or cancel the sale if you're not satisfied, get that promise is writing on the Buyer's Guide. If the dealer refuses to write the changes on the guide, you might reconsider buying from that dealer. (About half of all used cars sold each year are sold "As Is.")

Some states, including Connecticut, Kansas, Maine, Maryland, Massachusetts, Minnesota, Mississippi, New Jersey, New York, Rhode Island, Vermont, West Virginia, and the District of Columbia, don't allow "As Is" sales for many used vehicles. Some type of warranty must be given in these states. In Louisiana, New Hampshire, and Washington, if the dealer fails to provide proper state disclosures, the sale is not "As Is." To find out what disclosures are required for "As Is" sales in your state, contact your state Attorney General.

What are full and limited warranties?

Warranties must be written on the warranty section of the Buyer's Guide. Because terms and conditions vary, it may be useful to compare and negotiate warranty coverage. Dealers may offer a full or limited warranty on all or some of a car's systems or components. Most used car warranties are limited and their coverage varies. A full or limited warranty doesn't have to cover the entire car. The dealer may specify that only certain systems are covered. Some parts or systems may be covered by a full warranty; others by a limited warranty. A "full warranty" includes the following conditions and terms:

- Anyone who owns the car during the warranty period is entitled to warranty service.

- Warranty service will be provided free of charge, including such costs as removing and re-installing a covered system.

- You have the choice of replacement or a full refund if, after a reasonable number of tries, the dealer cannot repair the car or a covered system.

- You only have to tell the dealer the warranty service is needed in order to get it, unless the dealer can prove that it is reasonable to require you to do more.

If any of the above statements do not apply to your warranty, you have a "limited" warranty.

What are implied warranties?

Implied warranties are state laws that hold dealers responsible if cars they sell don't meet reasonable quality standards. These obligations are called implied warranties. They are unspoken, unwritten promises from the seller to the buyer. However, dealers in most states can use the words "As Is" or "With All Faults" in written notice to buyers to eliminate implied warranties. There is no specified time period for implied warranties.

The most common type of implied warranty is the warranty of merchantability: The seller promises that the product offered for sale will do what it's supposed to. That a car will run is an example of a warranty of merchantability. This promise applies to the basic functions of a car. It does not cover everything that could go wrong, though. Breakdowns and other problems after the sale don't prove the seller breached the warranty of merchantability. A breach occurs only if the buyer can prove that a defect existed at the time of sale.

Should I buy the service contract?

Like a warranty, a service contract provides repair and/or maintenance for a specified period of time. Warranties are included in the price of the car, but service contracts cost extra and are sold separately. Service contracts should only be purchased if the contract offers protection that begins after your warranty runs out or if potential repairs on the car will cost more than the service contract. Read your warranties carefully before signing a service contract or you may just be handing extra money to the dealer.

Do I need to get dealer promises in writing?

YES! Absolutely YES! If the dealer won't put the offer in writing, you may want to reconsider purchasing a car there. Don't give in to pressure sales tactics. If the dealer says you have to buy the car today because others are looking at it, let the "others" buy it. There's always another car — and a more reputable dealer to buy it from.

> *Spoken promises are hard to enforce.*
> *Get everything in writing.*

Should I test-drive the car?

Absolutely. Test drive the car under varied road conditions — on hills, highways, in town, and in stop-and-go traffic. Examine the car inside and out to see if all the gadgets work. Ask for the car's maintenance record. If the owner doesn't have copies, call the garage where most of the repairs and/or maintenance were done to see if they have a record.

Should I have the car inspected before I buy?

Yes. *Before you buy*, get a **mechanical inspection** done on the car by an independent mechanic. This inspection will determine the overall reliability and/or mechanical condition of the car. While this will cost you some money (around $100 or so), it's better to spend a little bit of money now to find out it's not a good car. Otherwise, you may be spending a lot later when you have problem after problem with the car. If the dealer won't let you drive the car off the lot for an inspection, ask if the dealer will take the car to the inspection facility you designate. (You will still have to pay the inspection fee.) Don't let the dealer pick the inspection facility.

Once the car has been inspected, ask the mechanic to provide a written report with a cost estimate for all necessary repairs (if any). Be sure the report includes the make, model, and VIN (Vehicle Identification Number found on a small metal plate on the driver's side dashboard) of the car. Make sure you understand every item on the report. If you decide to make an offer to the dealer after the inspection, you can use the estimated repairs to negotiate the price of the car.

To find a pre-purchase inspection facility, check the yellow pages of the phone book under *Automotive Diagnostic Service* or ask friends and associates for referrals. There are no standards for pre-purchase inspections, so ask what the inspection includes, how long it takes, and what it costs.

What should I know before signing an agreement?

If you do finance, make sure you understand the following aspects of your loan agreement *before* you sign any documents:

- The exact price you're paying for the car (including interest and loan costs).

- The amount you're financing. (The exact price minus your down-payment.)

- The amount of the finance charge. (How much will this credit cost you?)

- The APR (the cost of credit, measured as a yearly rate).

- The number of payments you'll be making (24 months, 36 months, 60 months, etc.).

- The amount of each monthly payment.

- The total sales price (the sum of the monthly payments plus the down payment).

Dealers, lenders, and banks/credit unions offer a variety of loan terms and payment schedules. Shop around and compare offers. Negotiate the best deal you can. Be cautious of advertisements offering financing to first-time buyers or to people with bad credit. These offers often require a large down-payment and a high APR. And keep in mind that if you have bad credit, no car dealer in the world can repair your credit for you. He can, however, make a lot of money from you. If you agree to financing that carries a high APR, you may be taking a big risk and jeopardizing your credit rating even further.

What if I buy from a person, not a dealer?

Buying a car from a private party is very different from buying a car from a dealer. Private sellers generally are not covered by the "Used Car Rule" and don't have to use the Buyer's Guide. You can have the car inspected before buying. Private sales usually are *not* covered by the implied warranties of state law. That means a private sale probably will be on an "As Is" basis, unless your purchase agreement with the seller specifically states otherwise. If you have a written contract, the seller must live up to the promises stated in the contract. Most private sellers, however, don't use contracts. If the car has a warranty or service contract, is it transferable to you? When you buy from an individual, you buy at your own risk. If something goes wrong with the car after you buy it, the seller is typically not responsible for any repairs or refunds.

How do I pay for a car?

You have two choices for financing a car: (1) You can pay in full or (2) you can finance a loan and pay over time (usually 24 to 60 months, depending on the amount of the loan). When you're first starting out, it might be wise to save your money to pay cash for a used car. If you finance, the total cost of the car increases because you'll also be paying for the cost of the credit (interest and other loan costs). For financing, you'll need to consider the following:

- How much money can you put down on the car (your down-payment)?

- How much can you afford for a monthly payment (and still be able to pay rent, eat, buy insurance, etc.)?

- What is the length of the loan? (The financing company may determine this for you. It's usually a shorter amount of time for a used car loan.)

- What is the APR (annual percentage rate) for the loan? (APRs are usually higher on used cars.)

To calculate loan and/or lease payments, go to *www.autosite.com*. The site has a calculator that figures up payments for you. When figuring out the price of a car, you also need to keep the following in mind:

- What is the cost to insure this car?

- What is the cost to register this car with the state?

- What is the cost to get license plates/tags for this car?

- Do I have to pay sales tax when I buy the car?

- Do I have to pay property tax on the car?

Can I return the car if I don't like it?

Dealers are not required to give you a three-day right to cancel. The right to return the car in a few days for a refund exists only if the dealer grants this privilege to buyers. Before you purchase from a dealer, ask about the return policy, get it in writing, and read it carefully.

If you have a problem that you think is covered by warranty or service contract, follow the instructions to get service. If a dispute arises, there are several steps you can take: First, try to work it out with the dealer. Talk with the salesperson or the owner of the dealership. Many problems can be resolved at this level. However, if you believe you're entitled to service, but the dealer disagrees, you can take other steps:

- Contact the manufacturer who backs your warranty or service contract.

- Contact your local Better Business Bureau, state Attorney General, or the Department of Motor Vehicles to file a complaint.

- You can consider using a dispute resolution organization to arbitrate your disagreement if you and the dealer are willing. (Under your warranty, this may be the first step required before you can sue the dealer.)

- If you bought your car through a franchised dealer, you may be able to seek mediation through the Automotive Consumer Action Program (AUTOCAP).

If none of the above steps are successful, you can sue the dealer in Small Claims Court. There is a limit on the amount of money you can sue for, so check with your county's Small Claims Court. There is also a charge to file the suit, which you would pay when filing. You represent yourself in most Small Claims Courts. No attorneys are allowed.

The Magnuson-Moss Warranty Act may also be helpful. Under this federal law, you can sue based on breach of express warranties, implied warranties, or a service contract. If successful, consumers can recover reasonable attorneys' fees and other court costs. Use this as a last resort and only if you have an expensive problem, otherwise you'll spend more money trying to resolve the problem than getting the car repaired.

For more information on your options, visit the Federal Trade Commission's website at *www.ftc.gov* or contact their Consumer Response Center, Federal Trade Commission, Washington, DC 20580, (202) 326-2222.

What if something happens and my loan isn't paid off?
You're still responsible.

Repossessed Car
This is not something you want to happen! It stays on your credit report for seven years — and makes it hard to get a loan or credit for almost everything else you may need. If you can't make a car payment, call your creditor immediately to discuss other payment options. Many creditors will

work with you if they believe you will be able to pay soon. They may offer to move a payment to the end of your loan (for a small fee), or offer some other solution. (Your creditor does have the right to refuse to accept late payments, though, and may demand that you return the car.) If you default on your loan, laws in most states allow the creditor to repossess your car without letting you know in advance.

You still have to pay the loan if your car is repossessed. Your finance company will try to sell your car to someone else and apply the money from the sale of your car towards your loan. Keep in mind that if you owe more on the loan than the car was sold for, you have to pay the financing company the difference. For example, if your car is repossessed and you still owed $2,000 on the loan; the bank sells the car to someone else for $1,700; you still owe the bank $300.

Wrecked Car

If your car is totaled in an accident, the insurance company will pay fair market value. If you owe more than that on the loan, you will have to pay the financing company, even though the car is totaled. (It's not the bank's fault the car is totaled. It may not be your fault, either, but you are the one responsible for paying the loan in full.)

Can I sell my car before it's paid off?

When you finance a car, both your name and the name of the finance company are listed on the title. Legally, you both own the car. The finance company is listed as the lien-holder — and you cannot sell your car without having the lien-holder sign off on the title. So, if you decide to sell the car before the loan expires, and the amount of money you receive from the sale of the car is less than the amount you still owe on the car loan, you'll have to pay the finance company the difference before the title can be turned over to the new owner.

 ## What car insurance do I need?

What are the types of auto insurance?

Auto insurance is used to protect yourself against expenses you could not otherwise afford due to an accident. If you own a car, you *must* also buy auto insurance. (Requirements vary by state.) When you buy an auto insurance policy, you are actually buying several individual coverages. Each coverage protects you against different types of losses. A brief description of each type of coverage is listed in the charts on pages 516 and 517.

What auto insurance do I have to buy?

Check your state's laws or with your insurance agent to find out which coverages are mandatory in your state. Most states require Bodily Injury Coverage, Property Damage Liability, PIP (Personal Injury Protection), and Uninsured/Under-insured. Optional coverages include Collision and Comprehensive, as well as Towing, Rental Reimbursement, and Excess Medical Payment.

You are charged for each type of insurance, so if you want to purchase Towing, for example, you would have to pay for that coverage. If you have an older car, you may not want to purchase Collision or Comprehensive insurance. They cover damages to your car only, so if the car isn't worth much, you might save your money by purchasing a liability policy only. Talk with your insurance agent about what coverages you need.

> *A good rule of thumb is to buy insurance*
> *only for the losses you can't afford.*

Comparison shop for an insurance company, but make sure you get the right coverages and good service. Take the highest deductibles you can afford in order to lower the price of your premium. Before buying a car, call an agent and ask what it would cost to insure it. That may change your mind quickly about buying that car!

Read your policy. Insurance coverage is very specific. Policies are legal contracts filled with exceptions, exclusions, and limitations. Read and understand what your policy covers.

How are insurance rates determined?

Two factors are considered when determining what you'll pay for auto insurance — underwriting and rating.

Underwriting

When an insurance company considers an application for automobile coverage, it will take into account a number of different factors about you and

Mandatory* Insurance Coverages

Types of Coverage	Pays for ...	Covers ...	Compensates ...
Bodily Injury Liability $25,000/person** $50,000/accident **	Other person's medical expenses, rehabilitation, funeral costs, and other covered costs, if you're at fault in an auto accident. It also pays for settlements of lawsuits and your legal expenses.	You, your family, and others driving your car with your permission.	The other driver and/or driver's passengers; passengers in your car; Injured pedestrians.
Property Damage Liability $10,000/occurrence**	Damage to other person's car or property in an accident. It pays for repairs, replacement, or cash value of the other owner's property. It also pays for your legal expenses.	You, your family, and others driving your car with your permission.	Owners of damaged property who are not members of your household.
Personal Injury Protection (PIP or No-Fault)	Medical expenses, lost wages, rehabilitation, funeral expenses, and in-home assistance for you and your passengers injured in an accident, regardless of who is at fault. Passengers who own their own cars collect under their policies.	You, your family, and passengers.	You and your family. (Passengers use their own insurance if they own a car.)
Uninsured / Under-insured Motorist Protection	You or your passengers for medical, rehabilitation, and funeral costs. It also pays settlements of lawsuits resulting from an accident caused by an uninsured, under-insured, or hit-and-run motorist. You and your family are covered as pedestrians or when riding your bike.	You, your family, and others driving your car with your permission.	You and your family while riding in a car or pedestrians.

* Check your state's laws or with your insurance agent to find out which coverages are mandatory in your state.
** Higher limits are available.

Figure 15C

Optional Insurance Coverages

Types of Coverage	Pays for ...	Covers ...	Compensates ...
Collision	Repair of your car in a collision or rollover, regardless of who was at fault. If your car is totaled, it pays for replacement of your car at current market value, minus the deductible.	Your car, regardless of driver.	You and your family.
Comprehensive	Repair of auto damage caused by windstorm, flood, fire, hail, vandalism, hitting an animal, and some other events. If your car (or any part of your car) is stolen, the company will replace your car (or the stolen parts) at current market value, minus the deductible.	Your car.	You and your family.
Towing and Labor	Towing after an accident or if your car breaks down.	You and your family.	You and your family.
Rental Reimbursement	Rental costs incurred while your car is being repaired after an accident.	You and your family.	You and your family.
Excess Medical Payment	Necessary medical services over and above those paid under PIP coverage for injuries to you or your passengers.	You and your family.	You and your family.

Figure 15D

your driving habits. This process is called underwriting. Each company has its own rules for deciding whether to insure a person. The following factors may influence your auto insurance premiums:

- Your driving record. Drivers with accidents or tickets in the past three to five years will pay more for insurance.

- Where you live. Urban areas have higher rates than rural areas because of busy traffic, thefts, vandalism, and such.

- Your car. Rates reflect the cost of your car when new and how much it would cost to repair or replace it. Some cars damage easily, are expensive to repair, or are high-theft.

- How you use your car. Rates are higher for cars driven to work or used in business than for cars used only for errands and pleasure trips.

- Your gender and age. Males, especially those aged 16 to 35, will pay more for insurance than females because statistics show that age group has more accidents. Unfortunately, even if you're a skilled 20-year-old male driver with no tickets, accidents, or other blemishes on your record, you still pay a higher rate. That's just the way it is.

- Prior insurance coverage. Have you been cancelled or non-renewed from another insurance company? Don't withhold this from an insurance company. They will find out.

- Lifestyle characteristics. Insurance companies also consider your marital status, employment history, and credit rating when determining your rates.

Ratings
After the underwriting process is complete, the insurance company will place you in one of three basic categories of drivers. Those with the lowest risk factors will receive the lowest premium because they are the least likely to file a claim.

- Preferred. Preferred drivers are considered to be the safest drivers with the lowest risk. They have a clean driving record.

● Standard. Standard drivers are a moderate risk and usually drive family-type cars. They have a reasonably clean driving record.

● Non-Standard. Non-standard drivers are considered high-risk. These drivers might include young drivers (under age 25), drivers with little experience, drivers with tickets or accidents, drivers with a poor payment history, and drivers with a reckless or drunk-driving history.

Can I get discounts on my insurance?

By qualifying for certain discounts, you may be able to lower your insurance premium. Ask your agent for available discounts. Some of the common discounts include the following:

● Two or more cars on a policy.

● Motor Vehicle Accident Prevention Course.

● Driver Education Course (teenage drivers).

● Good Student (high school/college students under age 25 who earn a B grade point average or better).

● Airbags, anti-lock brakes, daytime driving lights, alarms, and other safety devices.

● Anti-theft devices.

● Low mileage (if you don't drive very many miles each year).

● Carpooler.

● Clean driving record after a few years.

● Accident-free record.

● Auto/Home/Rental insurance with the same company.

What if my insurance payment is late?

Payment for your insurance *must be received* by the insurance company *on or before* the due date. Allow enough time to mail the payment.

> *There is no grace period for payment of an auto insurance premium. If your premium isn't paid by the due date, your policy expires at midnight on that date.*

Can my insurance company cancel my policy?

An insurance company can terminate your policy, but only under certain circumstances. Coverage may be cancelled or non-renewed. Cancellation means the company terminates your policy before it expires. Non-renewal means the company refuses to renew your policy when it expires. Most states require insurance companies to give you a 30-day notice — which means you have 30 days to find a new company to insure your car . Laws vary by state, so contact your State Insurance Commissioner for more information. (The number is in the government pages of the phone book.)

Should I keep proof of insurance in my car?

Yes. State laws require you to carry proof of insurance. Most insurance companies will send you a card or statement verifying that your car is insured for a six-month period. Keep a copy of this in your glove box. You'll need it if you're in an accident. You might also need it if you get stopped for a traffic violation.

What if my stereo is stolen from my car?

Insurance companies will only cover the following types of electronic equipment under Comprehensive coverage: stereo equipment that is permanently installed in the opening of the dashboard or console for which the equipment was designed (factory-installed); and electronic equipment that is necessary for the normal operation or monitoring of the car's operating system. (If you do not carry Comprehensive coverage, your insurance will not cover these items.) If you carry rental or homeowners insurance, you may be able to file a claim for other items stolen from your car on that policy.

What if I'm in an accident?

Being in an accident can leave you feeling confused, shaken, and possibly even angry or scared. Yet, if you are not injured, there are some things that you should do at the scene of serious accidents to help get your claim processed quickly and accurately.

1. Stay calm. Stop your car in a safe place. Turn off the ignition. Get out of the car carefully. Check for injuries and administer needed first aid. Don't try to move an injured person.

2. Call 911 immediately. If there are injuries, ask that medical help be sent.

3. If possible, move your car to a safer place to prevent additional accidents and further damage to your car. If your car cannot be moved, turn on your hazard lights and ask the investigating officer to set up flares until the car can be towed.

4. If another car was involved, write down the car's year, make, model, and license plate number. Get the driver's name, address, phone number, and the name of the insurance company. If the driver doesn't own the car, get the name of the car's owner. Also get the names of any passengers in the car and any witnesses. Give the other driver your same information. (You are required by law to give insurance information, but if the other driver is irate, don't give him your address or phone number.)

5. Write down the names and badge numbers of any police officers and other emergency personnel at the scene. Ask the officer how to obtain a copy of the police report for your insurance claim.

6. If you think the other driver was under the influence of alcohol or drugs, insist that the investigating officer give a breath test to you and the other driver.

7. Cooperate with the police and others involved, but don't apologize for or acknowledge causing the accident in any way. You may be required to say what insurance coverages you have, but don't say how much insurance you carry.

8. If the other driver takes responsibility for the accident, don't accept any money he/she may offer you. By accepting money, you give up

your right to file a claim against the other driver, even if the damages turn out to be more extensive than you first thought.

9. Never agree to forget about an accident, even if there appears to be no damage. You may find out later that there were actually hidden damages or injuries. You may even find out the other person has filed a lawsuit against you.

10. Write down your version of what happened. Include all details: time of day, weather, hazards, road conditions, driving speed, number of cars involved. Draw a rough diagram of the accident scene, showing stop signs, traffic signals, warning signs, etc. Note any pre-existing damage on other cars. If a camera is available, take pictures showing damage to all cars involved, position of cars, skid marks, and anything else that documents what happened. Make copies of the pictures. Send one copy to your insurance agent.

11. Notify your insurance agent as soon as possible.

For accidents in parking lots, many police will not respond. Instead, the drivers are to exchange information and let the insurance companies resolve it.

How do I file a claim?

Contact your insurance agent or company about any accident, regardless of who is at fault. Notify the agent or company while the details are fresh in your mind. If you report a claim by telephone, follow up in writing. Cooperate with the company's investigation. The agent or company's representative will inform you of what steps to take. You might need to get estimates from local repair shops or a company representative may come to you to estimate the damages. If the other person is responsible for damages to your car or other property, you'll need to contact the other person's insurance company to file a claim. (Sometimes your own insurance company will handle this task. Ask your agent.)

The insurance company has 30 days to investigate your claim, or they must provide a reasonable explanation for delay. (It's in the best interest of the insurance company to investigate promptly so that valuable evidence is not lost or destroyed.) Insurance companies do not, however, have to pay your claim within a certain period of time.

Under the terms of the insurance policy, the insurance company, not you, has the right to decide whether to repair, replace, or issue cash for a damaged auto.

If you suffer any injuries and own an insured car, you should notify your own insurance company. Your PIP (Personal Injury Protection) insurance would pay for any medical expenses incurred by you, regardless of who is at fault. This is true even if you're a passenger and not the driver.

 ## What general maintenance does my car need?

What basic maintenance can I do myself?

A car that's properly taken care of will run more efficiently and last up to 50 percent longer. It will also be safer. Some basic maintenance tips you can do yourself include the following:

Interactive CD-ROM
Movie

- Read your owner's manual. Follow the recommended service schedules.

- Change your oil.

- Wash and wax your car to protect its finish.

- Replace worn wiper blades and fill your washer fluid as needed.

- On your battery, scrape away corrosion from posts and cable connections, clean all surfaces, and retighten connections. (Wear eye protection and gloves if you do this yourself. Batteries have acid in them.)

If you do your own maintenance on motor oil, anti-freeze, coolants, tires, and old batteries, dispose of them properly. Never dump used oil or anti-freeze on the ground, down drains, or in open streams. Look under *Recycling* in the yellow pages of your phone book for hazardous waste sites.

(According to the Automotive Information Council, 20 times the amount of oil spilled by the tanker *Exxon Valdez* in Alaska is improperly dumped into America's environment by do-it-yourselfers each year.)

What basic maintenance should a professional do?

Interactive
CD-ROM

Movie

- Keep your engine tuned up.

- Replace filters and fluids as recommended.

- Keep your air conditioner in top working condition and have it serviced by a technician certified to handle and recycle refrigerants.

- Check your air pressure once a month while your tires are cool.

- Rotate your tires every 5,000 miles, or the recommendation of your owner's manual or tire manufacturer. Don't put tires of different sizes on your car.

- Check your battery. The only accurate way to detect a weak battery is with professional equipment.

- Change your oil as specified in your owner's manual.

- Check the tightness and condition of belts, clamps, and hoses in the engine.

- Your brakes should be inspected if you notice grabbing, pulling to one side, longer stopping distances, or squeaking.

 ## What signs of car trouble should I be aware of?

Are there specific warning signs?

You know your car better than anyone else. You drive it everyday. You know how it sounds and how it feels when everything is running right. Don't ignore the warning signs or you can do serious (and expensive) damage to your car. If you notice any of these signs, tell your mechanic when and how the problem occurred:

- Unusual sounds, odors, drips, leaks, smoke, warning lights, or gauge readings.

● Changes in acceleration, engine performance, gas mileage, or fluid levels.

● Worn tires, belts, or hoses.

● Problems in handling, braking, steering, or vibrations.

What are common car problems?

The most common car problems include the following:

Vibrating Brakes

If your brakes vibrate, it's often a sign of a warped rotor (the metal disk that brake pads push against to stop your car). If your car shakes each time you brake, your brakes are no longer working efficiently and need to be replaced. If you have anti-lock brakes and shaking only happens when you stop suddenly, it could just be your brakes working the way they're supposed to.

Vibrating Steering Wheel

If your steering wheel vibrates or shakes while you're driving, it usually means that your tires aren't balanced. This can lead to uneven wear on your tires. The problem could also be faulty or worn steering suspension components. Check with a mechanic to see if your tires are balanced. If they are, have the mechanic check your steering suspension.

Car Pulling to One Side

If your car is pulling to one side when you drive, your tires may be worn or under-inflated. Your front-end might also be misaligned. If your car pulls when you brake, you might have a faulty brake component. Have your mechanic check it.

Car Making Loud Noise

If your car makes a loud noise while the engine is running, you may have a detached or defective muffler or exhaust system component. If your exhaust system is damaged, it can emit toxic carbon monoxide fumes into your car. Have your mechanic look at it as soon as possible.

Screeching Brakes

If your brakes screech, replace them as soon as possible.

Squealing Engine

If your engine squeals when it's running, it may have a worn or loose belt that needs to be replaced or adjusted. If your engine does squeal, get to a mechanic immediately because most newer-model cars only have one belt, which means you'll be stranded if it breaks. Check belts as recommended in your owner's manual.

Smell of Gas

If you smell gas while you're driving, it could mean that you have a leaking fuel line. This can cause a fire, so park your car and have it towed to a garage.

Steaming Engine

If you have steam coming from your engine, you might have a cracked or detached hose. This can cause your car to overheat and break down. If the engine temperature light on your dash board comes on while you're driving, your engine is already overheating. Pull over immediately and have your car towed.

When do I need a tune-up?

If your car is hard to start, stalls, gets poor gas mileage, runs rough, shakes while idling, and/or has poor engine performance, it may be time for a tune-up. Recommended tune-ups on air filters, fuel filters, valves, and certain ignition parts are every 15,000 to 20,000 miles. Spark plugs might need tuned up every 30,000 to 60,000 miles. Check your owner's manual or ask your mechanic.

 How do I find a good mechanic?

How do I find a good mechanic?

Start shopping for a good mechanic before you need one. Ask friends and associates for recommendations. Your car can be repaired at a car dealership, service station, independent garage, specialty shop (like a muffler shop), a national franchise (like Jiffy Lube), or by the guy next door.

Before letting anyone work on your car, go check out the shop. Are the technicians qualified and/or certified? Are conditions orderly? Is the equipment modern? Are policies concerning diagnostic fees, labor rates, payment options, and guarantees posted? Are the cars in the parking lot or those being worked on equal in value to your car? Does the shop handle the make and model of your car? (Some shops specialize in certain cars.) Does the shop handle the kind of repair(s) you need? Is the shop willing to send you to another shop if they can't handle your repair, instead of running up your bill pretending to know how to fix it? How are the technicians paid? Are they paid on commission? If so, your mechanic has an incentive to sell you replacement parts — whether you need them or not.

Are there customer service and/or community involvement awards posted? Is the shop a member of the Better Business Bureau? Does it have AAA-Approved Auto Repair status? Are the rates reasonable? Call several shops to get an idea of reasonable rates.

Routine jobs (relining brakes, oil changes, replacing exhaust systems/mufflers, etc.) can be done for less by specialty shops.

What do I need to tell my mechanic?

Good communication between you and your mechanic is vital. Before taking in your car, answer the following questions: When did the problem occur? Is it constant or periodic? Does it happen when you first start the car or after the car has been running for awhile? Does it happen at all speeds or just when you're driving slow, fast, 30 miles per hour, etc.? Does it happen only when you brake? Does it happen when you shift gears? When did the problem start? Tell your mechanic so the problem can be diagnosed and repaired.

Ask as many questions of your mechanic as you feel necessary. Don't be embarrassed to request definitions of technical terms. Don't rush the mechanic for an immediate diagnosis. Some checks may need to be made before the actual problem can be determined. Ask to be called about the problem, the course of action to fix the problem, and the cost to fix it *before* repairs begin. Keep all of your records and maintenance paperwork. Start a file for "Car Maintenance."

If you're disappointed in the service/rcpair you received, discuss the problem with the service manager. Give the business a chance to resolve the problem. Reputable businesses will make a sincere effort to resolve the issue and keep your business.

Is my mechanic taking me for a ride?

So, you take your car to the shop for routine maintenance — and then get a call saying the mechanic found "something else" while he was under the hood. He may or may not have. Unfortunately, mechanics consistently rank high on the Better Business Bureau's complaint list. Some common tactics are:

1. Your transmission needs an overhaul.

2. Your front-end needs work.

3. It's time for a tune-up.

4. Your battery is dead. If your mechanic finds "something else" that needs repaired, follow these guidelines:

   ● If your car was driving fine on the way to the shop, you probably don't have a problem.

   ● If you can get a sample of what's leaking, take it to another shop for a second opinion.

   ● Check with another garage for a second opinion.

   ● If your car is less than 10 years old, have a diagnostic test run on it for $30 to $70 first. A diagnostic test hooks your car up to a computer to identify any specific malfunctions.

   ● Get written estimates before any work is done.

If the mechanic is honest, he won't have a problem with putting an estimate in writing, giving you a sample, or your getting a second opinion. If he's dishonest, take your business elsewhere.

 ## Any special traffic safety issues?

How serious is traffic safety?

According to the National Safety Council, 17.6 million motorists are involved in car accidents each year. *Every day, drivers in this country kill 120 people and injure 6,300.* Traffic fatalities and personal injury significantly outnumber death and injury caused by violent crime.

- 1 murder every 21 minutes vs. 1 traffic fatality every 13 minutes

- 1 violent crime every 18 seconds vs. 1 traffic injury every 9 seconds

- 1 crime every 2 seconds vs. 1 traffic crash every 5 seconds

- 1 property crime every 3 seconds vs. 1 property damage every 7 seconds

Car crashes are the number one killer of Americans aged 15 to 20 — and have been for decades. In 1999, about 520,000 young adults were injured and more than 4,900 died, according to federal statistics. Alcohol was a factor in more than a third of the deaths. Safety experts say the major distractions that contribute to these deaths include alcohol, drugs, speeding, music, passengers, and cell phones. These young drivers also lack driving experience, so the risk for a crash becomes even greater.

How can I be a better driver?

Northwestern University Traffic Institute offers the following tips to be a better driver:

- Wear a seatbelt at all times. It's the law! It increases your chances of surviving a crash by 50 percent! (Insist that your passengers also wear seatbelts.)

- Slow down. Obey the posted speed limit. Watch for school zones. If conditions warrant, go slower than the speed limit (such as in snow, rain, fog, or heavy traffic).

- Pass with care, especially on two-lane roads. The chance of a head-on collision makes a two-lane highway the most dangerous place to drive.

- Check your rearview mirror every three to five seconds for changing traffic conditions.

- Avoid a crowd. Risk of a fatal crash for teens doubles with two passengers in the car. It doubles again with three.

- Don't drive when you're angry or upset. Strong emotions distract you.

- Turn down the music. Playing loud music may sound great, but it's very distracting. Can you hear the siren behind you? Also, don't change stations or CDs while driving.

- If you see a problem driver (swerving, tailgating, driving wrecklessly), slow down and let him/her pass. If you have a cell phone, get the tag number of the car and call 911. This driver may be an accident waiting to happen — and you could be saving someone's life.

- When passing, make certain you can see pavement between yourself and the other car in your rearview mirror before re-entering the other driver's lane.

- If you have to drive off the road, aim for something soft, like a bush. If you have to hit something hard, strike it with a sideways blow.

- It's the law to pull over for all emergency vehicles, regardless of the direction they're traveling. What if your loved one was inside that ambulance or it was your house on fire?

- Slow down at night and when weather conditions are bad. Avoid driving at night, if possible. Most fatal crashes involving teens happen after 9 p.m. on weeknights and after midnight on weekends.

- Drive with your headlights on in rain, fog, snow, on mountain roads — and at dusk and dawn. Also use your headlights on two-lane highways, which are the deadliest roads to drive on because of the number of head-on collisions.

- On entrance ramps to freeways, remember that highway traffic has the right of way, so maintain proper speed and merge smoothly. Don't pull out slowly in front of traffic.

- Never drink or take drugs and drive. And don't ride with someone who has. Too many people think they can handle driving while impaired. They can't.

Am I a distracted driver?

Driver distraction plays a role in about half of all U.S. auto accidents. Humans have an inability to concentrate on two things at once, so distractions in the car take your attention off driving. Major distractions include talking to a passenger in the car, eating while driving, tuning the radio, adjusting the heat or air conditioner, and talking/dialing a cell phone. When you're behind the wheel of a car, your first priority is driving — and nothing else.

Why should I wear my seatbelt?

First, because it's the law. And, second, because it really can save your life. According to accident statistics, if you don't wear your seatbelt, you are 25 times more likely to be fatally injured (dead) if you're ejected from the car in an accident. You may be hurled on the pavement, scraped along the ground, or crushed by your car or another one. And all with great force! You can also be thrown into a tree, post, or other roadside object and be fatally injured.

The forces involved in a crash, even at low-speeds, make it impossible for anyone to avoid striking the inside of the car. If you're traveling at 30 miles per hour and weigh 150 pounds, you'll hit the dashboard with a force of 4,500 pounds! Ouch! Also, one in four serious in-car injuries is caused by passengers being thrown against each other.

Insist that all passengers in your car buckle up. It's the law!

How do I adjust my mirrors for blind spots?

More than 63,000 accidents occur each year because of cars being in the driver's "blind spots." By properly adjusting your side-view mirrors, you can reduce the chance of an accident. Here's how:

Driver's Side Mirror

Place the left side of your face against the driver-side window and adjust the mirror so that you can barely see the left side of your car.

Passenger's Side Mirror

Sit in the center of the front seat (or lean as close to the center as possible) and adjust the mirror so you can barely see the right side of your car.

If you adjust your mirrors properly, you won't be able to see either side of your car in the mirrors while sitting in the driver's seat. What you will see are cars approaching from the rear on either side of your car.

Any cell phone safety tips?

Progressive Insurance conducted a survey of people who talk on cell phones while driving. While driving and talking on cell phones …

- 46% have swerved into another lane.

- 21% have cut someone off.

- 18% have nearly hit another car.

- 10% have run a red light.

… and that's just what they're admitting.

If you use a cell phone in the car, follow these important safety tips:

- *Driving is your first responsibility.* Pull over safely on the side of the road to dial and talk.

- Position your phone where it is easy to see and reach. Be familiar with your phone's operation so you're comfortable using it on the road.

- Use the speed-dial feature to program frequently-called numbers.

- When dialing manually, pull over and stop the car.

- Never take notes while driving. Pull off the road to a safe spot.

- Let your voice-mail pick up your calls when it's inconvenient or unsafe to answer the phone.

- Dial 911 or another emergency number to report crimes or other life-threatening emergencies, accidents, or drunk driving. (Emergency calls are free.)

● If you find yourself in a near-accident situation, *drop the phone* and *drive the car*.

Where are the blind spots of big rigs?

Recent studies show that car drivers are responsible for 70 percent of accidents between semi trucks and cars. The Federal Motor Carrier Safety Administration has created a public safety awareness campaign, the *No-Zone Campaign*, to help educate motorists on sharing the road with semi trucks. Here are some *No-Zone* driving tips:

Interactive CD-ROM

Movie

● Be aware not only of the semi truck, but the driver, too. If you can't see the driver in his side mirror, he probably can't see you.

● Be aware of the *No-Zones* on semi trucks where truck drivers are unable to see vehicles: left rear quarter, right front quarter, and directly behind the truck.

● Don't linger when you pass a semi. Use the one-minute rule: Don't drive alongside a truck for more than one minute.

● Don't cut in front of semi trucks. Truck drivers need at least 10 to 20 feet of space between the truck and the car ahead to maneuver safely. What happens if you both have to hit the brakes? At 55 miles an hour, it takes a large truck more than the length of a football field to stop. It takes a car only half that distance.

● Be aware of semi trucks making right turns. Don't try to pass or squeeze by them.

Figure 15E

● Be respectful of truck drivers. They have as much right as you to be on the road. Without them, you wouldn't have any of the things that make up your life: food, entertainment, clothing, your car, toilet paper, McDonalds … the list goes on. Almost everything you buy

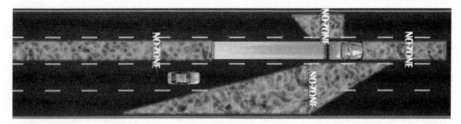

Figure 15F

and/or use is delivered by trucks! Be grateful they're on the road delivering goods to you every day.

Photos courtesy of the Federal Motor Carrier Safety Administration

● Don't change lanes abruptly in front of semi trucks. This is a leading cause of accidents — *caused by you, not the truck driver.* Also, drive as far to the left as possible when passing a truck so the buffeting effect that's created by wind whirling off the truck's wheels can't sway you off course.

● Respect the *No-Zone* behind a semi truck, which can extend as far as 150 to 200 feet from the back of the truck. In addition, drivers of vehicles following too closely behind trucks cannot see what's ahead. If the truck driver brakes suddenly, the car behind has no warning. Following too closely is a major reason for accidents between semi trucks and cars — *caused by you, not the truck driver.* If you're in front of a truck, stay four invisible car lengths in front. That's the minimum distance trucks need to stop.

● Give semi trucks enough room to maneuver. For example, when making a right turn at an intersection, semi trucks typically must pull to the left first so they have room to maneuver the trailer around the corner. When coming to an intersection with a truck in either lane, look at the truck's signal. If he's turning right, allow him room to turn before proceeding. Don't rush up beside him and try to turn in front of him.

● Never cross behind a truck that is backing up. Hundreds of motorists and pedestrians are killed or injured each year behind trucks. Truck drivers do not have a rearview mirror and may not see you crossing behind them.

● Driving inattentively (talking, eating, using a phone, reading, etc.) is another leading cause of accidents with semi trucks. *Driving is your first priority — so pay attention.* Failure to stop or proceeding too soon or too late through a stop sign or stop light are among top reasons for accidents between semi trucks and cars. Remember the driver's education motto: Stop, Look, and Listen.

● Call the *"How's my driving?"* number if you see a truck driver that's not driving safely. Calling the number does work. Fireman's Fund Insurance is so convinced the decals make drivers safer that it offers lower premiums to fleets that use them. Fleets that use the decals have 20 percent fewer accidents. The calls help truck companies spot problem drivers. If you call, answer questions about the incident, including where it happened, what type of vehicle it was, what the weather was like, and if the traffic was light or heavy. You can call the number to give compliments for courteous drivers, too!

Does sleep deprivation affect my driving?

Being sleepy at the wheel can greatly increase your chances of having an accident. The American Trucking Association offers the following danger signals as warnings that you could fall asleep while driving: your eyes close or go out of focus; you don't remember driving the last few miles; you find it hard to keep your head up; you can't stop yawning; your thoughts are wandering and disconnected; you find your speed going up and down; or you frequently drift out of your lane. The following tips can help you stay alert:

● Drive in the daytime. If you have to drive at night, make sure you're well-rested.

● Pull over frequently. Take a break from driving by pulling over in a safe area. Stretch your legs, breathe some fresh air, and take a short nap if you need to.

● Don't tense up. Sore neck and shoulder muscles add to fatigue. Concentrate on relaxing your hands and upper body. Relax your grip on the steering wheel, too.

● Beware of "highway hypnosis." Do you find yourself gazing at the white stripes and road signs? Keep your eyes moving every few seconds by looking in your mirrors and to the sides, then back to the road.

- Keep your car temperature cool. It's easier to nod off in a warm car. Turn on your air conditioner or roll down your window to help you stay alert.

- Take someone with you to talk to and keep you awake.

How can I avoid colliding with a train?

Trains cannot avoid people who get in their way — yet about every two hours, a vehicle or person is hit by a train in the United States, according to *Operation Lifesaver*, a non-profit, nationwide public education program dedicated to reducing crashes, injuries, and fatalities at railroad crossings and along railroad rights-of-way.

According to Federal Railroad Administration statistics, 431 people were killed and 1,303 were seriously injured in 3,508 vehicle-train collisions in 1998. More than half of these crashes happened at crossings that intersect with public roads — and had warning devices such as gates, lights, and bells operating properly at the crossings. Follow these guidelines at railroad crossings:

- Never drive around lowered gates. It is illegal and deadly. If you suspect that a signal is malfunctioning, call your local law enforcement agency, the railroad, or 911.

- Don't get trapped on a crossing. Proceed through a crossing only if you are sure you can cross the entire track safely.

- If your car stalls on the tracks, try to start it only if you can post two lookouts to watch for approaching trains. If you don't have lookouts and/or if you can't get your car started, leave your car and contact your local law enforcement agency immediately for assistance. If a train is coming, get out of your car and run along the right-of-way (beside the tracks) in the direction of the train so you won't be hit by your car after impact.

- When crossing multiple tracks, watch for a second train from either direction.

● Expect a train on the track at any time. Trains do not follow set schedules.

● Trains cannot stop quickly. It can take a mile or more to stop a train once emergency brakes are applied. Because of a train's weight and mass, it's impossible for trains to stop quickly, even at slow speeds. A majority of vehicle-rail crashes occur when the train is traveling less than 30 miles per hour — but it takes almost a mile to stop a 150-car train going that speed.

● Don't misjudge a train's speed and distance. A train's large mass makes it impossible to accurately judge its speed and its distance from you. For comparison, the weight ratio of a car running over a 12-ounce soda can is the same as a train hitting a car.

● Never race a train to the crossing. Even if you tie, you lose. A race to beat a train could be the last race of your life.

For more information, visit *www.oli.org.*

What do I do if my tire blows out?

A blown tire while driving at high speeds is a common cause of accidents. To get your car safely off the road, do the following:

1. Step *off* the accelerator. Allow the car to come to a gradual stop. You risk rolling your car over if you step on the brake and try to stop suddenly.

2. Drive in a straight line with both hands on the steering wheel. Jerking the steering wheel while you try to stop the car can also cause it to roll. Try to steer straight, and if you start to skid, steer in the direction of the skid until you get control.

3. Turn away from oncoming traffic. If you're headed for a collision, aim for something that will give way or steer toward something you can side-swipe to slow the car down.

What about motorcycle safety?

Federal statistics show that 2,472 people were killed in motorcycle accidents in 1999, the largest number since 1991. Motorcycle registrations continue to rise each year. The National Highway Transportation Safety Administration found that 41 percent of motorcyclists who died in crashes were speeding; almost half of those who died in single vehicle crashes were driving under the influence of alcohol; and almost one in six motorcycle riders were driving without a valid license.

The greatest number of deaths are among riders aged 20 to 29. These findings show the importance of rider training, proper licensing, and wearing protective gear (especially helmets).

 ## Can I be charged with vehicular manslaughter?

Just read the headlines:

> **Kansas.** *"Two teenagers wept as they were led from the courtroom, knowing they were facing mandatory life prison sentences for the death of a young couple in a traffic collision that occurred while the teens were fleeing police."*

> **Florida.** *"A 21-year-old man who admitted to running down and killing his friend after a fist fight pleaded no contest in a plea bargain to vehicular homicide. If convicted of the original DUI (Driving Under the Influence) manslaughter charge, he could receive 15 years in prison."*

> **Wisconsin.** *"A 20-year-old faces nine years in prison after he pleaded guilty to involuntary manslaughter, leaving the scene of an accident, and two counts of aggravated vehicular assault. The car he was driving sped from an alley, hit three teens, and then fatally slammed into a 75-year-old homeless man."*

> **Wyoming.** *"A judge signed a warrant charging an 18-year-old with DUI manslaughter and vehicular homicide for the car crash that killed a 15-year-old. If found guilty, he could face a 15-year sentence."*

> **Michigan.** *"A prosecutor and judge pleaded with teenagers to take heed of a tragedy as a 17-year-old teen was*

sentenced to jail for the death of her two friends. When she was 16, she got behind the wheel of a Chevrolet Blazer after spending the afternoon drinking with friends. It was the first day of a new school year."

Texas. *"An 18-year-old driver killed two teens and left three others hospitalized. He was booked at the scene on two counts of vehicular manslaughter, two counts of attempted vehicular manslaughter, and driving under the influence of alcohol."*

Colorado. *"A group of teens on a drunken spree smashed a stolen Jeep into a house, killing a pregnant woman in her bed, police said. Four teenagers were in the Jeep. The two 16-year-olds in the front seat are facing charges of manslaughter, vehicular homicide while drunk, and aggravated theft of a motor vehicle."*

Nevada. *"The driver in a crash that killed two students is back in court, charged with violating her probation. The 17-year-old pleaded guilty to two felony counts of reckless driving in connection with the accident that killed two of her friends."*

California. *"A high school student who sped repeatedly on the same stretch of road until he crashed and killed three classmates and another man was sentenced to eight years in prison. The 19-year-old pleaded guilty to reckless driving and four counts of vehicular manslaughter with gross negligence."*

Louisiana. *"A teenager who pleaded no contest to felony hit-and-run charges in the death of a 71-year-old woman was sentenced to two years for vehicular manslaughter and one year for felony hit-and-run."*

For more information, see Chapter 11, "Alcohol and Drugs."

How can I avoid road rage?

Road rage is very real — and very dangerous. You've seen overly-aggressive, angry drivers. They tailgate, speed, and cut other drivers off. You may even be one of these drivers. How do you keep out of their way or prevent a violent confrontation? Follow these tips:

- Be courteous behind the wheel.

- Honk your horn only when necessary, and with a short honk. Don't honk excessively.

- Move to the right lane after passing. Drive in the left lane to pass only, then move back into the right lane. Don't sit in the left lane for your entire trip.

- Signal before switching lanes. Other drivers can't read your mind, so tell them (with your turn signal/blinker) that you're going to change lanes or make a turn.

- Don't cut people off. When you merge, make sure there's plenty of room. If you accidentally cut someone off, make a gesture of apology (such as a friendly wave).

- Don't gesture your irritation or disapproval. Nothing gets a road-rager angrier than an obscene gesture. Don't even make eye contact. Try to put as much distance between you and the irate driver as you can.

- Keep your cool. An angry driver can't engage you if you refuse to get angry back. When an aggressive driver cuts you off, stay calm, smile, and say, *"Be my guest."* Make it part of your charitable contribution to your community.

- Don't take other drivers' mistakes personally. They have nothing to do with you … Just as your driving errors have nothing to do with anyone else on the road.

- Take up only one parking spot. If your car is that special, park at the end of the parking lot where there are a lot of empty spaces.

- When you get into or out of your car, don't let your door hit the car parked next to you.

- Don't tailgate. Maintain a safe stopping distance behind the car in front of you.

- Use your high-beam headlights only when needed and switch them to low-beam when an on-coming car approaches.

- Turn down your loud music at stoplights so you don't disturb or irritate drivers in nearby cars.

- If harassed by another driver, don't react. Don't accelerate, brake, or swerve suddenly. If the driver continues to harass you, drive to the nearest police station or a place with people. Don't drive home. If you have a cell phone, use it to call 911. Stay in your vehicle and avoid physical confrontation.

- Keep all of your car doors locked at all times.

- Allow plenty of time for every trip.

 ## How can I prevent my car from being stolen?

What are the facts about auto theft?

Nearly one in five stolen cars was left unlocked with the keys in the ignition. Over half of all car thefts occur in residential areas — possibly in your own neighborhood. About one in six robberies involves personal items or stereos being stolen from cars. More than two-thirds of car thefts happen at night. One of every five robberies involves the theft of motor vehicle accessories (stereos, wheels, and expensive options). Professional thieves remove factory identification and dismantle stolen cars so that they're unrecognizable. Good anti-theft devices slow down crime. The longer it takes to steal a car, the more likely a thief will look somewhere else.

How can I prevent my car from being stolen?

Every 19 seconds, someone steals a car in the United States. Auto theft is one of the fastest growing crimes in the nation. In the time it takes you to read this, five cars will be stolen. Guess who pays for replacing these cars at a cost of more than $8 billion a year? You do. We all do through rising insurance premiums. Indirectly, we also pay through higher taxes for police, prosecutors, courts, and jails. Most cars are broken into by amateurs who can be stopped or discouraged rather easily. You can greatly increase your car's protection by taking these precautions:

- Always lock your car, even if you're leaving for only a short time.

- Never leave your car running while unattended (on public or private property). It's against the law.

- Don't leave valuables or shopping bags visible in your car. Radar detectors, packages, radios, laptop computers, gym bags, cameras, and purses can attract attention.

- Always keep your keys with you. Don't leave them in the ignition.

- Roll your windows up completely.

- Park your car in a garage, if possible, and lock both the car and the garage.

- If you have to park on the street, park in well-lit, high-traffic areas.

- Don't leave your car for extended periods in public parking areas, such as shopping centers or airports.

- When possible, park in lots where an attendant is on duty.

- If vandalism or theft occurs from cars in your neighborhood, notify as many neighbors as possible. Neighborhood watch programs really do work.

- If your car is stolen or vandalized, report it to the police and your insurance company immediately.

Does my car need summer/winter care?

What summer care does my car need?

Summer's heat takes a toll on your car, so you should have your air conditioner examined each year by a qualified technician. The number one cause of breakdowns during summer months is over-heating. The cooling system of your car should be completely flushed and refilled every 24 months. The level, condition, and concentration of the coolant should be checked periodically.

What about driving in wet weather?

Traveling too fast for existing conditions on wet roadways can cause your car to hydroplane. Hydroplaning is the build-up of water between the tires and the roadway. Your tires lose contact with the road and ride on the water. The first rain after dry conditions mixes with the oily film buildup on the roadway and can be especially hazardous. Knowing the conditions that cause hydroplaning can help you prevent an accident:

- Water on the road, even a small amount from dew or fog, can create perfect hydroplaning conditions.

- Hydroplaning can occur at any speed, but danger increases with speed.

- Good tread or new tires will reduce your chances of hydroplaning. Save your money to get a good set of tires.

- A lightweight car is more likely to hydroplane than a heavier one.

When hydroplaning conditions exist, take the following precautions to stay in control: turn off your cruise control; follow the tracks of the car in front of you; don't steer, brake, or accelerate abruptly; slow down; and increase your following distance.

If you do hydroplane, remain calm, ease off the gas, avoid the brakes, and steer straight. If you must brake after you've regained control with the road, pump your brakes to avoid skidding or locking your brakes. In cars with anti-lock brakes, keep continuous pressure on the brake pedal.

What winter care does my car need?

A breakdown in the winter can be deadly. So, if you live in a climate that has brutal winters, you can make your travels safer by practicing the following tips:

- Monitor the weather. Check weather forecasts and road reports regularly.

- Travel only when necessary. Leave earlier than you usually do because there may be delays due to slower traffic speeds and collisions. Drivers who are in a hurry only make driving worse for everyone.

- Keep your speed down. Accelerate and brake gently. Make turns slowly, especially at heavily-traveled areas that may become icy from snow that has melted and refrozen. Your tires are less likely to spin when accelerating slowly. Brake by gently pumping on the pedal. If your vehicle has anti-lock brakes (ABS), don't pump them. Learn to use them correctly. Your vehicle owner's manual or car dealership can provide more information. *Steer into a skid*. If your car enters a skid, steer into the direction of the skid. Anticipate a second skid in the opposite direction as the car straightens out.

- Drive defensively. Increase the following distance between your car and the car ahead of you. Ice and snow greatly increase your stopping distances.

- Check your car's fluids. Make sure you've got enough antifreeze in your cooling system. Fill your windshield washer fluid tank. Other fluids that need to be checked include your radiator, transmission, brake, differential, and power steering. Change your oil and filters, if necessary.

- Keep at least a quarter of a tank of gas in your car at all times. It will prevent moisture in the gas tank, reducing the chances of your gas line freezing. It may also keep you warm if you get stuck in traffic or become stranded. Put a bottle of de-icer in your tank once a month to keep moisture from freezing in the fuel line.

- Keep your windshield, windows, mirrors, and lights clean and free of frost, snow, and ice. Visibility both *from* and *of* your car is very important. Use headlights when visibility is limited and wash with a wet rag. (Dry rags will scratch.) Carry an ice scraper in your car. Have good wiper blades for your windshields because they wear quickly in the cold.

● Your tires should have adequate tread for traction. Take a Lincoln-head penny and insert it with Lincoln's head down into the tread of your tire at the most worn part. If you see the top of Lincoln's head, you may need new tires. Tires can also lose pressure during cold weather. Check your inflation pressure frequently in the winter.

● Have your car's exhaust system checked. Small leaks can lead to carbon monoxide entering the car. Small amounts can lead to drowsiness, carbon monoxide poison, and fatal accidents. Also have a mechanic check your belts under the hood.

● Make sure front, rear, and side defrosters and defoggers work properly in your car. Clean the inside car windows. They defrost faster if they're clean.

● Make sure your battery terminals are free of corrosion. If there's a whitish powder on the connections, they need to be cleaned. Consider your battery's age and performance. A weak battery won't be able to start your car in cold weather. Batteries that are four or five years old should be load-tested by a mechanic to measure their strength.

Any winter driving tips?

Temperatures of 25 to 30 degrees are most hazardous because you only get half as much traction on wet snow than you'd get on solidly frozen snow. When the temperature drops below freezing, drivers should be aware of potential danger spots: ice on overpasses, bridges, elevated highways, and drainage culverts. Ice will always form more quickly in these areas.

"Black ice" is clear ice that forms on asphalt roadways and other dark surfaces. It often forms during the early morning as a result of freezing dew or mist during the night. If you encounter a slick spot, don't try to stop too quickly if you're sliding. If the back end of your vehicle is sliding, steer in the same direction as the slide. If the front end is sliding, take your foot off the accelerator. The car will come back into place. To stop on a slick road, put your car in neutral and lightly apply the brakes.

Do I need a winter survival kit in my car?

Just in case you get stranded in winter weather, keep the following items in an old backpack or box in your trunk: traction mats or a few metal coffee cans full of sand or kitty litter to provide traction under your tires if you get stuck; candles and matches or a lighter; blankets; extra winter clothing; gloves; a first aid kit; a flashlight; non-perishable food and a can opener; jumper cables; a red bandana to tie on your antenna if you live in an area that has high snow drifts; a flare or reflective device; a shovel; a tow rope or chain; snow chains (if allowed in your area); and a gallon of drinking water.

 Additional information for this Chapter

Books

- *The Complete Idiot's Guide to Trouble-Free Car Care* by Dan Ramsey and Thomas L. Bryant

- *Consumer Reports New Car Buying Guide*

- *Consumer Reports Used Car Buying Guide*

- *Kelley Blue Book*

- *Lemon-Aid: Car Guide 200x* by Phil Edmonston

- *Peaceful Driver: Steering Clear of Road Rage* by Allen Lyles (Audio CD)

- *Road Rage and Aggressive Driving: Steering Clear of Highway Warfare* by L. James and D. Nahl

- *Road Rage to Road-Wise* by John A. Larson and Carol Rodriguez

Web Links

- *www.pueblo.gsa.gov*

- *http://lemonaidcars.com*

Interactive CD-ROM

Click to the web from the CD-ROM!

Web Resource

- *www.hwysafety.org*

- *www.kbb.com*
  (Kelley Blue Book)

- *www.autosite.com*

- *www.nozone.org*

- *www.edmunds.com*

- *www.itsnotanaccident.com*

- *www.leasesource.com*

- *www.teendriving.com*

- *www.drivehomesafe.com*

- *www.federalreserve.gov/
  pubs/leasing*

- *www.oli.org*
  (Operation Lifesaver /
  Train Safety)

- *www.ftc.gov*
  (Federal Trade Commission)

- *www.acvl.com*
  (Association of Consumer
  Vehicle Lessors)

- *www.nhtsa.dot.gov/cars*
  (National Highway
  Transportation Safety
  Administration)

Am I a responsible citizen?

As an American citizen, you have responsibilities to yourself, fellow Americans, and your country. One of those responsibilities is to vote. Section A covers questions you'll need to know to register to vote. Section B covers topics that are necessary to be a responsible citizen.

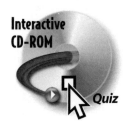

Interactive CD-ROM

Quiz

Section A. Registering to Vote

What city do I live in? _____

What county do I live in? _____

What state do I live in? _____

What country do I live in? _____

What school district do I live in? _____

Am I a Republican, Democrat, or Independent? _____

Yes	No	
○	○	Am I registered to vote?
○	○	If I've moved, have I registered at my new address?
○	○	If I've changed my name, have I registered under my new name?
○	○	Does my vote make a difference?

Section B. Responsibilities as a U.S. Citizen

Yes	No	
○	○	Do I pay taxes?
○	○	Am I loyal to America and proud to be American?
○	○	Am I a responsible family member?
○	○	Do I respect and obey the laws of my community?
○	○	Do I respect the rights and property of others?
○	○	Do I believe in equality for all people?
○	○	Do I respect individual differences and ways of life different from my own?
○	○	Do I take part in my community?
○	○	Do I take an active part in government?
○	○	Am I well-informed on important issues?
○	○	Do I use natural resources wisely?
○	○	If I'm male and 18+ years old, have I registered with Selective Service?
○	○	Do I know the words to the "Pledge of Allegiance?"
○	○	Do I know the words to "The Star-Spangled Banner?"
○	○	Do I honor veterans?

This quiz offers information only — so there is no score. However, if you checked *No* on any answers, you might want to reconsider the choices you're making.

Government

Sometimes it's easy to forget how great our country is as we become embroiled in political scandals or economic woes. But when you get right down to it, there is no better country in the world. Your vote does count, so know how your government works and what to do if you want to make something happen in local, regional, state or national government. Be proud to be an American!

 What are the levels of government?

What are the levels of government?

You live under three levels of government: local, state, and federal. All three work together to provide services and laws. The powers of each level of government are clearly defined by the Constitution of the United States — and all levels of government must obey it.

What does each level do?

Each level of government has its own responsibilities:

Local Government

Local government operates in counties, towns, townships, villages, boroughs, and cities. Local government has authority over the affairs of the community, including schools, police and law enforcement, fire protection, libraries, zoning and building codes, parks and playgrounds, sewage systems, public utilities, health and welfare services, and streets and traffic. Some services, such as electricity and public transportation, may be provided by privately-owned companies. Local government officials include the mayor, city council, sheriff, county clerk, and district attorney, among others.

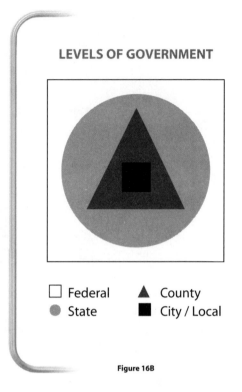

LEVELS OF GOVERNMENT

☐ Federal ▲ County
● State ■ City / Local

Figure 16B

State Government

State government has authority over most affairs within the state's borders, including elections, education, police, public building programs, health and safety, and highways. State government officials include the governor, lieutenant governor, legislators (House of Representatives and Senate), treasurer, auditor, secretary of state, attorney general, director of public health, and superintendent of public instruction.

Federal Government

The Federal government has authority over the entire nation. The work of the federal government is shared among three branches, each with its own responsibilities. The executive, legislative, and judicial branches work together to make the country run smoothly and to assure the rights of citizens are not ignored or disallowed.

- **Executive Branch.** The President is the chief executive officer of the United States and must take an active role in all phases of government. The President approves or vetoes all bills passed by Congress; is commander-in-chief of the U.S. military; keeps Congress informed about the state of the nation and the economy; proposes a "wish list" for the federal government's budget (which is initiated by the House of Representatives); conducts U.S. foreign relations and makes treaties; and can pardon those guilty of crimes against federal law.

There are 14 executive departments in the federal government, with each having specific areas of responsibility. They are the Departments of Agriculture, Commerce, Defense, Education, Energy, Health and Human Services, Housing and Urban Development, Interior, Justice, Labor, State, Transportation, Treasury, and Veteran's Affairs.

- **Legislative Branch.** The U.S. Congress is very powerful. It creates all federal government entities. Its most important responsibility is to make laws. These laws do not simply tell us what we can and cannot do. They determine how high taxes will be, what highways and dams will be built, what military equipment to sell to other nations, and more. They finance government, regulate trade and industry, defend the nation, and declare war and make peace.

- **Judicial Branch.** The judicial branch provides "equal justice under law," which means that all U.S. citizens are considered equal and are guaranteed equal protection by the law. This branch rules on disputes under federal law, and has no jurisdiction over state or local laws.

 What is the court system?

What are federal courts?

The federal court system consists of three main levels: the U.S. Supreme Court, 12 U.S. Courts of Appeals, and 91 district courts. (Each state has at least one district court.) The U.S. Supreme Court is the highest court, and works as an appeals court reviewing cases that have been tried in lower courts. The U.S. Courts of Appeals review cases that are appealed from district courts. There are no jury trials in the Courts of Appeals. The district courts are the base of the federal court system and are the only federal courts in which jury trials are held. They do not hear appeals from other courts.

What are state courts?

The state court system consists of numerous courts, including the State

Supreme Court and State Court of Appeals. District courts are trial courts with general jurisdiction over civil and criminal cases, including divorce and domestic relations, damage lawsuits, probate, guardianships, care of the mentally ill, juvenile and family matters, and small claims. Municipal courts are the lowest level and deal with violations of city ordinances committed within the city limits. Cases usually involve traffic and minor offenses. No jury is allowed.

How do I register to vote?

Can I vote when I turn 18?

Three requirements are mandatory to be eligible to vote in any state. You must

If you don't vote, you have no right to complain.

1. be a United States citizen;

2. be at least 18 years old; and

3. be registered to vote.

Many states also have other requirements. For instance, in the State of Kansas, you must

1. be a U.S. citizen;

2. be a Kansas resident;

3. be at least 18 years old on or before the date of an election;

4. not be sentenced to prison for one year or longer (unless civil rights have been restored), or for a crime punishable by death;

5. not claim the right to vote in any other jurisdiction under any other name; and

6. not be excluded from voting due to declared mental incompetence by court of law.

How do I register to vote?

Registration is required before you can vote by completing the National Mail Voter Registration form at any of the following locations: county election offices, driver's license offices, state offices providing public assistance, state offices providing state-funded programs for the disabled, armed forces recruitment offices, and locations designated by the election office. Some states offer registration at public libraries, post offices, unemployment offices, public high schools, and universities. Many private groups, such as the League of Women Voters, also distribute application forms. (For county election offices, look in the government pages of the phone book under *County/Municipal Clerk, Supervisor of Elections,* or *Commissioner/ Board of Elections).*

To register by mail, call or write your county election officer for a form. You cannot register on-line at this time, but you can download the on-line version of the application at *www.fvap.ncr.gov,* print and complete it, and mail it to your local election office. (The following states/territories do not accept the computer-generated version: American Samoa, Delaware, Guam, Louisiana, Mississippi, Nevada, New Mexico, Ohio, Puerto Rico, and the Virgin Islands.)

Registration and deadlines vary by state. (See *www.registervote.com* for state requirements.)

Why wasn't my application processed?

Local election officials may be unable to process registrations because

1. the form was not completed as requested by the applicant's state of residence;

2. the local election official could not determine a voter's eligibilty to vote because the voting residence address was incomplete, incorrect, or illegible;

3. a current mailing address was not provided;

4. the form was not signed and/or dated;

5. the form was illegible (the writing couldn't be read).

Do I need to re-register to vote for each election?

No. Most states have permanent registration. That is, you only have to register once unless you move or change your name. Some states do, however, require you to register again if you failed to vote in any November general election or if you haven't voted in a certain number of elections. Contact your county election office to see if it is necessary to re-register.

Where do I vote?

You vote at "polling places" that are determined by local officials. For the address or location of your specific polling place, contact your county election office.

Who do I vote for?

Vote for the candidate that has a message you agree with. Getting information about candidates and issues has never been easier. Watch the nightly news, read the newspapers, go on-line. Commentators and analysts will examine every statement until there is no question about where a candidate stands on issues. Brochures are usually distributed to voters a few weeks prior to an election also, with the candidates, issues, and polling places listed.

What is voted on?

Your vote will help determine who the nation's leaders will be and how billions of dollars will be spent on programs and policies. Federal offices that are voted on include the President and Vice President, House of Representatives, and Senators. State offices include the Governor and Lieutenant Governor, Attorney General, Treasurer, Commissioner of Insurance, and Secretary of State. Local offices include a mayor, state representatives, city offices, and county offices. Local issues are also voted on, including sales taxes, road improvements, and school issues.

What if I'm out of town on Election Day?

If you are out of your voting district on Election Day, you can still vote. Request an *Absentee Ballot* from your county election office. By completing and returning the application, you can have your ballot mailed to you starting 20 days before an election. You may then vote by mail or in person at the county election office starting the Tuesday before Election Day, or up to 20 days before the election, depending on your county's rules.

Does my vote really make a difference?

The most common reason for not voting is a person's belief that his or her vote will not make a difference in the outcome of the election. Every American who is eligible to vote has a responsibility — and an opportunity — to make history. One vote really does count. Here are a few examples of the power of one:

- One vote made the difference in the election of three presidents, Thomas Jefferson, John Quincy Adams, and Rutherford B. Hayes. The man who cast the deciding Electoral vote for Hayes was elected himself by only one vote.

- One vote brought statehood to California, Idaho, Oregon, Texas, and Washington.

- In 1868, President Andrew Johnson escaped impeachment by one vote.

- In 1920, one vote ratified the 19th Amendment, giving women the right to vote.

- 1n 1923, Adolph Hitler was elected as the Nazi party leader by one vote.

- John F. Kennedy would have lost the Presidency in 1960 to Richard M. Nixon if just one voter from each precinct in Illinois had voted differently.

- In 1994, republican Randall Luthi tied with independent candidate Larry Call for a seat in the Wyoming House of Representatives. A recount verified the tallies were correct. The Governor declared Luthi the winner after a ping-pong ball with Luthi's name on it was drawn out of a cowboy hat.

What is the Electoral College?

What is a primary election?

Primary elections are used for almost all elected offices — federal, state, and local. The primary election takes place first and is usually held in the spring. It allows voters to choose the candidates from each party who will run for public office in the later general election.

What is a general election?

The general election is used for almost all elected offices — federal, state, and local. During a Presidential election, when you cast a vote in the general (or popular) election, you are not voting directly for an individual Presidential candidate. Instead, voters in each state actually cast their votes for a group of people, known as electors. These electors are part of the Electoral College and are supposed to vote for their state's preferred candidate. General elections are held the first Tuesday following the first Monday in November. Presidential elections take place every four years. Congressional elections take place every two years.

What is the Electoral College?

The Electoral College only applies during a U.S. Presidential election. In the Electoral College system, each state gets a certain number of electors, based on its population. Each elector gets one electoral vote. For example, a large state like California gets 54 electoral votes, while Rhode Island gets only four. All together, there are 538 Electoral votes. In December, following the general election, the electors cast their votes. The votes are counted on January 6th, and the Presidential candidate who gets more than half (270 votes) wins the election. The President-elect and Vice President-elect take the oath of office and are inaugurated two weeks later, on January 20th.

In a Presidential election, voters cast ballots for 538 electors, not directly for President. A candidate has to win a majority of Electoral votes, not a majority of popular votes, to become President. Electors are expected to cast their ballots as decided by their state's voters, the popular vote.

 Am I a Republican or a Democrat?

What are political parties?

Political parties are an important part of the American democratic process. A political party is an organization made up of citizens who have similar ideas on public issues and who work together to put ideas into effect through government action. To achieve their purposes, political parties encourage voters to elect those officials favored by the party to public office. Parties also work to have laws passed that they favor.

The two main parties are Republican and Democrat, and are voluntary. You may declare a party when you register to vote, or you may sign a declaration at the voting place the first time you vote in a primary election. You are free to join the party of your choice. Citizens usually join a party because they agree with most of that party's ideas. (Of course, not all members of a political party agree on every issue.) Joining a political party is not a requirement to vote, so you can also choose not to affiliate with any party.

What is a Republican?

The *Merriam-Webster Dictionary* defines a Republican as one who favors a restricted governmental role in economic life. The Republican party is often called the G.O.P., which stands for Grand Old Party (a nickname Republicans gave their party in 1880). Go to *www.rnc.org* for more information.

> In this world, nothing is certain but death and taxes.
>
> ~ *Benjamin Franklin*

What is a Democrat?

The *Merriam-Webster Dictionary* defines a Democrat as one who practices social equality. Go to *www.democrats.org* for more information.

Are there other parties I can join?

There are many smaller political parties you can join. Two of the more common ones include the Green Party and the Libertarian Party, and are included on many state ballot forms. For more information, go to *www.greenparty.org* or *www.lp.org*.

Why do I have to pay taxes?

Why do I have to pay taxes?

You *have* to pay taxes to raise money so the government can provide the services you want. Your tax dollars (raised by many different means) are used to pay for police, fire and rescue squads; court systems; armed forces;

food, beverage, and drug inspections; health departments; public schools and libraries; building and maintenance of roads and highways; conservation of wildlife, forests, and natural resources; and emergency relief and aid for droughts, floods, and other natural disasters. (A large portion of tax dollars pays for welfare, disability, social security, and education.)

What taxes do I have to pay?

Individual income taxes are paid on the money you earn. These taxes can include federal, state, and local income taxes. Federal taxes include income taxes, Social Security taxes, and Medicare taxes — and everyone has to pay them. State and local taxes are determined by voters — and are different in each city and state. Many cities and states also require you to pay sales taxes, property taxes, and motor vehicle registrations. Some states require sales taxes on everything but food items, and some states have no sales tax at all. Estate, inheritance, and gift taxes are also collected by the government.

 ## What are my civic responsibilities as a U.S. citizen?

As a U.S. citizen, you are expected to do the following:

- Be loyal to America and proud of its accomplishments.

- Be a responsible family member.

- Vote. By voting, you have a voice in government.

- Pay your income taxes and other taxes honestly and on time.

- Respect and obey the laws of the community, state, and country.

- Respect the rights and property of others.

- Believe in equality of opportunity for all people.

- Respect individual differences and ways of life different from your own.

- Take part in and improve life in your community.

- Take an active part in government.

- Be well-informed on important issues.

- Use natural resources wisely.

- Serve on a jury, if called.

Who signs up for Selective Service?

Men who are American citizens (regardless of country of residence) are required by law to register with the Selective Service within 30 days of their 18th birthday. Aliens (citizens of other countries) who are permanent residents of the United States are also required to register. Registration forms are available at any Post Office. On-line registration is also available at *www4.sss.gov*. During times of war, any man who is physically able can be called upon to serve in the armed forces. (See Chapter 3, "Have I registered with Selective Service?" for more information.)

What is the **Bill of Rights?**

The *Bill of Rights* consists of 10 amendments that are added to the Constitution to protect certain freedoms and rights, although these are not "absolute" freedoms. There are limits based on the rights of others and on what is good for all.

First Amendment

The First Amendment guarantees you several rights:

- *Freedom of Religion.* Freedom of Religion allows you the right to practice any religion, or none at all.

- *Freedom of Speech.* Freedom of Speech allows you to express your thoughts and ideas, except to injure others. You do not have the right to tell lies or spread false rumors about others, or you may be sued in court for slander.

- *Freedom of the Press.* Freedom of the Press allows newspapers, television, books, magazines, and such to express ideas in writing.

- *Freedom of Assembly.* Freedom of Assembly allows you to hold meetings in a peaceful manner.

Second Amendment

The Second Amendment guarantees the right to keep and bear arms (guns).

Third Amendment

The Third Amendment says you cannot be forced to provide housing to soldiers in peacetime.

Fourth Amendment

The Fourth Amendment protects you from unreasonable searches and seizures. In most cases, you and your property cannot be searched and your property cannot be taken away from you by the government without a search warrant.

Fifth Amendment

The Fifth Amendment protects you if you're accused of a crime. Before you can be brought to trial, you must be formally accused of a crime (indicted) by a grand jury. The grand jury decides if there is enough evidence to go to trial. It protects you from having to testify against yourself (self-incrimination). It protects you from double jeopardy so that you cannot be tried twice for the same crime. It states that you cannot be denied life, liberty, or property without due process of law and that you can only be punished for a crime after receiving a fair trial. It also guarantees the right of eminent domain, which means that the government cannot take your property for public use without paying a fair price for it.

Sixth Amendment

The Sixth Amendment guarantees that if you are accused of a crime, you have the right to a prompt, public trial by a jury. If accused, you must be informed of the crime(s) you are charged with committing. You have the right to hear and question all witnesses against you and to call witnesses to appear in court.

Seventh Amendment

The Seventh Amendment guarantees you the right to have a lawyer if accused of a crime.

Eighth Amendment

The Eighth Amendment states that the court cannot set bail too high. (Bail is the money or property an accused person gives a court to hold as a guarantee that he or she will appear for trial. After the bail is paid, the person can leave jail. The bail is returned to the person after the trial.) It also forbids "cruel and unusual" punishment.

Ninth Amendment

The Ninth Amendment states that you may enjoy many other basic rights that are not listed in the Constitution. The list of these rights is limitless, but a few examples include the freedom to live or travel anywhere in the nation; work at any job for which you qualify; and marry and raise a family.

Tenth Amendment

The Tenth Amendment states that all powers are not expressly given to the federal government. Some powers are reserved for the states or for the people.

What does the U.S. flag symbolize?

What is symbolic about the American flag?

The American flag is a symbol of the nation. The flag has 13 stripes, seven red and six white, which stand for the original 13 American states. The 50 stars represent the states in the nation today. According to the U.S. Department of State, the colors of the flag are also symbolic. Red stands for courage, white for purity and innocence, and blue for justice.

What are the words to the "Pledge of Allegiance?"

The "Pledge of Allegiance" was written in 1892 by Francis Bellamy, a magazine editor.

> *I pledge allegiance to the Flag of the United*
> *States of America and to the Republic for which*
> *it stands, one Nation, under God, indivisible,*
> *with liberty and justice for all.*

The words *"under God"* were added in 1954.

What are the words to "The Star-Spangled Banner?"

Our national anthem, "The Star-Spangled Banner," was written by Francis Scott Key in 1814.

Oh, say, can you see,
by the dawn's early light,
What so proudly we hailed
at the twilight's last gleaming?
Whose broad stripes and bright stars,
thro' the perilous fight;
O'er the ramparts we watched,
were so gallantly streaming.
And the rockets red glare,
the bombs bursting in air,
Gave proof through the night
that our flag was still there.
Oh, say, does that star-spangled banner yet wave
O'er the land of the free
and the home of the brave?

> This will remain the land of the free only so long as it is the home of the brave.
>
> ~ *Elmer Davis*

 ## Why should I honor veterans?

Interactive CD-ROM
Movie

Pause to remember the brave men and women who served our country in the armed forces. Pay tribute to the sacrifices made by all who fought to protect our freedom. Maintaining freedom requires great sacrifice, often including the lives of those who defend it. It is these patriots, the men and women of the U.S. military, who continue to serve and defend the freedoms we cherish. While we can never fully repay the debt we owe to these courageous Americans, we can recognize the price they paid — and honor them for it. Respect their heroism, their love of country, their belief in freedom. (See Chapter 14, "Charities & Giving Back" for ways to say *"thank you"* to our nation's veterans.)

▶ Additional Information for this Chapter

Web Links

Interactive CD-ROM

Click to the web from the CD-ROM!

Web Resource

- *www.firstgov.com*

- *www.fec.gov*
  (Federal Election Commission)

- *www.house.gov*

- *www.sss.gov*
  (Selective Service System)

- *www.info.gov*

- *www.rnc.org*
  (Republican National Committee)

- *www.senate.gov*

- *www.democrats.org*
  (Democratic National Committee)

- *www.dnet.org*
  (Democracy Net)

- *www.lp.org*
  (Libertarian Party)

- *www.greenparty.org*

- *www.registervote.com*

- *www.fvap.ncr.gov*
  (Federal Voting Assistance Program)

- *www.FreeStockPhotos.com*

About the Author

Sally Taylor has been giving advice to adults-in-training for years — helping them help themselves as they struggle into adulthood. She believes that if you don't have the knowledge, you can learn it. She founded Silly Goose Productions, LLC, in 2000 — to provide information to others in an educational, entertaining, and affordable manner. *On My Own:*™ *The Ultimate How-To Guide for Young Adults* is her first book. Her background is in marketing and public relations, with a Master's degree in Management and a Bachelor's degree in Communications and Business Administration. Sally and her husband, Kerry, live in an old stone house in northeast Kansas (the part with hills and trees!) with three cats, Snickers, Texan, and Giggles.

Photo by Kerry Taylor

The Sandbox

A little boy was spending his Saturday morning playing in his sandbox. He had with him his box of cars and trucks, his plastic pail, and a shiny red plastic shovel. In the process of creating roads and tunnels in the soft sand, he discovered a large rock in the middle of the sandbox.

The boy dug around the rock, managing to dislodge it from the dirt. With no little bit of struggle, he pushed and nudged the rock across the sandbox by using his feet. (He was a very small boy and the rock was very huge.) When the boy got the rock to the edge of the sandbox, however, he found that he couldn't roll it up and over the wall.

Determined, the little boy shoveled, pushed, and pried, but every time he thought he had made some progress, the rock tipped and then fell back into the sandbox.

The little boy grunted, struggled, pushed, and shoved. But his only reward was to have the rock roll back, smashing his fingers. Finally he burst into tears in frustration.

All this time the boy's father watched from his living room window as the drama unfolded. At the moment the tears fell, a large shadow fell across the boy and the sandbox. It was the boy's father.

Gently but firmly, the father said, *"Son, why didn't you use all the strength that you had available?"*

Defeated, the boy sobbed back, *"But I did, Daddy! I did! I used all the strength I had!"*

"No, son," said the father kindly, *"you didn't use all the strength you had. You didn't ask me for help."*

With that, the father reached down, picked up the rock, and removed it from the sandbox.

~ Author Unknown

Thank You

Kerry, my husband

First and foremost, thank you, Kerry! Your faith in me is astounding — and I am truly blessed to have you as my husband and my friend! Thank you for believing in me!

And thank you to ...

Giggles, my cat

You are quite the slave-driver ... but a wonderful supervisor ... and an even better distraction. If only I could bottle your purr and sell it! And to Snickers and Texan, who worked even harder than Giggles to distract me ... but what wonderful distractions you are!

Erek, my nephew

It is because of you that I have the courage to take this risk. I know you're watching over me and I am forever grateful. I miss you!

Alisa, my niece

You're my best cheerleader! Thank you for finding all the websites and keeping my spirits up when I was feeling low. I'm so glad you're my niece!

Luke, my nephew

You are such an inspiration to me. Your heart "gets it." And you have taught me as much as I've taught you. Thank you for being so supportive of me ... and for your investment! (I promise to put it back in your college fund!)

Paul, my nephew, and his dog, Bob the Boxer

Thank you for your enthusiasm with this project ... And, yes, to Items 1, 3, and 5 of your proposed contract ... We're still going to have to negotiate the other two! Look out business world!

Mom and Dad

You gave me all the things I needed ...and I am forever grateful! I am as proud of you as you are of me!

Cindy, Tammy, Jimmy, and Lorey, my siblings

Thanks for teaching me about the world. I have learned so much from each of you — and it's a wonderful feeling to know that you're there when I need you. It's really great to be friends with all of you! (And, to Cindy, Mark, and Lorey, thank you for having such terrific children. They have brought so much joy to my life — and I am so lucky to be their aunt! Thank you for sharing them with me!) Debbie, thank you for your continued words of encouragement (and for putting up with Jimmy!) and Randy, thank you for your support (and for putting up with Tammy!). (Oh, and Mark, thank you for being the banker on Luke's and Paul's investments! It will pay off!)

Morgan

Who'd have thought we'd be where we are 13 years after meeting? Isn't it funny how our paths continued to cross over the years ...You've become such a dear friend ... and you've made this project much easier by being such a huge part of it! Thank you!

Alisa C.

You have been my mirror for so many years now. Can you believe it's been 15 years since we met in Japan? You have been the friend I've trusted most ... and you and your family continue bringing joy to my life!

Carla

Remember when we were sitting on your balcony dreaming big ... and you came up with the idea to put the book on CD-ROM? What a great idea! I owe you one! I'm so glad we're friends!

Jordan

I walked into your office with a list of 16 chapters ... and you made me believe this project could be done! Your enthusiasm in contagious ... and

I am forever indebted to you! Thank you for helping make this dream come true! And for becoming such a great friend!

The team at Digital Lagoon: Jordan, Jaime, Julie, Tony, Randall, James, Kevin … and all the others …
You are such a talented group of people — and I feel very fortunate to have this opportunity to work with you. You've taken an idea and turned it into reality … and even better than I could have imagined!

The team at Pneuma Books: Brian, Mike … and the others …
I love the book! It's so much fun! I am in awe of your talents! You, too, have surpassed my expectations for this project!

The proofreaders: Cindy, Kathryn, Morgan, Peggy, and Tammy
Thank you for making this book so much better than I could have done by myself. I marvel at your insightfulness. You ladies are good! Thanks for catching my typos and making such wonderful suggestions. And, thank you for doing it on such short notice …

Linda Vande Garde, MA, LSCSW and Nina Bryhn, M.D.
You two helped save my life. I don't know if I would have made it through Erek's death without your guidance. You are among the finest in your professions — and I am so grateful that I found you. I can never thank you enough.

Max and Carolyn, my in-laws
Thank you for being such great supporters … and for Kerry. After 13 years of marriage, I still don't know how I got so lucky …

Laurie
Thanks for calling to check up on me. Your weekly phone calls just to see how I'm doing really mean a lot to me. I can't wait until we have enough free time to head back to NYC!

Elaine
I still can't believe you wrote that poem, *Ode to an Author*. It's my first acknowledgement that I'm an author. (And it's hysterical! Although, I'm still waiting on the missing item …) Thanks for being such a great friend … and knowing just when to bring chocolate!

Bridget

I have grown so much since we met. And to think we'd have never met if I hadn't shown up in Salt Lake to surprise Kerry. I have learned so much from you — and I treasure our sleepovers! Thanks for continuing to help me "do my best!"

Danny

From the days of pink houses, orange carpets, and spiders in trees, you've been such a dear friend! Thanks for keeping me laughing! And for your faith in me and this project!

Toni

When I was 20, you gave me some really great advice — and my life is better because of that. You have such a kind heart … Thank you for all you've done for me over the years.

The Bunko group: Barb, Nelson, Peggy, Chuck, Morgan, Stan, Laurie, Steve, Patti, and Thom

Thanks for your feedback and support … and great food … and some stress relief! I'm so lucky to have such great friends!

Mary M.

I can't begin to tell you how helpful your inspirational stories and quotes have been to me. You seem to know just when to send them …

Steve Atha

I don't know if you realize it, but you've been a mentor since we started working together years ago. I've learned a lot from you. Thank you for offering your unsolicited advice: *"You already have a head full of good ideas. Trust yours. There's no shortage of good ideas. What's rare is someone who can decide to take action and then go forward and do it."* You and your team at Express Card & Label Co., Inc. are the best!

Tim Hallbom

Thank you for your guidance, patience, expertise — and your kind heart. You have helped me make such huge changes in my life … and I thank you. (And Kerry thanks you, too.)

Diana Halstead and Barb Rollings

Thank you for sharing your heartache over the loss of your sons. I know your pain — and I admire the strength it takes to tell your story. I believe we will make a difference …

Lynn Smith

I'm in awe of your courage to tell your story — and even more so in your ability to overcome so many obstacles in such a young life. One person can make a difference — and you certainly are! I'm looking forward to meeting you in May …

Steve, Becky, Gunther and all at Central Plains Book Manufacturing

Thank you for teaching me about the book industry. I'm still in awe of your willingness to help me. You've made this project much easier … and I look forward to many print runs with you!

Alex and Cathi at BookExpo America

Alex, thank you for helping put together a wonderful first show with just 2½ months' notice! You were terrific! I'm saddened that you've moved on … but I wish you well in reaching your dreams! And I look forward to working with Cathi on BEA 2002!

Beate Pettigrew, Adjunct Professor at Johnson County Community College

Thank you for coordinating your theatre students for the talent in this CD-ROM. They are terrific — and your help is greatly appreciated! And thanks to the young adults who came in to read the same lines once, twice, three times: Chris M., Alisa, Jason, Gretchen, Olivia, Laura, Derrick, Amberay, Lisa, Megan, Chris E., Jenny, Joe, Phillip, Whitney, and Danielle. And to Karl and his "Mr. Radio" voice. I wish you the best in achieving your dreams!

Tom at EMI Manufacturing

Thank you for teaching me about CD-ROM replication. I can't wait to tour the plant while my CD-ROMs are printing! How exciting!

Pam

The Silly Goose logo is perfect. She is continually complimented. Thank you for your talents!

Lloyd Rich, publishing attorney

Thank you for your guidance into the rules and regulations of the publishing industry. You've been such a tremendous help!

Pat Gideon, President, Silver Lake Bank

You play hardball ... and I admire that! Thank you and your team, Cindy, Janet, Wendy, and the others for taking a risk on this project. It couldn't have been completed without your help.

Judge Tommy Webb

What a pleasure to meet you and your wife, Judy. Your insight into the book is greatly appreciated — and I can't thank you enough for writing the Foreword. You are such an inspiration to so many — and I'd love to help you launch the LUNCH Program. What a great idea!

Tammy at Print Time

Thanks for doing a wonderful job of managing my printing projects!

Dina at Coughlin Indexing Services, Inc.

Thank you for coming through at the final hour to creat a great index! It certainly makes this book easier to use.

Peggi and Connie

If only bureaucracy didn't exist ... but, even so, what a thrill to know you! Thank you for your enthusiasm! I'm looking forward to racing with you!

Chris

And thank you, Chris. You are such a brave young man! I admire your courage — and wish you a world of happiness. It is because of you that I am a better person!

The Power of One

One song can spark a moment.
One flower can wake the dream.
One tree can start a forest.
One bird can herald spring.

One smile begins a friendship.
One hand clasp lifts a soul.
One star can guide a ship at sea.
One word can frame the goal.

One vote can change a nation.
One sunbeam lights a room.
One candle wipes out darkness.
One laugh will conquer gloom.

One step must start each journey.
One word must start each prayer.
One hope will raise our spirits.
One touch can show you care.

One voice can speak with wisdom.
One heart can know what is true.
One life can make a difference.
That one can be you.

~ Author Unknown

Credits & Copyright Approvals

 Credits

Production Partners

1. Silly Goose Productions, LLC, PO Box 44, Tecumseh, KS 66542. *www.silly-goose.com*.

2. Digital Lagoon, 14685 W. 105th, Lenexa, KS 66215. *www.lagoon.com*.

3. Pneuma Books: Complete Publisher's Sevices, 22 Sycamore Dr., First Floor, North East, MD 21901. *www.pneumadesign.com/books*.

4. Coughlin Indexing Services, Inc., 619 Severn Avenue, Suite 201, Annapolis, MD 21403. *www.indexing.com*.

5. Central Plains Book Manufacturing, 22234 C Street, Strother Field, Winfield, KS 67156. *www.centralplainsbook.com*.

6. EMI Music Distribution, 1 Capitol Way, Jacksonville, IL 62650. *www.emimfg.com*.

7. Bankrate, Inc., 11811 U.S. Highway 1, Suite 101, N. Palm Beach, FL 33408. *www.bankrate.com*.

8. Express Card & Label, Co., Inc., 2012 NE Meriden Road, Topeka, KS 66609. *www.expresscl.com*.

8. Print Time, 13354 College Blvd., Lenexa, KS 66210. *www.printtime.com.*

CD-ROM Talent

Chapter 1: Moving Out — Chris Morrow
Chapter 2: Finances — Karl Fruendt
Chapter 3: Career Guidance — Alisa Smith
Chapter 4: College & Skill Guidance — Jason Hardiman
Chapter 5: Dreams & Goals — Gretchen Mais
Chapter 6: Time Management — Olivia Li
Chapter 7: Relationships — Laura Ortiz
Chapter 8: Sex — Derrick Reynolds and Amberay Lake
Chapter 9: Health — Lisa Tunis Fosnough
Chapter 10: Personal Safety — Megan Eckard
Chapter 11: Alcohol & Drugs — Chris Evins
Chapter 12: Depression & Suicide Prevention — Jenny Bartlett
Chapter 13: Pet Care — Joe Clark
Chapter 14: Charities & Giving Back — Phillip Weaver
Chapter 15: Car Ownership — Whitney Rowland
Chapter 16: Government — Danielle Jolly

 **Advisory Committees**

Professional Advisory Committee

M. Kathryn Aranda
Nina Bryhn, M.D.
Lt. Col. Rich Davis
Cindy A. Doperalski
Col. Rufus Forrest
Peggy Hanna
DeWitt M. Harkness
Donald Hrenchir, D.V.M.
Gerald F. Kelly, Jr.
Mary T. Migliorelli
Elaine N. Toland
Linda Vande Garde, MA, LSCSW
Bridget Woods, CMHT
Tammy L. Young, MSN, FNP, RN

Young Adult Advisory Committee

Krissy Banman

Devin R. Cooper

Luke A. Doperalski

Paul M. Doperalski

Mario Ouellett

Alisa M. Smith

Jill Tunis

Lisa Tunis Fosnough

 Photographers

Shirley Baxley

Staff Sgt. Tisha Bay, 190th Air Refueling Wing, Kansas Air National Guard

Don Brent

Alisa Caldwell

Cathy Callen

Ken Cedeno

Morgan Chilson Rothenberger

Debbie Cooper

Sr. Chief Photographer's Mate Terry Cosgrove, U.S. Navy

Amy Diederich

Lana Dillner

Federal Motor Carrier Administration

Tina Fineberg

Eric Gay

Vicki Haid

Diana Halstead

Chuck Hanna

Scott Holmes

Frank Honn

Cindy Hrenchir

Doug Jacobs

Wayne Jarvis

Mike Kifer

Will Kincaid

Gary Landeen

Pat Landeen

Bertra Manning

Photographer's Mate 2nd Class Robert R. McRill, U.S. Navy
Peggi Moore
Earl Richardson, *www.earlrichardson.com*
Barb Rollings
Jane Schnellbacher
Dianne Smith
James Smith
Jered Taylor
Kerry Taylor
Thom Taylor
Elaine Toland
Val Tunis
Wamego Smoke Signal
White Dog Productions, LLC
Wolfe's Cameras, Camcorders & Computers
www.AnimationFactory.com
www.ArtToday.com
www.FreeStockPhotos.com
www.Kimmygems.com
www.ThanksCompany.com

 ## Videotaping Partners
Barb Banman
Krissy Banman
Baron BMW
Robert Bell, D.D.S., and Staff
Cindy, Luke, and Paul Doperalski
Jordan, Beth, Brooke, and Alex Gershon
Donald Hrenchir, DVM, and Burlingame Road Animal Hospital
Janel Mertel
Rick Tague, M.D., MPH
U.S. Marine Corps Toys for Tots
Jennifer Davis and Wayside Waifs, Kansas City's Humane Society

▶ Copyright Approvals

*Acknowledgement is gratefully made for permission to
include the following wonderful books:*

Awakening From Grief: Finding the Road Back to Joy by John E. Welshons.
© 2001 by John E. Welshons. (Open Heart Publications,
ISBN 1-928732-57-7)

The Carousel by Richard Paul Evans. © 2000 by Richard Paul Evans.
(Simon & Schuster, ISBN 0-684-86891-1)

*Dig Your Well Before You're Thirsty: The Only Networking Book You'll Ever
Need* by Harvey Mackay. © 1997 by Harvey Mackay. (Doubleday,
ISBN 0-385-48546-8)

Don't Take It Personally: The Art of Dealing with Rejection by Elayne Savage,
Ph.D. © 1997 by Elayne Savage. (New Harbinger Publications, Inc.,
ISBN 1-57224-077-6)

Forgiveness is a Gift You Give Yourself by Michele Weiner-Davis. © 2002 by
Michele Weiner-Davis. *www.divorcebusting.com*

The Healing of Sorrow: Understanding and Help for the Bereaved by Norman
Vincent Peale. © 1966 by Norman Vincent Peale. (Doubleday)

I Will Remember You by Laura Dower. © 2001 by Laura Dower. (Scholastic, Inc., ISBN 0-439-13961-9)

Life Strategies: Doing What Works, Doing What Matters by Phillip C. McGraw,
Ph.D. © 1999 by Phillip C. McGraw. (Hyperion, ISBN 0-7868-6548-2)

*The 9 Steps to Financial Freedom: Practical & Spiritual Steps So You Can Stop
Worrying* by Suze Orman. © 1997 by Suze Orman. (Crown Publishers,
ISBN 0-517-70791-8)

The Now Habit: A Strategic Program for Overcoming Procrastination by Neil Fiore. © 1989 by Neil Fiore. (J.P. Tarcher, ISBN 0-87477-504-3)

Success Gems: Your Personal Motivational Success Guide by Jewel Diamond Taylor. © 1999 by Jewl Diamond Taylor. (Quiet Time Publishing, ISBN 188-47843-01-3)

There is Nothing Wrong With You by Cheri Huber. © 1993 by Cheri Huber and June Shiver. (Keep It Simple Books, ISBN 0-9636255-0-0)

There's a Hole in my Sidewalk: The Romance of Self-Discovery by Portia Nelson. © 1993 by Portia Nelson. (Beyond Words Publishing, Inc., ISBN 0-941831-87-6)

Time Management From the Inside Out by Julie Morgenstern. © 2000 by Julie Morgenstern. Reprinted with permission of Henry Holt & Co., LLC. (ISBN 0-8050-6469-9)

What's The Difference Between Men And Women? by Dave Barry.© 1995 by Dave Barry. (Random House)

"There You'll Be" Written by Diane Warren. Sung by Faith Hill. Realsongs © 2001 International Rights Secured. Not for broadcast transmission. All rights reserved. DO NOT DUPLICATE. NOT FOR SEPARATE RENTAL.

All possible care has been taken to trace the ownership of all quoted sources in this publication and to make full acknowledgement of each use. If any errors have inadvertently occurred, they will be corrected in subsequent editions, provided notification is sent to the publisher. Please e-mail sales@silly-goose.com or write Silly Goose Productions, LLC, PO Box 44, Tecumseh, KS 66542. Thank you.

Our Greatest Fear

Our greatest fear is not that we are inadequate, but that we are powerful beyond measure.

It is our light, not our darkness, that frightens us. We ask ourselves, *"Who am I to be brilliant, gorgeous, handsome, talented, and fabulous?"*

Actually, who are you not to be?

Your playing small does not serve the world. There is nothing enlightened about shrinking so that other people won't feel insecure around you. And, as we let our own light shine, we consciously give other people permission to do the same. As we are liberated from our fear, our presence automatically liberates others.

~ Nelson Mandela

Index

before marriage, 228
multiple choice, 175
Quicken (software), 76
Quitting
job, 136–137
smoking, 306, 324–332
Quote, for renters insurance, 20–21

R
Railroad crossings, accidents at, 536–537
Rain, driving in, 543
A Rainy Night in New Orleans (poem), 503
Raise, asking for, 135
Rape, 344–347. *See also* Sexual harassment
behaviors increasing tendency of, 345–346
date, 287, 345, 374
Raw eggs, 28
Reality, escaping from, and substance abuse, 360
Rebelling, and substance abuse, 359–360
Reconciliation form, 66–67
Recordkeeping, 49–50
Rectal exam, 299, 300
Recycling, 32
References, 118
Refrigerator, 29
Refund, tax, 60
Rehearser, 235
Relationship quiz, 220
Relationships, 221–261. *See also* Partner(s)
conflicts in, 244–249
good, 221–230
Religion, 249–250
freedom of, 559
"Relinquishment papers," 282
Rent, 3
late, 11

in lease, 7
payment plan for, 11
raise in, 7
Rental application, 6
Rental property. *See also* Lease
finding, 1–3, 4
with furniture, 11–14
inspecting, 8
Rental Reimbursement coverage, 517
Renters insurance, 18–21, 103
Repairmen, criminals impersonating, 340
Repairs, 5, 8, 11, 12
"Replacement cost," 18–19
Reporting, lost or stolen debit and ATM cards, 70
Repossessed car, 513–514
Republicans, 557
Residence halls, 165
Residential Pages, 14
Respect, in roommate-relationship, 17
Responsibility
civic, 558–559
for emotions, 316
taking, 186–190
for temper, 248–249
at work, 130–134
Résumé, 116–119
Retirement, 94–99
Retirement benefits, 101
Risk-taking, 359–360
Rituals, 411
Road rage, 540–541
Rollings, Barb, 389–392
Romance, 224
Roofies, 374
Roommates
finding, 17
signing lease, 6
Roosevelt, Eleanor, 186, 225
Roosevelt, Theodore, 192

Order Form

Fax orders: 785-379-5224 (Fax this form.)
E-mail orders: sales@silly-goose.com
Website orders: www.onmyown.com
Check or money order: Silly Goose Productions, LLC,
Attn: Sales, PO Box 44, Tecumseh, KS 66542

Please send me

On My Own.™ *The Ultimate How-To Guide for Young Adults*
(Book w/CD-ROM) .... #_____ @ $34.95
The Ultimate Bill-Paying Tablet .... #_____ @ $5.95

Sub-total .... $_____
Kansas residents add 6.8% sales tax* .... $_____
USPS Priority Shipping & Handling (1st book) $3.95
Each additional book $1.00

Total .... $_____
*Sales tax for *On My Own*™ is $2.38 per book.
Sales tax on *The Ultimate Bill-Paying Tablet* is $.34 per book.

Payment
❏ Check or Money Order Enclosed
Credit Card: ❏ Visa   ❏ MasterCard
Name on Credit Card _____
Card # _____Exp. Date_____
Signature _____

Shipping information
Name _____
Ship-to Address _____
Ship-to City _____State_____Zip_____
Phone _____

Attention: Schools, businesses, and non-profit organizations
On My Own.™ *The Ultimate How-To Guide for Young Adults* is available at special discounts when ordered in bulk quantities. For information, please e-mail sales@silly-goose.com or call 785-379-5224.